Change Management

Dedication

To our beautiful girls,
Annabel, Imogen and Laura

Change Management

A Guide to Effective Implementation

Third Edition

Robert A. Paton and James McCalman

Los Angeles • London • New Delhi • Singapore

First published 2008

SAGE Publications Ltd
1 Oliver's Yard
55 City Road
London EC1Y 1SP

SAGE Publications Inc.
2455 Teller Road
Thousand Oaks, California 91320

SAGE Publications India Pvt Ltd
B 1/I 1 Mohan Cooperative Industrial Area
Mathura Road
New Delhi 110 044

SAGE Publications Asia-Pacific Pte Ltd
33 Pekin Street #02-01
Far East Square
Singapore 048763

Library of Congress Control Number: 2007938687

British Library Cataloguing in Publication data

A catalogue record for this book is available from the British Library

ISBN 978-1-4129-1220-4
ISBN 978-1-4129-1221-1 (pbk)

Typeset by C & M Digital (P) Ltd., Chennai, India
Printed in Great Britain by The Cromwell Press, Trowbridge, Wiltshire
Printed on paper from sustainable resources

Contents

List of figures

List of tables

List of mini cases

Notes on authors

Robert Paton is currently Professor of Management and the Director of the Complex Services Innovation Network (CSIRN) in the Faculty of Law, Business and Social Science at the University of Glasgow. He researches, publishes and lectures in the field of managing change, knowledge transfer and in organizational innovation. He has collaborated widely with co-researchers and various organizations and currently directs Glasgow's engagement with the *European Management Journal*. At present he is concentrating efforts on examining how best to achieve maximum benefit from the effective knowledge transfer within complex change scenarios, in particular he is increasingly focusing on services science and innovation. He has recently published in the *Journal of Information Technology, European Management Journal, Journal of Knowledge Management* and *International Journal of Project Management*. In addition, he has worked on programmes and consultancy associated with Associated Newspapers, Clydesdale Bank, ESCP (Paris), Glaxo Wellcome, Glasgow Housing Association, GSBA (Zurich), IBM, ScottishPower, Scottish Health Board Consortium and SCMG.

Dr James McCalman is Chief Executive of the Windsor Leadership Trust which provides a unique programme of meetings and consultations, held at St George's House, Windsor Castle for leaders to develop their own leadership wisdom and insight. Leaders from all sectors take part, including business, government, military, religion, and not-for-profit. He has been involved in managing change programmes within organizations at several levels from strategy formulation to the introduction of shopfloor teamworking.

He is the author of four books, seven book chapters and over 30 journal articles related to organizational behaviour and change in organizations. Dr McCalman has been involved in teaching and consultancy in the UK, United States, most of Western Europe and Southeast Asia in the areas of organization development, change management and teamwork. He has worked for several blue chip organizations including Managing Director of Sotheby's Institute of Art, British Petroleum, China Light and Power, Compaq Computers, Guinness, Motorola, National Semiconductor, NEC and the Bahrain government.

Dr McCalman's current research interests involve the politics of organizational change and the use of politicking by managers.

Foreword

Christopher Rodrigues CBE
Chairman, VisitBritain

'A good hockey player plays where the puck is. A great hockey player plays where the puck is going to be.'
Wayne Gretzky, Canadian ice hockey player

We live in a world full of change. The ability to lead change even became a platform on which the 2008 US Presidential Election was fought. Mastering change management is a key skill for the twenty-first century and living with change is a key survival skill.

This book addresses some of the key issues related to change from a practical, hands-on and realistic perspective. It will help the reader understand how to lead change; engage with change and survive change.

One of the key elements of change management about which we are all still learning is how to achieve it on a global basis. While the desired outcomes may be the same the world over the means of getting there can be very different. International organizations need the sensitivity not to drive through change using the culture of their home market. Europeans, Asians, North Americans and South Americans are not the same; they don't have the same value systems and they don't react to change in an identical manner. That much I learned for certain when I was CEO of Visa International.

I therefore very much welcome this updating by Robert Paton and James McCalman of their successful text on *Change Management*. The focus remains very firmly on the 'nuts and bolts' of organizational change – competing resources; politics; conflicts of interest and understanding. But the reader also benefits from change being examined from two very different angles – the organized *systems perspective* and a focus *on people development.*

I think the book also succeeds by providing detailed case analyses and in particular illustrations of change for growth and innovation. These stories of real world change in action give readers pause for thought and helps them reflect on the change management issues they raise and the potential lessons for their own organization.

The third edition also brings change itself in terms of introducing new subject areas that have come to the fore since the publication of the second edition eight years ago. *Gender*, with its impact on management style and change, is a welcome addition. So too is the focus on *organizational power and politics* which can have a significant impact on the success or failure of change programmes particularly in the area of competing narratives which the authors also address. Finally, they examine *complexity from a knowledge perspective* – how to overcome internal barriers to release organizational potential.

The book remains true to its original beliefs – change can be managed, but only by the driven and the willing. The debate on the best ways to manage change continues. Individuals and organizations will address the issues in a myriad of ways. Readers can use the material in this volume – coupled with their own experience – to evaluate the arguments and address the practical aspects of change implementation.

I wish you every success in your endeavours.

Christopher Rodrigues
Chairman, VisitBritain
http://www.visitbritain.com/

Acknowledgements

The ability to get on well with people is a distinct benefit in both teaching and writing about the management of change. We therefore, once again, need to thank a host of friends, colleagues and acquaintances.

Particular thanks must go to André Alexander, at the time a research associate, for his contribution to the Smokies case; Stacey Bushfield, doctoral researcher, for her assistance and contribution to the new edition as a whole, without her input a third edition would not have been possible; David Boddy, University of Glasgow, for his shared interest in the competing narrative phenomena; Linda Dempster, an executive with the Child Support Agency, for her contribution to the gender and change chapter; Stephen McLaughlin, Adam Smith Senior Research Fellow, for his leading contribution to the knowledge management inputs and the IBM case material; and lastly Sara Marian Todd for providing, from her own research works, the basis for the coverage of the learning organization.

From a professional point of view we would like to thank the following individuals and organizations for their assistance:

Argyll and Clyde Health Board, in particular Rosemary I. Jamieson

British Airports Authority, in particular Liz Drummond

British Gas, in particular James Kelly

Caledonian Airmotive, in particular David J. Crews

Ethicon, in particular Rosaleen McNeill

Babcock Industries plc, in particular Brian A. Wilson

Glenlight Shipping Ltd, in particular Alex Fawcett former Managing Director

McGriggor Donald Solicitors, in particular Carole Thomson

National Health Service, in particular Sean McCollum

Scottish Homes, in particular Aileen McFadden

SmithKlineBeecham, in particular John Hunter

Southern General Hospital Trust

Terley, R. Ltd (Texstyle World), in particular John Gilchrist

United Kingdom Atomic Energy Authority, in particular Stephen Rutledge

Robert Paton, University of Glasgow, Department of Management
James McCalman, Windsor Leadership Trust 2008

PART 1

THE IMPACT AND DEFINITION OF CHANGE

Introducing Change Management

Change may be regarded as one of the few constants of recorded history. Often society's 'winners', both historically and contemporary, can be characterized by their common ability to effectively manage and exploit change situations. Individuals, societies, nations and enterprises who have at some time been at the forefront of commercial, and/or technological expansion, have achieved domination, or at least competitive advantage, by being innovative in thought and/or action. They have been both enterprising and entrepreneurial.

Management and change are synonymous; it is impossible to undertake a journey, for in many respects that is what change is, without first addressing the purpose of the trip, the route you wish to travel and with whom. Managing change is about handling the complexities of travel. It is about evaluating, planning and implementing operational, tactical and strategic 'journeys'.

Change has been studied and researched for many years. Philosophies, theories, models and techniques abound; all aim, with various degrees of credibility and success, to deliver sustainable organizational change (Todnem By, 2005). We appear to have hit a hiatus, in terms of change management activity with a dramatic increase in interest directed towards organizational development related research: the net results being the learning organization, knowledge economies and management, complexity theory and the 'virtual' organization. Armenikas and Bedeian (1999) in a review of both theoretical and practitioner research models related to change concluded that organizational change literature and the underpinning research continue to be highly responsive to the demands of management and also the workplace and market. Demand for change literature remains high as managers continue to strive for that 'perfect' change as many continue to consider reported failure rates, as high as 70 per cent, rather excessive (Balogun and Hope Hailey, 2004).

Our purpose in writing this book is to try to begin to resolve some of the questions that managers ask when faced with the concept and reality of change. How can managers cope better with the journeys that they, their staff and organizations will have to travel? We have deliberately set this book out in a framework, which offers models for tackling the different change scenarios facing organizations. However, we have also set out to provide examples of how and where the models are used. What we wanted from this book, for ourselves and for the reader were four things:

1   valid and defined models for the effective management of change;

2   proactive approaches to change that relate to internal and external business performance;

3   practical, step-by-step means of handling change;

4   illustrations of the use and validity of the models through current, real-life case studies.

If we are successful, the reader will leave this book with the sense that the management of change is a complex, dynamic and challenging process rather than a set of recipes. In most examples of successful change management, those responsible have developed clear and shared visions of where they are going and have linked these to implementation strategies designed to produce the desired results. We believe that change management is never a *choice* between technological, organizational or people-oriented solutions, but involves combinations for best fit; integrated strategies designed to produce results. In this sense, the management of change adopts the contingency approach to organizations: it all depends. However, recognition of what it depends on is the subject of this book.

Successful exploitation of a change situation requires:

• knowledge of the circumstances surrounding a situation;

• understanding of the interactions; and

• the potential impact of associated variables.

One can try to predict and prepare for the future. Indeed history teaches that failure to do so will undoubtedly result in commercial ruin. However, it is best to remember that such predictions produce at best a blurred picture of what might be and not a blueprint of future events or circumstances. Future scenarios are dynamic as are one's abilities to manage them! Only the effective and progressive management of change can assist in shaping a future, which may better serve the enterprise's survival prospects.

The Importance of Change

Change will not disappear nor dissipate. Technology, civilizations and creative thought will maintain their ever-accelerating drive onwards. It could be argued that a state of continuous change has almost become routine (Luecke, 2003). Managers, and the enterprises they serve, be they public or private, service or manufacturing, will continue to be judged upon their ability to effectively and efficiently manage change. Unfortunately, for the managers of the early twenty-first century their ability to handle complex change situations will be judged over ever decreasing time scales.

The pace of change has increased dramatically. Since the publication of the second edition of this book there have been a number of global change events that have had and are continuing to have an impact on the way we all live, work and play. In particular how will we, at all levels and dimensions of our societies, manage the future scenarios associated with:

- the phenomenal growth of the worldwide web and associated technologies and the impact this has had on the way we work and play;

- climate change impact upon an increasingly fragile earth and governmental, social, and organizational responses to the associated challenges;

- the growth and establishment of new economic and global forces, in particular, China and India;

- 9/11 and the subsequent 'war on terror' and possibly more importantly the 'aftermath';

- the movement towards social responsibility, what is termed 'conscious capitalism'.

The Web is enabling globalization to march on apace, shaping the way we work and trade, while environmental pressures threaten the reliability of the physical supply chains that underpin globalization and the growth of China, India and the Pacific Rim economies. How can trust and understanding be rebuilt in the aftermath of 9/11? Could the world's great religions shape future trade and commerce? Global change can seem remote from the individual or enterprise. But how might the software engineer, working for a global organization (reliant on both the stability of world markets and supply chains), logged on to the company portal in Dublin (dependent on technology to bridge the problem solving gap), solving a problem networked with colleagues in Delhi, Budapest and New York (whom they will never physically meet nor travel with to the office), all, for a client based in Sichuan (who has sourced the solution via the web), view this new exciting world? How would you manage such an individual, their network or indeed the client interface?

Businesses and managers are faced with highly dynamic and ever more complex operating environments. Technologies and products, along with the industries they support and serve, are converging. Is the media company in broadcasting, or telecommunications, or data processing, or indeed all of them? Is the supermarket chain in general retail, or is it a provider of financial services? Is the television merely a receiving device for broadcast messages or is it part of an integrated multimedia communications package? Is the airline a provider of transport or the seller of wines, spirits and fancy goods, or the agent for car hire and accommodation?

As industries and products converge, along with the markets they serve, there is a growing realization that a holistic approach to the marketing of goods and services is required, thus simplifying the purchasing decision. Strategic alliances, designed to maximize the 'added value' throughout a supply chain, while seeking to minimize costs of supply, are fast becoming the competitive weapon of the future. Control and exploitation of the supply chain makes good commercial sense in fiercely competitive global markets. The packaging of what were once discrete products (or services) into what are effectively 'consumer solutions' will continue for the foreseeable future (Paton and McLaughlin, 2008).

The above, combined with the general ability to replicate both 'hard' and 'soft' innovations within ever diminishing time scales, places the creative and effective management of change well towards the top of the core competencies required by any public or private enterprise. The networked age supported by integrated supply chains, distributed manufacturing and integrated product offerings is here to stay.

This new world is a fragile one. Old traditions, conventions and belief systems are being challenged. Regulatory pressures, as one would expect, are increasing as those deemed to be in control (governments, civil services, politicians, managers and social leaders) attempt to both direct and manage in an increasingly dramatic and dynamic environment. In this new age staying marginally ahead of the game could be considered not only an achievement but also a prerequisite for survival.

Woody Allen tells a story of a race of aliens who peacefully colonize Earth, on a cohabitation basis with the original populace. They are not technologically advanced, nor do they have substantially improved physical characteristics. However, they have an uncanny ability to be first for everything! First to launch new products; first to modify an old technology; first to secure the deal; first, and therefore the 'winners'!

READER ACTIVITY

Identify two or three colleagues, friends or relations who are, or have been, in management or business positions. Ask them, without prompting, what they find challenging about their job? What do they find most frustrating? Attempt to find out what strategies and/or skills they employ to manage challenging and frustrating situations?

How can we manage change in such a fast moving environment, without losing control of the organization and existing core competencies? There are, as one would expect, no easy answers and certainly no blueprints detailing best practice. Designing, evaluating and implementing successful change strategies largely depends upon the quality of the management team, in particular the team's ability to design organizations in such a way as to facilitate the change process in a responsive and progressive manner.

The Imperative of Change

Any organization that ignores change does so at its own peril. One might suggest that for many the peril would come sooner rather than later. To survive and prosper, organizations must adopt strategies that realistically reflect their ability to manage multiple future scenarios.

Drucker (1997: 20–4), for example, argues that, 'Increasingly, a winning strategy will require information about events and conditions outside the institution…Only with this information can a business … prepare for new changes and challenges arising from sudden shifts in the world economy and in the nature and content of knowledge itself.'

Bamford and Forrester (2003) agree stating that a 'realistic approach to change must take into account multiple and varied forces'. They note the importance, in relation to a realistic take on change, of the history of the organization, customers, suppliers, and the economic environment, while stressing the need to also take into account both national and international legislation. Balogun (2007) recognizes the inevitability of organizational restructuring in the face of ever changing competitive, economic and social factors: she stresses the need to consider the actual practice of change, the internal environment, and the need to align strategic aspirations with practical realities. In short, restructuring must take into account those at the 'sharp end': the middle management.

If we take an external perspective for a moment, the average modern organization has to come to terms with a number of issues, which will create a need for internal change. At the point of writing we can identify six major external changes that organizations are currently addressing or will have to come to terms with in the new millennium:

1 A larger global market place made smaller by enhanced technologies and competition from abroad. The growth of the European Union to incorporate countries from Eastern and Southeast Europe, the dramatic growth of economies such as, China and India, and reductions in transportation, information and communication costs, mean that the world is a different place from what it was. How does your organization plan to respond to such competitive pressures?

2 A worldwide recognition of the environment as an influencing variable and government attempts to draw back from environmental calamity. The legal, cultural and socio-economic implications of realizing that resource use and allocation is a finite issue and that global solutions to ozone depletion, toxic waste dumping, raw material depletion, and other environmental concerns will force change on organizations, sooner rather than later. How does the individual organization respond to the bigger picture?

3 Health consciousness as a permanent trend amongst all age groups throughout the world. The growing awareness and concern with the content of food and beverage products has created a movement away from synthetic towards natural products. Concerns have been expressed about the spread of 'bird flu', genetically engineered foodstuffs, and the cloning of animals. How does the individual organization deal with the demands of a more health conscious population?

4 Changes in lifestyle trends are affecting the way in which people view work, purchases, leisure time and society. A more morally questioning, affluent, educated and involved population is challenging the way in which we will do business and socialize. How will you and your organization live your lives?

5 The changing workplace creates a need for non-traditional employees. Organizations are currently resorting to a core/periphery workforce, tele-working, multi-skilled workers and outsourcing. A greater proportion of the population who have not been traditional employees will need to be attracted into the labour force. Equal opportunity in pay and non-pecuniary rewards will be issues in the future. Pension gaps and shortfalls will create pressures on people to work beyond the traditional retirement age. How will the individual organization cope with these pressures?

6 The knowledge asset of the company, its people, is becoming increasingly crucial to its competitive well being. Technological and communication advances are leading to reduced entry costs across world markets. This enables organizations to become multinational without leaving their own borders. However, marketing via the Internet, communication via email and other technology applications are all still reliant on the way you organize your human resources. Your only sustainable competitive weapon is your people. How do you intend managing them in the next millennium? The same way as you did in the last?

To the extent that we could have picked half a dozen other issues for discussion indicates the imperative for change in organizations. What is important, however, is recognition that change occurs continuously, has numerous causes, and needs to be addressed all the time. Lawler (1986) sums this up quite effectively by noting that,

> Overall, planned change is not impossible, but it is often difficult. The key point is that change is an ongoing process, and it is incorrect to think that visionary end state can be reached in a highly programmed way.

The difficulty is that most organizations view the concept of change as a highly programmed process which takes as its starting point the problem that needs to be rectified, breaks it down to constituent parts, analyses possible alternatives, selects the preferred solution, and applies this relentlessly – problem recognition, diagnosis and resolution. Such an approach may be considered to be simple, straightforward, and relatively painless. But what if the change problem is part of a bigger picture? For example how do recognition, diagnosis and resolution address the problem of global warming, 'It's not our problem, and we'll leave it for the politicians to sort out.' This is a simple and effective response but progressive organizations are already providing their own solutions and recognizing that climate change will not be resolved by governmental action alone. This is a problem that nations have difficulties trying to address. As an issue, it creates an imperative for change. There are two ways of responding to that imperative. The individual organization can wait for legislation to hit the statute book and react to the legislation, or it can anticipate and institute proactive change. Most organizations won't. That's because they are geared and managed to run on traditional, analytical lines of decision-making – if it isn't broken, why fix it? What we would like to suggest here is that before it even gets to the point where a slight stress fracture appears, organizations should be addressing the potential implications of change scenarios, and dealing with them accordingly.

The Impact of Change

What makes an organization want to change? There are a number of specific, even obvious factors, which will necessitate movement from the status quo. The most obvious of these relate to significant changes in the external environment. For example, global warming drives regulatory, social and commercial forces to converge upon those perceived to be the key producers of greenhouse gases. Automotive giants and the petroleum producers are increasingly searching for technological solutions to offset the negative impacts of traditional fossil fuels. Governments are emphasizing the need to lessen our carbon footprint resulting in higher taxes on fossil fuel; investment in public transport; and, the incentive driven search for more efficient energy sources. Such external pressures have existed throughout time. Pettigrew (1985) pointed out that there were no clear beginnings and ends to strategic change. Environmental disturbances were seen as the main precipitating factor, but he also believed that these were not the sole causes of, or explanations of change. Burnes (2004) and Dawson (2003) also point to what might be termed the discontinuous nature of change, citing the ad hoc nature of change events, occurrences of multiple change initiatives, and multiple triggers as evidence of discontinuity.

To attribute change entirely to the environment would be a denial of extreme magnitude. This would imply that organizations were merely 'bobbing about' on a turbulent sea of change, unable to influence or exercise direction. This is clearly not the case. Pettigrew (1985) went on to argue that changes within an organization take place both in response to business and economic events and to processes of management perception, choice and action. Managers in this sense see events taking place that, to them, signal the need for change. They also perceive the internal context of change as it relates to structure, culture, systems of power, and control. This gives them further clues about whether it is worth trying to introduce change. But what causes change? What factors need to be considered when we look for the causal effects which run from A to B in an organization?

We would like you to consider changes that have impacted upon you, your family or your organization or networks over the last year. How often were these changes a reaction to events outside your control? For example, can you cite instances linked to your company's, or your, response to:

- changes in technology used;
- changes in customer expectations or tastes;
- changes as a result of competition;
- changes as a result of government legislation;
- changes as a result of alterations in the economy, at home or abroad;
- changes in communications media;
- changes in societies' value systems;
- changes in the supply chain;
- changes in the distribution chain?

Internal changes can be seen as responses or reactions to the outside world and are regarded as external triggers. There are also a large number of factors, which lead to what are termed internal triggers for change. Organization redesigns to fit a new product line or new marketing strategy are typical examples, as are changes in job responsibilities to fit new organizational structures.

The final cause of change in organizations is where the organization tries to be ahead of the game by being proactive. For example, where the organization tries to anticipate problems in the market place or negate the impact of worldwide recession on its own business, proactive change is taking place (Buchanan and Huczynski, 2006).

Change and Transition Management

If the concept of change can be examined from an internal, external or proactive set of viewpoints, then the response of managers has to be equally as widespread. Buchanan and McCalman (1989) suggest that this requires a framework of perpetual transition management. Following from Lawler's (1986) concept of the lack of a visionary end state, what appears to be required is the ability within managers to deal with constant change. This transition management model, although specifically related to large-scale organizational change, has some interesting insights into what triggers change in organizations, and how they respond. It suggests that four interlocking management processes must take place both to implement and sustain major organizational changes. These processes operate at different levels, and may involve different actors in the organizational hierarchy. The four layers are:

> The trigger layer: concerning the identification of needs and openings for major change deliberately formulated in the form of opportunities rather than threats or crises.

> The vision layer: establishing the future development of the organization by articulating a vision and communicating this effectively in terms of where the organization is heading.

> The conversion layer: setting out to mobilize support in the organization for the new vision as the most appropriate method for dealing with the triggers of change.

> The maintenance and renewal layer: identifying ways in which changes are sustained and enhanced through alterations in attitudes, values, and behaviours, and regression back to tradition is avoided.

Transition management suggests that organizations have to plan for, divert resources to, and implement four sets of interlocking processes. These are designed to implement, to sustain, and to build on change and

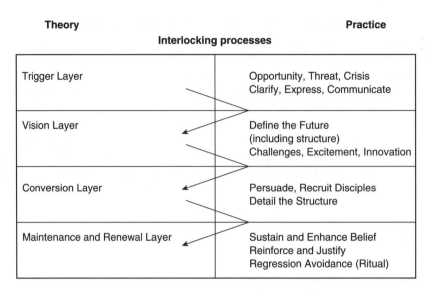

Figure I.1   Buchanan and McCalman's model of perpetual transition management

Source: Buchanan and McCalman 1989, *High Performance Work Systems: The Digital Experience*, Routledge, London, p. 198.

its achievements in an attempt to address the issues associated with change over time. The argument here is that these layers – trigger, vision, conversion and maintenance and renewal are necessary processes that occur in change management. The respective emphasis and priority attached to each of them will alter over time, but recognition of their existence goes a long way in determining the management action needed.

The model of perpetual transition management starts out with a number of questions. How do we explain successful change? How do we explain attempts at change in organizations that were doomed from the start? How do we explain change that is initially successful but wanes or fizzles out halfway through? Effective large-scale change demands a series of management actions linked to the four interlocking layers or processes (see Figure I.1).

In terms of the trigger layer, it is necessary to understand what is causing a need for change in the organization. These triggers need to be expressed in a clear way and communicated throughout the organization. For example, poor trigger identification and communication processes are best seen when the first that employees know of the difficulties facing the organization is when they are called in to discuss redundancy terms. People are generally willing and able to deal with change but many managers do not understand this. They are afraid that change is associated with some form of failure and they need to hide the changes. People will accept change when they know it is necessary and accept the explanation for the need for change.

It is necessary for these triggers to be expressed and communicated throughout the organization in clear and identifiable terms. For example, the trigger in many organizations is often a crisis, but it does not necessarily have to be a threat. People will respond to the challenge of a crisis but may react negatively to a threat. Expressing any potential crisis as an opportunity for change may assist the process itself. In this sense, the language in which the triggering mechanism is transmitted to the internal organization has to be clearly expressed as opportunity, and communicated widely. The chances of successfully implementing change are significantly improved when everyone concerned has a shared understanding of what may happen and why.

If the trigger for change has been clearly recognized and expressed, it is also a requirement for management within the organization to define the future. This does not call for crystal ball gazing but for the establishment of a vision layer. The requirement here is for definition and expression of where the organization intends to go. Just as shared understanding and awareness of the triggers for change help smooth the process, so do shared awareness and understanding of the new vision and the desired organizational goals. Management must visualize the future in terms of three criteria. The first is that change is seen to provide an effective response to the events triggering change. Second there is identification of the desired future condition of the organization in terms of its design, its products and its goals. Finally, it must provide challenges and stimulation. Change is assisted by a climate of enthusiasm and participation; resistance is a result of fear, prejudice, anxiety and ignorance.

The third layer of perpetual transition management is related to gaining recruits for the change. By this it is meant that those who have to work through the change process need to be converted to the ideas and concepts and own them. Defining a future that no one can 'buy into' will slow or hinder the change itself. Everyone involved in making change work has to feel part of it and accept the reasoning for the vision and how this is to be realized. It is at this point that the vision has to be detailed and aspects such as, the future structure and patterns of work are explained. There is a need at this point to recruit disciples to the vision. This is time consuming, as it requires detailed explanation. Failure to do so results in negotiation, re-negotiation, or decay. This is related to the, 'You've introduced this without consulting us first' syndrome. Managers at this stage need to get involved in two main activities. First, there is the planning team, the main core change unit. The most appropriate mechanisms here will depend on the organization and its consultation systems. Second, it is also necessary to talk to people about the change at every opportunity, formal or informal. This establishes a shared understanding of the change programme through debate.

The last question that perpetual transition management attempts to resolve is related to the decay associated with the management of mid-term change. Maintenance and renewal attempts to address the 'moving goalposts' feature of change. There are four main examples of this. First, the events that triggered change in the first place fade in the memory or lose their relevance over time. Second, articulation of the vision becomes less expressive when the originators move on. Third, replacements feel less committed to the ideas and have to be taken through the reasons for, and responses to, the triggers. Fourth, the change that took place settles down and becomes the norm in the organization. To avoid this sort of decay process there is a requirement for organizations to allocate resources to maintaining and renewing the original visions in an evolutionary framework. In this sense, management takes part in a process that is described as one of permanent transition. It is this point that can be regarded as the crucial concept. Getting managers to recognize that change is a constant feature in modern organizations, and one which they have to deal with, goes a long way towards addressing some of the factors that lead to resistance to change.

Outline of the Book

The book is divided into four parts. Part 1, which includes this chapter, discusses the impact and definition of change. Part 2 looks at intervention strategies designed to cope with systems-related change. Part 3 examines organization development models of change dealing with the behaviour of people. Finally, Part 4 offers a number of practical cases designed to explore further the validity of the models outlined in this book.

In Chapter 1, the need to address the nature of change is introduced. All organizations, from both an external and internal perspective, operate within dynamic environments. Prior to entering a change situation managers must classify the nature of the change facing their organization. It is the nature of the impending change that will determine one's initial management approach. Chapter 1 also identifies key issues that must be addressed in any transition process and discusses the importance of the problem owner to the change event. The problem owner(s) can be the manager, or managing group, deemed to be responsible for the change process and often facilitate the process via change agents.

In Chapter 2, 'Change and the manager', we look at the managerial competencies associated with effectively managing change. The importance of remaining in 'control' of ongoing dynamic change situations is reviewed. Management must manage change, no matter its source or impact, in a planned and controlled manner.

We have introduced a new Chapter 3 for this edition. This chapter, 'Managing change from a gender perspective', focuses on the skills, attributes and attitudes that many consider essential to the effective management of change. In particular we ask given this skills set whether gender could influence the managers' change capabilities?

The means of identifying change agents and defining the change environment are fully discussed and illustrated in Chapter 4. A systems-based analytical approach, involving the use of mapping and diagramming techniques, is suggested as being one of the optimal means of defining a change environment. The diagramming tools covered within this chapter may be employed to define an environment no matter the classification of the change. Each diagram introduced is illustrated with a practical example of its application. The value of the diagrammatic approach to change definition cannot be understated. It offers a communications vehicle, analytical processes, planning and control aids, and a means of defining complex organizational environments.

In Part 2 of the book we deal with systems intervention strategies. In Chapter 5 an interventionist approach to change is introduced and dis-cussed, namely, the intervention strategy model (ISM). This model is designed to tackle change from the 'hard', technical, end of the change spectrum, although, as we will see, it may be employed to deal with 'softer', people related issues. The origins and value of the model are discussed and this is followed by a sequential review of the model's component parts. Application issues, along with 'dos and don'ts', round off this chapter. Chapter 6 is dedicated to the exploration of practical cases that illustrate each stage of the model and examine key aspects of implementation.

Another method of dealing with project-based change is introduced in Chapter 7 when we examine total project management (TPM). To a greater or lesser extent all managers are project managers. This chapter describes the TPM process and outlines its rationale. Very often it is poor people management, not the degree of technical competence, which leads to less than effective project implementation. TPM offers a solution to this problem.

Chapter 8, another new chapter, explores the phenomenon of the com-peting narrative. As researchers and exponents of change will readily testify any post-change evaluation will, to greater or lesser extents, iden-tify divergent views as to the rationale for the change: its resulting impact, its value, and its consequences. Why, when the change was intended to be all encompassing and engaging, do those who managed events and implemented the outcomes perceive multiple realities?

In Part 3 we examine the need for an organization development model for change. In many Western organizations, the concept of management is so restrictive that control and decision-making operates as a hindering device on performance. The belief still exists that management and workforce are separate entities that sometimes come together to manufacture product or deliver services, but often act as polar opposites in some form of industrial struggle for superiority. Chapter 9 puts forward the proposition that it doesn't have to be like this. By examining some of the basic concepts of design and development, organizations can begin to combine the needs of the individual worker with those of business to find a mission that results in effective performance. This effective performance is reflected in results which are categorized in terms of numbers – profits, sales revenue, etc. – but also in terms of the quality of working life. However, to achieve this, managers have to suspend some of their inherent assumptions about work organization, the nature of work and how they attain commitment from the workforce. The basis of design is couched in the organization and its mission. As Matsushita (1984) comments, there has to be more to life than profit:

> Every company no matter how small ought to have clear cut goals apart from the pursuit of profit, purposes that justify its existence among us. To me, such goals are an avocation, a secular mission to the world. If the chief executive officer has this sense of mission, he can tell his employees what it is that the company seeks to accomplish, and explain its *raison d'être* and ideals. And if his employees understand that they are not working for bread alone, they will be motivated to work harder together toward the realisation of their common goals.

To be able to manage change effectively, organizations need to go through a process of identifying possible faults, looking at alternatives to the current situation, weighing up the pros and cons of these alternatives, reaching decisions on the future state of the organization, and implementing the necessary changes. This belies the pain and suffering that is often caused by the instigation of change. The resentment that is often felt during the management of change is not resentment to change per se but to the processes by which it is managed. Where people are involved, the potential for pain and the likelihood of resistance are increased tenfold. Peters and Waterman (1982), in their inimitable fashion, sum this up quite succinctly:

> The central problem with the rationalist view of organizing people is that people are not very rational. To fit Taylor's model, or today's organizational charts, man is simply designed wrong (or, of course, vice versa, according to our argument here).

In Chapter 10, we examine the organization development model (ODM). In this chapter we look at how organization development can assist the move from a situation that is regarded as undesirable to a new state that, hopefully, is more effective. The key to the ODM is looking at what change is required, what level the change takes place at, who is likely to be involved, and the processes by which change is instigated. Chapter 9 outlines the techniques of organization development and the steps that the change agent is likely to be involved in.

The concept of a change agent is similar to that of the problem owner, identified in Part 2 of the book. We change the name, not to protect the innocent but to imply significance to the role. In Chapter 11, we examine the role of the objective outsider. The organization development model suggests the need for an individual from outside the area of change who displays a number of unique characteristics. Chief amongst these are their ability to remain impartial or neutral and their ability to facilitate the process of change.

Another new chapter for this edition focuses on organizational reality and in particular politics and power. In Chapter 12 we look at 'Organizational power and politics' with a view to stripping away some of the tactics and techniques employed that can help or hinder change. Chapter 13 reviews the impact on OD and change in general resulting from the concept, development and value of the learning organization movement.

The subject matter of Part 4 of the book has been revised for this edition. Chapters 14 and 15 introduce two extensive case studies dealing with 'Managing knowledge and change: an IBM case study' and a 'Case study in business growth: change at Smokies'. In many ways Chapter 14, dealing as it does with knowledge management, could be seen as the natural 'next stop' in the evolution of the learning organization. Knowledge management and its exploitation, especially in relation to supply chain logistics, globalization and services science (Paton and McLaughlin, 2008), are considered by many to be fundamental to the sustained development of Western and certain emerging economies, societies and enterprises. The IBM case examines the barriers to change associated with effective knowledge management implementation. Chapter 15 addresses a particular omission from past editions, namely, the lack of a specific business strategy case. The Smokies case deals with a dynamic business situation that required the implementation of 'innovative' business solutions to a traditional enterprise. Part 4 continues, Chapters 16 and 17, with in-depth practical issues and cases illustrating the application of both the intervention strategy and organizational development approaches. Finally, we provide the reader with an epilogue which outlines the 10 key factors associated with the effective management of change.

1   The Nature of Change

A manager, or individual, whether at work, home or play, when faced with a change situation must first, no matter how informally, analyse the nature of the change. Only by considering the nature of the change can we determine its likely magnitude and potential impact. Successful determination of the nature of the change, at an early stage of the change cycle, should indicate the most appropriate means of managing the situation.

A full definition of the change environment is required prior to the final selection of a change management methodology. Defining a change environment is the subject of Chapter 4. There are many factors and considerations that must be taken into account prior to selecting a solution methodology. The aim of this chapter is to provide a means of evaluating the nature of an impending change situation so as to facilitate the marshalling of management expertise in readiness for the transition process. This will be accomplished by examining six key factors associated with successful change classification. They will be considered under the following headings:

1 *The selection and role of the problem owner*   The right person for the job in terms of their managerial skills, involvement and commitment to the problem or project.

2 *Locating change on the change spectrum*   Determining the nature of the change with regard to both its physical and organizational impact. Is it, for example, a purely technical or a more complex people related change?

3 *The TROPICS test*   A quick, yet effective, means of addressing the following key factors affecting the classification of a change situation: *t*ime scales, *r*esources, *o*bjectives, *p*erceptions, *i*nterest, *c*ontrol and *s*ource. By considering the change in relation to the above factors the manager responsible may determine, through an enhanced knowledge of the nature of the change, the optimal route forward.

4 *Force field analysis*: a *positioning tool*   A diagramming technique that assists in answering questions such as: what forces are at play and what is their likely magnitude? Who is for

the change and who is against? Can a proactive stance be adopted? The aim is to determine the nature and magnitude of the forces acting upon the change environment.

5   *Success guarantors: commitment, involvement and the shared perception*   Successful change management requires an understanding of the likely impact of the change on those systems most affected by it, and thereafter the development of a means of establishing a shared perception of the problem amongst all concerned. The visible commitment and involvement of those charged with managing the change and those affected by it are crucial to achieving effective transition management.

6   *Managing the triggers*   Change, as we discussed in the previous chapter, can be triggered by either internal or external events. The problem owner, or change agent, must understand both the likely impact of the trigger and how best to handle its subsequent, post-impact, management. The nature of the 'trigger' will influence the reaction of the organization and its staff, along with the associated supply chains, to the impending change, as well as assist in determining the appropriate course of action to follow.

The Role and Selection of the Problem Owner

How does one become a problem owner? There are essentially two routes. The first is the most straightforward and will positively influence the manager's evaluation of the change situation. Effective managers continuously monitor their operational environment from both an internal and external perspective. By doing so, they may identify change situations developing on the horizon and as identifiers of the change they at least initially become the change owners. Such ownership may lead to a more positive evaluation of its nature in relation to the degree of 'threat' associated with its arrival. Early identification and ownership tends to increase the probability of a change being seen in an opportunistic manner and therefore possibly being considered to be less threatening.

It must be noted that ownership of the change by a single change agent as outlined above does not ensure that all those ultimately affected by the change will identify with the owner's positive evaluation. Later chapters investigate the important role which organizational culture plays in the management of change. In organizations, where an effort has been successfully made to secure a culture that exhibits both enterprising and democratic characteristics, then one may expect to find a greater willingness and capability to share in the problem owner's initial view of the change.

The other route to problem ownership is the traditional one of delegation. The need for change is identified elsewhere and senior management appoints the problem owner. 'Ownership' does not belong to the individual, or group, charged with the management of the change and they simply become change 'minders' rather than change agents. Such situations are unlikely to produce positive opportunistic evaluations of the nature of the change, as it is difficult to be proactive and positive when you have been 'left holding the baby'. This can lead to rather messy situations developing!

For delegation to be effective in a change context, or for that matter in management in general, it must be accompanied by an 'educational' programme and a marketing exercise designed to pass over the ownership, responsibility and capability for the task at hand. Again, organizational culture plays a crucial role in determining the success of devolved ownership. When one feels part of a team working towards common goals then delegated problems will be viewed as common to all. On the other hand, if alienation and confrontation exists then achieving devolved ownership may be a long process.

Problem ownership affects our perception of a change situation. Positive feelings of ownership will result in a more opportunistic evaluation, whereas delegated ownership, which has been managed poorly, will highlight the threats and disrupt existing positions. The problem owner plays a pivotal role in the successful management of change. Given the obvious advantages of securing a proactive stance towards the change situation, it is essential to identify the most effective problem owner. They must possess both the skills to manage the transition process and the determination to see the change through. In short they must be the change *agents*.

All too often the problem owner is selected due to their proven skills in the general field of project management. It must be noted that this does not guarantee that they possess ownership of the problem at hand and are therefore motivated towards achieving the change objectives. An additional difficulty may arise if their 'skill' is of a technical or process nature. Successful change management requires far more than the understanding of network analysis, risk management and budgetary control. Alternatively, the selection decision may be based on who is least busy; resource constraints rather than logic determine the problem owner. The problem owner must be directly involved in the change process and must see clear linkages between their future success and the effective implementation of the change.

Positive problem ownership is clearly an important factor associated with successful change management. Ownership need not be directly linked to management ability and position. For example, when tackling a change on a ward, shop floor or even a battlefield those closest to the change impact could be better placed to assess, tackle and exploit the situation. It may on occasion be advisable to invest resources in developing the necessary management skills and providing additional support to the most appropriate individual or group. One volunteer is worth a hundred conscripts!

Often the problem owners identify themselves since they have initiated the change process. No matter their position within the hierarchy it is, in an ideal world, the initiator who should own the process. In circumstances where those at the core of the change do not have the necessary skills, authority or resources to manage the change process, then management must facilitate the change in such a way as to ensure their continued commitment and involvement. Initiators, although not directly involved in the actual management of the change, are ultimately still the problem owners and as such make committed and useful change advocates. When the pivotal role of problem ownership has to be delegated and/or assigned, then every care must be taken to select according to a detailed examination of the systems affected and the nature of the change. Such a key role should not normally be assigned solely to an individual or group from outside the affected system.

The manager responsible for the change has to this point been termed the 'problem owner'. Similar terms in common usage would include 'change agent', 'facilitator',' project manager' and 'team leader'. The terminology is relatively unimportant; their role is not. The previous paragraphs have hinted at the fact that the original problem owner may, for a number of reasons, not be the actual manager appointed to handle the change process. The remainder of this chapter, unless otherwise stated, will refer to the manager of the change process as the problem owner. When, as is generally the case, the owner acts as part of a management team then the individuals concerned and the team, as a whole will be termed 'change agents'.

Locating Change on the Change Spectrum

Our reaction to a particular change event will be influenced by its nature. When a change is of a purely technical nature, such as a machine or component upgrade, then the expectation would be that existing systems based knowledge would be applied in a reasonably mechanistic manner to implement the change. Change that requires the problem owner to apply their existing knowledge base in a systematic manner to problems requiring technical solutions, with minimal inputs from other quarters, may be regarded as the management of change in a static and isolated environment. The management process is simplified, as the impact is limited to a clearly identifiable and semi-autonomous component of a technical system. Systems based technical problems that call upon the application of knowledge of a highly structured and mechanistic nature do not create major managerial difficulties. Solution methodologies are

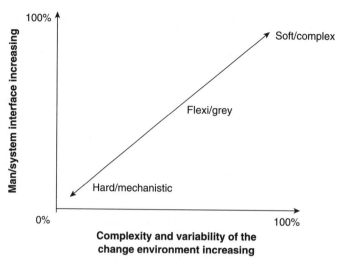

Figure 1.1　The change spectrum

based firmly on the systems school of managerial decision-making and analysis:

Definition:	a　objective clarification
	b　data capture and performance indicators
	c　systems diagnostics
	d　systems analysis
Design:	e　determination of solution options
	f　solution evaluation
Implementation:	g　solution implementation
	h　appraisal and monitoring

Technocrats who measure success against quantifiable and well-defined performance indicators apply the basic building blocks of definition, design and implementation to the problem. A technical change requires a systematic analysis and a mechanistic solution. That is not to say the solution will be easily arrived at, as the degree of intellectual input and technical expertise is likely to be significant, but rather that the methodology employed will be tried and tested.

Obviously, not all technical change situations are of the pure, totally systems-oriented, variety described above. The mechanistic solution methodologies of the systems school of management can be applied to a wide range of problems and provide optimal solutions to system interventions. A truly technical problem would be placed at the extreme 'hard' end of the change spectrum as shown in Figure 1.1.

Purely technical change, 100 per cent 'hard' or mechanistic change, exists towards the left-hand side of the spectrum. It will be characterized by a reasonably static change environment, clear quantifiable objectives and constraints, immediate implications, short time scales and minimal man–machine interfaces. In short a purely scientific or engineering problem. Such problems are reasonably uncommon as some form of human interface, even if it is only an operative who lubricates and checks a machine periodically, can generally be found if one digs deep enough.

At the extreme 'soft' end of the spectrum, one finds change situations that have a 100 per cent people orientation. Objectives and time scales will be unclear; the affected environment will be highly dynamic and difficult to specify, with subjective performance measures. Typical of the kind of problems found towards the 'soft' end of the spectrum would be ones in which personal relationships and emotional responses are predominant. As in the case of purely technical change, 100 per cent people change is also uncommon, as most individuals and groups interface with systems of a physical nature.

Solution methodologies applied to the softer end of the spectrum must reflect the highly volatile and dynamic nature of the change environment; they will originate in the organizational development school of thought. The systematic and mechanistic solution methodologies associated with scientific management will not provide answers to predominantly soft change situations. In fact they are more likely to create greater instability if applied.

By far the majority of change situations which managers are called upon to address fall within the 'flexi' region of the spectrum. A tendency towards either end of the spectrum indicates the appropriate solution methodologies that should be adopted. Part 2 of this book deals with systems based approaches designed to deal with situations which tend towards the harder end of the change spectrum, and Part 3 tackles change from an organizational development perspective, 'softer', people focused, situations and approaches are examined.

As often is the case in management, a contingency model or theory is required to cover all the ad hoc situations that may arise. Within the final sections of this book a contingency approach to change management will be argued. No single school of thought holds the answer to change management. One must not be afraid to adopt a systematic methodology when faced with people-oriented, messy situations. It must of course be flexible enough to incorporate organizational development techniques and concepts as and when appropriate. One can, if necessary, abandon all pretexts of systems methodology in the face of an increasingly dynamic environment. Similarly, the

Table 1.1   'Hard' and 'soft' problem attributes

Hard/mechanistic problems	Soft/complex problems
Objectives, constraints and performance indictors will be predominantly quantifiable	At best subjective, interrelated and semi-quantifiable objectives etc. will be available
A tendency towards static environmental forces	A volatile and complex environment will prevail
Time scales known, with reasonable certainty	Fuzzy time scale will predominate
The environment of the chain will be well bounded with minimal external interactions	The environment of the change will be unbounded and characterized by many internal and external interactions
The problem or change will be capable of clear and concise definition	It will be difficult to define problem characteristics
It may be defined in systems/technological terms	It will be defined in interpersonal and social terms
Resources required to achieve a solution will be reasonably well known	Resource requirements will be uncertain
Potential solutions will be limited and knowledge of them obtainable	There will be a wide range of solutions, all of which may appear relevant and interconnected
Structured approaches will produce results	No clear solution methodology will be visible
Consensus on the best way forward will be easily reached	Consensus on the way forward and a shared perception of the problem will not exist

management of organizational change can be enhanced through the adoption of systems based solution techniques when more static environmental circumstances are encountered.

Table 1.1 highlights the attributes associated with change situations from both ends of the spectrum. It should help clarify the position regarding the classification of change.

A brief review of the factors associated with a pending change, conducted as seen fit by the problem owner, would be sufficient to classify the change position on the spectrum. Exact positioning is not required. The more complex the change is, the greater the probability that the problem owner will have to call upon assistance, with more direct knowledge of the situation, to assist in clarifying the nature of the change. Force field analysis, which is discussed later in this chapter, may assist in determining the appropriate change management team. Such analysis may have to be augmented by the application of the diagrammatic techniques outlined in Chapter 4.

The TROPICS Test

The TROPICS test can be applied as an early warning device to access both the impact and magnitude of the impending change. It is capable of determining the most appropriate solution methodology for entering the change management process; this may have to be altered as the problem unfolds, by examining certain key factors associated with the transition process. It requires a minimal expenditure of management time and resources, as it does not need detailed quantifiable information as input.

The factors that should be considered by both the problem owner and any associated management team are as follows:

- *T*ime scales

- *R*esources

- *O*bjectives

- *P*erceptions

- *I*nterest

- *C*ontrol

- *S*ource

By considering TROPICS the manager, or the appropriately identified management team, will get a feel for the nature of the change and thus be able to establish the optimal route forward. Table 1.2 illustrates the use of TROPICS.

Management faced with straight As or Bs are shown a clear path to a solution methodology of which they can be reasonably certain. TROPICS can only provide a starting point and a tentative indication of the generic type of methodology to follow. Difficulties arise when the output is garbled in some way, with the user facing a combination of As and Bs. The

Table 1.2   The TROPICS test

Tropics factor			Solution methodology (tendency towards)
Time scales	Clearly defined – short to medium term	Ill defined – medium to long term	A = hard
			B = soft
	A	B	
Resources	Clearly defined and reasonably fixed	Unclear and variable	A = hard
			B = soft
	A	B	
Objectives	Objective and quantifiable	Subjective and visionary	A = hard
	A	B	B = soft
Perceptions	Shared by those affected	Creates conflict of interest	A = hard
	A	B	B = soft
Interest	Limited and well defined	Widespread and ill defined	A = hard
	A		B = soft
		B	
Control	Within the managing group		A = hard
		Shared outwith the group	B = soft
	A	B	
Source	Originates internally	Originates externally	A = hard
	A	B	B = soft

Note: 'Hard' refers to a systems-based, mechanistic, solution methodology.
'Soft' refers to an organizational development, complex, solution methodology.

examples below provide combinations of outputs and suggest possible user interpretations:

Case (a): time scale A, with all other factors B

This scenario would indicate an emergency situation, a time of crisis. Organizational development approaches are called for but the time scale indicates a need for an immediate action. A hard hitting dictatorial solution to overcome the short-term difficulties, followed by a longer period of education and cultural change to gain acceptance of the new state.

Case (b): source B, with all other factors A

This could represent an external technical change to a system, possibly as a result of a manufacturer's technical update. A systems approach to implement the change along with a limited education programme for operatives and maintenance may be required.

Case (c): control B, with all other factors A

This may represent an internally driven change that requires external permission to proceed. A satellite plant may wish to diversify into product design rather than act as an assembly plant. A system-based methodology may provide the answers to the internal systems change's but it is unlikely to convince the parent organization of the need to change.

TROPICS offers the manager an efficient and effective means of entering the change situation. Inputs need not be based on hard factual evidence; all that is needed is an educated assessment of the change's likely impact and general characteristics. It is important to get a feel for the change as early as possible as Mini Case 1.1 illustrates.

MINI CASE 1.1:   SCOTTISH HOMES

Scottish Homes, the then national housing agency, was facing major changes in the 1990s. For example, the Citizen's Charter held public bodies accountable for the raising of standards and the wise distribution of funds; compulsory competitive tendering for public bodies threatens in-house service functions; and the government inspired transfer of its housing stock to tenant managed housing associations; created a challenging operating environment for the agency. In the face of such massive change the board of the agency, in 1995, instigated a strategic review.

   A senior manager with the agency employed the TROPICS test, in association with a force field analysis, as a means of establishing a 'feel' for the problem. Changes were being imposed, but the organization was attempting to internalize them and determine a way forward:

TROPICS analysis:

Time scales:	Ill defined and at best medium term	Hard
Resources:	Unclear and variable	Soft
Objectives:	As yet unclear – need to be qualified	Soft
Perceptions:	Believed to be common	Soft
Interest:	Widespread amongst staff and stakeholders	Hard
Control:	With the executive and government, but must be localized to affect changes	Soft
Source:	Internalized within the agency	Hard

(Continued)

(Continued)

Force field analysis:

Driving forces			Restraining forces
Internal ownership	->	->	Individual security fears
Control over outcomes	->	->	Rationalization now affecting all 'business' units
Desire for continuous improvement – board	->	->	Change fatigue spreading
Opportunity to expand	->	->	Local opposition to centrally generated remit initiatives

For the manager concerned the above clearly showed that any organizational response to the externally driven, but now internally owned, at least at 'head office', impending changes fell into the 'grey' area of the change spectrum. The organizational implications of such dramatic change, affects the original core business (promotion, development and management of rented housing stock). Eventually, the stock must go. In turn the business units created to service the core business are under threat from a lost 'market' and the need to compete with external enterprises to secure business. However, if the problem is treated as purely one requiring a repositioning of the organization, then there is a danger that due to the unclear situation regarding resources and time scales, and the competitive threat, that the opportunity is lost and the agency is forced into a purely reactive role.

The agency recognized that it must undertake a form of corporate renewal in an attempt to ensure that the organizational design and strategy matched the new environment. It did also recognize the need to drive this change through as a matter of urgency and set about identifying change agents, prime movers, to instigate change within their spheres of control. Scottish Homes now sees itself as being not only a support service to housing initiatives, but also as being involved in local economic regeneration, finance and legal services, etc.

Frequent use of this model, with managers from a wide range of enterprises, Philips, IBM, JVC, National Semiconductor, British Airports Authority and Clydesdale Bank, suggests that although a change situation may be defined as tending towards the 'soft' end of the spectrum it need not mean that an organizationally based solution methodology is best. Very often the key factors are time and money. If time scales are tight and resources are limited then, even though all other indicators point to the complexity of the situation, a more mechanistic solution methodology will be selected. In such a situation it is best to employ a methodology that is at least capable of addressing the more complex issues while pursuing a direct path to the goal.

Force Field Analysis: a Positioning Tool

As we have seen in the previous sections it is important that the nature of the change facing the organization, department and/or problem owner is defined according to its position on the change spectrum. A realistic approach must be adopted when facing a change and the manager must take into account the many and varied forces at play (Bamford and Forrester, 2003). Force field analysis is a positioning tool that assists the management of change by examining and evaluating, in a basic yet useful manner, the forces for and against the change. Such analysis, as seen in Mini Case 1.1, can then be integrated with the spectrum positioning tool and/or the TROPICS test. It is also of use when considering the position of the problem owner and/or management team with reference to the power sources, both internal and external to the change, which may influence their ability to effectively manage the situation. The situation is further complicated by the fact that complex change situations, or at least the approach adopted to solving them, cannot be separated from wider organizational strategy (Burnes, 2004).

The organization or individual view of a change situation will be strongly influenced by the source of the change and their position relative to it. Ownership of the problem or project is the key element in establishing our reaction to change. When an individual or group have initiated certain actions, which in turn have to be managed, then they are more likely to display positive attitudes towards the situation and view the whole transition process as an opportunity to be exploited.

When the feeling of ownership is combined with the knowledge that one controls, or at least has influence over, the surrounding environment then the driving forces for the change will be significant. However, one must be aware (the TROPICS test can be of assistance here) of the degree of control within the managing group. Control shared with others, especially those above in the hierarchy, when they exhibit greater restraining forces will lead to conflict and potential blockages.

Table 1.3 illustrates the attitudinal responses and key features that can be attributed to the source of a change.

Table 1.3 Features and attitudes associated with a source of change

Internally generated change	Externally generated change
Proactive stance	Reactive response
Positive feelings	Negative feelings
Greater driving forces	Greater restraining forces
Viewed from an opportunistic position	Viewed from a problem solving position
Greater certainty	Greater uncertainty
Greater control	Reduced control
Less disruption	Greater disruption
Closed boundries and fixed time scales	Vague and variable boundaries

Externally generated change produces the greatest degree of negative feedback from those affected. External change need not solely relate to change generated outside the organization. A department, section or individual will regard external change as being any development forced upon them from outside their own environment.

Proactive attitudes and actions permit the management of a situation in an opportunistic and progressive manner. A proactive management team identifies and exploits opportunities associated with a transition between two states well in advance of the environment impinging upon them.

Figure 1.2 illustrates a generic representation of a force field diagram. Please note that the format of the diagram is of little interest. The value of

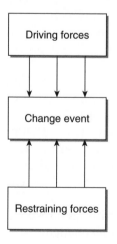

Figure 1.2 A force field diagram

such a diagram is in its power to force the problem owner into considering the position of other power sources with regard to the change at hand.

By producing a force field diagram for each individual, group or function affected by the change, the problem owner can analyse the relative magnitude of the conflicting forces, as well as develop an understanding of the underlying arguments, fears, and influencing factors. The systems diagramming tools introduced in Chapter 4 will assist the identification of interested parties.

Generally speaking, change that has been generated by the 'system' most affected is likely to produce driving forces that outweigh any restraining forces, the opposite being true for externally generated change.

Success Guarantors: Commitment, Involvement and a Shared Perception

Possibly one of the most fundamental steps in achieving the successful implementation of change is that of obtaining a shared perception amongst those affected, concerning their viewpoint regarding the issues and implications associated with the change. If the problem owner can reach a point at which all parties with a vested interest in change, view it in such a way as to see common objectives and mutual benefits then a great deal of progress will have been made.

One major obstacle to the formation of at least a partially shared perspective is the 'common sense' approach to both change management in particular and decision making in general. All too often individuals and groups attempt to sell their own particular brand of 'common sense' as if they are the only possible providers of wisdom and truth. Unfortunately, each individual or grouping affected by a changing environment is bound to possess its own particular brand. All that can result from such an approach is a mini brand war, with no clear winners and a confused market.

There are a number of influential factors, which will come together in such a way as to mould the way in which individuals, groups and organizations view particular change situations. The main factors are as follows and may be applied to all concerned and/or affected by the impending change:

- *Organizational culture*   Is it open or closed, enterprising or mechanistic, democratic or autocratic, progressive or entrenched, conducive to group work and common goals, or oppressive?

- *Source of change*   Is it internal to the affected groups and/or individuals, or externally generated and less easily controlled?

- *Social background*   Is it one that inhibits collaboration with other groups and/or individuals, or welcomes the opportunity to develop as one moves towards mutually beneficial goals?

- *Educational history*   Exposure to topical management ideas and practices combined with both a good general education and proven managerial ability may lead to proactive stances. However, inward looking internally focused development reinforcing traditional practices and customs, may work against prior educational understanding and external ideas.

- *Employment history*   Has historical experience coloured the way in which change will be viewed? Will the 'them and us' mentality interfere with the attainment of a shared perception?

- *Style of management*   The style of management exhibited by those directly involved in the change situation will obviously influence those whose co-operation and assistance they require. They may mirror the global organizational style of management, or possibly be at odds with it, but to be successful they must achieve general commitment and involvement within their terms of reference.

- *Problem ownership*   The importance of the problem owner, and where appropriate the management group, has been emphasized throughout this chapter. The involvement and commitment of the problem owner is essential, as is the managerial suitability of the problem owner to the task at hand.

- *Experience*   The track records identified with those individuals, groups and the organization affected by the change, judged in terms of their past ability to cope with change will influence the expectations of all concerned. If experience of a particular situation is lacking then, culture and style permitting, external sources of expertise must be approached and engaged.

A crucial factor associated with the successful implementation of change is the ability of the problem owner to overcome any personal prejudices regarding the change. However, they also need to ensure that the views and indeed prejudices exhibited by all other affected parties are taken on board. These need to be understood, countered or incorporated where appropriate. For most managers engaging with change can be an emotional business. It is only recently (Clarke et al., 2007) that the extent to which this emotional 'work' can impact upon the individual managers engaged in winning hearts and minds, which generally necessitates the manipulation of others, has been fully recognized.

To summarize, the problem owner must:

- Recognize that not all the suggestions offered and views expressed can be totally wrong, at least not all the time, just as the problem owners are unlikely to be totally correct at all times.

- Ensure that they are seen to be actively encouraging collaboration. Change management of all but the simplest projects is a multi-disciplinary group activity; everyone must be pulling in the same direction.

- Listen, even to the detractors and sceptics; one never wins an argument by shouting but by listening and counteracting intelligently.

- Be honest with yourself and those around you. Seek assistance and input from those most appropriate if you feel that in terms of capability you may have a problem.

- Be seen to have as much support and authority as possible. Senior management must be clearly identified with the project.

A change management consultant, while making a company presentation, provided the following quote that he attributed to Bertrand Russell, to emphasize the dangers of adopting a common-sense approach:

> When an intelligent man expresses a view which seems to us obviously absurd, we should not attempt to prove that it is somehow not true but we should try to understand how it ever came to seem true.

By following this advice the problem owner can begin the process of modifying perspectives through both education and understanding and moving along with those involved towards a shared perception of the situation and the ultimate solution of the problem.

Managing the Triggers

Those involved in the management of change need to ensure that they have established, within reason, the exact nature of the change they are about to face. They must not lose sight of the fact that change must be viewed as an event capable of causing multiple dislocations to the organization's culture, structure, systems and outputs. Leavitt's (1965) model, Figure 1.3, highlighting the impact of organizational change illustrates this point:

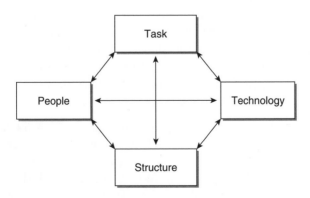

Figure 1.3   The Leavitt model

Leavitt views organizations as comprising of four interacting variables; a change that affects any one will, to a greater or less extent, interact with the others creating knock on affects. Change the task, or purpose of the organization, and the competencies (people), technology (the processes which accomplish the task) and structures (communication, power, reporting systems) must also adapt and change.

Change may be directed at any 'entry point' and have a resulting, possibly predictable, knock on effect elsewhere. Understanding the complexity of this organizational network is the first step in anticipating the likely response to any applied trigger. Once pulled, the change 'trigger' will set off a chain reaction of interrelated events, which may quickly, if not managed, create discord and inefficiency. A shock wave will reverberate, as Leavitt identified, throughout the organization. What are these triggers and can they be managed? Triggers may be classed as being either internally or externally generated, in addition, they may be further subdivided into whether or not a proactive or reactive stance is likely to be adopted to them – who pulled the trigger?

Some possible triggers could be:

- *Government legislation*   The case of the BSE scare facing the British meat industry in the late 1990s illustrates this point. In managing the crisis the government acted by strengthening existing health related legislation and by introducing new systems of registration and monitoring. European Union decisions relating to the new accession states will impact across Europe and beyond. Emission control legislation, carbon free policy and associated tax laws are bound to have an ongoing impact upon us all, industry and consumer alike.

- *Advances in process or product technology*   The converging of technologies within the communications and electronics industries is creating both new markets and revolutionizing existing ones. By combining broadcast, communications technologies and sheer processing power, the mobile phone has now permanently entered the world of work and play as an integral part of our networked world. Mobile and wireless technologies have combined to revolutionize the workplace. IBM predicts that 70 per cent of their workforce will soon work almost solely from home fully integrated with IBM's global network. Traditional distribution and supply channels have been revitalized by the growth in the power and reach of the web and ICT. Michael Porter predicts the demise of the university, as we know it today. He sees an electronic future capable of networking the learners with centres of knowledge and the demise of the traditional university system.

- *Changing consumer requirements, expectations or taste*   The British meat scare not only affected the producers and distributors. Consumers developed tastes for alternatives to beef and accordingly modified their purchase patterns. The environmentally friendly 1990s led to consumer demands for more resource friendly products and packaging. By 2007 this in turn has grown into an increasing demand for ethical government, corporate responsibility and environmentally friendly policy in general. The electric car, always technologically viable, is now a commercial reality. Consumers are now demanding more integrated and immediate delivery of services, for example, banks and financial institutions are entering partnerships with supermarket chains to deliver integrated financial packages.

- *Competitor or supply chain activities*   Organizations are developing strategic alliances, with both representatives of their own supply chain and providers of related services and products. This is done in an effort to meet more cost effectively the requirements of a sophisticated and technologically adept market place. They are essentially challenging the past and creating new and exciting ways of doing business – they are changing. Western manufacturer continue to divest of their manufacturing capability and capacity to low labour cost economies such as China and India, as do service providers who transfer transaction handling services overseas. IBM now sees itself not as a computer manufacturer but rather as a solutions provider, competing on knowledge acquisition, solution design and delivery.

- *General economic or social pressures*   In the global economy and market place, societies are becoming less isolated and more interdependent. Economic downturns in the United States, or political upheavals in Russia, mounting German unemployment, or French rural decline, or the prospect of a truly integrated Europe not only affect their immediate locality. They can create a ripple effect throughout an increasingly sensitive global society. These points are further developed in a very interesting case concerning 3M and the implications of an integrated Europe developed by Ackenhusen et al. (1996a).

- *Unpredictable environmental catastrophes*   Unpredictable, or at least unavoidable, catastrophes have, and always will, be a source of disruption and despair. If they cannot be avoided then they must be effectively managed when they occur. California has elaborate disaster plans that will, hopefully, help it cope when the 'big one' comes. The repercussions of Chernobyl are still being felt, not only at the source, but also across Europe. In Bhopal, India, negligence at a chemical plant resulted in disaster and the greatest economic power in the world is still dealing with the fallout of hurricane Katrina. Whether through negligence or as a result of global warming catastrophes are here to stay and in an increasingly global world with lengthy and complex supply chains and distribution channels their impact can but only increase.

- *Acquisition or merger*   It would appear that the appetite for mergers and acquisitions, or at least some form of strategic partnership, is once again growing. As China and India flex their growing economic muscle and Western organizations move to strengthen their foothold in Asia one can expect a few surprises. For example, the communist Chinese hold US government stock that maintains the low interest economies that has fuelled Western growth in this new millennium. An Indian multi-millionaire has purchased White and McKay whisky to add to his global drinks empire, and, the once rather conservative Royal Bank of Scotland now partly owns the Bank of China.

The manner in which a 'trigger' impacts upon a situation will, to a certain extent, depend upon its source, as well as its nature. Internally generated change is likely to be managed far more proactively, creatively and effectively, due to clear ownership, and prior knowledge and understanding. This point will be returned to at a later stage.

READER ACTIVITY

Throughout our lives we experience change. List below three significant 'triggers', along side of which identify their source and rank your feeling of 'control':

Trigger	Source (Internal/External)	Ranking (5 – high level of control; 1 – bystander status!)
1		
2		
3		

No matter the source, or nature, of the trigger it will initiate the change process. Buchanan and McCalman (1989) illustrate this through their model of perpetual transition, previously detailed in the introductory chapter (Figure I.1). The model offers a basis for managing change. From initial identification of the trigger the organization must clarify the situation, then express it in understandable terms and finally communicate its nature, impact and rationale. Next, it must formulate its response to the change focusing as far as possible on creating an innovative and opportunistic environment within which ideas and actions will be generated. Having decided on where and how to proceed the organization must convert the stakeholders and a shared perception of the change must be reached. Finally, the impetus for change must be maintained.

Being alert to the potential triggers is the first step an enterprise can take on the road to effectively managing change. Early identification and classification permits the creative, or at least proactive, management of subsequent events. According to Kanter (1983) effective organizations, or at least the masters of change within them, are adept at handling 'the triggers of change', namely:

- departures from tradition
- the crisis of a galvanizing event
- strategic choice
- prime movers
- action vehicles.

Kanter's triggers activate the senses of the change master. They are ready to exploit changes to the operating environment; they are also aware of the prime movers within the organization, and are capable of exploiting and enhancing their initiatives. Crisis situations are harnessed and used as a means of securing rapid response without incurring organized resistance. The value of a well selected vehicle for change, for example, quality improvement or customer awareness programmes, are not overlooked. However, Kilman (1995) questions the ongoing value of excessive use of action vehicles and suggests that workforces merely become apathetic towards them as their sustained use turns them into little more than fads. Practitioners often echo this viewpoint.

Prior to considering the need for, and the means of, defining the nature and environment of a change event, it is worthwhile pausing to consider the benefits of creating and managing your own crisis. Often organizations have to change fast. For example, an unwanted take-over bid may require immediate and dramatic responses. By anticipating and managing the situation in such a way as to create the environment of a *crisis* the organization may create a willingness amongst the stakeholders to act as one in defence of the enterprise. The crisis may act as a galvanizing event and lead to rapidly agreed responses.

READER ACTIVITY

Organizations are, with good reason, reluctant to discuss the creation and management of crisis situations. Practitioners will admit to minor falsifications: the pre-arranged panic which coincides with the visit of a superior, with the hope of securing additional funds or the deliberate stimulation of a crisis environment to encourage staff to give that little bit more.

Have you ever manipulated the true facts to get what you want? Consult your acquaintances, and ask what they have been up to.

As always, the key to good management lies in the ability to read environmental signals, categorize them, and take appropriate action. Don't wait for the trigger to be pulled. The best you will then be able to do is avoid the bullet, look for the initial move, act fast and be the first to draw!

The lessons

It is always advisable to ensure that you know what you are talking about, especially at those points in life when your utterances may shape your future career and lifestyle. The best way to ensure this is by doing your 'homework'. The successful management of a change event commences as soon as the decision is made to tackle the problem, or react to an opportunity or threat, through the simple task of doing your 'homework'. By identifying the nature of a change, the manager, or change agent, begins the process of determining the most probable solution methodology.

Given that managers operate in increasingly complex and dynamic environments, both within and outside the organization, time is one vital commodity that they never seem to have in abundance. If we spend too long on the 'homework' then we might just miss that once in a lifetime 'party'. A balance must be struck. In an ideal world it would be nice to know all that can be known about an impending event, but reality dictates otherwise. The best we can hope for is to identify and research the key issues, or variables, make our decisions based on informed but incomplete information, trust to judgement and experience, and pray! We need tools that allow us to review, appraise and respond to situations quickly and appropriately. The intervention strategy model, introduced in Chapter 6, could be one such tool. It is worth stressing that it is not uncommon for past changes to come back into play at a later date. The manager may think a state of embeddedness has been achieved only to find that the discontinuous nature of a particular change situation has once again raised its head (Luecke, 2003).

2 | Change and the Manager

Organizations and their managers must recognize that change, in itself, is not necessarily a problem. The problem more often than not is a less than competent management of the change situation. Why is this the case? Possibly, and many practising mangers would concur, the problem is related to managers' growing inability to appropriately develop and reinforce their role and purpose within complex, dynamic and challenging organizations. This problem can be compounded by failing to address and adapt working environments in the face of impending change: the organization exhibits inertia which in turn leads to the direct targeting or working practices for change (Buchanan et al., 2005). According to Burnes (2004) change is now an ever-present feature of organizational life, at both an operational and strategic level. Managers must realize that one cannot separate strategic change management from organizational strategy; both must work in tandem. The importance of the human side of change cannot be underestimated, one must identify and manage the potential sources and causes of potential resistance and ensure that 'motivators' are built into new processes and structures (Forlaron, 2005).

Competency and Change

Throughout the 1980s and 1990s organizations, both national and international have striven to develop sustainable advantage in both volatile and competitive operating environments. Those that have survived, and/or developed, have often found that the creative and market-driven management of their human resources can produce the much-needed competitive 'cushion'. This is not surprising. People manage change, and well-managed people manage change more effectively. Buchanan and Huczynski (2006) identify the key managerial competence of both the 1990s and the 2000s as being the ability to handle change, which in turn creates an increasing demand for the development of associated competencies. Kühl et al. (2005)

introduce the idea of 'lateral leadership', creating processes to stimulate trust, understanding and power shifts, to disrupt rigid patterns of thought and stimulate change. This once again places change at the centre of today's managerial competency framework. Change leaders are seen as being a key feature in organizations. They both set the tone and are indeed part of it: they create and live within the social dynamics of the enterprise placing change at the heart of the organization (Woodward and Hendry, 2004).

Managing change is a multi-disciplinary activity. Those responsible, whatever their designation, must possess, or have access to, a wide range of skills, resources, support, and knowledge, for example:

- Communications skills are essential and must be applied both within and outside the managing team.

- Maintaining motivation and providing leadership to all concerned.

- The ability to facilitate and orchestrate group and individual activities is crucial.

- Negotiation and influencing skills are invaluable.

- It is essential that both planning and control procedures are employed.

- The ability to manage on all planes, upward, downward and within the peer group, must be acquired.

- Knowledge of, and the facility to influence, the rationale for change is essential.

The list of competencies, or attributes, could be further subdivided, or indeed extended, as there is no such thing as a standard change event. Personal managerial attributes and skills will be returned to at a later stage.

Change and the Human Resource

Organizations over the past few decades have been moving towards flatter, leaner and more responsive structures. This has undoubtedly made many of them more efficient, in terms of their resource utilization and more effective in terms of their responsiveness to market demands. Technology has played a major role in ensuring that a coherent business approach and managerial performance can be maintained from a reduced resource base. The key to success in such moves has been the mobilization of the human resource (Peters and Waterman, 1982; Kanter, 1983, 1989; Pettigrew and Whipp, 1993). The revolution in organization design has been achieved by creating responsive working environments which emphasize the need to co-operate across and within functions; focus on service and quality; and search for holistic and integrated responses to trigger events; while encouraging participation, ownership and shared accountability (Spector, 1989; Handy, 1990).

Will the 2000s be any different? One would expect not. Managers and the organizations they serve will continue to strive to remain competitive in an increasingly global and complex market place. They will achieve sustainable growth only by embracing the power of communications technology, developing devolved supply chains and strategic alliances, and maximizing the return they receive from their accumulated knowledge base – their human capital. The knowledge they seek to exploit will be embedded across their supply chain and the barriers will be many, but ultimately success will depend upon their ability to tap into the human resource and release the potential (McLaughlin et al., 2006). As ever the 2000s will place the leadership and the human resource, in particular their alignment with organizational vision and strategy at the heart of successful change management (Graetz and Smith, 2005; Wren and Dulewicz, 2005). Employees must be on 'top form' and this can be achieved by considering their well being, stress levels, motivation and organizational loyalty (Tiong, 2005). Tiong suggests, as in some ways do Clarke et al. (2007) that in today's complex and challenging environment only by considering the employees' 'well-being' will organizations ensure productivity and alignment of interests during periods of change.

IBM, Ford, Honda, Motorola and Steelcase (the world's biggest manufacturer of office furniture) have, amongst many others, adopted team-based solutions to the management of their manufacturing facilities. Responsibilities increase as the team matures and gains confidence. Teams are being asked to participate in the process of innovation and change; employers are seeking, and ensuring that they get, enhanced performance through greater involvement and empowerment (Piczak and Hauser, 1996; Anderson and West, 1996). Lines (2004) identifies a strong relationship between participation and goal achievement and a negative relationship with resistance. British Aerospace and the BBC, along with Diageo, Fiat and Volvo, have all positively embraced the movement towards autonomous business units. The airlines, possibly with British Airways in the vanguard, have revolutionized their service in terms of the degree of emphasis that they place upon customer service and awareness. Many organizations, Power Systems, Telecom Sciences and Motorola for example, have dropped the terms foreman and supervisor, in favour of titles such as 'team leader', which is a visible manifestation of workforce empowerment.

For the manager this has led to an increasing emphasis being placed on project and teamwork, communications, customer awareness, auditing and quality procedures. The need to supervise, provide individual direction, motivate and control has diminished. Managers and leaders are being asked to facilitate events rather than direct; share responsibility and accountability rather than shoulder the burden; shape behaviours while building trust; and, develop and administer participative planning and control systems that build capacity (Higgs and Rowland, 2005; Kühl et al., 2005; and, Wren and Dulewicz, 2005).

There may be a danger that managers, amidst all this activity, lose track of their key responsibility and reason for being there in the first place. Managers are there to ensure that both they, and the processes and activities, for which they are responsible, add value to the organization as a whole. Managers of the twenty-first century are busy; they face challenging operating environments, multiple tasks and cross-functional responsibilities. In addition, they are increasingly encouraged to empower others and facilitate success. Ford and Greer (2005) suggest that we now may be in a situation in which organizations are failing to fully utilize traditional formal controls when managing change. It is becoming less clear who is actually responsible for adding value. Is it the organization as a whole? Is it the systems? Is it a combination? Is it the manager?

READER ACTIVITY

Pause and consider the following questions. What is your experience of working within teams? Who was ultimately responsible? How well informed were you? Did you feel involved? Did the team achieve its objectives? Would you have tackled things differently?

Ensuring Managerial Value and the 'Trinity'

Value is added, in a managerial context, by ensuring that all organization systems, both tangible and intangible, are aligned with their market's requirements and are capable of being appropriately developed. In today's highly competitive environment adding value is about ensuring the effective and sustainable management of change (see Mini Case 2.1).

MINI CASE 2.1: GLENLIGHT AND ERICSSON

The case of GlenLight Shipping (Boddy, 2005) deals with the final and dramatic attempts of a long established traditional enterprise to diversify into a potentially lucrative business. It hinted at one of the most frustrating obstacles that can confront a change agent – apathy. Lack of interest in the proposed change, is difficult to deal with as it manifests itself in neither the form of support nor opposition. In GlenLight the majority of the managerial stakeholders were too involved in maintaining the status quo and avoiding conflict. They had ceased to add value and became apathetic. They most probably felt that events were no longer controllable and were happy to merely react.

The significance and immediacy of the change facing GlenLight, combined with the relative remoteness of the enterprise's principal stakeholders, hampered activities to secure ownership of the change amongst the workforce.

The case of Ericsson, Australia, contrasts markedly from that of GlenLight. The 1990s saw massive deregulation of the Australian telecommunications industry and for Ericsson this effectively threatened its privileged relationship with Telecom Australia (Telecom accounted for over 60 per cent of Ericsson's business). Over the years Ericsson had to a certain extent grown complacent, as business was easy to obtain and service. The new, deregulated environment would be far more aggressive and cost conscious. Ericsson had to develop a marketing focus fast.

The Chief Executive set about revitalizing the organization. A vision statement was developed and a leading change programme instigated. The programme was designed to articulate the vision and prepare the management team for the implementation of change. They developed 'mental tools for change' and charged their management with identifying a project that would act as a vehicle for transferring the tools to the workforce. Ericsson succeeded in adding value to its processes and people and thus protected and developed its market presence (Graetz, 1996).

Successful change requires adherence to three key managerial rules – the 'holy trinity'. The religious metaphor is merely intended to convey the importance of adhering to the rules. Those at the centre of significant change events must 'buy in' to the process, without of course losing their objectivity, and believe with passion in the course of action about to be undertaken. If they don't approach their task with commitment others are unlikely to be convinced, resulting in apathy and discord (Beer and Eisenstat, 1990; Kotter, 1995). Senior management's role in ensuring visible commitment and direction is pivotal (Sminia and Van Nistelrooij, 2006), it is their role to set the tone and show belief. The trinity may be portrayed diagrammatically as in Figure 2.1.

All to often the process, or the activities associated with a change, assume more importance than the change itself. It is often far easier to 'talk a good game' and plan for a future event than to focus the mind on ensuring successful implementation. The first rule of the 'trinity', *maintain your focus*, highlights the need to address such questions as: Why are we changing and

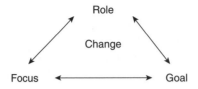

Figure 2.1   The 'trinity'

what do we expect in return? It takes effort to maintain the focus in a dynamic managerial and business environment. Attention and commitment will diminish as time elapses. Interest can be maintained by forcing the pace, organizing special interest events, reorganizing the core management team, employing 'creative' communications strategies, and above all else ensuring continued senior management support.

No less important than maintaining focus within the 'trinity' is the second rule of role awareness. Understanding the nature of the term 'value added' assists not only in clarifying managerial roles but also in maintaining the focus. Change for change's sake seldom results in any meaningful improvements. Change is costly, disruptive and potentially dangerous; it would be unwise to embark on the journey without first establishing that success would be both probable and beneficial.

READER ACTIVITY

Do you have a career plan? Do you really know why you are reading this book? What are you hoping to achieve and why? If you know the answers to these questions and are happy with your replies then you probably have set, and are pursuing, your goal – Read on!

The third rule of the 'trinity', *maintain your goal*, may seem obvious but it is often overlooked. Given that both the focus is maintained and roles remain clear, why raise the issue of goals? The effective development and achievement of business strategies, as described in numerous texts, depends upon successful implementation, which in turn is dependent upon the effective management of the resulting change. Focus and roles apply to the change at hand, but by considering goals the discrete change is placed in the wider context of policy and strategy. There is little point adding value to a system that is at odds with the strategic direction of the enterprise, or in maintaining focus on a target set between moving 'goal posts'. Change, whether strategic, tactical or operational, must be set in the context of general corporate strategy (see Mini Case 2.2).

MINI CASE 2.2:   HEWLETT-PACKARD

Hewlett-Packard is recognized as being a highly successful company. They led the way into open systems and were first to adapt to reducing industry margins. They are an organization, which at least on the surface adhere to the 'trinity'. They have a clear goal articulated from the top, namely, to stay ahead of the game and be both aware and responsive to long term trends. They strive not to lose focus by encouraging the enterprising spirit of the initial founders. Innovation and drive are welcomed. Managers and staff in general, are aware of their role, which is to ensure value to the end user. They stay close to the customer by organizing themselves into many multi-disciplinary and self-financing business units.

Fundamental rules, useful though they are, provide no more than guidance to those managing complex changes. However, the value of such rules or edicts is enhanced within organizations where the cultural environment encourages creative and progressive solutions to pending business opportunities or threats (Peters and Waterman, 1982; Kanter, 1983).

The Cultural Web

Consider 'first impressions'; many would argue that they are never wrong. Can you get a feel for a person, group, company or institution from an initial meeting? Could you attribute political leanings and social attitudes simply by observing an individual's car, clothes and look? By standing at the front door of a restaurant, pub, café or theatre could you get a feel for the likely level of service and quality that would be provided? If the answers to these questions are 'yes', then join the international stereotyping club. Stereotyping only exists because in the perceived majority of cases the initial impression is vindicated in some tangible way. Organizations can be classified, if only subjectively, by the way they 'feel' and 'behave'.

READER ACTIVITY

Consider the last bank you were in. How did it look and feel? Do you think that a deliberate effort had been made to create this feeling?

When you think of organizations such as Mercedes and Virgin what images to they conjure up? How do these enterprises reinforce this image and why?

Organizations are cultures; they can be studied and manipulated as such. Just as the individual can adapt to their social surroundings, altering their appearance, beliefs and behaviours, so to can organizations (Kanter et al., 1992). However, it is worth emphasizing the importance of 'culture' as it relates to the creative management of change. Every enterprise, public or private, will possess an unique cultural blueprint, which dictates how it interacts with its environment and manages its people. Understanding the relationships between the cultural web and a changing environment greatly assists the organization to manage change (Johnson et al., 2006). Higgins and McAllaster (2004) point to the importance of fully understanding and addressing the cultural artefacts associated and potentially impacting upon any particular change situation.

In the 1970s British Airways lost touch with the aspirations and requirements of its potential market. An apathetic, take it or leave it, culture had developed. This was not too dissimilar, at the time, to the prevailing cultures in British Rail and the Fiat group. However, at British Airways, extensive customer awareness programmes, along with a revamping of image and enhanced quality initiatives, undertaken in the 1980s, led and supported by their Chairman, Lord King, resulted in a dramatic change in fortunes. A tangible cultural shift was greeted positively by customers.

Johnson et al. (2006) argue that strategic developments can only be successful if they recognize and address the cultural aspects of the change at hand. Figure 2.2 illustrates the pivotal role played by the cultural 'recipe', the genetic blue print of the organization, when exploring complex change situations.

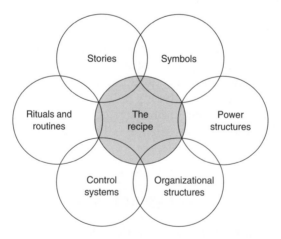

Figure 2.2   The cultural web

Understanding the nature of any change is the key to ensuring that both the situation will be properly analysed and a plausible implementation strategy developed. The 'recipe' is made up of two categories of ingredients. First, the physical or tangible, such as administrative systems; quality procedures; control mechanisms; organizational structures; dress codes; decor; communications systems; and written statements of aims, objectives, missions and philosophy. They are however only the manifestations of the second category. The intangible, 'soft', aspects of the 'recipe' may be thought of as the 'stock' of the dish. These ingredients are difficult to define but generally include factors such as informal value systems; interpersonal and group rituals; the politics of power and symbols of success. The cultural web of an organization is dependent not only upon the ingredients but also upon the manner in which they are mixed.

The Web and the Past

The web will protect itself and it will reinforce its values and relationships, and in effect it will resist change. Rosabeth Moss Kanter (1983) addresses this issue by asking the following question. Can we be sure what we are seeing is indeed the reality of the situation? History is written, or at least influenced, by the victors. Kanter suggests that to understand change, especially the 'softer', intangible aspects, the investigator must realize that what they are viewing or experiencing is the product of post hoc rationalization, a 'revised history' and a manufactured culture. How important is this? To predict the outcomes of any event it is necessary to understand the past and learn from previous mistakes and build on past successes. However, just as the historian must attempt to see beyond the victors' story, the manager, tackling a complex change situation, must investigate the true reality of past events. Reports, memos and documentation, along with personal and group recollections will have been formed with a view to selling, justifying and embellishing previous courses of actions and decisions. The culture will protect itself. Also, organizations and their managers tend only to learn from their obvious failures. Successes are welcomed and hailed but not often fully understood.

READER ACTIVITY

Consider the following questions. Have you ever made a mistake and attempted to hide it? Have you ever blamed others for your failings? Have you ever done something because it was the 'done thing to do'? What memories do you cherish? Are they ones that recall good times and create positive feelings?

(Continued)

> *(Continued)*
>
> We all want to belong and do what is best for the groups we belong to. This involves reinforcing shared values and projecting positive and successful images of ourselves. Organizations and their employees are no different.

Dig, seek the truth, and discover the reality. Unlock the myths; examine the nature of the politics and power plays; research the failings of past strategies and determine the rationale behind the 'recipe'. Higgins and MacAllaster (2004) discuss the need to address cultural artefacts, the myths and sagas relating to past success and failures, and who the villains, heroes or heroines were. Often these cultural artefacts act as barriers to change and they have to be modified or replaced before true progress can be made. Clearly culture and change are interrelated. How might the proactive and innovative organization be typified? Are there sets of culturally related attributes associated with effective change management?

Cultural Attributes of Change

Peters and Waterman (1982) and Kanter (1983, 1989) would suggest that there are common culturally related attributes associated with organizations recognized as being masters of change. The attributes may be presented as follows:

1 *A clear and communicated strategic vision* People must know where they are going and why. Suppliers, customers and stakeholders obviously benefit from a clear understanding of the organization's philosophy, purpose and strategic undertakings. The vision, based on a thorough understanding of the operating environment and organization capabilities, sets the context for strategic developments, organizational cultures, management approaches and lays the foundation of the desired means of sustaining competitive advantage.

2 *Visible senior management involvement* Sustainable change can only be achieved when senior management becomes visibly involved in the process. Executives must exhibit, and encourage within others, a bias for action (Peters and Waterman, 1982). The levers of change must be connected from the top to the bottom of the organization (Pettigrew and Whipp, 1993). The executive grouping, led by the chief executive, must support their change agents in their endeavours (Sminia and Van Nistelrooij, 2006).

3 *People based competitive edge* In an increasingly bland corporate world, where products, technology, packaging and image, are cloned and replicated, enterprises are finding it more difficult to identify a truly sustainable competitive edge. The people they employ and develop offer a means of sustaining a competitive advantage that is dynamic, potentially unique and difficult to emulate. An empowered, autonomous, knowledgeable and participating

workforce, encouraged to exhibit entrepreneurial tendencies, is more likely to respond to change and exploit potential opportunities.

4 *Marketing ethos* No matter the nature of an enterprise's business, nor the sector to which it belongs, it would be wise to maintain a watchful eye on the market place it serves. If it does not take care of its customers then someone else will. Everyone in an organization has a customer; satisfy the internal customer and build a 'marketing ethos' throughout the organization. Focus on the customer's needs and develop a culture designed to meet them.

5 *Consensus driven management* Driven by the previous four attributes, an organization would be wise to foster a shared view of the corporate ethos, to strive to establish a consensus on the best course of action and the optimal means of achieving the desired outcomes. A shared perception is not easy to achieve, as there is always a tendency, especially for those in positions of power, to dictate rather than communicate. Gaining a consensus takes time and commitment. It involves the re-engineering of the cultural web and in extreme cases may require the wholesale dismantling of existing organization structures and procedures in an effort to jettison 'baggage'.

6 *Awareness and reflection of social responsibility* By widening the definition of the corporate stakeholder to include society in general, who after all in some shape or form may be regarded as the market place, corporations are now attempting to reflect societal expectations. In addition, regulatory bodies again seeing society as their market are endeavouring to ensure that enterprises, of all types, conduct their business in accordance with society wishes. The cultural web is now, more than ever before, reflecting, in a tangible way, its responsibility to the environment, consumers, employees and the wider public (Martin and Hetrick, 2006).

READER ACTIVITY

Identify three well-known companies. Now do a little research. How do these companies stay ahead of the competition?

For example, Gillette through staying in touch with technology and the customer, ensure that they have at least 20 new shaving products in development at any one time. Pepsi, showing commitment from the top, have appointed a Director of Innovation for Europe. Virgin's Richard Branson brands all products with enthusiasm and commitment: he is the guarantee!

Greater emphasis continues to be placed on the importance of communication within the cultural change framework. Achieving and maintaining the above noted cultural attributes requires the organization to develop responsive communications systems (Pettigrew and Whipp, 1993). In addition, technological advances within the communications media are offering ever more interactive and imaginative means of 'getting the message' across (Morant, 1996). There is a widely recognized need to ensure effective corporate communication within a constantly changing environment (Moorcroft, 1996; Richardson and Denton, 1996).

The Role of Communication

Organizations increasingly have to deal with communication relating to change in the same way as they do in the market place. They have to be creative, purposeful and responsive, in particular they have to 'fight' to be heard. Employees are bombarded with information. To ensure your message is heard, understood and acted upon one has to take communication seriously. Ensuring enhanced communication in times of change is therefore essential (Graetz and Smith, 2005). Communication is a two-way process. Stakeholders must be in a responsive loop. They must be listened to and engaged. Goodman and Truss (2004) stress the importance of considering both the content and process of corporate communication in times of change, and indeed at all times. Particular attention should be paid to: ensuring the timely communication of change related messages; matching communication channels to the recipient's needs and listening patterns/opportunities in an appropriate manner; and, ensuring that uncertainty is minimized and the negative impact of the 'rumour mill' nullified. A common, shared, language will greatly enhance the communication process: enhancing understanding and potentially easing the process of acceptance and engagement (Eriksson and Sundgren, 2005).

It is worth noting from a change perspective, that there are a few well-defined guidelines or rules that have been developed over the years, which should assist individuals and organizations when communicating change events:

- *Customize the message*   The key here is understanding. Who is the audience? How will they react? What do they know? Ensure that the message has been encoded in a manner appropriate to the skills and knowledge level of the audience. Try not to use jargon and, if possible, place yourself in the recipient's seat. How would you react to the 'message'?

- *Set the appropriate tone*   The interpretation of a communication depends upon both the content and the tone. Offence can often be caused if the tone has been perceived to be inappropriate, for example, patronizing, flippant, condescending or impudent. Think before you act and always remember that the whole body sends the message: dress, body language, medium and words set the tone.

- *Build in feedback*   Communication is a two-way process. Assuming the message to be conveyed is not simply an instruction, statement or a 'news item', then the sender must consider how responses are to be made and noted. In change situations, given the need to allay fears and uncertainties, it is essential that the manager has some means of ensuring that the message was received, believed, accepted and understood. Managers must both plan and control the communications process. In change situations one must exercise some control by seeking feedback and maintaining an effective dialogue.

- *Set the example*   If you are asking others to respond to the communication, or brief their staff, ensure that as the sender you have done as requested. Be consistent and at all times practise what you preach!

- *Ensure penetration*   The media selected to deal with the communication must be capable of achieving the required penetration within the organization. It must also reflect the time horizons of the change. Is real time communication required? Is written feedback expected?

In the 1980s the Philips executive team regularly utilized the organization's personal television channel to communicate across Philips' global network. Glaxo Wellcome, in the 1990s, adopted a cascading distribution system. Corporate communications are cascaded down and through the organization via networked employee groupings. Peugeot UK also adopted this approach. Here executive decisions receive a colour-coded urgency rating which determines the speed at which they must be communicated to the workforce. When Delta airlines were faced with significant redundancies in 1994 they took positive steps to control and manage the situation. A communications centre, with freephone numbers, was set up to provide immediate responses to employee questions. Open forums were organized and Vice Presidents were dispatched to allay fears. In addition, the senior management team visited all Delta sites within two days of the announcement. The IBM of the twenty-first century, has an impressive array of technologically driven communications and network services in place to ensure not only effective and efficient communication but also to deliver and support a knowledge based solutions environment.

READER ACTIVITY

Have you ever been misunderstood? Did you send wrong signals, or where they simply decoded incorrectly? Consider your communications skills. Do they need improving? If so, then ensure that corrective action is taken; take the opportunities provided by your studies to practise in a non-threatening environment. Volunteer for presentations. Lead the team. Assist in report writing.

If organizations do not manage their communications, others will. The media, unions, the 'rumour mill' and competitors are only too willing to assist the 'silent' corporation in their time of need.

Effective communication, designed to inform, consult and promote action, will assist in overcoming both resistance to change and ignorance. Mobilizing the 'troops', while dealing with and overcoming resistance, apathy and ignorance, can be a daunting task for any manager. It is essential that organizations recognize the need to foster and develop the managerial talents required to facilitate change.

Resistance to Change

An organization can create an operating environment, both internally and throughout its supply chain, which encourages an opportunistic stance to be adopted. However, no matter how welcoming an organization is to change, it will still face a degree of employee, supplier, distributor, stakeholder and consumer resistance to change. It may manage to reduce the frequency and potency of such resistance but it will never eradicate the fear of the unknown.

Why do people resist change? Quite simply because they fear the unknown and are comforted by the familiar. Also very often successes and power bases are routed in the past and present, not necessarily in the future. Why risk losing position, control and reputation?

> It ought to be remembered that there is nothing more difficult to take in hand, more perilous to conduct, or more uncertain in its success, than to take the lead in the introduction of a new order of things. Because the innovator has for enemies all those who have done well under the old conditions, and indifferent defenders among those who may do well under the new. (Machiavelli, *The Prince*)

Kanter (1983) echoes Machiavelli's thoughts. She points out that it is always far easier to say yes, in the first instance, to a new idea for in the early developmental stages its impact will be minimal. Once the development work starts to produce results then the detractors will appear and a host of negative comments and actions materialize. No matter the extent to which an organization has designed procedures, structures and cultures to encourage openness, responsiveness and innovation, there will always be detractors. All too often we forget that: 'We are not creatures of circumstance, we are the creators of circumstance' (Disraeli).

When facing an uncertain personal change it is easy to forget mankind's successes in shaping the world. Unfortunately, organizations, individuals and groups often fear change for many rational reasons:

- *It can result in organization redesign*   Tampering with the design will modify, at least in the short term, existing power bases, reporting structures and communications networks. In extreme cases issues regarding security of employment will be raised and undoubtedly questions concerning redeployment and training emerge.

- *It creates new technological challenges*   New techniques, procedures and skills acquisition can bring out, no matter how briefly, the 'Luddite' that lurks just beneath our outer veneer of confidence. One should never underestimate the power of technological change to cause disruption. Often the technology is well understood by those promoting its introduction and they cannot understand the concerns of those who must manage end use of it!

- *It confronts apathy*   A great many employees grow apathetic in their approach to working life. Careers falter: positions of apparent security and ease are achieved. Competencies are developed, and employees become apathetic to their working environment. They do what they do well, or have convinced their peers and manager that they do, and deep down they would prefer the status quo. Change may have the audacity to wake them up from their slumbers!

- *It permeates throughout the supply chain*   Change for change's sake is both foolish and potentially expensive. The effective and efficient management of the supply chain ensures that the final consumer is delivered a product or service that meets their expectations. Stakeholders within the supply chain, including the final consumer, tend to be sceptical of any change that results in the 'equilibrium' being disturbed. Management must be careful to ensure that the effects of a change, although beneficial to a particular member, do not cascade throughout the chain causing negative results further downstream.

- *It challenges old ideas*   By their very nature organizations have traditionally encouraged stability, continuity and the pursuit of security. Continuity of procedures, services, products and staff leads to a stable operating environment. Remember that the basis of today's success lies in the past and this encourages management to reinforce the lessons of the past. For example, senior management do not retire. They take up non-executive positions on the board; non-executive directors are recruited for their past knowledge of the business environment; organizational design attempts to reflect the perception of historical success; and, recruitment policies endeavour to reinforce old beliefs by ensuring the appointment of like minded personnel. Success in the future will depend upon a management understanding the lessons of the past, but if too much emphasis is placed upon the past then these lessons will simply reinforce old ideas.

- *It encourages debate*   Debate is healthy when well managed, but it does tend to identify those lacking in understanding or knowledge. Once again the assumptions of the past and those who promote them will be challenged.

READER ACTIVITY

Compile a list of words which you would associate with an impending 'technological change'. Classify them according to whether or not you consider them positive or negative (you may also denote them as neutral).

Once you have completed the task consider how you decided whether they were positive or negative.

Managers must be aware of the impact of their actions. Resistance to change, as has been noted, can be reduced through creative organizational design and development, but it can not be eradicated. Effective communication often holds the key to successfully unlocking the door to change.

Change needs to be portrayed in positive terms, a necessity to ensure long term survival. In so doing gurus, chief executives, governments and individuals must be aware that not all resistance to change need be negative. Rational, principled and shared resistance to proposed developments may well signal that the 'common good' may not be best served by implementing change. For example, the design team who constantly fights cost cutting measures on the basis of maintaining product safety and performance levels should have their concerns openly and fully addressed. Had Ford done this in the 1970s the legendary case of the Pinto's safety related lawsuits may have been avoided. British Airways' drive to regenerate the airline by focusing on creating the world's number one airline could have influenced staff decisions to engage in competitive actions against Virgin, which would be later described as a campaign of 'dirty tricks'. Change for change's sake, change for short term commercial advantage or indeed change which may adversely affect the 'common good', should be resisted, not only on moral grounds, but also on the basis that the adverse long term financial consequences are likely to outweigh any short term gain.

The Change Agent or Master

The term 'master of change' may be traced to Kanter (1983). However, there are many other terms that have been used to denote those responsible for the effective implementation of change. For example, change agents, problem owners, facilitators, project mangers. The focal point of a change need not be an individual; a work group could quite easily be designated as a special task force responsible for managing the change. However, generally within, or above, any work group there is still someone who ultimately is accountable and responsible. What are the essential attributes of a change agent/master and are there any guidelines for them?

Buchanan and Huczynski (2006) suggest the need to encourage participation and involvement in the management of the change by those who are to be affected. The aim is to stimulate interest and commitment and minimize fears, thus reducing opposition. It may also be necessary to provide facilitating and support services. These could assist in promoting an individual's awareness for the need for change, while counselling and therapy could be offered to help overcome fears. Management must engage in a process of negotiation, striving towards agreement. This is essential where those opposing have the power, and influence, to resist and ultimately block the change. Such beliefs and initiatives were at the heart of British Telecom's 'for a better life' programme, which was in effect a vehicle for change (Mason, 1998).

If consensus fails then one has little alternative to move on to explicit and implicit coercion. Somewhere in between the two extremes management may attempt to manipulate events in an effort to sidestep sources of resistance. For example, play interested parties off against each other or create a galvanizing crisis to divert attention.

The techniques need not be employed in isolation. Kotter and Schlesinger (1979) emphasize that they may be most effective when utilized in combination. The core tasks facing a change agent, or project manager, according to Boddy and Buchanan (1992), are to reduce the uncertainty associated with the change situation and then encourage positive action. They suggest a number of steps to assist:

1 *Identify and manage stakeholders*   Gains visible commitment.

2 *Work on objectives*   Clear, concise and understandable.

3 *Set a full agenda*   Take a holistic view and highlight potential difficulties.

4 *Build appropriate control systems*   Communication is a two-way process, feedback is required.

5 *Plan the process of change*   Pay attention to:

- establishing roles – clarity of purpose
- building a team – do not leave it to chance
- nurturing coalitions of support – fight apathy and resistance
- communicating relentlessly – manage the process
- recognizing power – make the best use of supporting power bases
- handing over – ensure that the change is maintained.

MINI CASE 2.3:   AN NHS STORY

Boddy and Buchanan (1992) stress the need for control and feedback. This becomes crucial when communications are channelled from the managing group to other parties. A project manager, leading a team in a National Health Service Trust Hospital, assumed that information was being conveyed upwards by a senior member of medical staff. When it became apparent that no feedback was materializing the manager challenged the medic. It transpired that although initially agreeable to the assigned role of 'messenger' the medic now considered such a task as being one more associated with an administrator. More worrying, and much to the joy of the medic, the senior management team had not realized that it had not received any reports. Everyone was simply too busy to follow-up on all the initiatives they had sanctioned!

Are there any personal attributes that can be associated with the successful change master? Kanter (1983) suggests that masters exist throughout the organization (but are crucial at the top) and constitute in effect a latent force. Kanter typifies masters of change by their ability to:

- question the past and challenge old assumptions and beliefs;
- leap from operational and process issues to the strategic picture;
- think creatively and avoid becoming bogged down in the 'how-to';
- manipulate and exploit triggers for change.

Kanter has further developed these thoughts (1989). She suggests that the 1980s change master must now adapt to cope with the complexities of the 'post entrepreneurial' organization of the 1990s; they had to become a 'business athlete'. Seven traits are associated with such 'athletes':

1 able to work independently without the power and sanction of the management hierarchy;
2 an effective collaborator, able to compete in ways that enhances rather than destroys co-operation;
3 able to develop high trust relations, with high ethical standards;
4 possessing self-confidence tempered with humility;
5 respectful of the process of change as well as the substance;
6 able to work across business functions and units – 'multifaceted and multi-dextrous';
7 willing to take rewards on results and gain satisfaction from success.

To summarize the effective change agent must be capable of orchestrating events; socializing within the network of stakeholders; and managing the communication process.

Need the change master or agent be an internal appointment? Is it possible to acquire on 'loan' effective facilitators of change? The objective outsider has a lot to offer an enterprise engaged upon a change exercise. However, there is a need for competent internal change agents to be assigned to the project so as to ensure co-operation, effective implementation and successful handover upon completion (Buchanan and Boddy, 1992). The role envisaged for the external change agent, namely to assist in fully defining the problem is as follows: to help in determining the cause and suggesting potential solutions; to stimulate debate and broaden the horizons; and to encourage the client to learn from the experience and be ready to handle future situations internally; is complementary to that of the internal problem owner. It is the responsibility of the potential client to establish the need for an objective outsider, by considering their own internal competencies and awareness of the external opportunities.

MINI CASE 2.4:
MIXED MESSAGES AT BOART LONGYEAR

In an effort to enhance performance, Boart Longyear, a mining machinery manufacturer, attempted to implement self-directed teams, capable of not only acting for themselves but also of facilitating and managing ongoing initiatives. Each team went through 60 hours of training, which covered leadership, decision making, interpersonal skills and facilitation. Despite the effort teams were reluctant to take on the responsibilities and the lack of leadership led to decision-making delays. A great source of frustration originated from the fact that the employees were far happier being told what to do.

With perseverance the teams began to perform: members contributed as they did not wish to be accused, by the team, of under-performing. Former supervisors found a role as information providers and resource procurers and productivity increased by 12 per cent.

To conclude, those involved in the management of change need to heed the above guidelines and attempt to acquire the desired attributes. However, they must not lose sight of the fact that change must be viewed as an event capable of causing multiple dislocations to the organization's culture, structure, systems and outputs. Once again Leavitt's model, introduced in Figure 1.3, highlights the impact of organizational change and illustrates the interdependency of variables.

Change may be directed at any 'entry point' (people, task, technology and structure) and have a resulting, possibly predictable, knock on effect elsewhere. Understanding the complexity of this organization network is the first step in anticipating the likely response to any applied trigger for change. Chapter 4 attempts to come to grips with the potential identification and subsequent management of triggers for change through the use of mapping techniques. While Chapter 8, Competing narratives, links the outcomes of systems interventionist practice with the experiences of those who have managed change in an effort to understand, how can so many different views of a particular change event exist? The introductory chapter, together with the last two, have in many ways concentrated on the role of the manager and organization. Along with the examination of the role we have introduced the context of change and touched on some of the skills that one would require to manage a change event. The next chapter concentrates on those skills that have been identified as being useful to a change agent. Rather than merely list and examine the skills a rather more novel approach has been adopted. Which gender is best equipped, from a skills and attitudes standpoint, to best cope with managing change?

3 Managing Change from a Gender Perspective

Chapter 2 noted the importance of strategically managing change and identified the attributes of an effective change agent. Using an initial, holistic, almost multi-disciplinary, investigation this chapter examines the differences in the way in which men and women approach and manage change. From an academic standpoint the chapter suggests that the manner in which change is approached, and, the techniques and models employed to handle it, can be subject to varying interpretation, and acceptance, dependent upon gender. Management development practices related to change, in particular, the supporting models and assumptions, may have to take into account and address the 'gender question'. Practitioners may wish to note that change programmes could be impeded by the promotion of non-inclusive solution methodologies and approaches.

The Importance of Gender

The gender balance in the workplace is changing. According to Rosabeth Moss Kanter (1993, 1994) this is one of the most significant demographic phenomena ever to face organizations. By the early 1990s almost 70 per cent of the eligible female population participated in the labour market. In some regions of Britain female employees outnumbered males (Viewpoint, 1993). The labour force survey of May 1997 showed that women accounted for 47 per cent of all employees. The number of women managers has, as one would expect, been increasing. According to the Institute of Management, in 1997 women accounted for over 15 per cent of all managers, as opposed to less than 2 per cent in the early 1970s. The National Management Salary Survey 2000, commissioned and published by the Institute of Management and Remuneration Economics, indicates women now account for 22 per cent of all managers. In addition, female representation at boardroom level is also on the increase, up 8 per cent over ten years to almost 10 per cent.

There is no evidence to suggest that the trend towards an increasing proportion of women managers, or indeed that the advancement of female managers, is likely to diminish. As people ultimately manage change, not technologies, systems or organizations, and given the increasing complexity and pace of change, any differences in the way in which gender affects change management may have an impact upon performance. Charles Handy links the need to manage change with the emerging gender balance question:

> They [organizations] want people who can juggle with several tasks and assignments at one time, who are more interested in making things happen than in what title or office they hold, more concerned with power and influence than status. They want people who value instinct and intuition as well as analysis and rationality, who can be tough but also tender, focused but friendly, people who can cope with necessary contradictions. They want, therefore, as many women as they can get. (1994)

The management of change has in recent years received, from both academics and practitioners, an inordinate amount of attention. As demonstrated within this book (and similar publications) there are a multitude of models, tools, guidelines and inspirational diatribes, all designed to ensure successful 'change'. Likewise, gender issues in the workplace have also faced a great deal of scrutiny (Dempster, 1998). However, there has been little or no research linking gender differences to the management of change (Dempster, 1998; Lane, 2005).

Identifying, managing and exploiting change scenarios, together with anticipating and managing the transition to a more competitively secure future, are widely recognized corporate success prerequisites (Drucker, 1998; Handy, 1996; Pascale, 1999). Given the increasingly influential role women play within organizations, it is surely worth asking the question: Do men and women approach and manage change scenarios differently? And if so, do we have to modify the way in which we manage change?

Linda Dempster (an executive with the UK Benefits Agency), prompted by a recent exposure to change, began to wonder if the female skills set might not be better suited to change. Could women be better managers of change, and if so, what next? This chapter reports the outcomes of an explorative investigation of the issues surrounding the above questions (Paton and Dempster, 2002). The following section reviews the relevant gender and change management literature and sets the stage for the explorative study.

Management Styles and Gender

Marshall's 1995 study was concerned with 'Women managers moving on'. She was particularly interested in why senior female managers parted company with their employers, and indeed their careers. Marshall herself admits:

> The prominence of organizational change themes in the stories as a collection was initially a surprise to me. (p. 154)

Although not central to the study a common theme emerges. There was strong evidence that these women felt that they had to change their management style to have both themselves and their 'changes' accepted. Marshall discusses the tensions between the male and female management styles. The women saw themselves as open, collaborative, person-oriented and empowering. They felt that to succeed as change agents they must adopt more male orientated styles (styles which they described as directive and aggressive). Anecdotal evidence from Amy Segal's (1996) investigation of feminism and consciousness raising at work also tends to link male dominated organizational cultures with a growing tendency to question gender related roles and career/personal development.

Gordon (1991) echoes Marshall's, and her managers', interpretation. Gordon argues that many successful women have aligned themselves with prevailing organizational cultures and indeed have become 'prisoners of men's dreams'. Both authors suggest that different gender specific management styles exist. Differences such as these may influence the way in which the sexes approach and manage change.

Gordon and Marshall are not alone in their view that gender style differences exist. Vinnicombe (1987) employed the Myers Briggs approach to examine how managers perform their role. She found that significantly more women are visionaries and catalysts. They define power differently and are much more collaborative, and far less authoritative, than men. Eagly (1987) and Gibson (1993) again stress that *communal* behaviours, those concerned with the welfare of other people, are more usually attributable to females. *Argentic* behaviours, focusing on goals and control, tend to be associated with males. Eagly and Johnson's (1990) study of gender and leadership style concluded that women adopt a far more democratic and participative style of leadership than that of men. A more recent investigation (Singh and Vinnicombe, 2001) into the degree to which gender influences a manager's use of impression management highlighted the tendency for female managers to:

> ... wait to be noticed, delivering quality performance, quietly putting themselves out, volunteering and acting as good organisational citizens, whilst others push themselves forward. (p. 193)

This is yet further evidence of gender difference, a difference which given the above noted tendency for females to prefer more participative styles, may not only impact upon change management but also career progression.

One of the most cited studies dealing with gender and leadership is that of Judy Rosener (1990). This extensive research study focused on both male and female leaders. The study found female leadership was characterized by attempts to encourage participation, share power, energize and enhance the self worth of others. Males on the other hand view their job in transactional terms and rely heavily on formal authority. Rosener further developed her observations and argument in *America's Competitive Secret* published in 1995. The gender behaviours are associated with two different leadership styles, namely, command control and interactive. She suggests that women tend to prefer the interactive style but have been influenced by a plethora of publicity encouraging them to adopt a more male orientated style. In her view 'Implicit in this idea is the assumption that the "right" or "best" way to run an organisation is the white male way' (Rosener, 1995: 31). Drawing on her previous research Rosener provides empirical evidence that shows women to be different from men but not superior or inferior. The alternative qualities are of equal value.

Rosener's command and control and interactive styles may be compared with the transactional and transformational leadership styles (Burns, 1978), or indeed with calculating or committing management styles (Mintzberg, 1989). Interactive, transformational and committing styles encourage involvement and participation; they excite, empower and encourage individuals to commit to organizational success. The opposite is true of command, transactional and calculating approaches. According to Bateman and Zeithaml (1993):

> Transactional leadership does not excite, transform, empower or inspire people to focus on the interests of the group or organisation. (p. 429)

Alimo-Metcalfe (1995) further emphasized the gender divide. The comparative study of female and male constructs of leadership qualities once again identified women in the transformational camp and males firmly in the transactional. Alimo-Metcalfe's more recent research indicates that there may be differences between the UK and US in terms of not only how we measure/interpret transformational leadership but also how it may be perceived. The multi-factor based Transformational Leadership Questionnaire-Local Government Version (TLQ-LGV) highlights the importance placed in the UK on aspects of leadership associated with a genuine concern for others:

> UK understanding of transformational leadership appears to be based on what the leader does for the individual, such as empowering, valuing, supporting, and developing. (Alimo-Metcalfe and Alban-Metcalfe, 2001: 18)

Given the emphasis placed upon developing a transformational style, or culture, when managing change, or when formulating and implementing strategic initiatives (Kanter et al., 1992; Mintzberg, 1994; Pascale et al., 1997; Boddy, 2005), one could speculate that women may be better equipped to manage such situations. Hinkin and Tracey (1999) reinforce this point. They identify a number of key behaviours, ones that may be more readily identified with females, associated with transformational leadership. In their view managers should communicate a sense of where the organization is going, while developing the skills and abilities of subordinates, and encouraging innovative and participative problem solving. It is these leadership behaviours that can truly transform organizations.

Gender may have a role to play. In terms of leadership and general managerial style there appears to be evidence that women are more in tune with participative, empowering and visualizing strategies. Given that such strategies were recognized in the previous chapter as being advantageous when managing change there may possibly be a case to be made for adapting, change related, management development provision, and models, to reflect and address potential gender style differences.

READER ACTIVITY

Take some time out. Pause and consider the other gender. When working or studying with colleagues of the opposite sex how have they behaved in group situations? Have they sat back and listened? Have they taken control? Do they like the sound of their own voice? Or, have they been inclusive and consensus seeking?

Nature or Nurture?

Gender research in relation to management, as in other spheres of the social sciences, has progressed beyond style studies. Miller (1998) points out that it is difficult to tease out what in our behaviour is exactly due to genetics or is culturally shaped. This nature over nurture argument has been ongoing and for the last four decades the nurture argument has held sway. The biological approach has nevertheless captured interest at various times over the years. With regards to the gender impact on the management of change, the crucial point is that differences do exist. Several books and articles about gender differences and the brain have dealt with the genetic or biological approach (Durden-Smith and Desimone, 1983; Kimura, 1987, 1992; Moir and Jessel, 1991; Weiner and Brown, 1993).

Research has established that there are cognitive differences between males and females (Cahill, 2005; Kimura, 2002). In general males perform better on certain spatial tasks and mathematical reasoning and women perform better on verbal fluency tasks and tests of perceptual speed. Professor Christine de Lacoste-Umtasing discovered that the mass of nerve fibres that connect the brain hemispheres (the corpus callosum) is larger in women than in men. This suggested that women might process information differently because there is more communication between the right and left halves of the brain. Shaywitz and Shaywitz (1995) produced evidence of these differences. They used a Functional Magnetic Resonance Imaging (MRI) scanner to produce images of both the structure and the neurological activity of the brains of male and female subjects while they solved language problems. The male subjects' brains were active on the left side only. Women used both sides to solve the same problems.

Similar experiments by O'Boyle and Gill (1998), where the brains of children solving mathematical and spatial puzzles were monitored, showed that boys used one side of the brain only whilst girls used both. Because the girls are using verbal strategies to solve spatial problems they are complicating the problem. The boy's mind is focused; the girl's is networked. Moir and Moir (1998) draw on these and other experiments and research to conclude that there is overwhelming evidence that male and female brains are not the same. This supports Rosener's (1995) suggestion that women order information in their brains in a different way; arriving at answers in a holistic fashion. She goes on to suggest that as the processing information in a linear manner has tended to be labelled rational and logical, the judgements of women who think intuitively might be considered as being untrustworthy.

Scientific research has shown that the male brain begins as a female brain, but foetal testosterone changes its structure. Language skills are restricted to the left side of the brain, spatial skills to the right. The female brain has stronger connections between the two halves; the male brain has stronger connections within each half. This happens long before society or culture has influenced the brain's development and results in the male brain being able to focus attention more closely. Experiments have shown that men find it difficult to do several things at once (Lempert, 1985; Moir and Moir, 1998; O'Boyle 1987, 1991). The conclusion reached is that the male brain is designed to go step by step, to concentrate on one job, to see it through, and then go on to the next.

As noted above, research suggests that women think and process information in a more holistic manner and appear to be more intuitive. Thus is there not, once again, a message here for the effective implementation of change? Holistic problem solving, creative and intuitive thinking, are all associated with the competencies required of the successful change agent, all discussed further within Part 3 of the text (Kanter, 1993; Schein,

1988). In addition, complex change situations, those in which the objectives, boundaries and commitment of the change are less well defined (see Chapters 1 and 2), require the problem owners to develop and implement their solutions in a multidimensional manner. They must multi-task! The literature tends to suggest that women managers are likely to be far better suited to multi-tasking than their male colleagues. Could change management techniques and approaches encourage more effective multi-tasking by adopting and adapting female related problem solving and planning philosophies?

When one combines the above with the gender research relating to communication there is an even greater case for addressing gender and change. Researchers who have examined sex differences in communication among mixed sex groups arrive at similar findings. Vinnicombe and Colwill (1995) found that men talk more, use more words to make a point, make more summarizing and orientating comments, and interrupt more than women. Rosener (1995) draws on the works of Tannen (1994) and Gray (1992) to explain that men communicate to obtain information, establish their status, and show independence whereas women communicate to create relationships, encourage interaction and exchange feelings.

In the previous chapter we stressed that communication, between the managing team, the team and those facing the change, and, the team and their superiors and peers, must be managed effectively to ensure understanding, commitment and a shared perspective. The above evidence points towards the female gender as being better placed to facilitate and exploit communication within a changing environment. It may be that change related models and techniques, many of which are mechanistic and formulaic, should attempt to encapsulate a more dynamic, open and participative approach towards communication.

One could argue that much of the change management literature, especially the literature within organizational development origins or influences, already recognizes the need for open, participative and transformational approaches to change. However, when sanitized and delivered by trainers and consultants, within traditional male dominated organizational cultures, the transformational message may find itself rationalized and systematized. There appears to be a need, in busy and performance driven organizations, to be seen to be doing something and doing it quickly. Could we be merely paying lip-service to 'best practice' and focusing on the immediate task at hand (Paton and Dempster, 2002)?

Mental Models

The case for a gender-based examination of change management practices and models is further reinforced by a brief review of 'mental models'.

People carry images, assumptions and stories in their heads. Senge (2006) describes these as mental models of the world. Generally people are not conscious of such models or the way in which they might influence their behaviour. Buchanan and Huczynski (2006) point out that the process of interpreting events through these models normally happens instantaneously and without conscious deliberation.

Perceptions are created from interpretation or impression based on the understanding. This understanding is based on knowledge and experience. It is easy for individuals and organizations to become trapped in blind alleys, repeating successful approaches from the past that are no longer appropriate. Krogh and Vicari (1993) propose that this can be applied to the firm that 'reconstructs its reality by applying internally generated norms and distinctions'. There is therefore a danger that the acceptance, or otherwise, of the new is based on internal and historical norms. In a corporate world largely dominated, for some considerable time, by the male of the species, one could surely assume that the prevailing models are likely to be influenced accordingly. Likewise the management toolkit for dealing with and managing change will also have been so influenced.

It would not be surprising to find that women may find themselves at odds with a 'change toolkit' possibly based upon, and heavily influenced by, mental models that they do not readily identify with. However, the main point here is that the corporate and commercial world that we inhabit has undoubtedly been primarily influenced and shaped by males. Responses to change scenarios will likewise be influenced by the prevailing male orientated organizational culture. Females, given the opportunity at a senior management level, may view things differently.

What Can We Conclude from the Literature?

There are obvious dangers in attempting to study gender and change in a non-controlled organizational environment. However, as previously stated, this chapter represents an explorative study not a definitive work. It hopes to raise questions worthy of further debate and study.

The gender related literature upon which the case for investigation is made is not universally accepted. For example, Calas and Smircich (1996) and Fletcher (1994) cast doubt upon the validity and value of the female advantage literature that forms the basis of this chapter's case. But the main argument that they mount does not directly criticize the evidence that gender differences exist but rather disputes the merits in pursuing a potentially separatist methodology and philosophy. Burr (1998) also warns of the dangers of reading too much into sex difference research findings:

> 'Given the extent and prevalence of assumptions about women and men in contemporary society we should not be surprised if findings are interpreted in the direction of existing stereotypes', (p. 29).

However, Burr notes, that after careful consideration:

> Despite these cautions, it seems reasonable to accept that women and men differ in some psychological characteristics. It is also difficult to ignore the claims about difference that arise from our common experience of social life. (p. 30)

Given the focus and intent of the study outlined in this chapter it was decided to accept (while noting the wider problems) that gender differences do exist and that they may have an impact upon management. Many, often practitioners, hold the view that an organization may manage change and look the way it does because it has found the 'best way of working'. Indeed some contributors to the research also suggested that women may adopt more male associated behaviours and styles simply because they had found them to be superior in terms of achieving optimum outcomes. Even if the aforementioned views are partially true they did not constitute an argument for totally discounting the literature review findings. Gender differences do seem to exist and they may impact upon change management.

The effective management of change, and the creation of change accepting cultures, calls upon management styles, competencies and approaches that appear to be most readily associated with female styles and behaviours. The gender research, previously noted, strongly suggests that gender influences management style and decision making. A gap exists. Gender is well documented and so too is change, but change and gender seem to have been largely ignored. So far all that has been established is that there are gender differences and that they may influence the way in which managers manage.

READER ACTIVITY

What do you think? Will there be any meaningful differences between the genders in relation to how they approach and manage change?

Think of your own interpersonal and managerial style. Do you have a preferred style or approach and if so is it fixed, or do you adapt depending on the context and environment?

The Study

The investigative study was designed to establish the extent to which there was a link between gender and change, and to investigate the likely impact of such a link on the way we approach and manage change. By focusing on how we manage change it was hoped to find evidence of specific illustrations of gender preferences and differences.

The sample

The sample was drawn from executive branches of the British government's Department of Social Security (DSS) (now the Department for Work and Pensions), in particular, the Benefits Agency (BA) and the more recently formed Benefit Fraud Inspectorate (BFI). The BA is responsible for administering and delivering social security payments, and other benefits, in accordance with directives. The BFI is charged with ensuring that benefit payments are not fraudulently claimed.

As part of the civil service both the BA and BFI have been subjected to dramatic and sustained change over recent years. Governmental quests for better value for money, the establishment of internal markets, and, a desire to see a greater degree of accountability and more open government, have revolutionized the sector. One obvious outcome of the recent changes has been the move away from large monolithic departments to truly executive agencies (Gunn, 1988). The majority of civil servants are now employed in such agencies, which operate on 'a much more decentralised basis with greater flexibility and greater potential for genuine financial management and control' (Jones, 1996).

The executive branches, such as the DSS, have been subject to wide reaching and varied change since the early 1990s. Employees are familiar with change and have been exposed to multiple initiatives and considerable 'management development'. Although initially externally generated much of the change has become internally driven. Resistance has diminished as more proactive cultures developed.

The DSS provided an ideal sampling frame; the organization had experienced and managed substantial change. The changes had been well supported, in terms of management development and resources, and the managers had been encouraged to reflect, learn and build upon their experiences. The majority of the management cadre selected for the study had attended internally and externally provided change management programmes (approximately 60 per cent of the sample), numerous briefing sessions (whole sample), and individual and team awareness/building events (whole sample). They all went on to manage, both individually and collectively, significant change events (organizational change, regulatory change; systems/process change, and cultural/conceptual change).

The organization supported and encouraged, through a number of multi-functional management team events, reflection and learning. The aim being to learn and build for future change management programmes.

In addition, it was also important that the sample be drawn from an organization in which female managers had permeated throughout the structure. A 1998 survey produced by the DSS Equal Opportunity Unit indicates a predominantly female workforce (66 per cent); however, as one proceeds upwardly through the managerial grades female employees become increasingly under-represented. At the lowest managerial grades one finds that approximately 50 per cent of the workforce is female. This percentage drops at the senior grades to an under 30 per cent female representation.

Respondents were drawn from the total population of senior managers operating within a BA business unit, the Glasgow Benefit Centre, and the Glasgow wing of the DSS BFI. Of the total population approximately 30 per cent were female. In the lower senior management positions, and in the upper senior management positions, the gender balance tended to be equal. However, in the middle male managers outnumbered female mangers by 2:1. Male managers were marginally better qualified across all the grade ranges with 61 per cent holding a professional or managerial qualification (55 per cent of the female managers held similar qualifications).

The questionnaire design was informed not only by the literature review but also by, first, non-structured interviews with four senior managers (equal grading and gender split). All had attended a self-development course entitled 'Men and Women Working Together' (run for DSS staff by Bristol College in 1996). It was hoped that the individuals would be 'in tune' with the issues and well disposed towards the research. They clarified and prioritized the issues that they felt were significant and these, in general, supported the researchers' initial interpretation. The issues were grouped under the headings shown below. Second, the questionnaire, in particular the validity of the four groupings/headings, was piloted with a group of eight middle managers, equal gender split. This group was used to test questionnaire relevance, understanding and process.

The research questionnaire consisted of four sections dealing with:

- *Task completion*   How did they view (holistically) and approach (multi-tasking) tasks? Respondents were encouraged to relate their responses to a recent organizational change event with which they were familiar (ongoing restructuring initiatives affected all the respondents).

- *Tools and techniques*   Which analytical and communications devices did they use? Once again respondents, based on their selected change event, were asked to identify, given their general change management approach, what tools and so on they employed and how they managed communication.

- *Approach to change management*   What stance did they adopt, directorial or participative? This section attempted to identify the degree to which the respondent directed events and to what extent they actively encouraged the participation of others. Of particular concern was the extent to which managers were willing to listen to others and thereafter the extent to which the opinions, and so on, of others influenced the outcomes and actions.

- *Change environments (or cultures)*   Which did they prefer, closed/directive or open/consultative? The literature review indicated that gender might influence one's preference for particular types of operating/working environments. Respondents were asked, developing from the above section, to indicate their general preference regarding both personal and organizational approaches to change management.

The questions were predominantly closed and directed. In the main, respondents were asked to reply in accordance with a list of predetermined alternatives, both multiple choice and rating scales were employed. Although such an approach restricts the respondent's scope of response and curtails the collection of valuable qualitative information, it does tend to encourage completion and provide useful factual information. It should once again be noted that the aim was to conduct an explorative study. In total 80 questionnaires were distributed, 70 returned and of those 31 were from females.

The findings

As demonstrated throughout this book, change management approaches and theories generally stress the need to multi-task and to view change holistically. Do females tend to do this more than males? Yes, when faced with change situations the female gender tended to respond on a less task-focused basis. Less than 10 per cent of the females and 30 per cent of males found multi-tasking 'difficult'. Almost 14 per cent more males than females indicated a preference for completing one task prior to moving on. When faced with the need to multi-task and schedule, 94 per cent of the females agreed that they had no problem with this while only 70 per cent of the males felt 'comfortable'.

Gender research suggests that a lower percentage of males would have been inclined to approach multi-tasking requirements as positively as the sample. Nonetheless, there is still a marked preference on the part of the females to adopt a more holistic and multi-tasking approach to complex change. The study did not explore the nature of the multi-tasking approach adopted, it merely explored associated attitudes. Further research would be required to establish the true nature, extent and effectiveness of the approaches adopted by both males and females.

When asked to review the analytical and communications techniques they adopted when dealing with change a more marked difference between the sexes emerged. The sample was divided into those who had received specific training in change management techniques (58 per cent of the females; 59 per cent of the males) and those who had not. The study then concentrated on those who had been exposed to change related management development. It was necessary to focus on the 'trained' as the questionnaire was phrased in a manner which assumed knowledge of the terminology, theory and practices associated with change.

Males tended to favour, when planning and managing change, techniques that gave the impression of order and control, while at the same time distanced the change process from the actual impact. Diagramming techniques, charting methodologies and orchestrated 'news letters' all scored higher with the males than the females as a means of communicating and debating change. Newsletters, non face-to-face forms of communication, were favoured by 83 per cent of the males. Almost 90 per cent of the males preferred structured diagramming techniques, with charting methodologies used by over 65 per cent when scheduling activities. Female managers tended to employ such techniques between 10 to 30 per cent less. Female respondents seemed to prefer the 'softer' approaches, such as scenario planning, workshops, brainstorming and information meetings.

Once again the gender research, suggesting as it does that females tend to associate more with the 'softer' aspects of management, was supported by the above results. Males identified with process based techniques more so than the females, while the females tended to associate more with the more collegiate, inter-personal and outcome driven approaches.

In an effort to establish the individual respondent's preferred approach to change the questionnaire used 'approach descriptors' to encourage respondents to identify with a favoured methodology. Approach descriptors outlined scenarios, which could be classified as systematic, empowering, top-down or bottom-up. Would female managers more readily identify with approaches associated with more open ended and participative initiatives? The results suggested that female managers supported and welcomed change approaches that could be grouped under the general heading of 'empowering'. However, when asked to identify their preferred management style and the type of change initiative they most welcomed, the results were more telling. Over twice (33 per cent) as many female managers than male identified strongly with change situations in which they saw themselves as 'pioneers', in dealing with semi-open projects in which they know, within limits, the destination but are unsure of how to get there.

The Conclusions

The exploratory study did confirm, to a limited extent, the gender research findings. In particular females favoured 'softer', empowering approaches; they preferred non-diagramming based mapping and analysis techniques (less systematic and formulaic). They appeared to be better equipped for multi-tasking than their male counterparts (moving forward on a number of initiatives, possibly related, in 'simultaneous' time frames), and, in general favoured more holistic (big picture), participative and open approaches to change management.

The study, along with the literature review, supports the generally held view that on many dimensions males and females are different. They work, socialize and think differently. Not surprisingly, they tend to manage change differently (Dempster, 1998; Paton and Dempster, 2002). The initial aim of the research was to clarify the extent to which men and women differed in their approach to the management of change. Quite clearly there is a difference of both style and approach. Given the increasingly influential role women play within organizations facing change then such a finding is worthy of investigation. Under the previous sections of this chapter a number of questions were raised concerning potential change related gender issues.

Gender research suggests that females differ from males. If this is the case, would change approaches and techniques, in the main historically influenced by male management cultures and styles, be at odds with female preferences? The research supports the view that gender preferences are capable of dictating differing solution models/techniques. Also, the gender literature suggests that females may have an aptitude for, or at least a preference for, management approaches that are more dynamic, holistic and emergent, rather than mechanistic and closed. Once again this exploratory study would tend to support this view.

In addition to providing supporting evidence for the proposition that gender can influence the way in which we manage change, this study also raises some wider concerns:

- How exactly will gender impact upon the effective management of change?

- Who should take note?

- What might we need to do?

The concluding sections of this chapter attempt to address, in a discursive manner, the implications of the research and suggest a future research agenda.

There are a number of caveats, regarding the rationale and outcomes associated with this piece of research. This chapter presents a case, based on an explorative study, for recognizing the potential advantages of ensuring gender is considered when managing and/or researching change. However, the manner in which the gender literature review was presented tended to accept rather than debate the wider arguments associated with promoting 'sex differences'. Given the nature and scope of the research such an omission was permissible. The findings, indicating as they do that there is evidence to support the view that gender may influence both one's approach to change and perception of it, tended to support our view. In addition, the sample size was relatively small, but it was drawn from a well-informed, professional and reflective organization.

The Implications for Change

There are at least three groups for whom this study has potential implications. The first is individual managers, whether male or female. Personal managerial style may at times be in conflict with not only those others involved in the change, but also, with the change itself. There is more than anecdotal evidence that females prefer a more open, collegiate and holistic approach. Males tend to favour a more direct, task driven and closed approach. Quite clearly managers operating in mixed sex environments may wish to modify their managerial approach to achieve optimal outcomes. However, certain change scenarios actually favour specific managerial responses or approaches. Managers may have to modify both style and approach to maximize their effectiveness regardless of gender.

Second, when facing change the organization must ensure that the managerial approaches adopted, the communication media and the message, the support structures, and the training and development, all reflect the needs of the particular employee and managerial staffing profiles. By ignoring gender differences the organization may find that it alienates, or at least disadvantages, a significant proportion of the workforce. Third, the last grouping is academics and trainers. The majority of training programmes, designed to equip managers with the 'tools' for change, whether provided internally or externally, tend to offer mechanistic, systems oriented and results driven solution methodologies and techniques. These are easy to grasp, easy to teach and impressive when used. Academics often deride such approaches and profess more holistic, sociologically driven, strategically focused and less pragmatic approaches and processes. Neither the academic nor trainer is wholly wrong. Change is all embracing, dynamic, challenging and exciting. The change must drive the solution methodology, within the constraints of the cultural and systems environments affected. General staffing profiles and the specific genders of the key players have, as yet, failed to feature as significant factors in the literature associated with theoretical and practical change management. It may be time to reflect gender preferences and approaches in the development of change management theory and approaches (Paton and Dempster, 2002).

Gender differences must not be seen as being either good or bad. Neither sex has a managerial profile that confers a definitive blueprint for success. However, by failing to address and capitalize upon gender capabilities individual managers, organizations and educators may be overlooking an influential factor in achieving optimal and lasting change. There are no definitive answers or models. Women do not make better managers and men do not always get it right. What is needed are gender aware models, approaches that harness, taking into account the particular nature of the change being faced, the appropriate attributes, styles and beliefs of both the female and male manager.

Further research is required to determine how best to harness the intrinsic benefits each gender can bring to the change management debate. Yes, men do use lists, yes men do multi-task, but do they do it well? Women can be domineering, they can be task focused and they can adopt mechanistic approaches to change, but when should they? We are still some distance away from determining a generic change model that reflects, in an informed and integrated manner, gender considerations. The development and implementation, if appropriate, of a gender influenced model would have to be informed by a more in-depth investigation of how managers actually employ the previously detailed tools, approaches and styles.

The next chapter presents a range of approaches designed to facilitate the mapping and better understanding of change. Next up is Part 2 and the intervention strategy approaches. On the whole the approaches that are covered tend towards a structured socio-technical approach to change management. How might the investigative study outlined above impact upon one's reading of these chapters? Yes, they deal with structured approaches, but they are also intended to be holistic. They promote performance driven change and possibly suggest that there may even be a right answer, but yet they are inclusive and participative. On completing Part 2 readers may wish to consider where they stand on the importance and issue of gender and change.

4 | Mapping Change

As we have seen in the previous chapters it is important that the nature of the change facing the organization, group or individual is defined according to its position on the change spectrum. The use of techniques such as the TROPICS test and force field analysis, along with the need to consider the role and position of the problem owner and any other associated change agents, have been discussed. Physical or mechanistic change, exhibiting both systematized technical attributes and a low degree of man–machine/systems interface, should be addressed by adopting a systems based solution model from the scientific management school. On the other hand, more complex and generally messy change, involving complex personalized relationships and organizational cultures warrants the adoption of a more people based model from the organizational development stable.

The solution methodology associated with both ends of the change spectrum is therefore identifiable through a relatively limited examination of the change environment. Unfortunately most change occurs within what has been referred to as the 'flexi' area of the spectrum.

Messy change situations – those which may be classified as 'flexi', present management with a multitude of complex, interrelated and conflicting problems and issues. The 'mess' resembles, in its complexity of relationships, the structure of a spider's web. The spider builds a complex structure, which if the imagination is stretched, may be regarded as its organization. The structure is organized in such a manner that it provides a collective strength that may be brought to bear against intruders, be they a potential launch or an aggressive predator. An organization is built on a foundation of systems which, just like those of the spider, have a common primary structural role and may respond in a like manner when faced by an intruder, or indeed change.

When the predator begins to snip away at the threads of the web its strength weakens. Initially the problem for the spider will be a structural one, classified as a hard change. As the threads continue to be destroyed then the change moves along the spectrum to the soft end. As the web disintegrates the primary objective becomes threatened and the spider will have to reappraise the situation. Once the destruction is almost complete, all that can be done with the remaining components of the system is to use them as a means of escape. For the primary objective to succeed all the systems must be integrated and pulling in the same direction.

The systems which constitute the organization of today are complex: they each have their own formal and informal objectives which, when managed effectively, achieve the primary objective. Change in any one system, or in its relationship with others, may therefore impact on the total structure and eventually on organizational performance.

To understand the nature of a change situation that falls between the two extremities of the spectrum, the systems and their relationships must be examined as a whole. When the interaction between the human resource and the system undergoing the change takes place then the need to fully define the change in terms of its interactions with existing systems, individuals, groups, departments and the organization as a whole, becomes a necessity. How can management begin to cope with this complexity? The answer, in part, is to represent complex change situations in diagrammatic form and view the whole process of change in systems terms.

This chapter examines a number of tools that facilitate the thorough definition, analysis and communication of the impact of messy change. The management tools covered may be applied to either hard or soft change situations, and in so doing further the problem owner's understanding of the affected environment. They are often associated with systems change, due to their origins in systems analysis and design. It would be rash to limit their use to systems change alone for they can be profitably employed as a precursor, providing valuable diagnostic information, to the adoption of an organizational development approach.

The change problem may be viewed in terms of the systems and associated components and elements which it affects. Management can then represent the systems in terms of their physical and attitudinal characteristics alongside the principal relationships, in diagrammatic forms. Thus the inherent complexity of the problem is reduced to manageable dimensions through diagrammatic systems representation. Diagramming conventions, such as those used by systems analysts and programmers need not feature in 'change diagramming'. What is required is consistency within studies and subsequently standardization within the management unit. If a standard format exists and is widely used by management then it should be adopted, possibly with modifications, within the planning and managing change process. What is important is that the diagrams assist in the definition, analysis and communication of the change event.

Do not let preconceived notions of the complex nature of systems diagramming prevent you from employing such a powerful communications media and analytical tool. The diagrams described and demonstrated in the pages which follow have been selected for their simplistic, yet powerful, analytical characteristics. The principal construction and application rules that govern their usage remain more or less unchanged no matter the complexity of the problem. Formal conventions and terminology from the systems analysts' vocabulary have been intentionally ignored in an effort to reduce the entry barrier to non-systems readers.

No matter your background or future career path, your analytical and communicative competencies will be enhanced through effective utilization of diagramming skills. These simple techniques described in this section should be the starting point for experimentation in diagramming as an investigative tool and a communication medium.

If you followed the previous paragraphs, having had no cause to pause for a while to deliberate the meaning of a passage and/or reread to ensure understanding, then the written word has done its job. If on the other hand, you had difficulty grasping the 'message' on first reading then the written word, or at least the author's usage of it, has failed to satisfy fully. Diagrams can be used to simplify the written word; they assist in definition, understanding and communication.

Figure 4.1 attempts to communicate, in a logical and concise manner, the major points raised in the last few paragraphs.

The diagram tools, simply and concisely, assist in explaining the likely impact of the forces at play in any change situation. By employing multiple tools to the problem at hand one can attempt to better understand the events within the context of a dynamic environment. By viewing the change as a system and using diagrams to assist definition then we have a tool to facilitate definition, analysis and communication. Diagrams are useful tools. Let us now consider their role in systems investigations more fully.

The Role of Diagramming in Systems Investigation

Organizations are composed of numerous interrelated systems and subsystems, which in turn may be subdivided into components and ultimately into indivisible elements. These systems are designed to ensure the accomplishment of organizational goals and must, if the goals are to be achieved, operate in harmony. Machinery, technology, procedures, policies, operatives, supervisors and management are, depending on the view being taken, either systems, components or elements. Once a change impacts upon the equilibrium of a system, it, along with any interrelated systems, will be disrupted and their performance impaired. Diagramming tools assist in defining, analysing and manipulating the systems environment.

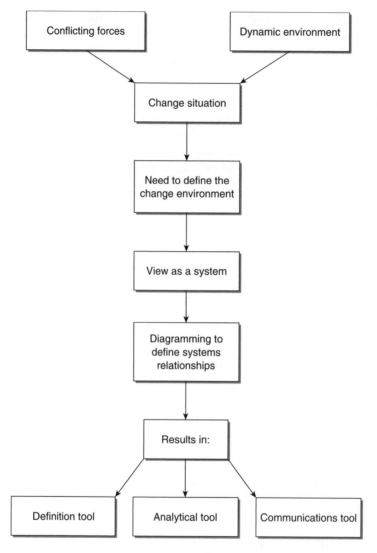

Figure 4.1   The need for diagramming

There are essentially four reasons why management should adopt certain diagramming techniques in their pursuit of the effective implementation of change:

1   Diagramming, along with the systems approach, can bring a much-needed sense of logic and structure to messy change problems.

2   By adopting standardized diagramming techniques the problem owner will develop a clear and concise view of change environments and at the same time introduce a

change handling methodology. This will simplify and standardize future change investigations, as well as provide the basis of systems specification and a relationships 'library'.

3 Unfortunately, verbal or long-winded descriptions of messy change tend to be messy in their own right. They are often ineffective in terms of their ability to provide the listener, or reader, with a clear understanding and generally are limited in their use as analytical platforms for future deliberations. Diagrams assist the process of understanding by providing a clear and structured map of the problem and assist analysis and implementation by effectively illustrating potential developments and options.

4 The communication of ideas/options is an essential component of the change management process. Diagrams can assist the communications process by providing a standardized, impersonal and credible interface between concerned parties.

In any problem solving or systems analysis exercise one may find an effective role for diagrammatically based analysis. It is in a manager's interest to develop both a practical understanding of the available techniques and a level of expertise in applying and exploiting them. A range of diagramming tools is available for use by the change management practitioner, as illustrated in Table 4.1.

Diagrams may be employed to fully define the change process and are particularly effective when applied to the solution of complex messy problems, which are capable of being considered in systems terms, those in the 'flexi' area of the change continuum and, of course, hard physical

Table 4.1 Diagram types

Diagram types	Descriptor
Input/output	Shows the inputs to a system and the resulting outputs, as well as any feedback loops
Flow, process and activity	A linked representation of a series of steps, activities or events describing a process
Force field	A basic visual representation of the driving and restraining forces relating to a change event
Fish bone	Generally used to work back from a problem situation determining root causes
Multiple cause	As above
Relationship mapping	Details the relationships between both 'hard' and/or 'soft' systems components
Systems mapping	Details the system(s) to be affected by a change
Influence (spider's web) charting	Charts the influences, and their linkages, on a particular system or situation

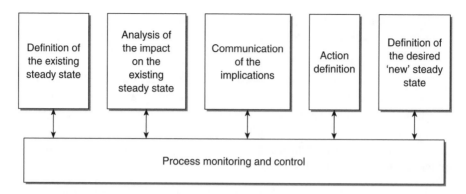

Figure 4.2   Transition process chart

problems. Figure 4.2 highlights each stage of the transition process in which diagramming techniques may be employed. For example, systems diagrams may assist in defining the existing steady state and may be followed by relationship maps, which would investigate the interactions between the steady state systems. Flow and process charts may both define the existing system and emphasize impact points associated with the proposed changes. All the aforementioned diagrams can be manipulated and studied to investigate the actual impact of the change; they also could be employed as communications aids. Action steps may be developed through the use of networking diagrams; these would also be used to monitor progress and once again all the diagrams could be utilized in defining the desired systems configuration.

Diagrams may be profitably employed by management when they are:

- defining and understanding the nature of those systems affected by the change (before);

- illustrating the means and stages associated with progress from the present to the desired situation (during);

- defining and understanding the nature of the desired solution/situation (after).

In other words diagrammatic representations may be used to assist the problem owner when they are engaged in:

- specification/definition

- understanding

- manipulation/modelling/analysis

- communication

- implementation

- standardization.

Diagrams, or even interrelated listings, provide an effective means of defining a change event. There are a host of diagramming techniques which assist in the understanding of change, as detailed in Table 4.1.

Diagrams not only assist in defining change events. They also offer a means of analysing, or plotting, developing situations, specifying end points, and lastly, but certainly not least, a means of communicating both within and outside the managing group. As long as the diagrams add value to the process of managing change they will have served their purpose.

By defining aspects of the system(s) undergoing change as above then the problem owner(s) will identify the extent to which the change will impact on: the relationships affected; the key influencing factors; the likely management team; and the potential reaction to the change itself. Diagramming facilitates not only definition but also leads to understanding because it allows the study of potential and actual behaviour, for both hard and soft aspects of the change.

A Review of Basic flow Diagramming Techniques

Three of the most common and revealing techniques employed by change management practitioners deal with 'flow' analysis. The first is the input/output diagram which provides an easy to follow means of investigating the input and output flows of physical materials and/or information with reference to any given system. The feedback mechanisms facilitating both control and performance measurement may also be included. Such a diagram is illustrated in Figure 4.3.

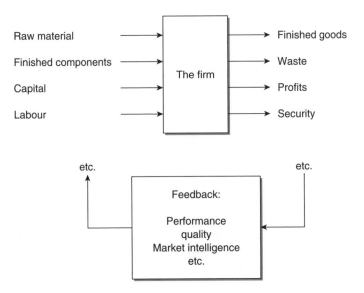

Figure 4.3 An input/output diagram with feedback

The second technique within this diagramming category is the traditional flow diagram, which permits the investigator to study the process steps and related activities, including interdependencies, associated with a particular system. Once again a pictorial representation provides a useful insight into a system at work, as the example contained within Figure 4.4 illustrates.

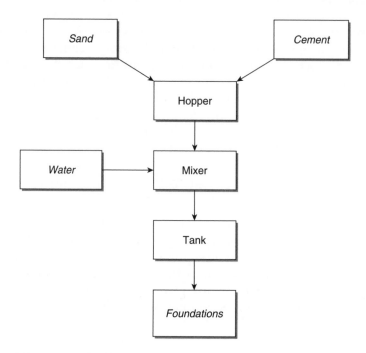

Figure 4.4   A sample flow diagram

Both the input/output and flow diagrams may be further developed to incorporate such information as:

- Who does what and why?

- What information do they require and why?

- Where does the information come from – channels, formats, etc.?

- What factors influence systems/individual performance?

The last diagram of this section addresses the 'softer' issues associated with systems investigation through the medium of 'flow' analysis. Activity sequence diagrams consider issues and stages of a process, or

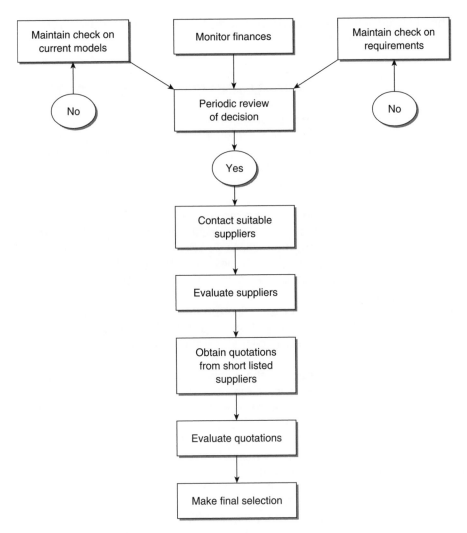

Figure 4.5   An activity sequence diagram

elements of a system, which are of non-physical/technological nature. For example, let us consider the purchase of a car depicted in Figure 4.5. In such diagrams the activities associated with key decision points relating to a particular sequence of events are emphasized for subsequent study.

All three diagrams described in this section may be employed throughout the transition management process to assist in the definition of the existing system, or to indicate the steps which must be taken in achieving the goal. Finally they may be used to help specify

the desired outcome. Further examples of their use are given in
Mini Cases 4.1 and 4.2.

MINI CASE 4.1:   ARGYLL AND CLYDE HEALTH BOARD

The Argyll and Clyde Health Board, in accordance with their statutory
obligations resulting form the introduction of the government White
Paper entitled *Working for Patients*, were required to ensure that the
processing of their Scottish Morbidity Records (SMRs) was enhanced
in line with new performance targets which were specified in the
White Paper.

The SMR is the document which records the details of each episode of
care for a patient treated in a National Health Service hospital. The aggregated data for all patient transactions are used as the basis for research,
epidemiological study and, possibly most importantly as the basis for the
planning and funding decisions taken by the centre for each individual
Health Board.

Completed SMR data for each Scottish Board had to be lodged with
the Common Services Agency (CSA) of the health service within two
months from the completed collation of any given month's SMRs. The
CSA collated the data for the 15 Scottish boards and funding was subsequently allocated according to the number and types of patient treated.
Prior to this, the performance target was somewhat more liberal, with
SMR data for one year having to be submitted to the CSA by the mid-
summer of the following year.

A computerized Patient Administration System obviated the need for
paper SMR documentation and manual processing within the Argyll and
Clyde Board. Its efficient operation was the ultimate responsibility of the
Information Services Division (ISD). The ISD may be regarded as the prob-
lem owners in this case. Their computer centre, via the SMR Standard
System, processed the returns for remote hospitals.

The problem owner, who was located within the ISD, produced the
associated diagrams. They formed the basis for subsequent analysis of the
existing systems conducted with a view to reducing SMR submission
times. The diagrams constituted part of the problem definition phase and
were used to illustrate the SMR production process. The activity sequence
diagram, Figure 4.6, illustrates the preparation of SMR data and its subsequent transfer to the ISD processing centre. Feedback was required to
validate centrally detected errors and queries. The input/output representation, Figure 4.7, depicts the entry of data into the SMR standard system.
Once fully validated output had been achieved for each hospital, it was
aggregated and transferred to CSA for analysis.

The problem facing Argyll and Clyde will be returned to in Chapter 16,
when the options for change will be considered and a solution identified.

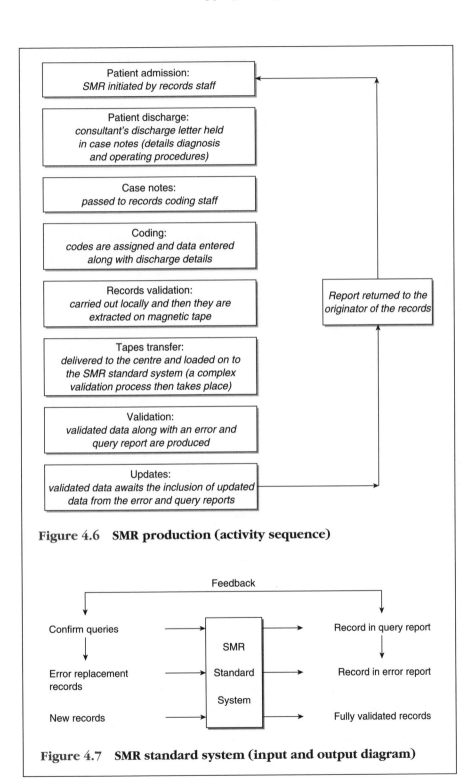

Figure 4.6   SMR production (activity sequence)

Figure 4.7   SMR standard system (input and output diagram)

MINI CASE 4.2:   VITAFOAM AND KAY METZLER LTD

This case demonstrates the versatility of the diagramming techniques so far covered. Here a hybrid form of illustration is used to depict the change forces at work, a force field analysis, and an input/output graphic.

   British Vita Plc, the parent company of both Vitafoam and Kay Metzler Ltd, wished to see a rationalization of both companies' operations. Amongst the many options available to the subsidiary organizations was a merger of operations at the current Vitafoam site. The problem owner, a member of the operational management team at the Vitafoam site in Paisley, Scotland, produced the diagram, shown in Figure 4.8, to assist in his understanding of the change forces at play in such a merger situation.

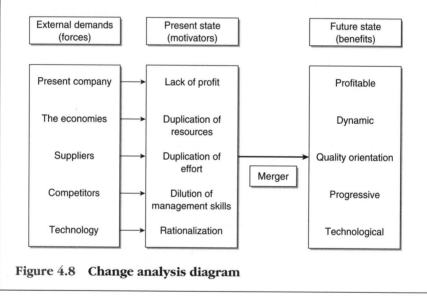

Figure 4.8   Change analysis diagram

Systems Relationships: The Key to Success

To fully understand the nature of a particular change situation, a problem owner must consider the relationships that exist between those affected by the change. By developing a relationship map, the problem owner may begin to appreciate the systems interfaces and complexities that are at work in the change environment.

By way of an example let us consider the relationship map in Figure 4.9, which may have been applied when the UK steel industry was undergoing privatization (it is not intended to be comprehensive).

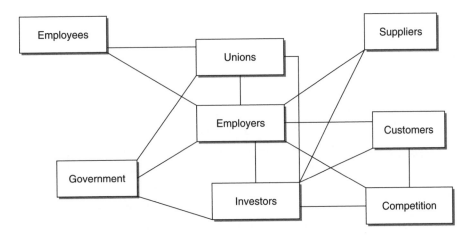

Figure 4.9   A sample relationships map

MINI CASE 4.3:   CALEDONIAN AIRMOTIVE LTD

Caledonian Airmotive Limited (CAL) was at the time a well-established company operating in the highly competitive international business of Aero Engine overhaul. The company was the subject of one of the detailed system related changes contained in Chapter 16.

As CAL will be dealt with in more depth in Chapter 16, all we require to know at this point is that the change deals with the total reorganization of the accessory shop within their Prestwick site. This shop mainly serviced one-off maintenance jobs that did not pass through the rest of the works. It did however depend on many of the general manufacturing services. Therefore, it was not uncommon for the demands of the accessory shop to interfere with the efficient production flow of the mainstream manufacturing activities. Management decided to minimize disruption to mainstream engine overhaul by creating an autonomous accessory shop, which would be totally self-contained and no longer a source of disruption to other service groups.

The relationship map, Figure 4.10, was produced at an early stage in the change process to assist in determining the key players and establishing linkages between them.

(Continued)

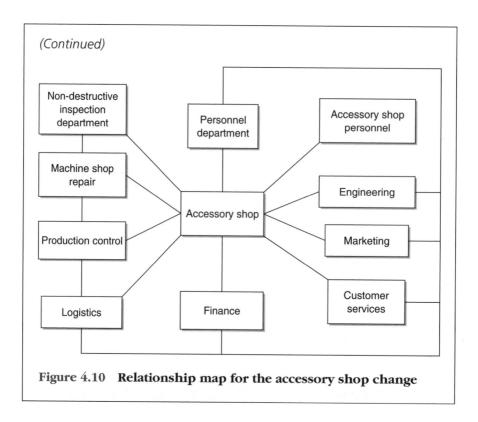

(Continued)

Figure 4.10   Relationship map for the accessory shop change

The complex change situation that emerged from Mini Case 4.3 indicated that although at the core of the problem was a significant system change, there was also likely to be a major organizational change. The identification of the need to integrate both schools of thought, systems and organizational, is a very common outcome of the diagnostic diagramming phase.

Systems Diagramming

Having considered the problem of defining and understanding the basic influences associated with change, the next step is to investigate, in more depth, the actual systems affected by the change. Systems diagramming is an essential component of the intervention strategy approach. The systems approach, through diagramming, brings a degree of sanity to messy change situations.

The principal diagramming techniques that will be employed within the intervention strategy model, the subject of Part 2 of this book, are as follows:

1 systems mapping

2 influence charts

3 multiple cause diagrams.

Each will be treated in turn and will be presented along with a practical case to illustrate their usage.

Systems Mapping

Systems maps need not be complex or difficult to construct. Their basic function is to present a pictorial representation of the system undergoing the change and can if necessary incorporate relevant interrelationships. The systems map is often employed in conjunction with the relationship map discussed in the previous section. The systems map identifies the systems and any subsystems associated with the problem and the relationship map analyses the nature of the linkages between the systems, their components and their elements.

A system consists of component parts, or indeed subsystems, which in turn may be further broken down. Subdivision ceases once the element level has been reached, an element being incapable of further division. The systems approach is examined in more detail in Part 2. System maps can therefore be produced for all levels of the change environment. For example, a map may be produced for the University of Glasgow Business School, a subsystem of the University of Glasgow, such as the one shown in Figure 4.11.

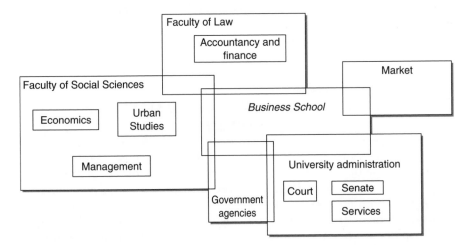

Figure 4.11   The University of Glasgow Business School systems map

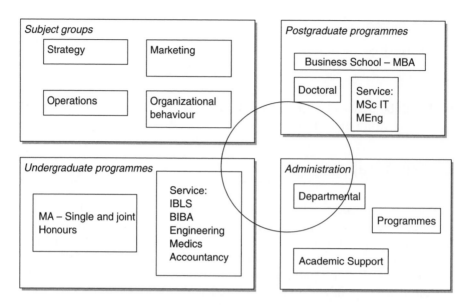

Figure 4.12   The Department of Management Studies systems map

This map could be further divided to show first the component parts of the Department of Management, which could then be further analysed in turn. This is represented in the further subdivision shown in Figure 4.12.

The problem owner and/or the management team concerned with the handling of the change must decide at which level of analysis the process should cease. Not only does mapping highlight the systems involved but also gives a clear indication of the parties who should be involved in the management process and at which point in the process they should be brought in (see Mini Case 4.4).

MINI CASE 4.4:   R. TERLEY LTD (TEXSTYLE WORLD)

A manager from this company, at the time an established retailer of a wide range of soft furnishings, while involved in a review of its existing stockholding procedures, constructed a simple cause and effect diagram. It is depicted in Figure 4.13. The map highlights the systems likely to be impacted upon by any changes to the warehousing of computerized stock control system. The rationale behind the proposed changes will be returned to when considering cause and effect diagrams.

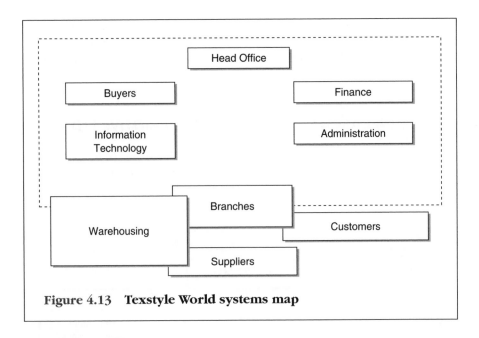

Figure 4.13   **Texstyle World systems map**

Influence Charts

The systems map is, in many ways, only of use when it is followed by the production of influence charts. Such charts illustrate influencing factors. For example, what influencing factors or groups could act upon a typical manufacturing firm? Figure 4.14 depicts the potential influences at play.

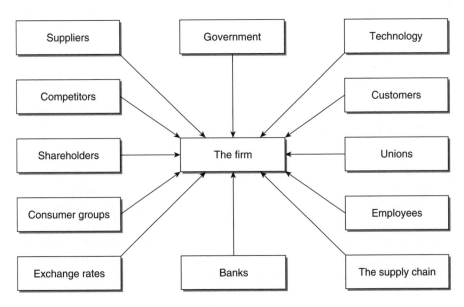

Figure 4.14   **Manufacturing influence map**

Influence diagrams connect the systems associated with the change and indicate lines of influence. Often, depending on complexity, both systems and influence diagrams can be shown as one (see Mini Case 4.5).

MINI CASE 4.5: CALEDONIAN AIRMOTIVE LTD

The change facing the accessory shop of Caledonian Airmotive has already been introduced in Mini Case 4.3. Figure 4.15 illustrates some of the systems and factors that influenced this subsystem of the manufacturing establishment.

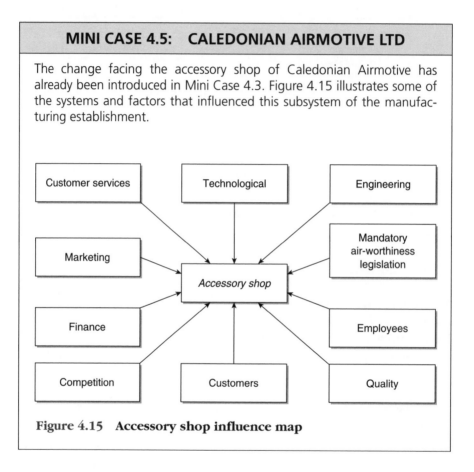

Figure 4.15 Accessory shop influence map

Multiple Cause Diagrams

A means of further developing the influence chart is to consider the causes associated with a change situation or problem. Multiple cause diagrams examine the causes behind particular events or activities and express them diagrammatically.

For example one may depict, as in Figure 4.16, the factors that interact to create the energy costs within the home. From this figure the demand factors could be examined as shown in Figure 4.17.

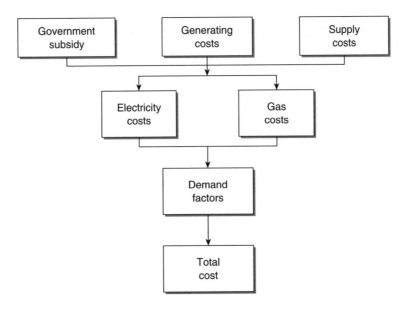

Figure 4.16   Energy costs multiple cause diagram

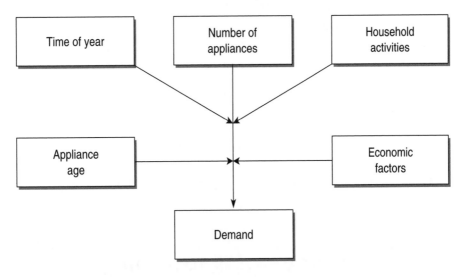

Figure 4.17   Demand factors multiple cause diagram

Mini Cases 4.6 and 4.7 illustrate the ways in which one may present multiple cause diagrams. Such diagrams are of great value in determining the driving forces or factors behind a particular change event. They identify 'cause chains' and assist in identifying the key elements.

MINI CASE 4.6:   McGRIGGOR DONALD (SOLICITORS)

McGriggor Donald, a large law firm, upgraded its office IT systems. The problem owner was the director of administration and she produced the multiple cause diagram detailed in Figure 4.18.

Although rather simplistic, it does quite clearly indicate the reasons for the upgrade and in so doing pointed the way forward with respect to the required features of the new system. It also proved a useful means for assisting in the communication of the impending change to the office staff and acted as a focus for initial management/staff discussions.

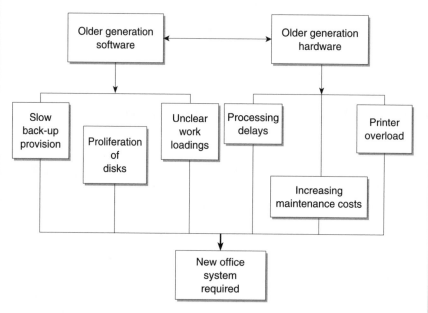

Figure 4.18   Office IT system multiple cause diagram

**MINI CASE 4.7:   R. TERLEY LTD
(TEXSTYLE WORLD)**

The Terley (Texstyle World) stock problem was previously introduced in Mini Case 4.4 and the associated systems map produced. The following cause and effect diagram depicted in Figure 4.19 neatly sums up the rationale behind the review of the existing computerized system. It utilizes a fish bone format.

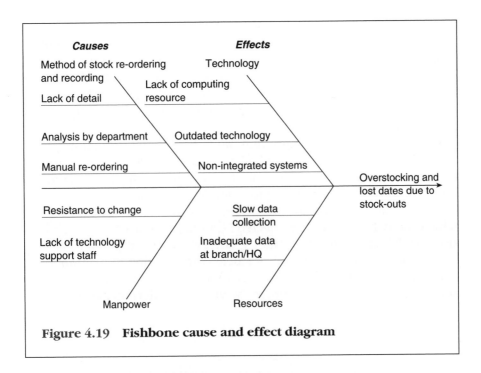

Figure 4.19   Fishbone cause and effect diagram

A Multi-Disciplinary Approach

Diagramming alone, while offering significant assistance to management, is unlikely to meet all our analytical and research needs in the field of change management. The successful management of complex situations calls upon many disciplines and the application of a wide range of theories and techniques: it truly requires a multi-disciplinary approach.

Environmental impact tests based on the previously detailed diagramming techniques, along with related investigative tools, such as STEPLE (social, technical, economic and political, legal and environmental analysis), SWOT (strengths, weaknesses, opportunities and threats), scenario planning, Delphi techniques, brainstorming sessions and general auditing tools, assist in determining the nature of an impending change event. They commence the process of defining the change, but stop short of fully specifying its likely impact. That impact will be felt by the systems that constitute the organization and support its continued success.

Change can be managed by adopting a systems interventionist approach (see Part 2 'Intervention strategies'), but only if this is done with full knowledge that the 'softer' aspects of any complex situation must be built into the solution methodology. When dealing with a specific situation falling within the complex region on the change spectrum, the intelligent use of systems based approaches will produce acceptable results. This is especially the case when environmental scanning suggests that both time and resources are significant constraints.

Major change events – those that are both complex and strategically focused – cannot be managed simply by applying interventionist models. However, intervention strategies can still assist in defining, investigating and planning for such complex situations.

When change occurs the first questions that require attention are what exactly has, or will be affected? Can the systems and its subdivisions be defined? More importantly, however, how autonomous are the systems in question? The final practical cases relating to diagramming and change, as depicted in Mini Cases 4.8 and 4.9, illustrate the value of adopting a diagramming approach when considering the impact of change.

MINI CASE 4.8:   BRITISH AIRPORTS AUTHORITY

British Airports Authorities (BAA) Plc recognized the potential benefits of harnessing the creative powers of the *team* as a means of further developing its competitive advantage and securing future success. To this end they instigated a 'freedom to manage' programme designed to stimulate change. The Terminal 3 senior management staff at Heathrow, London, piloted the initiative. The team first identified the critical success factors as depicted in Figure 4.20.

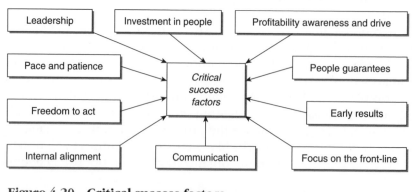

Figure 4.20   Critical success factors

These factors became the focus for further investigation by staff teams, led by an external consultant, with the aim of identifying what would have to be done to close the gap between the present position and the goal of achieving the freedom to manage. The pilot proved successful and was cascaded throughout BAA.

MINI CASE 4.9:   SOUTHERN GENERAL NHS

The cardiology department of the Southern General Hospital NHS Trust assisted in servicing the European heart disease capital of the world, Glasgow. They did not at the time, however, have any provision for cardiac rehabilitation. Such rehabilitation had been shown to be highly effective and reduced the likelihood of recurrence. In an effort to address this weakness, and in recognition that they were not the sole providers of cardiac care, the Trust, through its cardiology team set about addressing the problem.

In an effort to understand the impact of change, the team set about identifying the systems which would be affected by the introduction of a cardiac rehabilitation service. They produced the diagram illustrated in Figure 4.21.

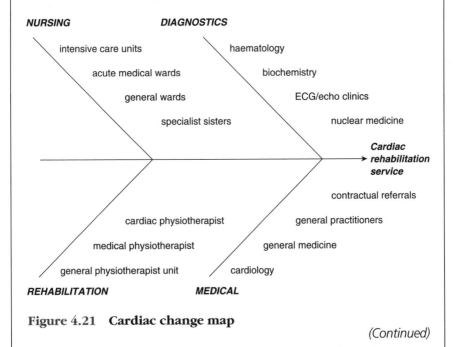

Figure 4.21   Cardiac change map

(Continued)

(Continued)

By diagramming the systems implications of the proposed change, the cardiology team quickly identified the key players. In so doing they identified additional team members and those who must be kept informed. They had begun to manage the change.

READER ACTIVITY

Consider an airliner about to be struck by lightning – what electrical systems could it safely do without?
   List three:

1
2
3

Why the above? Hopefully, because you have selected systems which do not directly impact upon the ultimate purpose of the prime system, that is to fly (and land). For example, autonomous systems may include video facilities, catering services, cabin lighting, or the machine that goes 'bleep' in the cockpit!

PART 2

INTERVENTION STRATEGIES

PART 2

PREVENTION
STRATEGIES

5 | The Systems Approach to Change

In change management, the systems approach is the term given to the analysis of change situations that is based on a systems view of the problem. The intervention strategy model (ISM), which forms the basis of this chapter, is based on the premise that messy change situations may be effectively managed through the application of systems thinking (Ackoff, 1999).

The application of the systems approach is not limited to the 'hard' end of the change spectrum. All management processes and structures may be described in systems terms. Therefore a systems analysis of the change situation, no matter how complex and people-oriented the transition may be, will provide meaningful results for the problem owner(s). It would be incorrect to suggest that the application of an intervention model such as ISM to an extreme organizational change would produce in itself a detailed solution. It could, however, provide a framework for initial investigation, and/or a mechanism for more detailed analysis of specfic change issues within Part 3, which examines organizational development approaches and issues.

Interventionist approaches tend to be based on systems thinking, a socio-technical approach to dealing with and managing change, and as such come with a particular language and underpinning assumptions. So, prior to considering in detail the ISM methodology a brief run through of basic systems-related terminology would be in order.

What is a system?

From the perspective of managing change, a system may be defined as being an organized assembly of components, which are related in such a way that the behaviour of any individual component will influence the overall status of the system. It is impossible to think of any physical mechanism or process that cannot be described in systems terms. Similarly, most managerial processes and functions may also be described in a systematic manner. All systems, physical or 'soft' must have a predetermined objective that the interrelated components strive to achieve.

Given that a system must have an objective and that it is interrelated with other systems associated with its environment, then the accomplishment of the objective must be of interest to all concerned. It is this shared interest that warrants the application of a systems approach. Any system that impinges on the activities of others must be investigated in the light of its associations. Changes in any given system will affect both its own internal workings and very possibly those of interrelated external systems. There is therefore a need to accurately define the system environment experiencing a change prior to the development of a transition path. This requirement highlights the importance of the previous chapter that illustrated the use of diagramming techniques for the purpose of achieving systems definitions. Such techniques assist the problem owner in defining the nature and impact of systems related changes from both a physical and organizational perspective. Karp (2006) stresses the importance of ensuring that the leaders of change, when confronted with complex and possibly chaotic scenarios, should adopt a systematic approach and view. A systems approach provides clarity, understanding and sense of direction. More importantly it provides a means of tackling knowledge management related change events and gets things started (McLaughlin et al., 2006). Fenton (2007) investigates the power of process mapping approaches as applied to change events. This process view of the system produces powerful results and can, if applied properly, assist greatly in managing change.

The automobile, when considered in terms of its basic transportation role, provides a simple example of interrelated systems dependencies, as Table 5.1 illustrates. The definition of the system under study depends, to a great extent, on both the position of the reviewer in relation to the system and the purpose of the study. If the review is taking place from a position that is concerned simply with the car as a means of transportation, then the driver is a subsystem. However, a doctor appraising the medical competence of a prospective driver may consider the 'driver' as being the system. A manager selecting a delivery driver may consider the 'driver' to be the system. However, to complicate things further what the driver has to handle is a heavy goods vehicle and is also required to assist in loading and unloading, so both the manager and the doctor must consider and take a wider systems review. The car itself may be seen as a subsystem if one considers the household and its operations as the greater system. The term 'element' is also introduced to describe the gearshift. An element is that part of a system or component which cannot or need not be broken down any further.

Table 5.1   Interrelated systems dependencies

Systems level	Status	Objective
The car	System	To transport occupants and associated artefacts.
The driver	Subsystem	To manage and direct the system.
The engine	Subsystem	To provide the car's driving force.
The gear box	Subsystems	To engage and influence the driving force.
The fuel pump	Component	To provide petrol to the combustion chamber.
The gearshift	Element	To facilitate driver/gearbox interaction.

System objectives need not be singular, as they are in this example. The car's objective is to provide transport but this may be subdivided and thus provide a greater insight into the system as a whole. It is important to consider not only the prime objective but also any associated subobjectives as they may be of particular interest to both the internal analysis of the system under study and to any other related external systems. Let us again take the car as an example and consider a possible objectives tree as shown in Figure 5.1.

Transport may be the primary objective but economy and safety could be secondary aims, provided that the car still offers reasonable looks, adequate performance and offers personal esteem to the owner.

Objective trees, similar in construction to the one illustrated in Figure 5.1, are produced in most systems investigations. It is seldom enough simply to consider the primary purpose of a system or the macro-objective of a

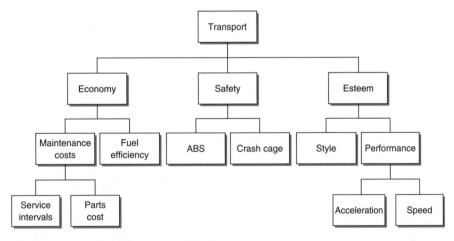

Figure 5.1   Car objectives tree

proposed change. The various elements of the associated change environment may place greater emphasis on particular sub-objectives; to ignore this possibility could lead to a problem owner ill-defining the relationships within the affected environment.

Systems Autonomy and Behaviour

The diagramming techniques previously introduced, along with the construction of objective trees, provide the problem owner with the ability to define the systems environment effectively, prior to and/or during a change event. Care must be taken to define the scope of the change environment in an accurate manner. To accomplish this, consideration and effort must be devoted to determining the degree of systems autonomy existing within the change environment. Within any given environment its systems and their internal workings will have both collective and individual boundaries. The problem owner must ensure that these boundaries are set when defining the change in such a way as to exclude any non-essential relationships. A change environment consists of all systems both directly and indirectly affected; it also includes all associated subsystems. It is part of the 'art' of systems diagramming to set the boundaries appropriately – to include all relevant factors but exclude all irrelevancies.

It is therefore necessary to determine the degree to which the core system under investigation may be considered in isolation. Throughout an investigation we must constantly ask the following questions, bearing in mind the objective, nature and impact of the proposed change:

- How autonomous are the systems?

- What relationships exist?

- How relevant are they?

- Will developments lead to re-definition of boundaries?

- Can the complexities of the change environment be simplified?

READER ACTIVITY

Consider your next family holiday, or one from the past, who must be considered and why, and what associated household related systems and relationships must be considered?

The problem owner, wishing to conduct a thorough systems definition, must at all times remember the purpose of the study. Systems are not of interest because of their inherent physical structures, but rather for what those structures achieve – their aims, interactions and behaviour. Systems autonomy must be considered in light of the study objectives.

The consideration of the degree of autonomy associated with a given system determines its boundaries in relation to the study objectives. What is actually being considered is the behaviour of the systems with particular reference to the nature and relevance of their internal and external relationships. A study of systems behaviour requires that the following three process areas be reviewed:

1   the physical processes constituting the operational system;

2   the communications processes handling the transfer of information and knowledge within and between systems;

3   the monitoring processes maintaining system stability through active knowledge based interventions.

By reviewing the process linkages one may begin to determine the degree of autonomy existing within the various constituent parts of the system. It is how the system behaves, in relation to both internal and external change stimuli that must be considered. A systems investigation should commence with a detailed specification and analysis of the change environment. Having determined the general environment, the investigator then focuses on eliminating irrelevancies. This is achieved by considering the study objectives with reference to the behaviour and autonomy of the systems under review.

READER ACTIVITY

Once again consider the holiday, how did the systems and their associated components behave?

Did the dog howl at the thought of the kennels? Did junior jump with joy at the thought of Disneyland? Who stayed quiet and reflective? Did Sara not want to go because of the destination, or because she would have to leave her boyfriend in the clutches of Susan her 'best friend'?

The Intervention strategy

The previous chapters have examined both the nature of change and the means of coping with its inherent complexity. Now what is required is some means of handling, in a structured manner, the analysis and implementation of a change situation. An intervention strategy may be regarded as the procedural methodology for successfully intervening in the working processes of the original system. The ultimate result should be a stable new environment, which incorporates the desired changes.

The remainder of this chapter is dedicated to the introduction and examination of a practical systems intervention model, termed the intervention strategy model (ISM). This is very much a hybrid model which is firmly based on the traditional investigative techniques associated with the schools of operational and systems management. It is based on a socio-technical platform, one which, although systems driven, endeavours at all times to be inclusive, participative and embedded within the organization. Socio-technical underpinnings are common with managing change models (Luna-Reyes et al., 2005; Ackoff and Emery, 2005). Elements and underlying premises associated with systems intervention strategy (SIS) developed by the Open Business School (Mayon-White, 1986) and the total project management model (TPM), which is the subject of Chapter 7, a product of the University of Glasgow Business School (Paton and Southern, 1990), have been incorporated within the ISM. All three models have been extensively tried and tested on countless practising managers, and their associated organizations. In addition, the models have been employed on a number of successful consultancy projects. User feedback has at all times been positive and the models have found a place in many professional managers' toolkits.

In previous chapters, the basic investigative methodology associated with the operational and systems management schools was implicitly introduced:

1   objective clarification

2   data capture and performance indicators

3   systems diagnostics

4   systems analysis

5   determination of solution options

6   solution evaluation

7   solution implementation

8   appraisal and monitoring.

As we can see, the methodology consists of three phases. The definition phase defines the objectives, the general problem environment and sets the investigative framework. This is followed by an evaluation or design phase, of which the first step is to determine the most appropriate analytical and/or research procedures to employ. Having made this selection the data collected in the definition phase are analysed to produce a range of potential solutions. These solutions are then subsequently evaluated against the performance criteria associated with the investigation's objectives and an optimal solution identified. The final phase is that of implementation during which the plan for introducing and monitoring the solution is devised.

Systems intervention models all share this basic three-phase approach. The actual terminology used to describe component parts of the model and the emphasis placed upon various elements within each phase may differ, but the underlying framework remains unchanged. However, the intervention strategies are much more than basic decision-making frameworks. They, for example, stress the importance of systems analysis, participative group work, iterative mechanisms, organizational issues and much more, as the following sections and the remainder of Part 2 will illustrate.

The ISM methodology emphasizes the linkages between the second and third phases. It stresses the need to consider implementation issues within the design and evaluation phase to ensure acceptance of the change at a later date. ISM also encourages the user to embrace many of the 'softer' techniques, approaches and indeed philosophies, associated with the organizational development school of thought (see Part 3). However, the model insists that users endeavour to assign quantifiable performance measures to even the most 'soft' objectives. The word 'system' has been deliberately omitted from the title, as the model can be applied to both specific systems related change and more general management problem-solving situations.

Change, be it technological, personal, organizational or operational, must at some point impinge upon a 'system'. A system's view of the process, operation, relationship and/or culture experiencing change is an essential feature of ISM. However, word 'system' often alienates those of a non-technical background. ISM does not require the user to be familiar with system analysis and design. The diagrams employed have been previously outlined and are neither overly technical nor complex, and their subsequent analysis need not be of a particularly quantitative nature.

READER ACTIVITY

How often have you been involved in a project, or event, which has failed to produce what you expected? Why has this happened? To what extent have unforeseen circumstances spoilt an otherwise promising project? With hindsight, could they have been foreseen?

By defining a change situation in systems terms, the problem owner may clearly define the nature of the change: those affected by the change, the boundary and scope of the change, the relationships affected by the change, etc. A systems-based intervention strategy is a powerful change management tool.

The Three Phases of Intervention

Successful systems intervention, or problem formulation and solution, requires the management team, or the individual, to proceed through the three interdependent phases until the management objectives have been achieved. The three basic phases of ISM are highlighted in Figure 5.2.

Problem initialization may sound impressive and conjure up images of a complex management process, but in reality its meaning is relatively simple. It means that a change situation has been identified and that the process of managing the change is about to commence.

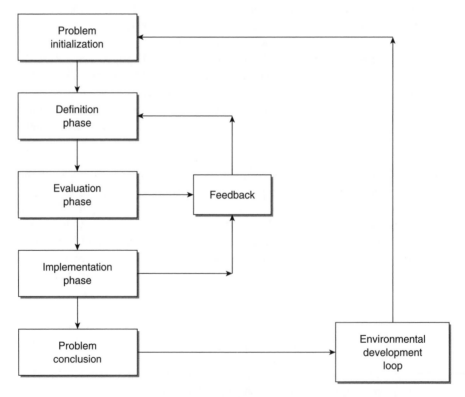

Figure 5.2 The basic phases of the intervention strategy model

A problem owner and possibly a supporting group will have been identified and charged with handling the transition from the old to the new. Chapter 2 stressed the importance of ensuring that the problem owner was committed to the task at hand and possessed, or had access to, the necessary managerial expertise and skill to manage the transition process. For the purposes of this review of ISM the problem owner will be deemed to be the actual manager of the transition process. Those individuals, along with the problem owner, who are eventually identified as being part of the managing team will be termed the change agents. The nucleus of the management team will be formed during problem initialization. The constitution of the team may alter to reflect the environment affected by the change and the skills required managing the problem.

The definition phase involves the in-depth specification and study of the change situation, both from a historical and futuristic viewpoint. The second phase generates and evaluates the potential solution options. The third phase, implementation, develops the action plans which should successfully exploit the outputs of the design phase. Owing to the inherent dynamic nature of operational, organizational and business environments, it is essential that, during each of the phases, the systems affected be constantly monitored. This should involve not only an internal managing team review. It must engage with external stakeholders, to ensure the validity of associated assumptions, objectives, information and analysis. At any point, it may be necessary to iterate back to an earlier stage for the purpose of incorporating a new development, or factor, which may influence the validity of the original outcomes.

Iterations are an essential feature of an effective change or problem management strategy. For this reason, it is often advisable to conduct a 'quick and dirty' analysis of the change, prior to a more formal and detailed investigation. This should reduce the need for numerous time-consuming iterations once the 'intervention' has formally commenced.

Figure 5.2 shows an environmental development feedback loop, linking the final outcome, the 'new environment', with that of the 'initial situation'. The purpose of this loop is simply to illustrate that the change cycle is never complete. Dynamic environmental factors will, over a period of time, necessitate the need for additional change and so the process will once more commence. As operational, organizational and competitive environments continue to develop, management must adopt a proactive stance, thus anticipating and managing change to their advantage. The ability to handle, in an effective manner, the transition between 'steady state' situations should be regarded as a potential source of competitive advantage.

The Intervention Strategy Model (ISM)

The individual stages associated with each phase of the model are shown in Figure 5.3. The adoption of the model will provide a means of managing the change cycle in a structured, logical, interactive and open manner. It facilitates the total planning and control of a systems-oriented change.

A number of important points must be noted relating to the effective and efficient use of the model prior to investigating each of the individual stages. They are as follows:

- Iterations may be required at any point, within or between phases, owing to the inherent dynamic nature of change events. Once the desired position has been reached, further environmental developments may cause the transition process to be re-entered at some later date.

- Problem owners and any other associated change agents should be involved throughout. It is essential that they be committed to the initiative, as they are the driving forces.

- There is a tendency to rush through the diagnostic phase, with problem owners basing assumptions on their own brand of 'common sense'. Time spent getting it right first time is seldom wasted. Specification and description are crucial to the understanding of a change situation.

- It is always advisable to attempt to produce quantifiable performance indicators in stage 3, as they will simplify the evaluation process in stage 6.

- It is virtually impossible not to start thinking about solution options during the diagnostic phase, especially on a 'live' problem. There is no harm in this, but do not skip stages. Put the options aside until stage 4.

Having generated a host of options, some form of 'sensitive' screening must take place. Often one will find that certain options may be eliminated, for implementation reasons, or because they are dependent upon uncontrollable factors. Such options should be removed prior to more formal evaluation. Occasionally, options may have been entertained for 'political' reasons. For example, suggestions that are less than suitable may have to be tolerated to avoid alienation, or because they come from key players who expect to be listened to and acknowledged. Such options may be edited out at this stage; they may be lost or forgotten for long enough to allow more plausible alternatives to take hold.

The options and solutions generated and evaluated within the second phase need not relate to individual and unrelated entities. It is often the case that chains of interrelated options and solutions have to be dealt with and care taken to ensure they are evaluated as a total entity.

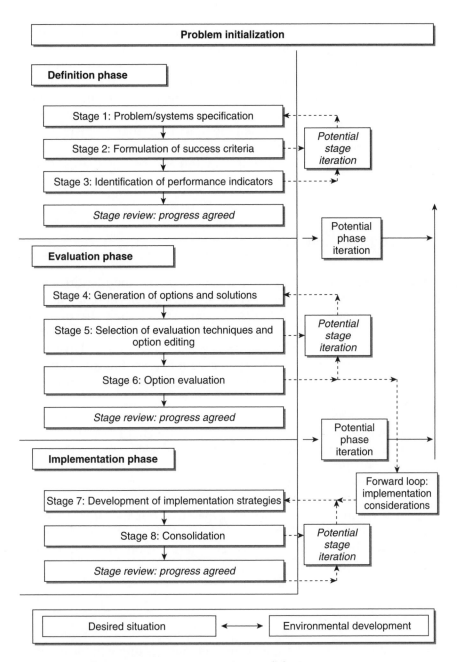

Figure 5.3   The intervention strategy model

The distinction between the second and third phases is rather blurred. The second phase concludes with option evaluation.

Implementation phase commences with the development of implementation strategies. However, for effective implementation to
take place it must itself be considered during the evaluation phase.
Options may on occasion have to be considered in the light of their
ease of implementation. Users of ISM must be prepared to jump
forward during the evaluation phase to consider implementation.
This can often be accomplished by ensuring that implementation
related performance indicators are built into the definition phase
thus ensuring that they will have an impact during the evaluation
stages.

The Stages of ISM

The key to successful change management is first the identification of
the appropriate problem owners and second the selection of a management methodology to provide the means of handling the transition.
Provision of adequate resources and support is crucial. The management team charged with handling the change may not have senior
management representation. In such case it is essential that key stakeholders are kept in the 'loop' and their visible support secured and
managed.

Assuming the 'players' have been identified, they must decide on their
subsequent course of action. ISM should be selected when the impending or existing change situation exhibits tendencies towards the harder
end of the change spectrum, what was termed the 'flexi' region of the
change spectrum in Chapter 1. The systems approach can also be
employed to tackle the initial stages of softer organizational problems.
Long-term solutions would not be generated, but the problem owner
would have 'kick-started' the change process, by starting to define and
manage the complexities of a messy change situation. This can be useful
when time is of the essence.

Definition phase

Time spent defining a change event – its nature, impact and repercussions – will pay dividends as the management process develops.
Accurately describing the change allows the managing team to adjust
membership if required, assess cultural impacts, examine, through system mapping techniques, relationships, attitudes and causes, and begin
to address the change holistically.

Specification then moves on to the formulation of the success criteria. The principal objectives are identified, along with any sub-objectives and/or constraints, and against each are assigned success criteria.

Stage 1: problem/systems specification and description

Management must, through the problem owner(s) and with the assistance of interested parties, develop their understanding of the situation. The change, or problem, must be specified in systems terms and the complexity reduced so as to isolate and determine the systems interactions, relationships and cultures.

It is at this stage that one employs the previously outlined diagramming techniques as a means of assisting definition and analysis. Meetings and interviews will be conducted, experience sought and historical data examined, in an effort to construct an accurate picture of the present system and the likely impact of the changes. As this is likely to represent the first formal notification of the change one must tread lightly, unfreeze the present system in such a way as to minimize the likelihood of resistance and non-co-operation. Mistakes here in communicating the impending change to interested parties will create both immediate and future difficulties. The problem owner requires co-operation if the true nature and impact of the change is to be defined. In messy change situations, diagramming and defining the change must be seen as a group/stakeholder activity.

Stage 2: formulation of success criteria

The success criteria associated with a particular change situation may be defined in two ways. The first, and most common, involves the setting of objectives and constraints. The second is merely a corruption of the first in that it generates options, or paths, which are tagged on to the original objective. For analytical and communicative purposes it is always best to produce objectives and constraints. They are simpler to understand and can be more readily associated with performance measures. Options are messy to deal with and have to be broken down at a later stage to determine specific measures of success.

An example of an option masquerading as an objective could be a phrase such as 'Improve productivity by reducing manning levels'. A solution or option has followed the objective. This tends to result in the problem owner(s) focusing in on this option without fully considering alternatives, a dangerous and unimaginative course of action.

Objectives may be derived from the rationale behind the change and constraints generally emerge from the resources that have been allocated to the task, or more accurately the lack of them. It would be fair to say

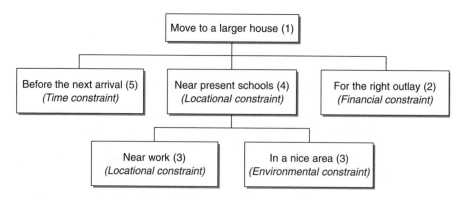

Figure 5.4   Prioritized objectives tree

that the normal constraints facing management in change situations are time and money. Constraints may also be traced to both the nature of the systems and the cultures affected. Even when objectives and constraints appear to be clear and unambiguous the problem owner(s) must ensure that any less obvious sub-objectives, along with any associated constraints, have been identified.

It is always advisable to construct a prioritized objectives tree, with associated constraints incorporated. Figure 5.4 illustrates such a tree. It considers the objectives and their ranking which may be associated with the need to upgrade the size of the family home due to a pending 'population explosion'. Priorities are numbered, with the number '1' indicating the greatest priority. Constraints are shown in parenthesis.

This objectives tree can, during evaluation stages 4, 5 and 6, be developed to include the options for achieving the objectives. In turn the generated option paths can then form the basis of an implementation strategy.

Stage 3: identification of performance measures

Having decided what the objectives of the exercise are, it is necessary to formulate appropriate measures for each one. If this is not done at this point, then how can the problem owner evaluate the options generated subsequently?

Where possible it is best to identify quantifiable measures, such as costs, savings, volume, labour and time. When this is not possible then the measures should be graded in some way, e.g. ranking could be employed. Measures can be entered on the objectives tree, thus providing one descriptive representation of what is to be achieved and how its success will be measured. This provides an ideal focal point for the subsequent evaluation phase and also communicates in a logical fashion the aims of the change.

READER ACTIVITY

Consider a forthcoming change, at work, home or in another arena of personal activity. Now complete the following:

- Through diagramming identify the key players, their relationships and lastly their anticipated reaction to the proposed change.
- Identify the primary objective of the change and any associated sub-objectives; for each identify a valid measure of success.
- Identify and relate any constraints associated with the project.
- Develop the above by conducting further environmental tests, for example, TROPICS, SWOT or STEPLE.

Now, briefly detail how you would proceed. Who would be involved? How would you structure the option evaluation phase and where would you place the change on the spectrum?

Evaluation phase

The definition phase should have highlighted the key players in the change process: they should, in some way, be involved in the generation of potential solutions to the problem. However, dependent upon the outcomes of the definition phase, they may need to be joined by additional stakeholders: indeed, some of the original team may have to be dropped.

Stage 4: generation of options or solutions

A wide range of techniques (Table 5.2) are available to the problem owner(s) which assist in option generation. It is outside the scope of this text to investigate the above techniques; however, the reader will see many of them detailed and practised within this and other chapters.

Table 5.2   Option generation

Attitude surveys	Ideas writing
Brainstorming (experience)	Interviews
Comparison analysis	Market research
Delphi	Supply chain research
Desk research	Story/scenarios telling
Focus groups	Structured meetings
Gap analysis	Talking wall

Many of the benefits associated with adopting a collective solution methodology will be lost if the groups and teams involved are not operating effectively. Very often, especially when those coming together do not generally function as a work team, it is best to engage in some form of structured team building. This should first break the ice, and second raise the level of performance. Facilitating the learning development process is crucial to the success of group-based approaches. Vennix (1996) develops this point and proposes adopting systems-based dynamics into team building, a focus on structure and process to gain results.

It is important not to take too blinkered a view of the change during the option-generating sessions. A variety of possibilities and opportunities should be considered. There is no need to worry about 100 per cent relevance, as any sub-optimal options may be screened out in the subsequent evaluation.

The participating individuals and groups must see such sessions as being constructive and influential. They should not become cosmetic smoke screens for the tabling of preconceived options. If this happens, those involved may withdraw support and take a more reactive stance. To this end sensitivity must be shown towards the promoter of even the most ridiculous options.

Stage 5: selection of appropriate evaluation techniques and option editing

Having identified the potential options or solutions, which may of course be presented as 'strings' of options rather than discrete solutions, the investigator must then evaluate them. First, a brief comparative study of the options and the predetermined success criteria will act as an initial screening device. It is important not to alienate those who have contributed suggestions. Second, a range of evaluation techniques must be selected and applied, for example:

- Examination and manipulation of the previously developed diagrams should assist in determining the impact of the solution option(s) upon the systems environment.

- Physical and computer simulations may assist in determining operational viability – especially in situations where real life experimentation could be 'costly'.

- Risk, investment, cash flow and cost-benefit analysis should assist in determining the likely return on investment and the projected cash flows.

- Project management techniques, such as network analysis, will test the potential benefits, time scales and resource implications of implementation.

- Environmental impact analysis may be employed to establish the 'hidden' environmental cost of adopting particular solutions.

- Strategic and cultural fit must be considered: will proposals match intended strategic outcomes and does the existing culture support the changes?

This initial formal screening should eliminate sub-optimal options, as well as developing an understanding of the interrelationships and order of option paths and linkages. Remember that options need not be standalone activities: they may form paths, courses of activities that must be considered as a group. The analysis within this stage need not be quantitative. Subjective assessments of an option's suitability may be conducted when there are non-quantifiable performance indicators. Subjective assessments of an option's suitability are best conducted in an open and participative manner, thus ensuring that accusations of bias and skullduggery are minimized.

Stage 6: option evaluation

This stage constitutes the final hurdle of the evaluation phase. Here, options are evaluated against the previously determined change objectives in particular, the performance measures previously identified in stage 3.

A tabular format may be used to conduct the evaluation. Objectives, along with their associated performance measures, are entered as a prioritized listing on the left. Individual options and/or option chains are entered along the top. Factual data and/or calculated weightings are entered in the appropriate box corresponding to the option's performance against a particular objective measure.

The example shown, Table 5.3, illustrates the use of such a format for the selection of a new family car based on four objectives and a choice of four models (the options). The safety rating could be based on the EuroNCAP ratings. Esteem indicators could be based on subjective and personal preferences influenced by the motoring press. A grading system would have to be employed. Given the indicated priority for each objective the selected

Table 5.3   Evaluation table

Objective/measure	Priority	Option A	Option B	Option C	Option D	Optimal
Cost £s (constraint: < £25K)	3	10K	22K	15K	12.5K	A
Performance 0–60mph, seconds, top speed, mph	1	10 99	8 130	8 116	12 109	B
Safety	4	Low	High?	High	Medium	C
Esteem	2	Low	High	Medium	Medium	B

option would be model B. Modifications to any of the variables can be easily introduced and the priority system altered to illustrate greater differentials. For example, let us assume that the driver, due to a recent addition to the family, increases the priority on safety to 1 and cost to 2, while downgrading performance and esteem to a negative digit. The selection may then alter to option and model D.

This simple example illustrates the visual impact of the tabular presentation and indicates how it may be used as a focal point for discussion and the consideration of 'what if?' scenarios.

The process of option evaluation must be conducted with reference to subsequent implementation. A forward loop is incorporated within the model to emphasize the importance of this factor. This can be formally addressed by ensuring that implementation objectives are built into the original objectives tree, thus resulting in the production of at least subjective measures of success relating to implementation issues. Unless implementation objectives or constraints, with their associated measures of success, have been included in the definition phase then the strategy will be untested against the rigors of implementation. Will it be accepted? Is there time to train staff? Has it been fully communicated and understood? And, of course, can we afford it?

Implementation phase

Assuming all has gone well, the foundations of an achievable strategy to deal with the change will have been laid. One danger – and practitioners will testify to its prevalence – is that too much time will have been spent on developing a solution and precious little has been left for implementation. In such cases all the good work will have been in vain. The 'trinity' of change, previously noted, must be adhered to throughout the application of ISM. Stay focused, remember the goal and ensure task completion.

Stage 7: development of implementation strategies

By this stage in the change management process, or in any other form of problem analysis or systems investigation, the detailed foundations of a successful conclusion to the project will have been laid. Objectives are clear and current, options selected and reviewed and the system well defined and understood. Now all that is left is to package the outcomes into a coherent whole and introduce the changes to the system.

It may sound simple, but it never is. It is at the point of implementation that all those affected will recognize the full impact of the change. Only now will the problem owner discover the extent to which a shared perception was reached. In problems with truly 'hard' systems there will be little or no resistance. The physical change will go ahead, but as one gravitates towards the 'softer' end of the change continuum the risk of latent resistance is always a worrying factor.

To ensure the successful implementation of change via ISM the following key success factors must be adhered to:

- The foundation of effective change management lies in a comprehensive definition of the change situation: 'act in haste and repent at leisure'.

- Participation of those likely to be affected is crucial.

- Change calls upon a wide range of competencies to be employed. A team-based approach is likely to produce best results, assuming it is 'facilitated' by a skilled exponent of change.

- Visible and tangible senior management support is essential.

- An open mind must be kept, effective communication striven for and the change must be 'marketed'.

- Sensitivity and understanding should be displayed when dealing with those who may feel threatened by the change.

- Failure to provide the resources, development and training required to handle the change will be disastrous. Prepare staff to cope.

- Organizational structures and forward looking strategies which welcome change and see it as an opportunity will greatly enhance the environment for change and thus ease the change agent's task.

There are essentially only three basic implementation strategies available and they are as follows:

1   pilot studies

2   parallel running

3   big bang.

Pilot studies provide the greatest opportunity for a subsequent review of the change. Assumptions and procedures can be tested, arguments developed and the likely future acceptance of the fully implemented change increased. But they also delay full implementation, and they allow those who may wish to resist to adopt delaying tactics and marshal their forces. In addition, the environment does not stand still; delays to implementation may render the original solution sub-optimal and therefore necessitate a review of the whole process.

Often the proposed changes will have a dramatic effect on not only those parts of the system directly affected but also on all associated systems. Under these circumstances one may adopt a parallel-running implementation strategy. Slowly phase out the old system, as the new becomes more reliable and understood.

Big bang implementation maximizes the speed of change but it can also generate the maximum resistance to the change, at least in the short term. Like most things in life, compromise generally provides the answer, and a blend of the three strategies is normally found.

Later chapters will deal with the development of implementation strategies in more depth, from both a systems and organizational development perspective. But for the present, remember that to gain a shared perception of a problem and commitment for its solution, it is essential to involve those affected by it in the decision-making process and to ensure that they have the knowledge, skills and tools to handle the change. This point is illustrated in Mini Case 5.1.

MINI CASE 5.1:   BRITISH AIRPORTS AUTHORITY

Having identified a need to change, to match organizational, managerial and employee strategies with those of the business, BAA faced the question of how to energize those responsible for managing the future within an environment which challenges the past and threatens their position.

BAA ensured that their empowerment programme was driven and owned by their middle to senior management team. To ensure that their customer focused business produced results, they intended to empower staff, democratize the communications processes, and ensure business results. Such moves can threaten the position, authority and stability of the middle management team, which are ultimately responsible for implementation.

BAA ensured that middle management were at the centre of the design, development and implementation of their 'freedom to manage' programme: they owned it, they transferred it to others, they developed their 'new' role and guaranteed personal and organizational success.

Stage 8: consolidation

Armed with an implementation strategy designed to maximize the probability of success and acceptance, the agents introduce the change, but we have not yet finished. Old systems and practices just like old habits, die hard. It takes time for a new system or change to be fully accepted. Skilful communication, visual support from above and provision of adequate support to those affected, are required throughout this stage. Initial changes must be followed up, and both protection and enforcement of the new system will be required. It is up to the problem owners, the agents of the change, to nurture the growth of the new, while encouraging the peaceful demise of the old. Implementation is not the end of the process. Lessons learnt must be openly discussed and communicated. Mini Case 5.2 helps illustrate this point.

MINI CASE 5.2:   VISION

Implementing change obviously calls upon both basic and advanced planning and control techniques. However, managing significant change events requires the energizing of many disparate individuals and groups to achieve the predetermined goals. Richard T. Pascale (1994) identifies the need to 'manage the present from the future' when dealing with major 'transformation' programmes. He suggests that British Airways in the 1980s, Thomas Cook in the 1990s, along with many others such as Haagen-Dazs, recognized the need to project their goals and identify achievable, yet challenging, visions of the future. From these visions a set of goals was identified and projected backward in time to the present. Each organization then determined whom, what and when to move forward. They took only what was needed and left the baggage of the past behind.

Successful implementation of change is dependent upon many variables. However, if one encumbers the prime movers with the emotional and moribund baggage of the past then they will pull and push it with ever increasing loathing towards future goals. It is far better to free them to select the best of the past and transport it to a future ideal.

The 'Quick and Dirty' Analysis

The impression may have been given that the adoption of ISM will force the change agents into a protracted period of consultation, negotiation and deliberation. In many instances the nature of the change will be such that its magnitude will necessitate a lengthy and meticulous transition process. In situations where either the nature of the change is such that its impact will be limited, or the time scales involved dictate a speedy conclusion to the problem, or both, the application of ISM may be conducted in what may be termed a 'quick and dirty' manner (Q&D for short). A small group can drive themselves through the model and arrive at a solution which may not be the optimal one, but it will at least have addressed and incorporated the key factors associated with the change environment.

A Q&D analysis can also be a useful starting point for the change agents tackling a more complex problem. It will indicate key factors and potential barriers to change. It will highlight the principal players and give an indication of resource requirements. Such an analysis will at an early stage set the scene for things to come and provide the change agents with a valuable insight into the complexities of the transition process.

The Iterative Nature of the Model

A principal aspect of the model is its iterative nature. Although the model has been described in a stage-by-stage sequential manner, one must not forget the feedback loops. These have been incorporated into the design to facilitate the return to previously completed stages in the light of environmental changes. In addition, each phase is concluded with a review. The first two phases conclude with an agreement from those involved that the stage sequence is complete and all agree with the decisions and conclusions reached. Ownership of the problem as it develops is thus maintained. The final phase concludes with a debrief activity. What were the management lessons associated with the transition process and how can things be improved the next time?

To date, this chapter has mainly highlighted the 'macro' aspects of the model's iterative nature, in particular the need to be aware of the continuous cycle of change that affects all systems. But the need for what may be termed 'micro' iterations also exists. Such iterations take place during 'real time', while the transition process is actually occurring. The model design incorporates feedback loops between each of the stages so as to emphasize the importance to the user of constantly updating and monitoring the system environment.

Environmental shifts impacting upon the systems under review must be assessed not only at the point of impact. One must look back to past decisions and on to potential outcomes to ensure all aspects of the impact have been assessed and dealt with. If the impact is such that the system definitions and relationships are altered then this must be appropriately incorporated in the subsequent stages of the model. Iterations may not all result in a complete reappraisal of the definition phase. For example, the iteration may be from the implementation to the design phase; such would be the case if resource allocations altered prior to implementation and rendered a selected solution path redundant.

Living with Reality

The reality for most managers, in today's changing world, with limited resources and time, is that they are simply 'snowed under' with work.

Although they know, at least in terms of having a knowledge of best practice, how to manage change, they simply do not have the time to do it justice. If applied on a 'quick and dirty' basis, possibly with only a core team involved and a competent and motivated change agent, then ISM can often show a clear way forward. It may not produce an optimal result for the long term, but it may secure short- to medium-term results. Voltaire (1698–1778) may help justify such a cavalier approach as in his view: 'Details are the vermin that destroy great work!'

Managing the Future

Managers, organizations and the societies they serve would be naive, even fatalistic, if they failed to realize the necessity of planning for the future. Planning for planning's sake must be avoided. The ultimate failure of centralist planning initiatives, such as those adopted in the past by the Soviet Union, China and even the American automotive giants such as Chrysler, along with many corporations in the 1960s and 1970s, illustrate the need to be responsive. Plans must be flexible and in tune with the environment in which they are to be implemented. Operating environments, in the broadest sense of the term, need to be understood and managerial actions reflect their complexities and intentions.

There is no evidence to suggest that the rate and the nature of change are likely to alter dramatically. Technologies, industries and societies will continue to converge. Organizations will continue to seek strategic alliances and maximize the benefits associated with a well-managed supply chain. Managers and employees will be judged, as they are now, on their ability to cope with and manage change. Adaptability, continuous improvement, life long learning and sustaining competitive advantage remain the watchwords.

Corporate winners, whether public or private enterprises, will have fostered and maintained a desire to succeed through progressive, dynamic and challenging initiatives. Strategies and cultures that welcome, address and imaginatively manage change will continue to triumph. We will return to the theme of maintaining a competitive advantage in Parts 3 and 4 of the book, but in the meantime the following quote seems to encapsulate the general message:

> The first law of the jungle is that the most adaptable species are always the most successful. In the struggle for survival, the winners are those who are most sensitive to important changes in their environment and quickest to reshape their behaviour to meet each new environmental challenge. (Cotter, 1995)

6 | Cases in Intervention

The previous chapter concentrated on the technicalities of the intervention strategy model (ISM). Each phase and its associated stages were described in a sequential manner. The iterative nature of the model was highlighted, which facilitates the return to earlier stages in the light of changes in either the internal or external environments. Key points concerning the model's application were emphasized. The need to consider certain of the models and techniques associated with Part 3 of this text, namely organizational development and design, which deal with the 'softer' people issues, was raised. Effective implementation can only be accomplished when both participation and commitment have been sought and won.

This chapter aims to illustrate the detailed use of ISM by introducing a number of short case studies from a range of 'real life' practical applications. They will be presented in a sequential manner in accordance with the ISM format.

The Definition Phase

Stage 1: problem/systems specification and description

Chapter 4 dealt with systems diagramming and in general the definition and initial analysis of change situations. There is therefore little point in dwelling on this area of systems definition. Stage 1 should produce a clear and concise definition of the affected systems and their relationships. To illustrate this point let us briefly consider the systems change described in Mini Case 6.1.

MINI CASE 6.1: BRITISH GAS

An example from the purchasing department of British Gas (Scotland) Plc illustrates how a systems problem should be entered. A policy decision was made and justified at the corporate level of the company, to the effect that the stockholding of items termed 'one-time-buys' (otherwise denoted as OTBs) would commence and that the more frequently used OTBs would be held at two central locations. The aim of this exercise was to reduce the delivery time of such items and thus improve the quality of service to the end customer. Traditionally, these were items ordered by purchasing clerks directly from suppliers as and when requested. The numbers involved and the frequency of orders did not, on a regional basis, justify internal stock holding.

The policy change, designed to improve delivery performance, would result in the bulk of the OTBs being held in a central warehouse facility with the regions ordering directly. Delivery time, in the region of 15 days when ordering directly from the manufacturer, would be reduced dramatically.

The purchasing manager, in effect the problem owner, was directed to manage the change and had an imposed target date to work towards. He quickly identified another two key change agents and brought them on to the team: first, the spares buyer who had line responsibility for the clerks who dealt with OTBs, and second the purchasing department's own systems development technician. They then, as a group, set about defining the exact nature and impact of the change. The first steps they took on entering and defining the change were as follows:

1 The ordering clerks were notified of the proposed change and the rationale behind it and the process was explained.
2 The change agents developed a flow chart with the assistance of the clerks, which detailed the internal OTB ordering system (in effect a subsystem of the total ordering system) to assist in the understanding of the existing process.
3 The change agents then constructed an activity sequence diagram to determine how the new system would impact on the old, thus determining the scope of the change.
4 Next they produced a systems map detailing both internal and external systems associated with the OTB ordering process.
5 A relationship map was then developed to aid their understanding of the nature of the linkages between the systems involved.
6 An investigation then took place into the relative magnitude of the conflicting forces that existed, to determine their effect on the likelihood of success. Force field analysis was employed.

(Continued)

(Continued)

On completion of the sixth step the change agents had a clear picture of the systems involved and their relationships and status. By this point it was obvious to all concerned that what they were faced was a reasonably 'hard' systems change, with minimal people issues. The clerks' function would be retained and retraining was unlikely to be significant. This case, along with the diagrams mentioned above, will be dealt with in more depth in Chapter 16.

Stage 2/3: formulation of success criteria and identification of performance indicators

Having fully defined the change environment as far as is both feasible and productive, we may enter the next stage. Mini Case 6.2, taken from ABC Ltd, details the objectives, constraints and measures developed to assist in solving a particularly 'hard' problem.

MINI CASE 6.2:   ABC LTD

This case involved the possible automation of calibration and monitoring systems on an engine test rig. The problem owner defined the problem, namely the test controller, who cited the following reasons in support of an ISM-based solution:

1 *Time scales*   As soon as possible to maintain competitive advantage over other test facilities.
2 *Clear objectives*   The introduction of an automatic recording system to a test rig with the purpose of reducing costs and improving the quality of data.
3 *System boundary*   Clearly defined and limited to the test facility.
4 *Source*   Internally driven by the testing facility management.
5 *Control*   Essentially fully under the control of the testing facility management.
6 *Resources*   Limited financial budget.
7 *Motivation*   A high degree of interest and commitment existed amongst staff.

The above review of the nature of the change facing the test controller deals with the issues raised by the TROPICS test introduced in Chapter 1.

All the above factors were considered, with the term 'motivation' being employed loosely to cover the areas of perception and interest. Diagrams were produced which vindicated the initial assumption that this was

---

indeed a 'hard' systems change. Subsequent production of the objectives and constraints listing, along with the associated performance measures, also indicated a straightforward systems change. The products of ISM Stages 2 and 3 are shown in Table 6.1.

Table 6.1 Objective and performance measures for ISM stages 2 and 3

Objective	Performance measure
a Quality improvement	% of correct data
b Test time reduction	Hours
c Reduced calibration time	Hours
d Removal of manual inputs	Hours
e Reduced fuel usuage	Gallons
f A more reliable system	% down-time
Constraints	
a Cost	£, limited hardware and software budget
b Resistance	Co-operation, potential employee/union resistance (recognized but not acted upon)

It is at this point that ABC Ltd strayed from the ISM path. Like-minded engineering managers who focused on the technical aspects of the system constructed the diagrams. They entered the formulation stage as one and did not think forward in sufficient detail to the implementation phase.

The millwrights, who were the shop-floor operatives most directly involved in the existing manual process, were not fully briefed nor adequately consulted during the planning process. The 'softer' issues were not identified in the definition phase as the emphasis had been on technical specifications and systems. The result was that the management of the project was impeded just as the implementation phase was being entered. The co-operation of the operatives and their union could not be relied upon. Insufficient attention had been paid to the operators' perception of a loss in status due to the automation of their task and the possible resulting redeployment of their resource.

The situation was resolved by an iteration back to the definition phase to incorporate the 'softer' elements of change. The implementation was put on hold until the involvement and retraining of the operatives had been effectively incorporated into the solution.

The evaluation phase

Stage 4/5: the generation and editing of options and solutions

As we noted in Chapter 5 there are a host of techniques available to the problem owner to assist in both the generation of options and their subsequent reduction of numbers. The appraisal and subsequent selection of the evaluation techniques employed, and their degree of sophistication and method of application will depend almost wholly on the nature of the problem and the availability of resources.

The ABC Ltd example introduced in Mini Case 6.2 followed the ISM protocol as outlined in the following sections.

Option generation

Owing to the perceived need for haste, given the expressed desire to maintain the enterprise's competitive edge, the generation of options was conducted in a single brainstorming session led by the test controller. Representatives of the following groups took part, their presence being justified by their key positions within the original systems definition:

- computer systems
- instrument technicians
- engine performance analysts
- testers.

The above group produced the following list of options:

- hire or buy equipment
- in-house designed system
- externally designed system
- partial system – data collection only
- complete system – no manual intervention
- external equipment maintenance
- in-house equipment maintenance
- tester-operated
- tester-operated with instrument technician back-up
- tester-operated with staff back-up.

The reader should note that the above list is not as extensive or as detailed as that produced by the team during their option-generation session. The technical nature of many of the options and their explanation was such that their reproduction would simply lead to confusion.

Option editing

Having generated the options, the group then set about editing out those which were unsuitable or impracticable given the existing system environment:

Option	Rejection criteria
Tester operated with staff back up	Shift working problems
In-house systems design	Insufficient expertise
In-house equipment maintenance	No facilities

As we can see, there is no need to become involved in complicated procedures and protracted discussions. These options were eliminated without recourse to any form of financial analysis.

Stage 6: option evaluation

Following on from the editing stage, the group moved on to the evaluation of the remaining options. The data required to formally evaluate the options were gathered and generated by the problem owner and the other change agents. Much of the information came from financial and operational analysis of existing in-house data and literature provided by equipment manufacturers. Various break-even style analyses were conducted to establish both cost and performance profiles for all the options. The necessary information along with the objectives and options were collated and presented in a tabular format as shown in Table 6.2.

The agreed solution was as follows: the recording system should be externally designed and 'complete', allowing auto-calibration and recording of data to be directly transferred to the mainframe computer. The equipment should be hired and operated by the tester with support from the instrument technician.

The implementation phase

The importance of this phase must not be underestimated. One of the most frequent failings associated with poor change management occurs

Table 6.2 Option evaluation (test rig)

Objective	Options	Buy	Rent	Data record only	Data record transfer	Complete system	Tester and technician
Improve data quality		N/A	N/A	90%	95%	98%	98%
Reduce testing time		N/A	N/A	1 hour	1 hour	1 hour	N/A
Reduce fuel consumption		N/A	N/A	150 gallons	150 gallons	150 gallons	N/A
Reduce calibration time		N/A	N/A	0 hour	0 hour	8 hours	N/A
System reliability		N/A	N/A	N/A	N/A	N/A	2%
Reduce costs	*Buy:*	N/A	N/A	£50K	£75K	£100K	N/A
	Rent:	N/A	N/A	*	*	*	N/A
Reduce manual input		N/A	N/A	0 hour	2 hours	2 hours	N/A

Note: N/A denotes not applicable. Rental costs would be approximately 30% less than the associated purchase cost.

at this point. The problem owner, along with any other relevant change agents, having just completed a major project evaluation, possibly very effectively, may rush into the implementation without fully preparing the way ahead. Implementation strategies are required which address issues such as timing of events, scheduling of activities, sourcing and delivery of resources and the development of the human resource support structures. Implementation issues need not be left until the final stages of ISM. They will naturally emerge during both the discussion and evaluation of options and solutions. Previous discussions regarding sound implementation strategy emphasized the need to build implementation issues and objectives into the actual evaluation process.

There is much more to developing an implementation strategy than engaging in network-based planning exercises and the construction of elaborate control charts and budgetary monitoring devices. No one would deny the value of such techniques or the importance of seriously considering the harder issues. However, the vast majority of competent managers are capable of dealing with both the planning techniques and monitoring mechanisms, either directly or by seeking expert assistance. The technical aspects of project planning are not generally associated with project failure. It is the 'softer' people-based issues that can have a detrimental impact on the successful implementation of a project.

The two cases chosen to examine the implementation phase have been selected not for their complexities of planning but rather for the emphasis they place on the management of people. The need to address the people issues was also illustrated by a study entitled the *Glasgow Management Development Initiative* (Brownlie et al., 1990). The researchers contacted many employers and their managers, through both focus groups and questionnaires, in an effort to establish the health or otherwise of management development activity. By far the most sought-after category of development was managing people. Managers themselves know that the key to success lies in their ability to effectively manage people in an enterprising manner towards the fulfilment of mutually agreeable objectives.

Stage 7/8: develop implementation strategies and consolidation

The first case, Mini Case 6.3 deals with Froud Consine Ltd (FCL). It demonstrates the benefits of generating a shared perception of a problem and ensuring that the principal players are 'on-side' prior to implementation. To make sense of the implementation phase, we must join the case at the conclusion of the formulation phase.

MINI CASE 6.3:   FROUD CONSINE LTD (FCL)

FCL is a medium-sized engineering company involved in the design, manufacture and installation of high-technology test equipment. Babcock International (BI) acquired the company in 1985. Prior to the BI take-over, FCL had experienced a succession of management teams endeavouring to improve the firm's performance, mainly through diversification. The company found itself providing a service as well as a product, but did not successfully restructure its manufacturing and management systems accordingly. FCL was a traditional engineering company: they had their own way of doing things and had managed to survive in their original base in Worcester for almost a century.

The problem owner, part of a four-man management team from BI, was faced with an organization set in its ways and fast developing a substantial inertia to change. There were of course many issues that the BI team addressed, but for this example the emphasis will be placed on the objective of improving the commercial control of contracts in line with the increasingly important customer-servicing requirements.

As one might have expected from the project objective and the nature of the company, the change was not going to be one of simply updating a few physical management systems. There would be a number of complex organizational issues. This was recognized within the management of the change process and every effort was made during the early stages of the systems change to identify and involve the principal parties who would play a key role in securing the successful adoption of the change. Although the organizational issues were significant, the management team opted for a systems-based solution methodology. In the aftermath of a take-over and faced with tight schedules the aim was to secure immediate improvements with minimal opposition. The more protracted and open nature of the organizational development solution methodologies were not considered to be appropriate. This is not to say that BI did not wish to see organizational change, but at the time of the take-over this was seen as being a longer-term objective.

The option evaluation table, Table 6.3, produced by the problem owner along with the change agents, reflects the importance of organizational issues within this particular change environment.

The preferred option was the establishment of a dedicated contract management function. As Table 6.3 illustrates, all the generated options dealt with the organizational issues associated with the proposed change. ISM produced a solution to what was at least superficially a non-systems problem. It identified the optimal route forward and by ensuring, in the traditions of best practice, that the principal change agents were involved and committed from an early stage it simplified the process of implementation.

Table 6.3   Option evaluation (restructuring)

Objectives	Options	A dedicated contract management function	Improve administration effort and employ progress chasers	Place contract responsibility on functional department heads
Contract control		Responsibility defined; good chance of success	No single point of responsibility	Difficult to view the whole problem; poor chance of success
Cost control		Requires contract budgeting system	No budget responsibility	No overall contract cost control
Customer service		Single contact point	Multiple contact point	Multiple contact points
Team spirit		Facilitating role; independent of functions	No effect	No cross-functional benefit
Internal communication		All significant communication via contract manager	Possible improvement within functions only	Possible improvement at middle management level only

Implementation was dealt with as follows:

1 Detailed planning to establish the new function. Conducted by the BI team and the proposed contract managers.
2 Immediate transfer of staff from their existing functions (see point 3).
3 The transferred staff, 10 in total, acted as 'product champions'. These individuals had in the past, out of necessity, been acting as contract managers for large orders. As a result they were keen to promote the concept and generated a great deal of enthusiasm in others. In addition they possessed both a practical knowledge of the existing systems and understood the organizational issues.
4 The contract managers, within their new department, developed the control systems.
5 Resistance to the change was minimal, as the new systems did not replace any existing control mechanisms. Remember that this function had not previously existed.

Over a period of time the contract management function established itself and in so doing produced a dramatic improvement in the handling of contracts. BI involvement continued until the change had been consolidated. They acted as an external driving force providing the change agents with authority and encouragement.

The change situation in Mini Case 6.4 was previously referred to in Mini Case 4.3 where examples from Caledonian Airmotive were used to demonstrate diagramming techniques. We shall return to the company in Chapter 16 and therefore, at this point, the review of their implementation strategy will remain brief.

MINI CASE 6.4:   CALEDONIAN AIRMOTIVE LTD

An autonomous accessory workshop is the desired outcome of the following implementation strategy:

1 Parallel running of the proposed autonomous system along with the existing integrated set-up designed to minimize production disruptions.
2 Building modifications to create purpose-built space for the new facility.
3 Installation of an additional testing facility to ease capacity problems.
4 Selection of additional supervisors for the new facility, with recruitment taking place from the existing systems personnel to minimize employee resistance.
5 Erection of a new storage area to service the facility.
6 Selection and training of store personnel.
7 Additional training of the mechanics about to enter the new autonomous working group.
8 Final organizational change.

The sequential nature of the implementation strategy reflected the physical aspects of the change. Training and development, points 4, 6 and 7 above, ran alongside the physical construction activities. Discussions dealing with the finer detail of the organizational change were also scheduled to take account of the construction completion date. As would be expected, the greater emphasis on physical systems within the Airmotive case produced a typical project planning solution, but people issues have been identified and are receiving attention alongside the technical aspects of the change.

Iterations

The example taken from the ABC testing facility (Mini Case 6.2) illustrated a typical iteration. Too great an emphasis was placed on one aspect of the problem, in this case the technical features of the proposed system, which resulted in a key systems relationship, namely the role of the operatives within the new system, being overlooked until implementation loomed. In any project dealing with new and/or complex issues iterations are inevitable. The ISM methodology recognizes the need to formally introduce mechanisms which facilitate a number of feedback loops, and which may be utilized without casting aspersions on the abilities of the project management team.

All to often, especially in the West, failure is taken in its literal sense. However, if one takes a broader, more informed view, then failure can be seen in a far more positive light: if we can learn from our 'mistakes', build on the lessons learnt and improve. The iterations that are built into ISM both recognize the dynamic nature of change and to a certain extent legitimize 'failure'. Managers often fear admitting that they got it wrong the first time round: in change, as in life in general, the ability to admit omissions, possibly errors, and then act positively to resolve the situation should be admired, not ridiculed. Remember that the vast majority of change initiatives that may be deemed by some to have failed have not: they will have brought progress, understanding and knowledge. Failure to achieve performance indicators, based on objectives that may be unrealistic, estimated and politicized, cannot be seen in a totally negative light.

7 | Total Project Management

Project managers, or practising managers with knowledge and experience of project based management approaches, have often expressed the view, when first faced with ISM, that it is little more than another three phase methodology: definition, design and implementation. They generally consider themselves to be proficient in the use of network and budgetary-based planning techniques and fully understand associated decision-making processes. However, with a little prompting they will very quickly admit that the problems they face when managing a complex project, a transition from one state to another, a change in effect, are often traceable to people-related management issues. When they are then forced to examine the planning and control tools they employ in project management, along with their decision-making methodologies, they realize that they do not incorporate the features necessary to ensure the organizational complexities are fully integrated with the physical planning mechanisms.

Even in the 2000s, many organizations, or at least divisions within them, do not fully recognize the need for holistic, people focused, change management. The ISM, introduced in Chapter 5, may be considered by some to be just a little too liberal, democratic and even possibly dangerous. Many managers may readily identify with the rationale behind its design, but consider the emphasis placed on a holistic systems review and participative style as simple common sense – a common sense that they acknowledge but do not necessarily observe or fully understand.

Staff, in particular Dr Geoff Southern, at the University of Glasgow Business School, detected an interesting development in the 'Operations Management' module. A practical assignment, designed to examine and improve the relationship between operating practices and business strategy, employed investigative techniques, namely ISM, from the 'Managing Change' module. The prevalence of ISM within the assignment was such that a decision was made to investigate. Focus groups were organized. The participants expressed the view that existing network-based planning tools, computerized or not, did not fully address the 'softer' problems, raised by the assignment. However, many participants operating within more traditional organizational cultures, in which 'Taylorism' and 'Fordism' were alive and well, felt uncomfortable with what was obviously a useful tool.

In response to this change trigger, work commenced on developing an integrated model, which was later termed the total project management model or TPM for short. The basic aim was to present to the project manager a package which integrates the participative features of ISM and the mechanistic planning tools associated with a more scientific management approach. A model such as TPM cannot teach a manager to manage in a more participative and less interventionist manner, but it can highlight the points within a typical project life cycle when a more liberal, trusting and open management approach should be employed (Firth and Krut, 1991). In many ways TPM promotes a more inclusive and trusting environment for those most likely to be impacted upon by the change event (as stressed by Lines et al., (2005). It forces project managers and problem owners to progressively 'open-up': this is especially useful when the organizational culture is more rigid, formal and traditional. Such an approach may minimize the impact of the initial intervention and enhance the likelihood of a sustainable outcome (Karp, 2005).

As far as the TPM is concerned a project manager is simply the individual charged with handling a specific project. They need not be, in the course of normal events, permanently designated as a project manager. They may or may not be skilled in the application of project planning techniques. However, the assumption has been made that they will be aware of the existence and seek out, when appropriate, project team members skilled in their application. Such assumptions concerning the capabilities and knowledge bases of professional and appointed project managers are in the authors' view valid given the context in which TPMs were both conceived and promoted.

The Value of Total Project Management

The introduction to this chapter noted that project management has traditionally been treated as a systematic process with the emphasis firmly placed on the physical activities of the planning process. The planning process has been in the past and often continues to be, according to practitioner feedback, solely conducted by those deemed to be directly responsible for the 'management' of the project. This project team will often consist of planners and possibly technical experts with specific expertise associated with the project at hand. They will not normally experience the actual implementation of their plans from a managerial viewpoint. The most cursory glance of the literature relating to information systems and operations management clearly demonstrates that even now we are still not fully engaging with user populations and as a result sub-optimal project outcomes are all too common (Boddy and Paton, 2004). Many of the individuals and groups who will be both affected by and involved in the implementation of the planning outcomes are all too often excluded. Yet surely it is this 'excluded' group who will ultimately determine the degree of success associated with the venture?

An example, which rather dramatically illustrates the need for consultation, involved the construction of an office block in the mid-1970s. The clients for whom the office block was to form a new headquarters, through their architects and consulting engineers, specified and subsequently had installed an air-conditioning system. Such systems were not common in Scotland at this time (although the year-round tropical climate does make them a necessity!) and people's knowledge of them was limited. On occupying the premises, the clients' staff, the ultimate users of the system, discovered that the windows did not open. They created such a fuss that at considerable expense a large number of sealed windows were removed and replaced with ones that opened. No one, from the clients to the contractors, had ever thought of asking the users what they desired in terms of workplace design. If they had, they may have discovered the need for some form of direct control over the working environment.

A holistic investigation of the project boundaries along the lines advocated by ISM and TPM would have indicated the need to consult the end users. By involving the users in the planning process and engaging in a programme of explanation as to the rationale behind the use of air-conditioning, the project managers may have reached some form of agreement and/or compromise prior to installation. Resistance to change is minimized when employees feel that they have exercised a degree of control over potential outcomes.

READER ACTIVITY

Pause and consider situations in which you have actively participated in resisting a proposed change. Were you fully aware of the rationale behind the change? Did you feel involved in the decision-making process? Were you just another 'after thought'?

Complex Projects

At what point does a project cross the 'boundary' from mechanistic to complex? There is unfortunately no simple answer to this question.

Table 7.1 Comparison between mechanistic and complex projects

Complex projects	Mechanistic projects
Unclear objectives	Clear objectives
Large number of activities	Limited number of activities
Activity sequences and boundaries are unclear	Clear activity sequences and boundaries
Activities tend not to be technically oriented and/or the technical aspects are not well defined (e.g. new communications and technologies)	Activities are technically oriented and the technical aspects are well defined and understood
Activities have indeterminate durations and resource requirements	Activities have fairly determinate duration and resource requirements are at least approximately known
Activity successes are largely dependent upon mobilizing and motivating people	Activity successes are linked to known technologies and systems, with limited human interfaces

Earlier chapters dealt with the classification of the nature of change and the subsequent definition of a change environment. A project manager should employ the techniques and follow the procedural steps outlined in these chapters. This will assist in placing the project reasonably accurately on the change spectrum. As we have seen earlier, a tendency towards the 'softer' end of the spectrum indicates a greater probability that it will fall into the complex category. In such cases a purely 'hard' approach will not provide an optimal solution; that is not to say that the project will fail, rather that the conclusion will be arrived at only after encountering both controversy and resistance. Any disruption to a project causes concern as delays generally result in penalties.

Complex projects may be differentiated from their more standard mechanistic ones by the dependency they place on gaining the co-operation and acceptance of those directly affected. The successful implementation of complex projects will ultimately depend on the effective management of organizational issues throughout the total planning process. Characteristics associated with complex and mechanistic projects are compared in Table 7.1.

The success of the project management process depends on the appropriate selection of a planning methodology. By fully defining the project in systems terms, the manager gains an insight into the complexities associated with the planning process. In situations where the project activities work towards the achievement of a specific and well defined objective and the technologies, along with the environment, are equally well defined, then traditional planning tools should suffice. If any doubt exists as to the nature of the problems facing the project team and/or the environmental impact is difficult to define, then it is always safer to adopt an intervention based strategy such as TPM.

Total Project Management

TPM recognizes that a technically oriented approach to the management of complex projects must be augmented by the adoption of 'softer' people-centred approaches. As already stated, projects consist of both technological (systems based) and organizational (people based) elements. A systems-based planning technique is needed to handle technological or physical change; after all, it is in fact the systems that are being manipulated. However, adopting when dealing with the human aspects of the project a purely systematic approach may lead to subsequent implementation diffi-culties. TPM addresses both 'hard' and 'soft' issues, by focusing on the technical and more physical aspects of a project from a systems point of view, and by adopting techniques associated with organization develop-ment (French and Bell, 1998) to address 'softer' aspects. Both aspects are treated in an integrated manner, utilizing cross-functional teams, drawn from key areas of the project environment, who will bring to the problem a range of appropriate managerial skills and knowledge bases to effectively manage the 'total' project (McCalman, 1988).

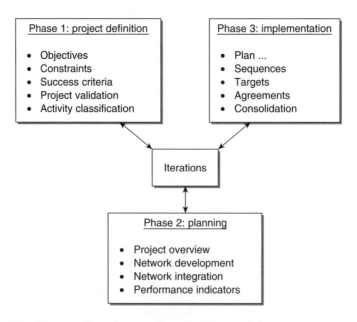

Figure 7.1   The total project management model

Table 7.2   **TPM phase descriptions**

Factors addressed	Techniques employed
Phase 1: project definition	For example:
Definition of the current position ...	Brainstorming techniques
• Specification of environment	Team building
• Evaluation of the project	System diagramming
• Definition of the project owners	Factor ranking
	Decision trees
Definition of the preferred position ...	Investment appraisal
• Project objectives	Stakeholder analysis
• Resource constraints	Competence analysis
• Resource requirements	
• Success criteria	
• Activity classification	
Phase 2: planning	For example:
• Integrated project plan	Gantt charts
• Performance indicators	Cash flow analysis
• Potential iterations	Critical path methods
	Resource scheduling
	Investment appraisal
Phase 3: implementation	For example:
• Presentation of the plan	Charting methods ...
• Application and monitoring of	process charts
review systems	cumulative spend charts
• Potential iterations	Variance analysis ...
• Autopsy of the project	exception reporting
	Socio-technical change models

The TPM is an iterative and systems-based planning technique, which integrates 'softer' management philosophies and techniques into a traditional project management process. The model is outlined in Figure 7.1. Again the familiar three-phase format, similar to that adopted within the ISM, is employed, with terminology and activity modifications to reflect the specific emphasis on project management as opposed to the management of change.

The first phase, accepting the addition of a project validation step, is almost identical to ISM. The evaluation phase of ISM has been replaced with planning which deals design and solution development via a prescribed networking approach. In a project the activities will be defined in the first phase. Implementation is dealt with in a similar manner in both models. Table 7.2 outlines the principal factors addressed within each phase. The following sections will address each phase from both a project management and ISM perspective.

Phase 1: project definition

The first step in managing a complex project is to define its scope in terms of the primary mission, associated objectives, constraints and performance measures. This involves conducting a detailed examination of the project environment in order to assist in optimizing subsequent management decisions. It is achieved by making a detailed, systems-oriented, analysis of the project environment that engages with any individuals or groups (representatives) who have a vested interest. Within this analysis the activities and resources required to complete the project will be identified and detailed. In stressing the need for such an environmental analysis, TPM is no different from ISM, and similar techniques would be employed in accomplishing the definition.

TPM possibly emphasizes the need to indulge in team-building activities to a greater extent than ISM. This reflects the fact that project managers are often dealing with environments that change in terms of their composition from project to project. As TPM suggests, the best way of ensuring that organizational issues are incorporated into the plan is to create and develop a cross-functional team representing key system areas and relationships. As this team is likely to vary between projects, every effort must be made to ensure a team approach to the planning process is developed (Boddy, 2005). To this end TPM advocates the use of brainstorming techniques and planning sessions, within the definition phase, which emphasizes a participative team involvement in specifying the project in terms of objectives, constraints, resources and environmental factors. Given the diverse nature of the project team, in terms of hierarchical position, disciplines and roles, a non-threatening and open means of generating information for the definition phase is required (Paton et al., 1989).

Project validation, utilizing investment appraisal techniques, is not normally associated with ISM. A project manager often finds it necessary to justify future actions by either proving the need to go ahead or by validating someone else's initial proposals. TPM also identifies the project activities and resources required within this first phase; these will be required to complete the network analysis associated with the next phase.

READER ACTIVITY

Have you ever been in a group situation where you felt uncomfortable voicing your ideas, solutions and thoughts? Why was this the case?

What could the facilitator/leader have done to encourage participation?

Could the process have been modified to encourage the 'team' to come forward with ideas? For example, non-attributable 'talking wall' approaches ensure the anonymity of respondents.

> Could the facilitator have adopted a less confrontational approach? We do not pay enough attention to developing facilitation skills. Interpersonal skills and facilitation techniques are often ignored; a manager, or team leader, is apparently meant to pick them up as they go along. This is, sadly, rarely the case.

Phase 2: planning

Having fully specified the project environment in the initial diagnostic phase, the project team can now confidently progress to planning. By evaluating the plans produced at this stage against the previously defined performance measures, the team will be able to effectively evaluate planning alternatives. In addition, since the total project environment has been considered, they should be aware of and ready to deal with any obstructions that may delay implementation.

Linear, logical and inflexible planning based approaches are often criticized. Burnes (2004) points out that they are of little use when facing a change that necessitates a rapid response and transformation. Others, for example, Higgs and Rowland (2005), express concern that linear approaches lack both flexibility and creativity which are essential when dealing with complexity. Both views are valid, but neither ISM nor TPM claim to be the only answer, nor do they purport to be the ideal solution to complex organizational change situations. In their own way they attempt to harness the power of systems theory, rationality and drive in a manner that recognizes the need to address aspects of organizational change within a planning cycle. For example, TPM utilizes team based solution methodologies within a holistic framework, as can be seen by the four-step planning process:

1 *Project overview*   This is conducted by the project team and consists of the identification of major components, key events, component relationships, and human resource requirements (Boddy, 1987).

2 *Network development*   This is conducted by a component team (i.e. a subgroup of the project team) identified during the previous step. This stage consists of task and resource requirement definition, followed by construction (Lockyer, 1991).

3 *Integration of component networks*   This is conducted by the full project team and consists of potential iterations back to component networks, formulation of the total project network, and referral back to objectives and measures identified in phase 1.

4 *Performance indicators identification*   This again is conducted by the full project team and consists of identification of specific performance indicators and iterations back to phase 1 and step 3 above. The indicators will be used for control and assessment purposes.

The planning phase of TPM follows the traditional project-planning route, utilizing networking techniques to facilitate the actual physical planning of the project. The actions required to address the organizational issues identified within the definition phase, along with any others discovered during this phase, should be incorporated into the network planning process. These may include educational and training programmes and/or the limited involvement of additional key players in the actual planning process. In the similar ISM phase there is unlikely to be such a clear path to follow as one must first determine the potential solution paths and appropriate analysis techniques, prior to even considering sequencing solution options.

Phase 3: implementation

The final phase, that of implementation consists primarily of the activities associated with effectively presenting the plan to interested parties, and to put in place the necessary monitoring and correction systems. It is reached only after an exhaustive examination of the environment has been completed, and the results have been incorporated into the planning stage. As factors concerned with implementation are part of the planning process they will have already been considered. Hence the presentation and monitoring mechanisms already developed to ensure successful implementation are integrated into the plan, and are more likely to be easily administered and understood.

Implementation involves the integration of the network analysis exercises of phase 2, together with a thorough appraisal and action plan relating to organizational issues, such as education, development and negotiation identified in earlier stages. Consolidation in the case of TPM involves the project manager in monitoring the control mechanisms and taking corrective action as and when required. TPM must deal with similar implementation issues as those addressed in ISM.

All too often project planning teams reach the final hurdle of implementation, only to find that a lack of consideration in the earlier environmental definition has led them to neglect a key variable or factor. By fully specifying the problem in systems terms and subsequently analysing the interactions to identify areas of interdependence and resistance, the project team will have the ability to forecast and deal with potential difficulties during phases 1 and 2. Any potential difficulties associated with implementation will hopefully have then been removed.

If external business and organizational developments alter the project environment between phases 1 and 3, then the TPM model, with its built-in iterations, can backtrack and incorporate the developments. Phase 3 ends with a post-mortem of the TPM cycle; any lessons learnt may be identified and incorporated into the project team's subsequent planning processes. The net result of the adoption of the TPM philosophy will be effective project management allied to the development of an integrated design team. The use of socio-technical models to effect the final implementation is included to emphasize the point that TPM, just as ISM, may require to employ, when dealing with a particularly messy change situation, techniques and processes associated with organizational development and design.

Administrative and Organizational Points

TPM is a multi-disciplinary approach to the process of project planning. A cross-functional team, bringing its own managerial skills and environmental knowledge, progresses through an integrative and interactive planning process, led by an accomplished facilitator, to produce a project plan geared to a total solution. This multi-disciplinary and cross-functional approach to project planning, along with the required establishment of a team approach, often necessitates the need for extensive management development of the core project team. The provision of technical planning skills is not enough, and managers must be made aware of, and provided with the skills to cope with, the 'softer', people-related issues (Boddy and Buchanan, 1986).

Project planning is conducted in a dynamic environment; the variability of both external and internal factors necessitates that the TPM concept incorporates iterative feedback loops. Iterations, as mentioned previously, are particularly important during the implementation phase, but they may occur within and/or between any of the aforementioned phases. They may be seen as the reaction to the dynamic nature of associated variables. Iterations may be minimized through the development of a proactive stance by the project team. Changes in the environment associated with the project must be managed and incorporated within the developing plan (Wright and Rhodes, 1985).

Total project management may be regarded as a hybrid planning tool. Its component parts are not revolutionary; it is the packaging of the systems and organizational disciplines into a cohesive whole that creates the positive results. Such a complete planning package, when effectively managed, cannot fail to increase the likelihood of successful project implementation. Networking techniques, computerized or not, can no longer be seen as an independently sufficient means of achieving effective project planning.

Organizational Development and Design: their Role in Systems Interventions

In both the ISM and the TPM much is made of the need to ensure parti-cipation and involvement, with the aim of achieving first a shared perception of the problem and second commitment to finding a solution. A systems based solution methodology cannot achieve this without recourse to management techniques and processes associated with the field of organizational development and design. Problem owners and project managers must endeavour to encourage those affected to accept the situation and thereafter assist in determining and implementing a solution.

Adoption of the 'softer' management approaches within a systems based investigative framework should encourage the management team concerned to integrate, involve and share more fully with those at the sharp end of the change.

Let us now consider five factors that influence the way in which people respond to change:

1 *Involvement*   Involve them in the process by explaining the nature of the change and dis-cussing its implications in an open and frank manner; gain participation by seeking out and fostering their ideas.

2 *Communication*   Communicate – don't lecture – by means of: meetings and discussions presentations; education and training.

3 *Perceptions*   Consider people's worries. Think about: individuals' objections and how one could deal with their fears; the benefits of the change and how they could be sold.

4 *Resource*   Recruit and transfer in advance to allow assimilation of the new environment and facilitate training.

5 *Schedule*   Avoid, if possible, scheduling the change and/or associated activities during work peaks: inconvenience and disruption are never welcomed.

These factors must be integrated with the 'harder', systems-based, approaches. In earlier chapters, organizational culture was noted as an important factor in promoting a climate of change, along with the need to formulate a proactive stance towards change and therefore encourage it to be viewed as an opportunity rather than a threat. Opportunistic and proactive actions are encouraged within cultures that exhibit enterprising features and open structures that foster challenging ideas. The creation of such cultures is far beyond the remit of systems based intervention models. The power and scope of the intervention approach increases dramatically when it is employed in a progressive and co-operative environment. The organizational development chapters that follow in Part 3 detail and discuss the rationale, strategies and approaches associated with accomplishing 'softer', people based change.

To provide a link between the systems intervention model and that of organization development, we recommend that the reader study Figure 7.2. This provides analysis of a step-by-step guide to managing change adopted by one of our case study organizations, MTC Ltd. Figure 7.2 examines the people element of change as part of a total systems approach. The harder issues addressed are grouped under resource and

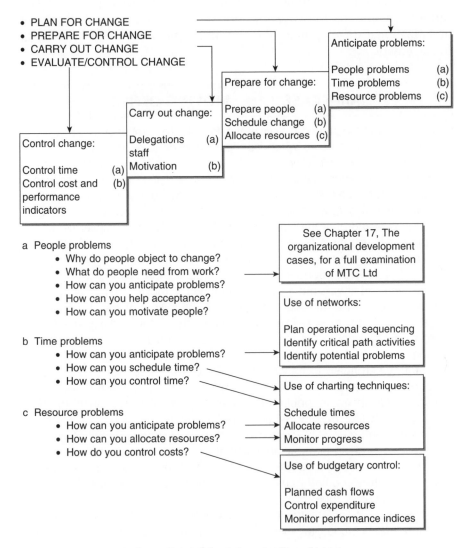

Figure 7.2   A step-by-step guide to managing change

time problems. These groupings reflect the more technical features of TPM and are used to manage the control, planning and implementation of the change project in conjunction with the people problems.

The following chapter may also be seen as a bridge to the organizational development chapters of Part 3. Competing narratives is the term we have coined for describing situations, which in truth are really the norm, when post-project or after the change, those responsible and those affected appear to have conflicting recollection of the rationale, process and outcomes. How can there be so many views of the same event? How can we learn from the past when we cannot agree on what actually happened? Chapter 8 examines the issues around these questions and further strengthens the case for seriously considering such things as organizational development, the learning organization and knowledge management.

MINI CASE 7.1:   MOVING OFFICE

A finance company, based in a city centre, identified a number of commercially related factors and trends which led them to decide to relocate to an out of town site. For example, clients were moving HQs out of town; technological advances were reducing transaction costs and simplifying the communications process; city centre costs were escalating; and lastly, but not least, it was anticipated that a purpose built 'greenfield' site would improve the quality of working life and offer the opportunity to further enhance IT capabilities and general productivity. A team, consisting of divisional heads, supported by IT specialists, set about identifying a site and planning the move.

Staff were kept informed but the communication process was rather one-sided and always put a positive 'spin' on the move. The management team conducted a thorough and professional review of the situation; it was a 'text book' exercise in what could be termed standard best practice. However, the move cost more than expected and took far longer than expected.

Staff, when finally faced with the reality of the move, objected on two counts – neither of which had been explicitly voiced during the planning process. Out of town would mean that they would be cut off from the 'buzz' of city life. The city centre offered a way of life, good pubs, restaurants and entertainment, combined with quality shopping – all of which were seen as being far more appealing than a greenfield site full of cows! Furthermore, how did you get out of town? The commuting links were poor; therefore you had to use a car – not nearly as appealing as jumping on a train, bus or tube!

The move went ahead. It had to. Contracts had been signed and commitments made. However, given that staff concerns were expressed close to the time of the move there were going to have to be some very tough negotiations. Staff had to be compensated for the move; car lease schemes and flexitime was introduced.

The project team should have taken a more holistic view; they were more concerned with the logistical task than the overall change. Delays and additional costs may have been avoided, or at least reduced, had a more holistic view and approach been adopted.

Another, less dramatic example of an office move offers further evidence of the need to think and act holistically. This move concerned a small training establishment. They were only moving a short distance, within the same office block, utilizing the same services and essentially it was a case of business as usual. The project manager did everything right. A detailed plan ensured minimal disruption to service. The staff knew of the move. They knew where they were going and when. They also knew why and agreed fully with the rationale underpinning the move.

So how could things go wrong? The project manager had overlooked a number of key questions. Who was going to get the window seat? Who was going to face the door? How would seating plans be decided? Once again, up to the point of the actual physical move everyone had kept quiet and had fully co-operated with the design and general layout of the new facilities.

After much debate and behind the scenes activity the matter was resolved. Seat allocation was decided by drawing names out of a hat, with prior agreement that there would be no further mention of the subject. Initially there were many petty grievances, but by focusing attention on the fact that staff had selected what they considered to be a fair selection process, the project manager rode out the storm!

8 | Competing Narratives

In a result driven competitive world organization, managers and employees strive to both grow and survive. Not only are things more competitive they are also in many ways more open and complex. Technology has unleashed a communications explosion that maximizes both exposure and impact. Globalization has dramatically increased the complexity of both trade and commerce resulting in ever increasing managerial challenges. In addition, globalization has also exposed organizations to the world stage ever listening, judging and increasingly aggressive. Is it any surprise that we all endeavour to manage the outcomes of our labour in such a way as to show them in a favourable light?

The managerial, indeed society's, new cancer is *spin*. Governments, organizations, leaders, managers and employees all, at some point, massage the truth. We all live in an increasingly competitive world. A world in which success, position, power and celebrity appear to be highly regarded. Being seen to succeed brings both reward and security. What has this to do with change? The successful management of change is based on trust. We trust not only in others but also the message they deliver. We trust the information upon which we base our decisions. But what if our information is based on spin and those rationale decision makers are not what they seem?

As if spin wasn't enough to contend with in relation to how we make sense of things we also have to deal with the fact that even if spin didn't exist our decision-making knowledge bases would still be corrupted. Knowledge of past events is based on the records and memories of those who have lived through them. But are they true reflections upon which to build our learning and shape our futures? Those who experience a change event will not necessarily share a common view about what happened. In addition, formal recording of recollections tends to take place in an environment contaminated by hindsight and post hoc rationalization.

This chapter and the case studies within it attempt to make sense of what we have termed the competing narrative.

Managing Outcomes

When managerial rhetoric promotes success and certainty, while in reality doubt exists, it is only a matter of time until the discovery of the vacuous nature of the rhetoric. Alternatively one may choose to try to manage the reality to fit the spin – the outcome will eventually be the same. When things start to deviate from the plan, those in charge often seek excuses or try to redefine the original objectives; they may attempt to 'paper over the cracks' or even flee before the extent of the failure is fully recognized. Less grand projects, those that may be bounded by a company, industry or market, also suffer from the need of those in charge to demonstrate outcomes related to the original expectations. Leaders, at any level, have a vested interest in visibly demonstrating success. They are judged by it. So to ensure that their 'public' deems them to have succeeded, they must show a positive result, and there are many ways of managing a successful outcome!

Managing successful outcomes, manipulating the perceptions relating to the change environment, or indeed, massaging the truth, are not new phenomena – as anyone who has discussed similar issues with participants on an executive development programme will testify! In some cases this may not matter, with dissenting or sceptical voices being part of the normal organizational teasing and positioning. The issue is more serious if the dissenting stories are symptomatic of deeper divisions or fragmentation within the business. Well-known examples in the area of information systems include Markus' study of the introduction of a corporate financial information system (Markus, 1983), Knights and Murray's long-term study of the introduction of new information systems at an insurance company (1994), and the study by Lloyd and Newell (1999) of a pharmaceutical company's efforts to introduce laptop computers to support the work of the sales force. More topical, or popular, instances of situations where dissenting voices were silent, or silenced, may include the Millennium Dome, Enron and Arthur Andersen, the British passport technology fiasco of a few years ago, the BA dirty tricks campaign waged against Virgin Airlines, or the recent revelations concerning what appeared to be recurrent safety failures in the American space shuttle programme. For every major event that reaches the public domain how many other project champions breathe a sigh of relief while exclaiming 'but for the grace of God …'.

At some point our experiences will be documented, outcomes logged and history written. Those that follow us will look to our accomplishments, read the files, and hopefully learn. But if the organization is recording for posterity what may be regarded as being at best a benign post hoc rationalization based on hype, conjecture and hindsight, then the same mistakes will be made again and again. It is often said that history is written by, shaped by, the winners. Management winners manage the outcomes and therefore shape organizational learning.

READER ACTIVITY

List below three occasions when you have massaged the outcomes of a decision or event to better satisfy your personal position and why did you do this?

1

2

3

Consider current world affairs. Identify three situations in which, in your view, world leaders or multinationals have massaged the truth and why do you think they have done this?

1

2

3

Competing Narratives: What are They?

An idea, which may help managers put such divergences of perception and action into context, is that of competing narratives (Boddy and Paton, 2004; Dawson and Buchanan, 2005). In themselves these are not a sign of weakness or management failure, but an inherent feature of complex organizations. In the main they only become significant when they are ignored, overruled or over time are lost to the natural learning process. By ignoring reality, failing to confront and deal with such narratives, managers and organizations in general risk repeating past mistakes and reinventing the wheel.

Those managing change have a choice. They can manage in a way that marginalizes or ignores competing narratives, or, they can recognize and see them as a legitimate source of alternative views. The choice is not dissimilar to that identified by Taylor (1999). Taylor highlights the point that the perception of senior managers may differ greatly from those below in terms of how they view the nature of significant change events. They will make *sense* of change differently and this will influence the stories they tell of it and therefore shape the way in which future change is dealt with and received. This point is echoed to a certain extent by Dawson and

Buchanan (2005) in their study of technological change and competing narratives:

> Corporate narratives concerning technological change are often constructed around a linear event sequence that presents the organization in a positive light to internal and external observers. These narratives often sanitize the change process, and present data from which commentators can formulate neat linear prescriptions on how to implement new technology.

This linear choice will not only affect details of the current project. A much more important concern relates to the wider context within which future initiatives will take place. A valued outcome of change is the ability of the organization to manage future change (Shenhar et al., 1997). Well managed, projects are a source of creativity and of positive attitudes towards change. Poorly managed, they generate apathy, distrust and scepticism towards the next proposal. Pettigrew et al. (1992) also researched this idea within the UK National Health Service. Their research into units that welcomed change (and those which did not) identified a number of factors that affected receptivity to change. These included:

- simplicity and clarity of goals and priorities;
- quality and coherence of policy (including the analytical process);
- supportive organizational culture; and
- fit between the change agenda and local circumstances.

Successfully addressing the factors above appeared to energize those affected by the change and hence influenced the ease of adoption. The receptivity model appeared to explain the differences in the rate at which different units in the service were able to introduce change. Managers, which had dealt effectively with these issues, had created a culture that was relatively receptive to change.

This chapter examines the relationship between organizational change and the extent to which competing narratives may impact on receptivity to change. Using a descriptive case study it shows how managers in three organizational groupings handled an initiative in a way that generated contradictory accounts of the change via competing narratives. We propose that the manner in which one manages and learns from competing change narratives will impact upon the above factors. It will influence 'receptivity' to change.

READER ACTIVITY

Can you recall a situation in which you sought advice prior to making a decision, and subsequently when acting upon your decision things did not go as planned?

   Has this ever happened, to your knowledge, due to a tainted information source?

Multiple Subjective Narratives

Accounts of a change event will vary between the people affected (multiple.) This is inevitable. Opinion and recollections will reflect both how they viewed the context and evaluated the impact upon their personal goals (subjective), in relation to both the change process and the ultimate outcomes. Accounts of corporate strategy and of the projects through which managers implement it are usually presented from a perspective that draws on the rational traditions of Western scientific enquiry. They present management actions as objective and rational, based on scientific methods of observation, measurement and analysis. The focus is on the scientific principles of management, with an implication that these are universally true and acceptable by all right thinking members of the organization.

There is another perspective that emphasizes the subjectivity of organizational events. Views of right or wrong, and success or failure, are not universal truths but are socially constructed, and so can be defined in different ways by different groups. Those who take this view believe that people live in fragmented worlds, from which they form diverse views of what may seem to be the same events. Knowledge is fundamentally fragmented and is produced in so many bits that there can be no reasonable expectation of a single, universal view. They seek to show that organizations experience fragmented and often contradictory streams of action.

This approach stresses fragmentation as a feature of organizational life. People are members of many subcultures within an organization, with different views and interpretations. These subcultures form in response to events, and to influences such as hierarchical or functional position (Ogbonna and Harris, 1998). Recognizing subcultures means that close examination of an organizational change may reveal that there are many sides to the story. It can rarely be captured in a single, agreed narrative, one that all the players accept (Alvesson and Deetz, 2000; Buchanan et al., 2005). There are usually contradictory versions of events with diverse views about the need for a change, the form it has taken, and the value of the outcomes.

READER ACTIVITY

Consider a past change within your organization, for instance, the introduction of a new policy or management system. Recall the initial consultation process and subsequent discussions. Did everyone have the same expectations of the change or did different stakeholders have different expectations and concerns? If so, could their opinions have been influenced by their past positive or negative experiences?

The narratives, which people use to reflect on change, will shape their view of future initiatives. Positive narratives, stressing the benefits will help to generate a culture that is responsive to change, accepts it, and looks forward to future innovation. Negative narratives may lead to apathetic or indifferent attitudes towards the future. Those responsible for implementing change shape the narrative, perhaps unintentionally, by the way they manage. The next section discusses how the process and context of change interact to influence and create a supportive culture.

An Interactive View of Change

Following writers such as Pettigrew (1987) and Dawson (2003), most academic accounts of organizational change now stress the influence of the context and process of change (Boddy, 2002).

The *context* refers to features that are external to the particular change project. Managers leading a change project work within the existing organizational context, but at the same time try to change aspects of that context to encourage behaviour that supports objectives. They create rules and incentives to encourage new behaviour. Other players interpret those rules in their interests, and these together now form their context. This interaction perspective, building on the work of Orlikowski (1992), expresses the idea that people and context affect each other – people shape their context, which then shapes their behaviour. How people react to the change is shaped by how they see the new context affecting their present and future.

How people see their context and the project is a primary source of their narratives. Some aspects of the context (here we will focus on the less tangible elements of people, culture, structure and power) will encourage positive and supportive narratives, others the opposite.

The context a person experiences is affected by time, hierarchy and function. Management seeks to implement change against a background of previous events. Past decisions shaped the organization context.

They affect its receptivity to change and its ability to change. The context occurs at each hierarchical level of the organization – such as operating, divisional and corporate. People at any of these levels make changes in their context – which may help or hinder the manager of a particular project. For example, a project at one level will often depend on decisions at other levels about the resources available.

The contextual elements also occur within functional (or similar) structural units. Members of each unit develop distinct cultures and ways of seeing their world – and so are likely to interpret a proposal from their unique perspective, rather than from a unified organizational one. A change may threaten political interests, so commentaries reflect what people believe the change has done, or will do, to the distribution of organizational power. There is no reason to expect that people see themselves within a unified, coherent context that encourages them to work towards the success of the project. They are just as likely to see the experience as a fragmented or contradictory experience. It is part of the manager's job to create a culture that encourages long-term receptiveness to change (Boddy, 2002). This idea is echoed by Taylor (1999). Taylor suggests a key role of senior management is to provide 'sensemaking' processes to situations in which there may be differing understandings of both rationale and desired outcomes.

The *process* refers to the ways in which managers make the substantive changes to the context. Achieving the objectives depend on making changes to several of the elements in the context – and the processes by which managers make these changes affect their quality and acceptability. These most obviously relate to the substantive nature of the present initiative – such as the quality and acceptability of a new information system or marketing strategy. It is also possible that they have indirect, but perhaps highly significant effects through the way they affect the receptivity or otherwise of people in the organization to future changes. In that sense, processes affect the context of future changes. Some processes will encourage a culture or structure that is receptive to both present and future change. Others will have the opposite effect, fostering indifference, apathy or defensive behaviour. A person's narrative will reflect how managers handled the process of change. The discussion of context and process, combined with previously mentioned ideas and examples, suggest propositions such as:

- A valued outcome of change is the ability of the organization to manage future change.

- Accounts of the change will vary between people, reflecting how they see their context and personal goals.

- Those implementing change reconstruct the context to encourage behaviour, which supports their objectives (i.e. they seek a positive narrative).

- The processes by which they do so will affect how others interpret a change and its context (and hence their narrative).

- These narratives shape socially organizational structures and cultures, and so affect the receptivity of people to future change.

The rest of the chapter illustrates the emergence and nature of competing narratives, based on participants' accounts of change scenarios. In particular, the chapter concentrates on the impact of the 'narrative' on the receptivity to change, as this underpins all five propositions.

Reporting the Case of the Competing Narrative

To illustrate the ideas presented earlier, we now provide a brief account of reactions towards change within three organizations: a major utility company, an educational establishment and an information services provider. All are major and internationally engaged enterprises. A project-auditing tool was used to illicit reposes. The audit, by employing a range of open-ended questions, examined from numerous change related perspectives, the case history of a recent, or ongoing, change event. Respondents completed the audit on an individual basis and then as a group examined, in a comparative manner, the outcomes.

Managers were asked to prepare an extensive, based on a standard audit format, written commentary on a single project within their organizations, with which they had all been involved and could comment upon from a knowledgeable perspective. Having written an individual account of the change they then in their groups prepared a further written commentary, including a critique, of those issues that they saw as having been significant across the group.

The audit deals first with the project specification. Respondents were asked to briefly describe the project and to outline their role in relation to the project and its outcomes. They then prepared a semi-structured account of the project under pre-defined headings:

- cultural change impacts: nature and handling effectiveness;

- structural change impacts: nature and handling effectiveness;

- power relationships: nature, impact and handling effectiveness;

- resource implications: extent, availability and impact;

- participant commitment: process and effectiveness;

- management process: participative, contemplative and imaginative, and/or, directive and task driven;

- communications: nature and effectiveness in relation to above;

- momentum: importance and sustainability;

- project champion: nature, role and effectiveness;

- implementation plan: detail, monitoring, milestones and capability;

- additional contributing factors: issues and so on not raised above.

The audit was administered towards the close of a series of change man-agement programmes. Respondents were fully aware of the terminology employed within the audit. Having individually responded the groups then conferred, critically discussing and appraising the projects, their views were captured on an open grid format, which took as the y-axis the headings above and for the x-axis:

- extent of narrative presence and impact;

- outcome of impact: positive or negative;

- overall effect on the project/initiative.

What the managers thought

There was extensive and intense debate amongst the groups and indi-viduals seemed both shocked and enlightened by certain revelations. What was being witnessed not only evidenced the existence of compet-ing narratives, but also the extent to which both the individuals and their organizations appeared to have failed to grasp and learn from past experience. Discussions were lively and often included phrases such as 'but have we not done that before?'; 'you don't understand'; 'is that not what we used to do?'; 'we tried that before'; and 'are you sure about that?'

Those who had been closest to the change in terms of ownership and ultimately accountability consistently held positive narratives across all the groups. Those purporting to hold positive views and feelings were at worst totally oblivious to the problems and concerns identified by their colleagues, and at best courteous in their dismissiveness. Competing narratives tended to be dismissed on the grounds that those managers who held such views had 'simply missed the plot'. Stated out-comes were merely desired and not written in tablets of stone. The 'big picture' held the key not specific predetermined objectives. On one occasion line managers were astounded to find out that one of their pro-posed choices as a company wide example of impending change had been according to a representative from the corporate centre 'shelved and superseded'.

Failure to see and understand the 'big picture' was put down to poor communication. As the major projects developed the original intent changed over time, at least according to those holding a more positive view, but the organizations failed to convey to those at the 'sharp' end the rationale for such change. At the outset, managers felt that they knew the 'big picture' but as the reality emerged they quickly 'lost touch' with the current state of play. The more pessimistic amongst the detractors felt that the reality was far different. Yes, communication was poor, but so too was senior management's commitment to major change initiatives. Over time commitment wanes and new initiatives develop and subsume previous projects. An often-quoted phrase from all contributors was 'flavour of the month'. Indeed many managers claimed to have at least once or twice in the past played a 'waiting game'. Why expend effort on a new corporate initiative when it is likely to be superseded in due course?

All the organizations represented in this research study appeared to suffer from the effects of competing narratives. All appear to suffer also, to varying degrees, from a lack of openness and possibly trust. Deviations from the pre-agreed plan or path appear to be managed on a need to know basis. This leads to confusion and a lack of trust and commitment elsewhere. Managers delay acting until they are sure they have to. This managerial inertia was illustrated by expressions such as 'keeping our powder dry'; 'buck passing'; 'back pedalling'; and 'keeping our heads down'. On a more positive note, the respondents, when pressed, acknowledged that the existence of competing narratives tended to be limited to major change events, events that impacted upon the whole organization, its structures, culture and direction. In addition, although such distractions were not welcome, they were not considered overly detrimental in the short term. However, the managers involved in the study did agree that in the longer term such dissension impacted upon general morale and could often lead to a lack of reflection and learning.

No apparent differences existed between the organizations represented in the study, the exception being the educational establishment. Here competing narratives existed but they were not seen to be of such importance – the 'nuisance' variety mentioned earlier in the chapter, they were seen as inevitable. Managers from this organization considered communications to be effective and deviations from plan understood by all concerned parties. In addition, they felt that such deviations had to be expected in complex change and could not identify any project or general initiative where organizational trust related issues had emerged. They considered their organization to be open and consultative.

The results of the study are summarized below:

1   A valued outcome of change is the ability of the organization to manage future change: competing narratives could contribute to a lack of meaningful organizational learning.

2   Accounts of the change will vary between people, reflecting how they see their context and personal goals: the closer to the change the manager is, the more likely they are to purport positive project narratives.

3   Those implementing change may reconstruct the context to encourage behaviour, which supports their objectives (i.e. they seek a positive narrative): the need for behavioural change is not always fully conveyed to all those involved.

4   The processes by which they do so will affect how others interpret a change and its context (and hence their narrative): gaps in knowledge and understanding will be filled as best as possible by those 'at the sharp end'.

5   Narratives can socially shape organizational structures and cultures, and so potentially affect the receptivity of people to future change. Why move when the scenery is changing all around you? Why trust the 'spin' and, why get involved when minds are made up?

READER ACTIVITY

Try to recall specific change events. How often did those involved endeavour to learn from the event and communicate the lessons to others?
    If this has happened:

1   Did you all share the same common experiences or did views differ?
2   Was the story line, the lesson, massaged to put on a positive spin?
3   Did anyone act upon your advice – were things done differently the next time?

Implications for Managing Change

Complex projects are challenging and impact upon the whole organization. They affect the way people work and think. Managers facing such challenges would be advised not to underestimate the impact that past change events have had in terms of generating competing narratives. As the change at hand develops such narratives have to be positively addressed and managed. More generally, and possibly of greater concern, it would appear that organizations are possibly failing to fully address the actuality and reality of change. They could be institutionalizing the 'post hoc rationalization' rather than the truth. They may not be learning nor managing knowledge effectively.

This study suggests that managers and change agents must ensure communications are timely and address not only the action required but also explain the rationale. What people don't know they will make up! Momentum in any major project will wane. Senior managers and those charged with implementing the change will be faced with many competing challenges and objectives, and their attention will be distracted. Momentum and commitment must be maintained if those affected by the change are to believe in its value and trust in the organization's vision and commitment. Let people know what you are thinking and why. Visible commitment, reassurance and direction must be maintained. Maintaining contact with the 'rumour mill' is essential.

Competing narratives cannot be eradicated. Everyone will view the change from their, not your, perspective. However, managers and organizations can influence and manage perspectives. Time spent understanding the nature of the change, how it impacts upon others and how they are likely to respond, is never wasted. Anticipate perspectives and manage the change environment accordingly. Failure to do so will not only foster narrative creation but also undermine fellow managers and subordinates. Taylor (1999) stresses the need for organizational leaders, and stakeholders in general, to understand how those concerned arrive at their *sense* of an event. Through better understanding of how we arrive at a *sense* leaders may be assisted in their drive to provide, meaning, understanding and *sensemaking*.

The representatives from the organizations in this study all acknowledged the need to debrief the project management team, both during and after the project. The respondents saw this as a valuable learning tool. However, all respondents expressed concerns as to how the debrief was managed and communicated to others. Narratives which competed with the views of those in charge of the project, or their superiors, tended not to feature as heavily as one might have expected in the 'final report'. Learning tended to be at best on an individual/project team basis rather than on a shared and formalized basis.

On a more positive note, the respondents felt that both they and their organizations knew what had to be done when facing complex change situations. However, they also felt that it was fine in theory but difficult to implement in practice. Cultural, structural and leadership factors were seen to be important but they were also more difficult to address. Attention therefore focused on the 'mechanics' of the change, the plan, the milestones and the deliverables. The 'softer' factors were acknowledged at the start of a change event. For example, visible senior management involvement, company wide communications and a general rise in awareness, were all evidenced; however, as the project developed this visibility and contact tended to dissipate.

This chapter describes an explorative study concerned, in the main, with the impact of competing narratives on an organization's receptivity to change. A vertical and horizontal cross-section of a number of organizations suggests that change related historical narratives both exist and compete for 'air-time'. Divergent narratives may emerge due to ineffective communication, poor organizational learning, shifting agendas or even potentially the proliferation of institutionalized post hoc rationalization. Receptivity to change, our willingness to engage with and shape the future, is linked to our ability to identify and address the impact of competing narratives.

Whether or not we deliberately, or otherwise, create and promulgate factitious realities, is not the issue here (although it may be worthy of future research). What is of importance is that realities based on a dichotomy of narratives impact upon organizational competence in a manner that may be detrimental to effective change (Boddy and Paton, 2004). This chapter suggests that competing narratives are linked to receptivity to change and that they can to a certain extent be managed. However, further research would be required to ascertain their true nature; in particular, to what extent are they a product of post hoc rationalization, a desire to mask the truth in an effort to illustrate personal and organizational success?

Part 3 dealing as it does with organizational development and learning, along with the IBM case, which focuses on knowledge management and change, explores many issues and approaches that may assist in combating the competing narrative. As the effective utilization of both learning and knowledge are key to successfully managing change and are in themselves often based on the *narrative* and its interpretation, organizations and their managers must strive to ensure that actions, decisions and cultures are based upon the real truth and not ill-shapen post hoc rationalization.

PART 3

THE ORGANIZATIONAL DEVELOPMENT MODEL

9 | People Management

The bulk of the scientific evidence suggests that the more the individual is enabled to exercise control over his task, and to relate his efforts to those of his fellows, the more likely he is to accept a positive commitment. This positive commitment shows in a number of ways, not the least of which is the release of that personal initiative and creativity which constitute the basis of a democratic climate.

(Einar Thorsurd, 'Job Design in the Wider Context', in L.E. Davis and J.C. Taylor, *Design of Jobs,* Penguin, 1972)

You firmly believe that sound management means executives on one side and workers on the other, on one side men who think and on the other men who can only work. For you, management is the art of smoothly transferring the executives' ideas into the workers' hands.

(Konosuke Matsushita, founder of Matsushita Electric, from 'The secret is shared', *Manufacturing Engineering*, March 1988)

No management works quite like self-management. And working at Semco means self-managing as much as possible. It isn't nearly as frightening as it sounds. In the end, it's self interest at work. It requires conceding that managers don't – and can't – know the best way to do everything. … by letting people off the hook of grand policies, procedures and rules, we release them to be accountable only to themselves.

(Ricardo Semler, *The Seven-Day Weekend,* Century Books, Random House Group, 2003)

An examination of any of the current, vogue examples of 'successful' companies reveals that two underlying themes are ever-present. First, there is an emphasis on meeting, to the highest standards, customer satisfaction. The quality criterion is what guarantees success in any business you care to mention. Second, the successful organization, no matter which country it comes from, how long it has been in existence, or what products or services it produces, takes care of its people. That is to say, success comes from customer satisfaction which is generated from motivated people. The ability of an organization to manufacture products or provide services, rests on its ability to gain commitment from the people within that organization. This seemingly simple process is complicated, however, by the approaches adopted by managers within organizations in terms of their behaviour and attitudes towards the individual.

There is the potential for conflict in all organizations. In fact, conflict occurs on a daily basis. The argument with your secretary over a report that is needed for the board meeting; the screaming match between marketing and the factory floor; the formal warning given for consistent lateness are all examples of conflict between individuals who theoretically share the same objectives. Buchanan and Huczynski (2006) view this as a potential organizational dilemma:

> Many of the 'human' problems of organizations can be identified as conflicts between individual human needs, and the constraints imposed on individuals in the interests of the collective purpose of the organization.

Similarly, March and Simon (1958) note that:

> An organization is, after all, a collection of people and what the organization does is done by people. Therefore, ... propositions about organizations are statements about human behaviour.

The simplistic logic in these statements is only lost on us when we begin to view organizations as something more than what they are. When the issues are confused by organization structure, management roles and the role of technology, we begin to lose sight of what the real basics are. If we build organizations for performance, then it is the people within such organizations that deliver the performance we require.

Part 3 of this book, and this chapter in particular deals, with three fundamental concepts:

1 Organizations are about people.

2 Management assumptions about people often lead to ineffective design of organizations and this hinders performance.

3 People are the most important asset, and their commitment goes a long way in determining effective organizational design and development.

People in organizations can be provided with the opportunities for growth and development if the organization itself is designed to do so. It is the recognition of this which drives the basic principles of organization development. We introduce here, the concept of design and development within the organization as it relates to people. The organization development model (ODM) is not new, nor is it radically different from the writings of many of the leading authors in the field. What it does do, is to place design and development in the context of managing change. To do so, requires that people, as well as structures and systems, change and this leads to the potential for conflict. Avoiding conflict is as much a state of mind as it is a manageable process. If the manager believes in employee involvement, the freedom to exercise control over tasks, then the design element should reflect this. The difficulty, as Konosuke Matsushita points out, at the beginning of this chapter, is that a lot of managers in organizations in the Western world believe in the division of labour – the separation of initiative from performance of the task, thinking from doing, manager from employee. This raises a number of questions which the following chapters will hope to address. Why is it so prevalent in Western economies? Can organizations develop into learning entities? What are the consequences of adopting these approaches? And lastly, can we do anything about it? Part 3 seeks to address these questions by looking at how and why an organization development model is needed. We begin by looking at why some form of people management is necessary in all organizations. From there we go on to look at the concept of organizations design and various reasons why OD is not paid enough attention.

The latter part of this chapter begins to look at some of the presumed weaknesses of Western management. In particular it addresses managers' perceptions as they relate to the desire for control in organizations, the way in which they perceive design as an analytical exercise, the lack of resolution to delegate responsibility, and the lack of philosophy and values about the organization. These are serious accusations that are laid at the door of managers in organizations in the Western world. They reflect a level of truth associated with them. Management in Western economies still operates to a large extent with traditional forms of work organization which are epitomized by the application of assembly style manufacture. This may be a gross generalization, and some of you may work in what can be termed as enlightened companies. But many will not, and this is what we need to address. One answer is to look at how other countries do it. The quote from Matsushita at the beginning of this chapter continues,

> We are beyond the Taylor model; business, we know, is so complex and difficult, the survival of firms so hazardous in an environment increasingly unpredictable, competitive and fraught with danger, that their continued existence depends on the day to day mobilization of every ounce of intelligence. (Matsushita, 1988)

Our first justification is based on the assumption that firms look for alternative models of design and behaviour where they perceive that a need exists. In the past the need for change did not exist; the old ways of manufacture brought profitable returns. This is no longer the case. The reasons are related to the growth of competition from abroad. Managers are beginning to ask questions of themselves and their organizations based on the need to search for solutions that will ensure competitive survival in the market place. Many firms do this traditionally because they know of no other way. This is the way that it has always been done, and it brought profitable return. However, when the market place demands change, for example, products geared to specific customer needs, traditional concepts such as, the long production run or the provision of a service regardless of customer need are no longer feasible, and change is therefore needed.

Second, we wish to see firms actively address these organizational and managerial issues in a positive sense by looking at alternatives; by using the intervention strategy and organization development models to consider options, and by implementing changes which make for effective organizations. We all have a vested interest in the survival and growth of organizations. By overtly opening up the discussion in this way we hope to suggest that there is a need to look at organization design and development and view it as being as important as product development. It is only in this way that managers begin to recognize its importance for effective performance.

Why Manage People?

Extremism is a popular concept in management. Both in the theoretical underpinnings and in the everyday practice, analogies are used which portray the two extreme elements of management characterized by an 'either or' exchange deal: good and bad management practice, hard and soft management techniques, manufacturing versus marketing trade-offs, technology or people. The reality is a continuum which Simon (1957) recognized as bounded rationality; that is, all managerial decisions are made by individual rationality based on economic (business) and social (humanistic) concerns. One of the outcomes of these concomitants of economic and social rationality is that there is a dependence and independence among individuals in organizations.

McGregor (1960) argued that the individual in American industry existed in a state of partial dependence:

> Authority, as a means of influence is certainly not useless, but for many purposes it is less appropriate than persuasion or professional help. Exclusive reliance upon authority encourages countermeasures, minimal performance, even open rebellion.

If this was true of the American organization of the 1960s, then it is also true of Western societies in the new millennium. The power of the individual has assumed greater prominence over the last decade, fuelled by the cult of entrepreneurialism, the alteration in demographic make-up of the working population, the increasing educational awareness of the workforce, and the erosion of the middle management layer in organizations. What we have in existence in today's society is a workforce which matches ideally that propounded by the early organization design and development writers,

> *Inter*dependence is a central characteristic of the modern, complex society. In every aspect of life we depend upon each other in achieving our goals ... the desirable end of the growth process is an ability to strike a balance – to tolerate certain forms of dependence without being unduly frustrated. (McGregor, 1960: 27)

This is one of the major issues concerning the management of people today. How does the manager tread the fine line between complete dependence of the individual on the one hand, and complete independence on the other? This brings us back to extremism again. Down one path (dependence), leads the conceptualization of the individual as specialist in the organization process. This is the Tayloristic view of structure and design of the firm, everyone in their place. Down the other path, many would see the manager's worst nightmare, organizations without management. As was hinted at earlier, the reality is the middle ground, what McGregor et al. would refer to as interdependence.

The need to manage people effectively is the desire to attain what is termed the 'helicopter' approach to management, that is being able to take the longer term view without becoming involved in the day-to-day operational issues. These are workforce issues and are most comfortably dealt with at that level. One manager explains how this process should work, and why it doesn't ...

Let me give you an example of how you manage it. It's dead easy and the analogy is so straightforward that even some of our managers can understand it. You have an important meeting to get to on Monday afternoon and you discover that your car isn't working on Friday night. What do you do? Obvious, you contact the garage first thing Saturday morning, get them to come round, take it away and fix it for you. You also find out if they can get it back to you later that day or Monday morning. You then go ahead and make alternative plans for your meeting if necessary, plan

(Continued)

> *(Continued)*
>
> what you are going to do at the meeting, and in reality enjoy the rest of the weekend. You now enjoy the Chablis over a good meal on Saturday night, oversleep Sunday morning, spend the afternoon over the *Sunday Times*, etc., etc. What you don't do, and this is where you get the message home, is stand over the mechanic while he repairs your car, telling him what to do. He knows what to do for Christsake! If it's good enough as a personal example then it's good enough in a workplace scenario. The manager has to let go. He has to let the people for whom he is responsible get on with their own jobs, secure in the knowledge that they have the competence, the capability and the commitment to deliver the goods on time. This leaves the manager free to do other things. Planning is an example, dealing with customers and suppliers, both internal and external to the business. The difficulty we have is that so many of our managers find it painful letting go of the everyday reins of what they consider management. It's basic insecurity on their part, they have to be seen to be doing something and overtly managing the work is the best showpiece they have; it's silly really.

One of the key elements of managing change is to develop a 'hands-off' management approach. Peters (1987: 369) notes that,

> In this new role, the middle manager must become: (1) expeditor/barrier destroyer/facilitator, (2) on-call expert, and (3) diffuser of good news. In short, the middle manager must practise fast-paced horizontal management not traditional, delaying, vertical management.

Similarly, Kanter (1989: 280) stresses the importance of change in organizations, away from formalized structures and rules towards greater personal commitment:

> In the traditional bureaucratic corporation, roles were so circumscribed that most relationships tended to be rather formal and impersonal. Narrowly defined jobs constricted by rules and procedures also tended to stifle initiative and creativity, and the atmosphere was emotionally repressive. The post-entrepreneurial corporation, in contrast, with its stress on teamwork and cooperation … brings people closer together, making the personal dimension of relationships more important.

The difficulty with these visions of the future are that making the change is difficult, painful, and not too many managers truly believe that the changes are essential to business survival. Why is this the case? If there is any truth to what we are saying here then why don't managers want to make the necessary changes that ensure survival, growth, customer satisfaction, and success? The answers have a self-accusing, almost frightening tone to them.

We Have Met the Enemy, It Is *Us*

Most managers when they look at their employees see a need for control. Tom Peters summarizes this approach quite eloquently,

> You have to ask yourself what you see, what you really see when you look into the eye of a front line employee. Do you see a ne'er-do-well that needs that span of control of 1 to 10 prevalent in your organization, that'll rip you off if you turn your back for more than three or four nanoseconds. Or do you see a person that could literally fly to the moon without a face-mask if only you would just train the hell out them, get the hell out of their way, and give them something decent to do.

> (Quote from 'Tom Peters – Business Evangelist',
> *Business Matters*, BBC Television)

It is this concept which lies at the heart of the control versus commitment argument of management. From an organization development-perspective, organizations are about people, about their development, enhancing their performance and building the organization on that performance. The essence of rigid control is an onerous one. It is obvious that every organization needs a set of rules and guidelines against which individual and group behaviour is judged. However, in most modern organizations, these tools and methods are traditional. No matter how well refined and expertly applied, they are insufficient mechanisms for the development of the organization towards higher standards of performance. Why? Let us look at a common and persistent example.

Task fragmentation is a popular system in firms (Buchanan and McCalman, 1989: 11). It can have a number of advantages for the organization that applies it. The individual employee doesn't need too much expensive, time-consuming training; those who leave are easily replaced because the job is simple to learn. Employees can do their tasks at great speed and less skill is required, hence lower paid workers. For the manager it is also easier to control employees who undertake simple tasks. However, fragmentation also has a number of serious drawbacks. For one, the job is repetitive and boring. The employee working on a fragmented task has no idea what their contribution to the organization as a whole is. This boredom costs money – absenteeism, apathy, carelessness, even sabotage. The employee develops no skills which can lead to promotion, a greater degree of contribution, or higher standards of performance. But, it is these facets which are exactly what we require from every employee to allow the firm to survive and grow in the global economy of the future. And yet, the procedure for fragmenting manufacturing or service tasks is common and accepted in most industries today. Telephone call centres are the latest example of task fragmentation to be established, this time in the service sector (McCalman, 1996).

One therefore has to ask oneself why are these techniques and practices still applied so widely? Many of the management theories developed in the last century are now widely known and practised. However, many of these, Taylorism for example, are inappropriate for today's organizations. Designed in the early part of the twentieth century they work on assumptions that no longer exist. So in this sense we practise the wrong stuff, and many Western organizations stick by these theories as if they were tablets of stone. For example, companies are structured in bureaucratic forms. Rules, procedures and role allocations are established throughout. How can companies like Dell, Microsoft or Sun Microsystems come from nowhere to become the world's leading multinational enterprises in the space of fifteen years with a fraction of the manpower that other electronics companies employ? The reason is they allow their people to make decisions. They are founded on the belief that success is a people factor.

There has recently been a growth in interest in the concepts of work organization and development. The reasons for this are fairly straightforward. The circumstances that organizations face today are related to speed and flexibility of response to changing market situations. Management concern is associated with being able to deal with changing markets, how to make best use of sophisticated levels of technology application, and how to meet the rising expectations of customers as they relate to quality, reliability and delivery. This means that issues related to the people element of firms become more important. As Kanter notes,

> You watch human resource policies now, move in British firms, from being a sort of backwater, 'they're the people who do the paperwork', to being a much more significant piece of strategic thinking for the firm because everybody is going to compete for people ... In fact the quality of people is going to make a bigger difference than the quality of products or the quality of services. (Rosabeth Moss Kanter)

Buchanan and McCalman (1989: 6) argue that these issues have meant a movement has occurred in the management of people in organizations. This movement is one away from 'personnel administration' (the hiring and firing) to 'human resource management' (development of the individual in the organization). As problems have become more serious, what was traditionally accepted as the boundaries placed on work organization have been widened. One could postulate that human resource management is no longer acceptable unless it is accompanied by organization strategy and improvement. The argument here is that traditional personnel departments have become involved in people and organizational development at the same time to assist the organization in dealing with more complex issues. Effective people management affects the overall operating profitability of the organization and must therefore involve management at all levels from the boardroom to the shop floor.

There are important issues at stake here. In earlier chapters we have emphasized how systems could help resolve what we classified as hard issues – questions such as, technology allocation, priorities, etc. In Part 3 we also want to place emphasis on the concept of what would be considered by many as soft issues. The concern here is with people management as part of the 'Big picture', getting the best from the human resource. These are not incidental issues. Effective human resource management makes money, guarantees profitability and ensures effective performance. We may classify these as soft issues by comparison to systems but the returns on getting it right in terms of organizational development are equally important as the issues dealt with in Part 2. The significant questions associated with people management are:

- How do we manage people to best effect ?

- What systems do we put in place to ensure that this effective management of the human resource occurs ?

- To the extent that effective human resource management systems have been widely known since the 1930s and 1940s, why are these systems and styles not applied?

The answers have a familiar, self-analytical tone to them. We manage organizations according to our perceptions about the individual and about the organization. We don't apply models where we believe they are likely to upset the apple-cart. In other words, *we have met the enemy – it is us.* The answer to the question, why are these systems not applied, is that there is a fundamental problem in the way managers think. It may be a rather simplistic way of putting it, but managers design and run organizations. If these organizations are unable to compete in the market place, then the design is wrong and the blame ultimately rests with those responsible for that design. This is what Konosuke Matsushita was getting at in the quote at the beginning of this chapter. In this sense the battleground is over the correct and appropriate division of labour. Megson (1988) argued that:

> Six major issues seem to be at the core of building organizations that perform exquisitely. These in my experience are the major educational hurdles we have to overcome if our quest for more effectiveness is to bear further fruit.
>
> 1　*The way we think is THE root cause*　We use analytical and mechanistic thinking inappropriately. With organizations we need to use systemic and synthetic thinking instead.
>
> 2　*Our models of organizations are too limiting*　Produced by analysis they run on analysis. Machines are their analogues.
>
> 3　*We have no purpose*　Preposterous? Organizations are inward looking and purpose can only be found beyond their boundaries. So if we don't look in the right place for purpose we will not have the right one, which is as bad if not worse than none at all.
>
> 4　*We have no vision or sense of mission*　Without this, any organization cannot achieve really high performance.
>
> 5　*We lack the resolution to delegate*　We simply do not treat our subordinates as we expect our bosses to treat us – and if they feel 'less than' their contribution is 'less than' as well.
>
> 6　*We have no values nor philosophy* – about work and people that are explicit, shared and identify the part people play in the scheme of things.

As a result, there are a number of elements associated with the choices that are made in relation to people management in organizations today.

First, because the root cause is the way we think, we tend to use models for organization design which are too limiting for our needs. Managers use and concentrate on the machine theory of design and place capital equipment above and before people in the design element. The machine system analyses the problem, produces the desired design and installs that design, in-company, by analysis. The difficulty here is that the reason for designing the organization in this way is to meet an internal purpose when purpose is to be found beyond the boundary of the firm. An example of this would be where managers design systems that are technologically driven but ignore human contribution and/or customer demands.

Second, very little time and attention is paid to the concept of design from an organizational perspective. The research and design of a *product* can take years from initial idea to final product delivery. Market research, advertising and placement of that product can command massive budgets in ensuring that everything is right when the product hits the market place. The amount of time spent *designing a new organization system to cope with change* is minimal, if it takes place at all! It is more often than not done *on the back of an envelope*, with little consultation with those likely to be affected by the changes involved, and little consideration given to the likely outcomes of the change. The reasons for this are related to the way managers think about their organizations. Analytical and mechanistic thinking are encouraged (especially at most business schools and on most MBA programmes) when they are highly inappropriate. If an organization is an organic system then systemic and synthetic thinking are necessary.

Third, the behaviour of managers in organizations suggests that there is a distinct lack of resolution to delegate within organizations. This was referred to earlier on and the examples by Thorsurd, Matsushita and Semler explain the impact that this has. There is an unwillingness to treat subordinates in the same manner that managers expect to be treated by their own superiors. This has knock-on implications for motivation. Place yourself in the position of a front line operator. Ask yourself the question – 'If I am treated as "less than" by my immediate boss, then is it surprising that my response in terms of commitment is "less than"?'

Fourth, managers lack any form of systematic thinking about core values and philosophy. They have few beliefs concerning the nature of work and people that are explicit, shared and identify the part that people in organizations play. If you don't understand yourself how you want your organization to operate, then how can others see how they fit into it?

It is these issues which need to be addressed in order to create a clearer understanding of what the big picture is, and how people fit into it. This leads us on to Chapter 10 which details the organization development model and how it can be used. The remainder of this chapter takes each of the comments associated with the main management issues outlined above and explains them in more detail. We look at why these issues occur, how they manifest themselves in organizations, and what is needed to change. The accounts given here are largely prescriptive in the sense that we specifically set out what is being done wrong, and what is required to make it right. They are also set in fairly provocative and challenging terms – deliberately so. We want you to think about them, see if they are true, see if they apply to your organization, and then think what can be done to resolve them. However, we have also attempted to be descriptive and present particular events and circumstances that the manager would be expected to come across during the course of the job. You should be able to sympathize and associate with these. You should also be able to recognize and begin to think about the changes that are needed. One important point needs to be emphasized here. Suspend your initial judgements and firm belief that, 'This wouldn't happen to me, so I can ignore it.'

The Models We Use are Too Limiting

The way managers think is very much conditioned by their approach to the management profession. It is most readily summed up in that well worn (and flawed sentiment) that 'It's management's right to manage.' The noun 'right' in this instance connotes a prerogative, authority or desire to control or dominate. The right is that of position power in many instances and is based on nothing more than title. This is reflected in the traditional Tayloristic model of organization popularized in the early twentieth century. This views people, especially those on the shop floor, as machine parts, elements, factors of production, cogs in the larger machine. In this sense, the individual only needs to know as much as is necessary to play their part in the process. It is the manager's role to organize, control and co-ordinate the bigger picture.

There are three reasons why models such as Taylorism retain their popularity. First, they are easy to apply. Taylorism, the division of labour, task specialization, and so on, appears as a plausible and cheap set of techniques. The ideas are fairly straightforward by comparison to some of the models which are linked to organization development. Specialization for example, increases the amount of work that progresses through the system. It also simplifies the production element. Everyone has a place and everyone should be in that place: 'It is always easier to blame workers who have the wrong skills, wrong attitudes and wrong values, than to blame a systematically prepared job specification' (Buchanan and McCalman, 1989: 12).

Second, it perpetuates status. The status is that which Taylorism affords to managers. A greater degree of responsibility taken on by the workforce, who can control the performance of meaningful sections of an organization's operations begins to threaten the legitimacy of management. It is easier (and more comforting to status) to have individual workers who have little or no identification with the whole organization and who have no idea how they fit into the bigger picture. Taylorism fragments tasks, hides contribution and maintains managerial status.

Third, managers are unaware of alternative forms of design and development for their organizations. This is not the manager's fault. The alternatives are couched in such obscure language (and journals) that their wider applicability is lost to the manager, and thus the credibility of such alternatives is eroded.

One of the difficulties with the old fashioned view of management was that it failed to recognize the full potential of the individual in the organization. It is commonly accepted that for most organizations survival and growth will stem from the full utilization of the intelligence, skills and commitment of the workforce – to perceive the labour element of production as an asset value instead of a factor cost.

It is not surprising that approaches to the concept of design are not new in organizations. The fact that firms have been in existence for 150 years or more would suggest that at some time during this period a body of knowledge on how best to organize and design the firm would have built up. There are a number of approaches that can be considered. Many are couched in the period in which they developed, and many show the signs of age. However, there are schools of thought which try to integrate differing variables associated with design to effect more appropriate forms of business performance.

Four models are briefly outlined in this section. We freely admit to not doing them justice here, and the reader should seek out more detailed explanations. The models have an historical, sequential development beginning with machine theory or scientific management (Taylorism), developing on to the human relations movement, the contingency theorists and finally, the Organization Development Movement.

Scientific management (Taylorism)

One of the first models of organizational and management behaviour was that developed in the early part of the twentieth century by Frederick Winslow Taylor. The concepts of what is now widely referred to as 'Taylorism' lay in the division between manual and mental work in the organization. The basis of Taylor's theories were that work could be divided in to sub units or specializations which could be performed by individuals. Taylor started from the basic principle that work could be scientifically determined and that 'one best way' to perform a task could be found. This would then be made standard practice and the individual and organization would benefit. We do not have the time or space here to go into the details of the model but would recommend you read any general organizational behaviour textbook for an introduction to Frederick Taylor and the concept of scientific management.

The human relations movement

The second school of thought related to organizational effectiveness and behaviour stemmed from the studies of Elton Mayo and Fritz Roethlisberger at Western Electric's Hawthorne plant near Chicago during the 1920s and 1930s (Roethlisberger and Dickson, 1939). Whereas the scientific management studies of Taylor focused attention on mechanistic, machine theories of organization, the Hawthorne studies drew attention to the humanistic approach and in particular to group behaviour and relations among group members and between group members and management. Effective performance was associated with understanding the linkages between the individual, their role among other members of the group at the workplace and the degree of independence given to the group. In the human relations movement, increasing individual satisfaction within the group led to increased performance and greater organizational effectiveness. The human relations movement was also important in recognizing job design and the working environment as key variables in organizational performance.

The contingency theorists

By the early 1960s further research in the area of organizational behaviour suggested the development of a series of contingency theories based on an open-systems concept or view of the organization. These organizational theorists advocated no single form of organizational structure or style of management. Concepts such as, structure and managerial style were dependent on the organization's business and its environment, or numerous other influencing variables. There were a number of contingency theorists, each with their own specific view of the influencing variables which determined the way an organization was designed. We shall look at two pairs of authors in particular – Burns and Stalker and Lawrence and Lorsch.

In an examination of 20 British firms during the 1960s, Burns and Stalker identified two types of effective organization – mechanistic and organic. Both types were effective under different circumstances. The mechanistic firm prospered in stable markets whereas the organic firm succeeded in rapidly changing markets and technologies. The mechanistic organization has the following characteristics:

- task differentiation and specialization;

- hierarchy for co-ordination of tasks, control and communications;

- control of incoming/outgoing communications from the top and a tendency for information to be provided on a need to know basis;

- interaction and emphasis placed on vertical reporting lines;

- loyalty to the organization and its officers;

- value placed on internal knowledge and experience in contrast to more general knowledge.

(Burns and Stalker, 1961: 119)

By contrast, the organic organization was characterized by:

- continuous assessment of task allocation through interaction to utilize knowledge which solves real problems;
- the use of expertise power relationships and commitment to total task;
- sharing of responsibility;
- open and widely used communication patterns which incorporate horizontal and diagonal as well as vertical channels;
- commitment to task accomplishment, development and growth of the organization rather than loyalty to officials;
- value placed on general skills which are relevant to the organization.

(Burns and Stalker, 1961: 120–5)

Burns and Stalker's research work was important in the sense that their studies identified differentiation between types of organization. It also stressed the belief that the organization could change its design, structure and approach in relation to its environment.

In a similar vein, the basis of Lawrence and Lorsch's analysis of organization (1967, 1969) was that structure and management depended on the environment the firm found itself in. Because of this, the more complex the environment, the more decentralized and flexible management needed to be. Patterns emerged which suggested that the nature of *differentiation* occurring in the organization determined the degree of centralization/decentralization that took place. This differentiation could be measured by an examination of:

- formal structure (rules, regulations, procedures, etc.);
- certainty of goals (Are they clear and easily measured or uncertain?);
- The timing of feedback (Are results seen in the short or long term?);
- interpersonal interaction (level of interpersonal and intergroup communication and co-operation).

One of the key elements to emerge from the work of Lawrence and Lorsch was that predictability of the task was a basic condition variable in the choice of organizational form. That meant that both internal and external criteria had to be taken into consideration.

The organization development model

The next chapter deals specifically with the historical development, systems and application of organization development. However, it is important to emphasize that it is a design model that has been developed extensively over the last 30 years. A wide body of literature exists on the subject of organizational development and design. It is important here to classify what we mean by organization development and the concerns it attempts to address. Warner Burke (1994) classifies OD as, 'a planned process of change in an organization's culture through the utilization of behavioural science technologies, research and theory.' The importance though is that:

> OD practitioners are concerned with change that integrates individual needs with organizational goals more fully; change that improves an organization's effectiveness, especially human resources; and change that involves organization members in the decisions that directly affect them and their working conditions (1994: 11)

OD provides us with a model in which the importance of relating work to people is fully recognized. They no longer become cogs but are an integated part of the organizational equation. Figure 9.1 is a schematic representation of this. The first point to note is that it is a bounded

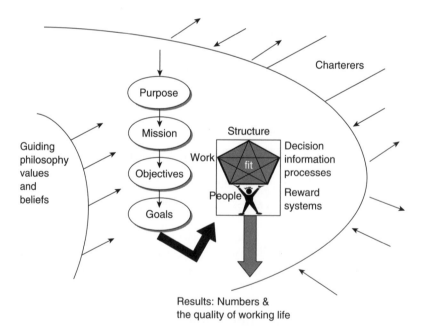

Figure 9.1 The organizational development model

Source: Megson, 1988.

model. It places the organization within an environment (this pays heed to the work of Lawrence and Lorsch) represented by 'charterers'. The word charterer is used to convey importance to those outside the organization, those that give the organization its reason for being and can take it away. Mechanistic models of organizations ignore them or assume that their needs, having previously been established, do not need to be reviewed. However, for survival, organizations need to identify expectations of charterers, and synthesize these into a statement of purpose.

Our Organizations Have No Purpose

If the accepted design norm is that most organizations are/were designed using the process of analytical thinking, breaking the job down into constituent parts for task specialization, then this machine analogy finds its purpose by reference to an internal focus. However, as many organization theorists point out, the purpose of an organization is found outside its own boundaries, in its ability to react with and to its environment. Therefore, design which focuses too much on internal issues is looking in the wrong place. This becomes clearer when we look at the purpose of organizations.

READER ACTIVITY

Take a couple of minutes to think about your own organization's purpose?
    You may have come up with some interesting conclusions. The first reaction is normally a straightforward one. The purpose is to make a profit, provide a needed service or to stay in business. Simplistic, yes, but hardly definitive. Delving a little deeper may bring you to the provision of goods and services of high quality that serve customer needs. This is getting closer to the reality of an organization and its purpose which is provided by the external environment and is directly linked to results and performance. What the organization has to take into account is that the conflicting expectations of the external environment (customers, shareholders, suppliers, governments, etc.) need to be synthesized into a single statement. Megson provides an example of the importance of establishing purpose: 'Purpose has to be on target because all other organization design flows from it. An unclear or wrong purpose ruins further design and effectiveness can no longer be achieved. A wrong purpose can be worse than none. With none the quest to find one may continue, a wrong one may stop further search and so seal its doom' (1988: 10).

Sherwood (1988) argues that one of the features of high performance organizations is the definition and organization-wide awareness of purpose:

> A shared sense of purpose entails sharing a vision that is based on a clearly stated set of values describing both the organization's mission (purpose) and the methods for realizing it. An organization's vision provides energy and direction ... It empowers individual employees and forms the basis of a planned culture.

Organizations have to be able to define their purpose in clear, unambiguous terms which enable them to create a precise design to fit the purpose. The most effective means of doing so is to look to the external environment to find the purpose of the organization (provision of product on time, negotiation of supply contracts that benefit both sides, etc.). This provides the work that an organization needs to accomplish, and then the organization executes the work. The other variables in Figure 9.1 operate to assist in the accomplishment of purpose. Define the purpose, do the work, achieve the result and effective performance results. This appears too easy. The reality is that design is complicated because of what we have argued earlier. We are not geared towards thinking in these terms. Pasmore (1994: 46–7) notes that,

> Neither managers nor employees are prepared for this task at the beginning of a redesign effort. Most have never worked in a flexible organization of the kind I am describing or read much about alternative ways of organizing or how to approach change. Some have never thought about these things before, and a few don't ever *want* to think about them ... If people know only what history has taught them, they are prisoners of the past.

However, these concepts of defining purpose and organization redesign are seen as 'woolly' and too far removed from reality and the everyday pressures of work. We would argue that this is because many organizations lack the vision or sense of mission to think in these terms.

Our Organizations Lack Vision or Sense of Mission

The mission statement in organizations is a popular tool for clarifying operational strategy. Mission, in an organizational sense, is for the people working in that organization to develop. The level at which mission is defined determines awareness and commitment to it. The most popular form of mission definition is that provided by the boss. It's quick but shuts out the rest of the organization. Mission defined by a senior management team takes longer but the payoff is more powerful. Mission determined by the whole organization is rare, takes an enormous amount time, and may prove impossible to develop. Whoever sets it, mission is about aspirational values within the organization. By not sharing these aspirations the opportunity to build an effective organization team is lost. In developing vision and mission the organization also has to look at the needs and wants of the individual. People do not get energized unless they see their own needs and wants in parallel with those of the organization. If purpose tells the organization what it needs to do, then mission gives the organization what it wants to do as well. There are opportunities to structure work that has to be done to fit the purpose in ways that meet individual needs. However, these needs are often ignored. Organizations need to develop their mission, to tap into the talents and energies of the people within it.

Managers Lack the Resolution to Delegate

Many managers do not treat their subordinates as they expect to be treated by their bosses. As a manager, the expectation is that your immediate superior will give you space – you can manage yourself – true? However, managers expect obedience from those who work for them. Managers see themselves as committed to the organization and to its purpose as well as their own. Yet managers expect loyalty from subordinates without considering their needs and wants. The manager expects to use their talents to the full, yet they tell people what to do. As a manager you see yourself as open, candid and courageous, yet we see subordinates as 'less-than'. This results in shutting off employees' candour and makes disagreement and argument feel like a test of courage or a career decision. Managers often treat employees as less-than in terms of their own initiative to contribute, and it is hardly surprising therefore, that their response is less-than. There is a need to empower subordinates so they see themselves as equals.

In Chapter 10 we will look at some of the practical applications of organization development. One of these is the use of autonomous or semi-autonomous work groups where employees are empowered to take responsibility for their own actions in a workplace setting. However, this is difficult for the manager to deal with because it involves a 'hands-off' approach. The structure of these work groups sets up the requirement for employees to be treated as equals. Managers have trouble with this because most of them do not really believe that they are or can be equal. Because of this managers do not have the necessary values which are consistent with the concept of delegated responsibility. Without this there is never full commitment, and hence the potential of employees remains unexplored.

Organizations Have No Values

This is a mistake. Everyone has their own values and philosophy which guide them through life. However, in a organizational setting what is lacking is a shared set of values and philosophy. Philosophy and values relate to how organizations deal with their beliefs about people and work. These fundamental beliefs and philosophy guide the design of organizational life. They need to be defined and shared with organizational members in order that people understand and make sense of their working life; how and where they fit into the big picture. Megson, in describing the guiding values and beliefs at Digital comments that:

> They are based on a *Philosophy* that I describe as follows:

> People are the most important asset we have. They want and need to grow. Without growth interest wanes and talents waste away. With growth interest flourishes and talents develop. People really do care, they do exquisite work – if it is designed to enable them to grow. In other words, personal growth is the engine that drives organization performance. (Megson, 1988: 16)

It is the ability to put these guiding values and beliefs into practice which is at the heart of the organization development model which we deal with in the next chapter. The key is to design work that fits people and not the other way round. If we accept that effective performance comes from people being energized towards their needs and wants as well as those of the organization, then the design has to take account of this.

The Concept of Design in Organizations

All firms have to consider the element of design. To the extent that every firm exists, it has a design associated with it. The small business operating out of a garage and employing ten people has a structure and is designed according to the owner's wishes. The corporate multinational operating across five continents and employing 400,000 people also has to consider design. The commonality is associated with the attainment of standards of performance and the need to deal with complexities of size and division of labour (Galbraith, 1977). The organization has to conceive an approach to satisfy the attainment of a number of factors. There are three factors: the goals and purposes for which the organization exists, the patterns of labour division and co-ordination of different units within the organization, and the people who will do the work (Galbraith,

1977: 5). The concept of design in organizations is associated with establishing a fit between these three areas of choice. The essence of design is the assessment of fit between the three areas, the examination of alternatives where the fit does not operate effectively, and the implementation of those alternatives in the form of a new design.

A couple of mini case study examples best illustrate the need for fit and the concept of organization design.

MINI CASE 9.1:   BELL ATLANTIC AND PARTICIPATIVE CHANGE

Rosabeth Moss-Kanter conducted an interview with Bell Atlantic's CEO Raymond Smith who, on his appointment had seen the urgent need for change. He realized that the growth of his company's core businesses would not sustain it into the competitive global economy of the twenty-first century. Smith designed four initial strategies to improve Bell Atlantic's position:

- improved efficiency;
- improved marketing to protect market share;
- new products and services;
- new businesses operating outside of the United States.

The culture of Bell Atlantic had grown out of a long-standing monopoly with a centralized organizational structure. As a result, managers did not understand the initiative, innovation, risks and accountability necessary to meet new business goals set by Smith. The company also indulged in parochial, cross-departmental competition which raised costs and prevented new initiatives.

Plans were made to seek to change the behaviour of the organization to realize Smith's strategies. He was personally involved in the design of seminars in which 1,400 managers spent half a week discussing and debating what the values of the new organization should be. Five values were eventually agreed upon:

- integrity;
- respect and trust;
- excellence;
- individual fulfilment;
- profitable growth.

Some of these are essential to underpin organizational development efforts e.g. the individual should be treated with respect and dignity.

(Continued)

(Continued)

Once the company values had been agreed, Smith realized that the organization needed to move from general statements to concrete behaviours and work practices. Through participative management, Smith defined the obligations of the managers to the organization and encapsulated these in a formal document, 'The obligations of leadership'. Bell Atlantic took a year to get the required understanding and commitment from its management. Once this was done, an organized programme of internal communications for all employees was developed outlining obligations to each other, the opportunities ahead and the need and reasons for change.

The emphasis of the organizational structure was on teamworking and quality because Smith believed that:

> In a large business the most important determinant of success is the effectiveness of millions of day-to-day interactions between human beings. If those contacts are contentious, turf-orientated, and parochial, the company will flounder, bureaucracies will grow and internal competition will be rampant. But when employees behave in accountable, team-orientated and collegial ways, it dramatically improves group effectiveness.

These activities led to the design of 'The Bell Atlantic Way', an organized, participative method of working together that allowed everyone to maximize their contribution to team goals. Smith announced a ten year transition to this way of working. Forums were designed to introduce the Bell Atlantic Way to 20,000 managers and then to the staff. He wrote to all employees defining the basic business problems, the strategies identified to resolve them, departmental goals and individual objectives. Reward systems were then initiated, which focused on team and individual results.

When Smith unveiled his new organization, individual departments were empowered to create the organization they thought would be most efficient. The 'Champion Programme' was also introduced at the same time to identify potential corporate entrepreneurs, train them and develop their ideas into new businesses.

After these changes had been implemented, Smith noted that people were no longer parochial or territorial but more accountable and more team-oriented. Thirty-six champions were accepted into the Programme and there were 33 products and services in the pipeline, several near to commercialization.

The techniques Smith used at Bell Atlantic map well onto the perpetual transition management model outlined in Chapter 1:

Theory	Practice
Trigger layer	Core businesses would not sustain the company in the competitive global economy of the twenty-first century
Vision layer	Development of four strategies
	Articulate five values of the company
	The obligations of leadership
Conversion layer	Communications programme to all managers and staff defining the business problem, strategies to resolve it, departmental goals and individuals' objectives
	Definition and practise of 'The Bell Atlantic Way'
Maintenance and renewal layer	Reward systems
	Business measures e.g quality and customer service
	Development of the 'Champion Programme'

Moss-Kanter argues that competitive pressures are forcing organizations to adopt new, flexible strategies and structures. Bell Atlantic's move towards empowered, flexible teams seems to be an example of this.

CASE 9.2: A NEW TELECOMS ENTERPRISE AND DICTATORIAL TRANSFORMATION

Dunphy and Stace (1990) argue that incremental and collaborative or consultative modes of change implementation often generate conflicting views and ideas which are not always reconciled. As a result such change strategies are time-consuming. They argue that there is a role for dictatorial transformation and forced evolution in such situations. At Bell Atlantic Smith believed it was important to ensure that all of his employees were clear about his vision for change and his plans to achieve it claiming that:

> Even the best evaluation system will not produce the desired behaviour unless people understand our business problems and our strategies. (1991 *Harvard Business Review*)

A newly formed telecom enterprise provides an example of where dictatorial transformation and lack of participative change management has not worked well. If a programme of coercive or dictatorial change is adopted,

(Continued)

(Continued)

as Dunphy and Stace suggest, with no communication programme or planning for change, then the effort may well be doomed from the start. Kotter (1995) explains that 'without motivation, people won't help and the effort goes nowhere.' This view is also supported by evidence for the failure of many change management initiatives. Reasons often cited include:

- Poor communication – giving information gradually is risky.
- Misunderstanding of what change is about – change is a journey not an event.
- Lack of planning and preparation – management may look only to the end result, not at the required steps to get there.
- Lack of clear vision – if staff do not know where the company is going how can they get there?
- Quick-fix option – change means more than a T-shirt, quality poster, coffee mug, seminar or newsletter.
- Legacies of previous change – may have developed a sceptical, risk-averse culture.
- Goals are set too far into the future – short term wins are essential for success.

The new telecoms enterprise's main objective was to become a leading regional telephone operator. In 1994 the company was an informal adhocracy moving towards a functional structure. The advantages of such a structure were its flexibility and ability to cope with changing circumstances. This was outgrown as the company increased in size, launched more products and acquired more companies. The move from business into residential markets also had a major impact on the organization and the company developed a function based bureaucracy with control centralized through the CEO. Merging other acquired companies into the new structure became increasingly more time-consuming. The company did not use change management techniques to manage its transitions and no change agents operated within the organization.

   In 1997, a staff survey was undertaken by management. Some of the responses seem to highlight the effects of rapid change within the organization:

   Question: How frequently do you feel stressed at work?

Not at all	8%
Every few months	23%
Every few weeks	28%
At least once a week	32%
Every day	8%

Short temper, poor or careless work were cited as the main expressions of stress with 18% of those asked saying they occasionally become ill as a result of stress.

Question: What is the most important management action that could be taken to reduce workplace stress?

Discussion and communication	32%
More staff	19%
Improved resources	16%

Question: Indicate whether you think the following culture statements are true of the firm:

The organization is honest, open and trusting:

Very true	12%
Quite true	41%
Not sure	34%
Not very true	11%
Totally untrue	2%

These findings appeared to suggest lower than desirable trust levels. To explore this further additional cultural related questions were asked concerning:

whether staff felt empowed;
whether promises were delivered;
whether management 'walks the talk';
whether teamwork and co-operation were natural;
and if staff felt personally responsible for the success of the enterprise.

These questions received similar ratings. The 'walk the talk' culture statement scored badly with nearly a third of the company saying it was not true and nearly half saying they were unsure.

Employees did not feel involved in the company as much as they might otherwise be if communication was good. Values of teamwork and respect etc. were not lived or communicated throughout the business from the top down as they were at Bell Atlantic. This factor perhaps explains some of the scepticism regarding cultural statements and indicates that there could be a role for organizational development to play.

Bell Atlantic recognized the benefits of using change management techniques and of investing the time and effort to ensure their organizational

(Continued)

(Continued)

changes had a positive outcome. In the case of the new telecoms enterprise where organizational change was dictatorial and unmanaged, problems have occurred. The implication of this seems to be that a participative approach could be more successful.

In the case of Bell Atlantic, indications were that bureaucracies cannot adapt to change rapidly and that there was a need for them to move towards more flexible, team-based structures.

Finally, there may be a role for academics and managers to work together in developing successful approaches to organizational change. Bennis (1996) notes that, 'while the French moralist may be right that there are no delightful marriages, just good ones, it is possible that if managers and behavioural scientists continue to get their heads together in organizational revitalization, they might develop delightful organizations – just possibly.'

Conclusion

The concept of design in organizations has to be congruent with people. Work needs to be designed in a manner in which people are engaged in *meaningful* tasks. The organization must fit work to people, not the other way round. Anything less is sub-optimal. It doesn't guarantee high performance. When designing the organization, we must consider how the work of the individual employee adds to the purpose of the enterprise. Work has to contain within it elements that achieve business purpose and can be measured. For example, in manufacturing, the mechanistically determined fragmentation of tasks means that the individual employee knows their own job very well but not the whole. This means that people miss the impact that interactions have on their surroundings. The traditional mechanism for responding to this lack of interaction is supervision. The supervisor provides the overview and direction to the task players. Today the pace of change is such that this level of supervision is questionable. It is an inadequate use of employee capabilities and is overmanning gone mad. Work that is designed to allow the employee to build product, test it and ship it provides contribution and meaning. People understand where they fit into the system, and performance is easy to assess in terms of results that are important – quality, cost, time to customer, etc. It provides the employee with work that demands commitment.

This is largely where we came in. Management in organizations today is largely people management. If people are the important asset, effectiveness is related to:

- how managers perceive the individual;

- how people relate to one another;

- how we get the maximum contribution, and

- how we go about changing from a situation which is seen to be ineffective to one which ensures higher standards of performance.

In Chapter 10 we set out the organization development model as an approach to managing change. It is one which lays emphasis very much on people issues. In this chapter we have tried to lay the groundwork in a challenging manner. We doubt whether organizations are as black as the picture we have painted in terms of purpose, mission, delegation, etc. But when dealing with the people element of managing change it is important to continually question why we are doing things. It is how we perceive people that matters. It is how we perceive the organization that matters. It is how we perceive the manager's role that matters. We are fortunate to live in an era of rapid change. It gives us the raison d'être to ask questions, try new concepts, and most importantly be aware of the pervasive nature of change. The goals associated with the soft issues such as organization development, are related to communication within the organization, to decision-making styles and systems, and to problem solving. The values are humanistic and are aimed at developing maximum potential for the individual, the group and the organization as a whole. The requirement is for the encouragement of open relationships in the organization. Understanding the importance of people is the first step.

10 Organizations Can Develop

In the last few years, more and more organizational leaders have realized that it is not enough to carry out piecemeal efforts to patch up an organization problem here, fix a procedure there, or change a job description. Today there is a need for longer-range, co-ordinated strategy to develop organization climates, ways of work, relationships, communications systems, and information systems that will be congruent with the predictable and unpredictable requirements of the years ahead.

(Richard Beckhard, *Organization Development: Strategies and Models*, 1969)

Let us make no mistake: the cultures of consent are not easy to run, or to work in. Authority in these organizations does not come automatically with the title; it has to be earned … based … on your ability to help others do better, by developing their skills, by liaising with the rest of the organization, by organizing their work more efficiently, by helping them to make the most of their resources, by continual encouragement and example.

(Charles Handy, *The Age of Unreason*, 1989)

Perhaps the greatest competitive challenge companies face is adjusting to – indeed, embracing – non-stop change. They must be able to learn rapidly and continuously, innovate ceaselessly, and take on new strategic imperatives faster and more comfortably. Constant change means more organizations must create a healthy discomfort with the status quo, an ability to detect emerging trends quicker than the competition, an ability to make rapid decisions, and the agility to seek new ways of doing business … the only competitive weapon left is the organization … winning will spring from organizational capabilities such as speed, responsiveness, agility, learning capacity, and employee competence.

(Dave Ulrich, 'A new mandate for human resources', *Harvard Business Review*, February 1998)

Years of study and experience show that the things that sustain change are not bold strokes but long marches – the independent, discretionary, and ongoing efforts of people throughout the organization. Real change requires people to adjust their behaviour, and their behaviour is often beyond the control of top management. Yes, as a senior executive, you can allocate resources for new product development or reorganize a unit, but you cannot order people to use their imaginations or to work collaboratively. That's why, in difficult situations, leaders who have neglected the long march often fall back on the bold stroke. It feels good (at least to the boss) to shake things up, but it exacts a toll on the organization.

(Rosabeth Moss Kanter, 'The enduring skills of change leaders', http://www.goodmeasure.com)

Plus ça change? There is almost a 40 year gap between Beckhard, Handy, Ulrich and Kanter yet the issues being addressed have not really changed all that much. Beckhard, writing in 1969 identified that the business environment of the time had to deal with quite a few changes. This included internationalization of markets, shorter product life cycles, the increased significance of marketing, relationships of line and staff management, new organization forms, and the changing nature of work (1969: 5–6). Issues don't really change over time, only the degree of importance. How many of the changes identified by Beckhard are crucial today? We would argue that they all are.

READER ACTIVITY

Appropriate consideration of change ...
In the twenty-first century a number of changes are likely to have a serious impact on the way your organization does business. Consider for example the following trends:

An ageing population   In 2005, the UK population totalled 60.2 million with one in five under 16 and 11 million people over retirement age. In the next 20 years the number of people aged 85 or over is expected to double from 1 million.

The structure and size of the population has a major influence on the economic well being of a country. Population demographics have a serious bearing on the profitability of certain industrial and service sectors.

Technology gone wild   The development of computing and information technology will continue to spiral and this will create significant reductions

(Continued)

(Continued)

in geographical and temporal space. The time distance between Europe and the Far East will diminish to become insignificant.

Computing systems will become the main form of doing business through the Internet and technological advances will cause business to become less labour intensive. Advances in medical technology will mean we live longer and continue to be active long into what is now considered old age.

Environmental protection   Being able to develop business ideas at either the micro or macro level will have to be undertaken within rules of sustainability and protection of global resources such as the oceans and the atmosphere. Firms will be publicly prosecuted for infringements and those that can illustrate environmental enhancement will gain competitive advantage. Carbon footprinting will become a key aspect of social responsibility for organizations.

Flexible approaches to the workplace   Not only will work become increasingly more mental than manual, the concept of the workplace itself will alter radically. As fewer people are employed in manufacturing, the service sector will design and implement methods of working that remove the concept of a physical working environment and place this within the realms of technology.

People will no longer be employed by a single organization but will develop consultancy approaches to their work. This will lead to the development of lifelong learning patterns paid for by the individual themselves.

Management as a control process will cease   As individuals take on greater and greater levels of personal responsibility for the outcomes of their work, the need for traditional forms of management will end. Managers, to the extent that they exist, will act as co-ordinators of independent staff and will be judged on their ability to attain a number of performance criteria such as, inspirational capabilities, visionary sense, and the ability to delegate.

What are the major implications of these changes for your organization?

In the last chapter we seemed to indicate that there was a great deal to be done in the area of organizational development. Our argument was that because of the nature of managerial behaviour, the full level of effective performance of an organization was hampered. The major element of this behaviour was reflected in approaches to the management of change. More often than not these are non-participatory, lack clear goals and objectives, and are undertaken in a piecemeal fashion. Our suggestion in this chapter is that the element of people management via organizational development programmes is not given the same level of importance, or thought, as that attached to product development or market research development.

... Leads to effective responses to opportunities.

Let us look at some of the implications of the trends highlighted earlier. Most organizations are likely to be affected by changing demographic patterns to a greater or lesser degree. Three examples serve to show the crucial nature of being aware of the need for proactive change within organizations.

Private pension firms will increasingly take advantage of the mismatch between the working population and those moving to retirement. As governments struggle to manage the gap between tax inflows and outflows the private sector will service the individual's needs. The development of the individual pension and savings plans will catapult pension firms into even greater prominence.

Two of the major beneficiaries of an ageing population are likely to be pharmaceutical giants and healthcare companies. An ageing population spends more per capita on healthcare than any other section of the population. Organizations in private healthcare face a drain on their resources as an ever-ageing population begins to take advantage of the healthcare schemes that individuals have contributed to over the years. Similarly, there is a growth opportunity in nursing homes that cater for an older population but do so in a professional manner. However, a generally healthier, more health-conscious population might not be such a drain on firms in the healthcare sector. The National Health Service in the United Kingdom currently struggles under the strain of increasing demand. Will an ageing population bring about greater levels of privatization? Some may find it morally indefensible to remove the socialist icon of 'from the cradle to the grave' but others will identify opportunities for exploitation. The politics are not what are at issue here. The concern is what type of change response one contemplates – proactive or ostrich?

In retailing, an increase in the middle-aged sector of the population may hold benefits for companies that specifically target this range of the population. Marks and Spencer won't go to the wall in the next decade because it has refocused on its traditional customer base in the 30+ age range. Companies with ecological and environmental reputations, will match up well with a more environmentally aware population.

The importance of change management is not the extent to which these trends are accurate or will actually come to fruition. The importance lies in thinking about the implications of issues, such as demographics on company performance ten years down the road. How many of you, when thinking about demographics, thought about the impact on recruitment within your own organization?

In dealing with the often 'messy' problem of people management, many settle for the easy route of ignoring the problems and hoping that performance will somehow be maintained. What we argue in this chapter is that, given the current economic climate, organizations can no longer afford to ignore the human element as part of the change process. All change in organizations is about people. Technological change includes a people element to it. Product design or improvement is likely to affect those who have to manufacture those products or provide those services. In this sense then, the people side of change cannot be ignored. Nor should it. We firmly advocate in this chapter that firms begin to use more refined mechanisms for instigating change that consider, include, seek out and involve those likely to be affected – the organization's members. What we recommend here is the use of an organization development model (ODM). However, in doing so we are not attempting to break new ground. The techniques that we describe and explain here are neither unique nor innovative. These techniques have been well known for at least 20 years, but not so well practised by organizations. The techniques of the ODM, however, will require a change in emphasis in management thought. First and foremost, they require recognition that change implementation involves people and that gaining the involvement and active participation will assist the likelihood of success.

There are three areas that we will concern ourselves with. First, we look at where organization development stemmed from. To do so, involves an analysis of the work of a number of writers in the fields of behavioural and social science, what they suggest and how this impacts the individual, management and organization as a whole. Second, we detail what we mean by the organization development model and how it can help organizations to manage change more effectively. Third, we comment on guiding values and beliefs that assist the movement towards effective performance.

Sorry, There Are No Route Maps

Handy (2004) argues that organizations are like inverted doughnuts with people being treated in a different manner,

> The doughnut idea requires managers to treat insiders as outsiders, to negotiate with groups, specifying minimum delivery requirements, the central core of the doughnut, and the general aims of the project, paying for any increase over the specified minimum outcome. They would be treated as far as possible as independent contractors, as outsiders, but would still be insiders, full members of the organization with all that it meant for security of employment, career development and the sense of belonging to something bigger than themselves. The group would, however, have every incentive to improve productivity and be creative and would have

the space to experiment within their areas of discretion. Incentive and opportunity are the two necessary preconditions of creativity in organizations. The doughnut, properly designed, provides both. Mere exhortation offers neither.

To achieve this notion he also notes that firms tend to have a number of characteristics,

> The research on long-lasting, and successful organizations suggests that what enables a corporation to succeed in the longer term is a wish for immortality; a consistent set of values based on the awareness of the organization's own identity; a willingness to change; and a passionate concern for developing the capacity and the self-confidence of its core inhabitants, whom the company values more than its physical assets. (Handy, 1997)

To be able to meet future challenges managers need to create (or more realistically recognize the existence of and channel) commitment from the workforce towards new working relationships and more effective performance. Effective performance comes from having a committed workforce. This is accomplished by allowing people to have a sense of belonging to the organization, a sense of excitement in the job, and by confidence in management leadership. The difficulty with excellence programmes, as authors such as, Peters and Waterman have found out to their cost, is that although many management writers are aware of where organizations should be heading for in the future, there are no route maps. We can describe the processes by which change should take place and the issues that need to be considered by management and workforce alike, but you cannot buy a stencilled guide to change management for your own organization – it doesn't exist.

Many managers while accepting the overall argument about the need for change and the development of new organization structures and management styles, would like to see some substance. There is a common belief that there is a lack of adequate guidance on how to transform an organization and its employees, at all levels, in this direction. What we will stress is that the change movement process is not effortless. However, when one pays attention to the experience of change as it is lived, then a more comprehensive perspective of change emerges (Buchanan and McCalman, 1989: 50–7). One of the best ways of doing so is to look at examples of change management situations in some detail, analyse how and why they took place, and learn how to apply the benefits that accrued elsewhere.

What we attempt to address in this chapter is the process of organizational development from a people point of view. In the sense that we put forward a model here – the organizational development model – it is not a panacea. It is the description of an approach, a school of thought on change that has developed largely since the late 1960s. In this sense, we offer a set of descriptive commentaries. However, we justify this by arguing that in this area of change, there is much commonality.

READER ACTIVITY

The manager, the organization, and design issues
Before we go any further we would like you to undertake a short, relatively painless exercise to try to gauge your own assumptions about your organization and the people who work in it. Below are ten sets of paired statements. We would like you to allocate 10 points per paired statements. For example, if you agree more with the first statement then allocate more points to that one than the second.

                                                                    Points

1   There are very few people in my organization
    who come up with good ideas.   A.....

    Given the chance most people in my organization
    will come up with good ideas.   B.....

2   The majority of people in my organization can and
    do exercise self-control and self-direction.   C.....

    The majority of people in my organization prefer
    to be given direction.   D.....

3   People in my organization do not have enough
    experience to offer practical ideas.   E.....

    Getting people to contribute ideas leads to the
    development of useful suggestions.   F.....

4   For the manager to admit that an employee is right
    and they are wrong weakens their status among
    other employees.   G.....

    The manager's respect and reputation are enhanced
    by admitting to their mistakes.   H.....

5   A job that is interesting and challenging can go a long
    way in eradicating complaints about pay and benefits.   J.....

    Paying people enough for the job means that they are
    less bothered with responsibility and recognition.   K.....

6   If employees are allowed to set their own objectives
    and standards of performance, they tend to set them
    higher than their manager would.   L.....

    If employees set their own standards, they tend to be
    lower than those set by the manager.   M.....

7   The more a person knows about the job and is free
    to make decisions about it, the more you have to keep
    an eye on them to keep them in line.   N.....

    Knowledge of the job and freedom to make decisions
    means fewer controls are needed to ensure competent
    performance.   P.....

8   The restrictions imposed by the job limits the ability
    of people to show imagination and creativity.   Q.....

    In the workplace, people do not use imagination and
    inventiveness because they do not have much of either.   R.....

9   When responsible for their own quality, people tend to
    raise their standards.   T.....

    Quality tends to fall off when it is not supervised and
    imposed on people.   V.....

10 Truth is better than fiction and most people prefer the
    full story no matter whether bad or good.   X.....

    When there is bad news about the organization
    employees prefer the manager to keep it to him/herself
    until it needs to be broken.   Z.....

Scoring

Add up the total points scored for each of the letters in the column below:

A   ....
D   ....
E   ....
G   ....
K   ....
M   ....
N   ....

(Continued)

(Continued)

Q   ....

V   ....

Z   ....

                                = your X score

100 – X score   = your Y score

Score analysis

This simple exercise tells you something about the type of manager that you are. It is based on McGregor's Theory X/Theory Y classifications. If you have a high 'X' scoring then the assumptions that you make about people and the design of work in organizations operate around a certain set of values. The framework you use is one that views the individual in the organization as someone who needs to be directed, avoids responsibility, must be controlled and coerced into effort, and has an inherent dislike of work. If you have a high 'Y' score then your assumptions are that individual and organizational goals can be integrated and that the individual is a person that strives for better performance, has commitment to the organization for whom they work for, and can contribute more than is currently being asked of them.

We would certainly hope that your 'Y' score is higher than your 'X' score as it will assist in your willingness to use some of the ideas and concepts within the ODM. Either way, you should reflect on the scoring that you have just achieved. That score is based on the assumptions you make about individuals in your organization, and hence influences how you go about managing change in organizations.

Where Does Organization Development Come From?

There are a number of broad definitions of the term 'organization development'. However, there is a body of opinion from authors such as, Beckhard, Bennis, Blake and Mouton, French and Bell, Lawler, Schein, Walton, Warner Burke, etc. which regards OD as a process by which the members of an organization can influence change and help the organization achieve its goals. The ultimate aim is to achieve greater organizational effectiveness and this is accomplished by use of a number of different approaches. These set out to unlock issues that are currently hampering performance. The process of facilitation involves a change agent or agents who help members of the organization move forward towards an agreed set of goals and objectives that can then be implemented. This occurs at three levels – individual, group or organization.

The first level is that of the individual and what motivates individuals to higher standards of performance. This emphasizes two areas of thought, need and expectancy theory. Need theory concentrates analysis on issues associated with how jobs are designed for best effect, career development, and human relations training. Expectancy theory concerns itself with needs and rewards systems. The second level is that of the group and inter-group perspective. This emphasizes the importance of group behaviour, group belonging and its effect on the motivation of the individual. The group acts as the major leverage point for change. The third level is organizational. Emphasis is placed on management style and approach, organization structure, and the environment.

To get a better understanding of organization development it is useful to understand its historical progression. Rather than chart the history of the subject from time immemorial, we shall examine the development of OD in a number of subject areas and include a number of authors. We divide these into two phases. The first phase concerns the work of Douglas McGregor leading to theory X and Y, and the work of Eric Trist and Ken Bamforth at the Tavistock Institute which led to the development of socio-technical systems design. The second phase looks at the growth of subject-specific work related to organization development techniques from the 1960s onwards.

McGregor and the human side of enterprise

One of the many starting points for OD comes from the work of Douglas McGregor, author of *The Human Side of Enterprise* (1960) which set the tone for management thought during the 1960s. McGregor worked at the Sloan School of Management at Massachusetts Institute of Technology (MIT) and developed OD programmes for many organizations including Union Carbide and Esso. These training programmes usually took the form of team building events. McGregor along with Beckhard also worked on changing organization structures to enhance teamwork and increase decision making at the shop floor level. They termed this work, organization development. The publication of *The Human Side of Enterprise* clarified the role of management and created the concept of theory X and Y. In this, McGregor classified managers' attitudes and perceptions about the worker and the design of organizations as falling into two categories:

McGREGOR'S ASSUMPTIONS LEADING TO THEORIES X AND Y

Theory X assumptions

1 The average human being has an inherent dislike of work and will avoid it if he can.
2 Because of this human characteristic of dislike of work, most people must be coerced, controlled, directed, threatened with punishment to get them to put forth adequate effort towards the achievement of organizational objectives.
3 The average human being prefers to be directed, wishes to avoid responsibility, has relatively little ambition, wants security above all.

Theory Y assumptions

1 The expenditure of physical and mental effort in work is as natural as play or rest.
2 External control and the threat of punishment are not the only means for bringing about effort towards organizational objectives. Man will exercise self-direction and self-control in the service of objectives to which he is committed.
3 Commitment to objectives is a function of the rewards associated with their achievement.
4 The average human being learns, under proper conditions, not only to accept but to seek responsibility.
5 The capacity to exercise a relatively high degree of imagination, ingenuity and creativity in the solution of organizational problems is widely, not narrowly, distributed in the population.
6 Under the conditions of modern industrial life, the intellectual potentialities of the average human being are only partially utilized.

(Douglas McGregor, *The Human Side of Enterprise*, 1960)

The last exercise you completed placed you in one of the two camps. By creating a form of extremism in terms of management perceptions of the workforce and the design of organizations, McGregor intentionally set out to accomplish a particular objective:

It is not important that management accept the assumptions of Theory Y ... It is important that management abandon limiting assumptions like those of Theory X, so that future inventions with respect to the human side of enterprise will be more than minor changes in already obsolescent conceptions of organized human effort. (McGregor, 1960: 245)

At this point it may be useful to refer back to the exercise you completed and reflect again on which side of the fence you came out. We would suggest that if you came heavily out on the side of Theory X then the use of organization development techniques and the ODM would be difficult for you given its emphasis on participatory management techniques.

The Tavistock Institute and socio-technical systems

Not all theories and practices relevant to the OD model emanated from the United States. At around the same time that McGregor et al. were undertaking research analysis on issues such as, sensitivity training, a second influential body of research work was being undertaken at the Tavistock Institute of Human Relations in London. At Tavistock, researchers such as, Eric Trist, Ken Bamforth and A.K. Rice were developing the model of socio-technical systems design from their research work with Durham coalminers and textile workers at Ahmedabad, India.

The concept of socio-technical systems that resulted has had a great deal of influence on the field of OD as it relates to elements such as, work design and autonomous/semi-autonomous workgroups. The argument they put forward was that any organization exists both as a social and a technical subsystem and that both these subsystems need to be taken into consideration when organizations contemplate change. It is a powerful technique in terms of work design but lacks popularity. One of the reasons for this is that the approach itself directly challenges the status and responsibilities of managers at supervisory levels whose duties can be taken on by self-managing groups. During the 1980s and 1990s as problems within organizations grew in significance the concept received a new lease of life. Radical solutions that call for a redefinition of the management function as well as reorganization of work became more acceptable and gained management credence under these circumstances. However, applications of this particular type of work design model have largely been the prerogative of large, multinational organizations (Buchanan and McCalman 1989: 209–12). The Tavistock model is outlined in Figure 10.1.

In analysing the effectiveness of socio-technical systems and especially the concept of autonomous or semi-autonomous work groups in organizations, Hunt (1979) comments that:

> Probably more than any other method, this approach recognizes the common sense of individuals who for decades have been treated as morons by managers of large organizations.

Three important issues for organization development emerge from the Tavistock studies. We have not done the studies justice here and would suggest that the reader delve deeper into them. However, the three important issues that emerge are:

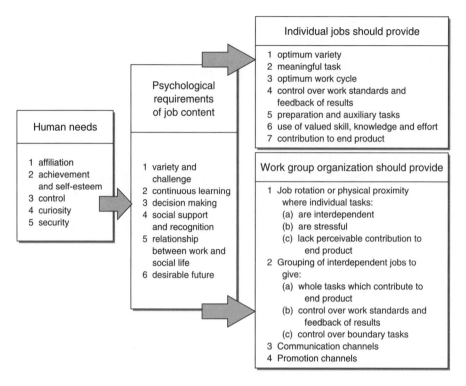

Figure 10.1   The Tavistock work organization model

1   It is managers that make decisions about work organization, job allocations, the formation of groups and the amount of discretion allowed to workers.

2   Mass production techniques can be replaced by alternatives that maintain or even enhance performance whilst offering a better quality of working life.

3   Working in groups is the best form of work organization to meet both technical and social needs within the workplace.

If we relate this to change management and how the OD model can best be used, we argue that: It is managers that make choices about change in organizations. There are also alternatives that they can consider when looking at work design. These alternatives can prove to be more effective. Therefore, the organization development model is about management choice. When faced with change situations within your own organization, you have the opportunity through the OD model to instigate change for the better. This is a choice that many firms in the past have made, and which has led to the use of organization development, as we now know it.

The term *organization development* gained contemporary and pronounced usage at the beginning of the 1960s when a number of researchers and authors dealt with the concepts of instigating change in organizations. They all fall within the area of organization development because of the inter-relatedness of their work, the similarity in the use of methodologies and techniques applied, and the acceptance by many of them for a need to define what was meant by the term. Schein and Beckhard for instance comment that,

> ... a number of us recognised that the rapidly growing field of 'OD' was not well understood or defined. We also recognised that there was no one OD philosophy, and hence one could not at that time write a textbook on the theory and practice of OD, but one could make clear what various practitioners were doing under this label. (Warner Burke, 1994: xvii)

This is precisely what we intend to do here. Because of the development of OD it is more appropriate to analyse this part of the historical progress via the subject material of some of its major proponents. In this instance, we have selected specific areas that we feel best represent what is meant by the OD model that we shall propose later on in this chapter. These areas are: individual motivation at work, job and work design, interpersonal skills in groups, and participative management.

Motivation of the individual

One of the key areas of organization development is understanding human behaviour. The work of writers such as, Victor Vroom (1969) and Edward Lawler (1969) was concerned with what motivated individuals to perform within their organization. Their research work led to the conclusion that motivation was dependent on situational and personality variables. In relation to this, Vroom comments that,

> The situational variables correspond to the amounts of different kinds of outcomes (e.g. pay, influence, variety) provided by the work roles, and the personality variables correspond to individual differences in the strength of their desire or aversion for these outcomes. (Vroom, 1969: 200–8)

Motivation was linked to three factors or assumptions concerning individual behaviour. The first pertained to what the individual saw as the expected outcome of their behaviour. For example, if an individual believes that the accomplishment of a certain task will lead to rewards then they will undertake that behaviour in the expectation that reward will be forthcoming. This belief is classified as performance-outcome expectancy. The second assumption was that the rewards associated with behaviour have a different value (valence) for different individuals. In this sense, what motivates some individuals may not motivate others to the same degree. One individual may place a greater emphasis on monetary gain than another would. Third, individuals had to have a certain degree of belief that their behaviour would have a reasonable chance of success. A manager may believe that he can finish a company report within ten days but his expectation that he can finish it within seven days is very low, no matter how hard he works on it.

Research work on motivation led to the conclusion that the individual would be personally motivated when they perceived that rewards would accrue, where they valued those rewards, and where they believed they could perform at a level where attainment of the rewards was feasible. Vroom also included a fourth variable related to past performance. That is the amount of reward that the individual expected to receive or had received in the past would also influence their behaviour within the organization (1969: 200–8).

Lawler's work also extended into analysis of job design and the importance of issues such as meaningful contribution and feedback in stimulating motivation in the individual. In relation to this, Lawler comments that,

> ... it has been argued that when jobs are structured in a way that makes intrinsic rewards appear to result from good performance then the jobs themselves can be very effective motivators. In addition the point was made that if job content is to be a source of motivation, the job must allow for meaningful feedback, test the individual's valued abilities and allow a great amount of self-control by the job holder. (Lawler, 1969: 425–35).

The work of writers such as, Lawler and Vroom is important in an OD sense because of its emphasis on motivating the individual towards higher standards of performance. Their work is also crucial because its focus of attention is on job design and structure as well as the provision of feedback as mechanisms for enhancing organizational performance. Similarly, their work suggests that reward systems are an important variable in effective OD change processes. These are issues we will look at in greater depth later in this chapter.

Job and work design

Work design is an important part of OD models. The research work in this area, especially that of writers such as, Hackman and Oldham (1975, 1980) looks at work design from a position of need and expectancy theory. The focus of attention, in this instance, is how work design leads to greater worker satisfaction. The variables associated with greater worker satisfaction are:

1 meaningfulness of the work;

2 responsibility for the work and its outcomes;

3 performance feedback.

Hackman and Oldham (1980) attempted to separate the main features of work as being:

> core job dimensions;
>
> critical psychological states, and
>
> employee experience,

to establish a causal link between job implementing concepts such as:

> natural work units;
>
> feedback channels;
>
> core job dimensions, such as task identity and autonomy;
>
> critical psychological states, such as, responsibility for the work and knowledge of the results;
>
> and personal and work outcomes resulting in high internal work motivation, high quality work performance, etc.

Figure 10.2 details the worker motivation, job satisfaction criteria associated with OD.

Interpersonal relations

The work of writers such as Chris Argyris is important to OD because of the emphasis placed on issues related to developing the individual within the organization. Argyris' work falls into two main streams as far as OD is concerned: individual development towards maturity at work and interpersonal relations within the group at work. Argyris argued that what prevents maturity in individuals in the workplace is the

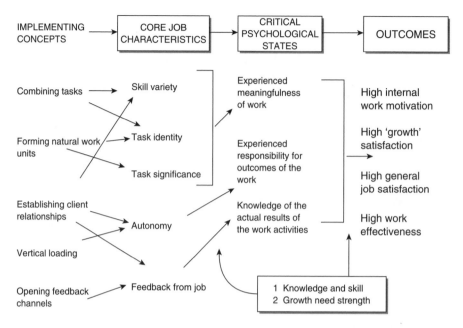

Figure 10.2   The complete job characteristics model

Source: Adapted from J.R. Hackman and G.R. Oldham (1980) *Work Redesign.* Reading, MA: Addison-Wesley

approach of management and the lack of interpersonal competence. Developing on from the work of McGregor, he argued that certain behavioural patterns of management emerge in organizations. A manager may espouse theory Y values but his pattern of behaviour (which Argyris referred to as pattern A) associates his managerial competence with that of theory X (Argyris, 1970). In this sense, management self-perpetuates its own need for control:

> The increased use of management controls deprives employees of any opportunity of participating in the important decisions which affect their working life, leading to feelings of psychological failure. It is not they themselves but the control systems (such as work study and cost accounting) which define, inspect and evaluate the quality and quantity of their performance. (Pugh and Hickson, 1989: 168–9)

In terms of change management, managers adopt a certain model of behaviour. Argyris (1978) and Argyris and Schon (1996) argue that managers seek solutions in the form of a model of behaviour where they:

1   take action based on valid information that has been freely and openly obtained;

2   take action after consultation with those competent and relevant to that action based on their informed and free choice;

3   sustain commitment to the choice made and monitor the preparedness of the organization for change and implementation of change itself.

The appropriateness of this approach for the model of OD we are proposing is clear. The solutions argued by Argyris and Schon assume that the manager in this instance adopts and displays an open and participatory approach to the process of change in organizations. There is a need here to remove the defensiveness associated with control orientation in order to obtain contribution from others likely to be affected by change. To do so, Argyris and Schon argue that the organization needs to be able to call on the assistance of outside agents, another characteristic of OD.

Participative management

Organization design is a key element of the development process. The ability of any organization to design itself to effectively meet the performance criteria which it sets will determine the success or not, of that change effort. Likert (1967) described four models of organization design:

1   *Exploitive authoritative*   Management uses the techniques of fear and threat to control members of the organization. Communication channels are downwards. Management and the workforce are physically and psychologically separate. Most of the decisions affecting the organization are taken at the top of the hierarchy and fed down.

2   *Benevolent authoritative*   Management uses the technique of reward as a control mechanism but the views and opinions of the workforce are subservient to those of management. Communication channels upwards are restricted to what is acceptable to managers. Decisions affecting the organization are taken at the top but may be delegated to lower levels for implementation.

3   *Consultative*   Management uses both rewards and occasional punishments whilst seeking some limited form of involvement. Communication channels are both upward and downward but upward communication is still limited to acceptability on the part of management. Policy is determined at the top with implementation and some limited form of workforce participation occurs at departmental level.

4   *Participative*   Management uses the technique of group rewards to attain participation and involvement of the workforce. High standards of performance, goal setting and improvement

of work methods are all characteristic of the participative organization. Communication channels flow upwards, downwards and horizontally. Decisions are made through group processes and integrated throughout the organization via 'linking pin' individuals who are members of more than one group.

Likert was also primarily responsible for one of the main techniques used in OD models, the survey feedback method. This will be looked at in greater depth when we examine the processes associated with OD.

The Organization Development Model: How Do Organizations Develop Effectively?

We now wish to look at some effective mechanisms and techniques for using organization development. What we are interested in is the concept of organization development, what it can do, and what specifics it can deal with. Here we begin to get into the technicalities or substance of the OD model. For example, in terms of what OD expects to address, French (1969) identified seven objectives behind the use of organization development programmes. These objectives, it was argued,

> ... reflect problems which are very common in organizations:
>
> 1 To increase the level of trust and support among organizational members.
>
> 2 To increase the incidence of confrontation of organizational problems, both within groups and among groups, in contrast to 'sweeping problems under the rug'.
>
> 3 To create an environment in which authority of assigned role is augmented by authority based on knowledge and skill.
>
> 4 To increase openness of communications laterally, vertically, and diagonally.
>
> 5 To increase the level of personal enthusiasm and satisfaction in the organization.
>
> 6 To find synergistic solutions to problems with greater frequency.
>
> 7 To increase the level of self and group responsibility in planning and implementation.
>
> (French, 1969: 23)

Organizational development is about changing the organization from one situation, which is regarded as unsatisfactory, to another by means of social science techniques for change. In terms of organizational change, it is important to remember the concept of anticipation. The manager has to be always thinking ahead. Pugh (1978) argues that the effective manager anticipates change, diagnoses the nature of the change, and then manages the change process. In this, and the next chapter, we argue that the manager is often too near to the problem to be able to anticipate, diagnose, and manage the change him/herself. What is needed is the assistance of an outside agent, either internal to the organization, or brought in specifically for that task.

In terms of managing change, the organization has to follow a five-step process of planned change that moves it through specific phases:

1 *recognition* by senior management that there is a need for change in the organization;

2 establishment of a change *relationship*;

3 *movement* towards the desired change by the organization and its members;

4 *stabilizing* the changes within the organization;

5 allowing the change agent to *move on*.

(Lippit et al., 1958)

When we look at change in organizations it is important to be able to understand why it is taking place. Pugh (1978) argues that there are four principal issues associated with the use of organization development and that to understand the basis of OD, one has to place it within the context of the organization itself.

PUGH'S FOUR PRINCIPLES FOR UNDERSTANDING ORGANIZATIONAL CHANGE

1 *Organizations as organisms*   The organization is not a machine and change must be approached carefully and rationally. Do not make changes too frequently because they become dysfunctional or cosmetic.

2 *Organizations are occupational and political systems*   The reaction to change relates to what is best for the firm, how it affects individuals and groups, and how it affects the power, prestige and status of individuals and groups.

3 *Members of an organization operate in occupational, political and rational systems at the same time*   Arguments for and against change will be presented using rational argument as well as occupational and political considerations.

(Continued)

(Continued)

4 *Change occurs most effectively where success and tension combine*
   Two factors are important here, confidence and motivation to change.
   Successful individuals or groups will have the confidence to change
   aspects of their work, which are creating problems. Unsuccessful members of the organization are difficult to change because to protect
   themselves they will use their rigidity.

Having established some basic principles related to the organization and
how its members will react to, anticipate and deal with change, it is now
useful to look at what attributes the model of organizational development has. Margulies and Raia (1978) identify 13 characteristics common
to organization development:

1   It is a total organizational system approach.

2   It adopts a systems approach to the organization.

3   It is positively supported by top management.

4   It uses third party change agents to develop the change process.

5   It involves a planned change effort.

6   It uses behavioural science knowledge to instigate change.

7   It sets out to increase organizational competence.

8   It is a long term change process.

9   It is an ongoing process.

10 It relies on experiential learning techniques.

11 It uses action research as an intervention model.

12 It emphazises goal setting and action planning.

13 It focuses on changing attitudes, behaviours and performance of groups or teams in the
    organization rather than individuals.

(Margulies and Raia, 1978)

Combining these characteristics with those mentioned by Lippit et al.,
French, and Pugh, we can put forward the following definition of
organization development:

DEFINITION

Organization development is an ongoing process of change aimed at resolving issues through the effective diagnosis and management of the organization's culture. This development process uses behavioural and social science techniques and methodologies through a consultant facilitator and employs action-research as one of the main mechanisms for instigating change in organizational groups.

This means that we are dealing with a philosophy of managing change that involves a number of skills and practices. It is hoped that you will be stimulated to enhance your knowledge of the subject area further and to that end we have recommended a number of OD publications.

When considering using OD as a means of managing change in the organization you need to be aware of its characteristics:

1 The focus is on interdependencies and not on the individual. Therefore, teamwork is encouraged.

2 A climate for change is sought rather than superimposed unilaterally.

3 Interpersonal relationships are built upon using behavioural science techniques for example, role playing, problem solving exercises.

4 Goals relate to communication, decision making and problem solving.

5 The value system is humanistic aimed at maximizing development and encouraging open relationships in the organization.

The organizational development process is a tricky one to get hold of. It means sometimes having to re-evaluate how you manage people to get the best from them. It means looking at change with an open mind, laying down preconceptions about change.

READER ACTIVITY

The following exercise is adapted from Huse (1975). Rule number one is to be honest with yourself. Do not try to second-guess the answers from what you think is wanted. Read carefully through the statements below and consider what your views on these are. As you read through each statement, you should allocate a mark to the statement depending on whether you agree with it or not. Mark your view in the column to the right using the following five-point scale:

(Continued)

(Continued)

5 Strongly agree
4 Agree
3 Neutral
2 Disagree
1 Strongly disagree

1   Personal growth is the engine that drives organization performance. This is best provided within an open and challenging environment.

   _____

2   The individual does not work in a vacuum and prefers to work within and is influenced by groups at the workplace.

   _____

3   The way organizations go about design lead to clashes of personality that are not of the individual's own making.

   _____

4   Work groups increase effectiveness by attaining individual needs and organizational requirements. Leadership in this instance is of a participatory nature.

   _____

5   Not considering people's feelings is likely to hinder leadership, communications and organizational effectiveness.

   _____

6   The formal organization forces people to conform. This prevents individual growth, innovation and wastes talent.

   _____

7   People are the most important asset an organization has; yet they are demotivated in formal organizations and do not take on more responsibility.

   _____

8   When problems arise in the organization the ability to be open and honest in discussion helps both the individual concerned and the organization as a whole.

   _____

9   To be effective, organizations have to enhance the level of interpersonal trust and co-operation amongst individuals at all levels.

   _____

10 The way we structure and design the organization can reflect the needs of the individual, the group, and the organization as a whole.

   _____

SCORING

Your rating of the items will give you an indication of your willingness to consider using OD techniques to manage change. First calculate your total score on the 10 items in the table. The range of total scores goes from 10 to 50; the higher the score, the more you are in agreement with OD values. The following scoring brackets indicate where you, as a manager lie in terms of willingness to use OD as a model for change:

Score   Rating

40–50   You are largely in agreement with the principles and practices associated with OD. The way you feel about managing the organization, the people within the organization and the concept attaining effective change is inline with basic organization development principles. You may pass GO and collect £200.

25–39   You agree with most of the OD principles and are quite willing to experiment with the concept for overall development of your organization. Some doubts as to the efficacy of some of the ideas, but a willingness to experiment. Pass GO and collect your £200 next time round.

10–20   You have serious doubts about the basic concepts of organization development. You are willing to give some attention to the concepts but basically you want to see some evidence before being fully convinced. Do not pass GO. Do not collect £200.

< 10   Go straight to JAIL, do not pass GO, do not even think of collecting £200! You probably know all the answers to *Trivial Pursuit*!

Organizations that use the OD process can be seen as falling into two 'black and white' categories. The 'white' category relates to the organization that has a well-defined OD strategy. This is tied into its overall business strategy and is used continuously as a mechanism of stimulating change at all levels. As with many innovative management practices, OD has been used more often in the United States, and by larger corporations facing constant change. In the 'black' category we have the organization, in such an internal mess that it needs to call on OD to address resistance to change. Resistance to change reflects bad management of the process of change. Where it does occur there are a number of factors that may help recover what is seen as a lost position.

The Organization Development Process

Organizational development, as it suggests, is about trying to progress change through more than one element within the firm. It is viewed very much as a long term, strategic mechanism for initiating change that places emphasis on the process of attaining change.

The purpose of training people in OD techniques is to help increase the organizational effectiveness by providing expertise and skilled resources. The amount of change that is undertaken is reflective of the environment of the firm. The type of work, the type and mix of skills, structures and systems, response times, performance measurement of operating units and people, and the way in which different parts of the organization are designed and operate are all factors which will have a bearing on organizational effectiveness. The main essence of organizational development is trying to maintain control over an organization that is in constant change.

A LEADING AMERICAN ELECTRONICS MULTINATIONAL'S JUSTIFICATION FOR A $300,000 OD TRAINING PROGRAMME

Why organization development is so important.

1 The volume of change in many organizations is massive.
2 The economic scene places demands on managers while they are reluctant to change from tried and tested methods.
3 The role of management is changing and new models are needed.
4 Change management takes time.
5 Some changes challenge basic assumptions – for example, the role of supervisory staff.
6 The need for control remains – the skill is remaining in control when so much change is going on.
7 More comprehensive strategic pictures are needed which integrate different changes in the organization and alleviate confusion.
8 Organization design and re-design are *as important and necessary as* product, process or system design and are the responsibility of management and people in organizations, not just specialists.

By this point you will have reached the stage where you understand that change in the organization requires both planning and management. It doesn't occur on an ad hoc basis. There is a role for the social sciences in instigating change in organizations, and organizational development is one of the key methods of instigating and attaining successful change. There are four situations where organizational development is needed:

1   The current nature of the organization is leading to a failure to achieve objectives.

2   Change is required to react faster to external alterations.

3   Where the introduction of factors such as new technology requires change in the organization itself.

4   Where the introduction of change allows a new approach to be adopted.

It was suggested earlier that you test your own values and assumptions concerning organizational development. Similarly, the importance of factors such as group work have been expressed as important elements of OD. The important point to note here is that change is a continuous process of confrontation, identification, evaluation and action. The key here is what is referred to in OD as an *action-research model*. French (1969) argued that this model involved collaboration between the consultant (who could be an internal or external change agent, as we shall see in Chapter 11) and the client group towards data gathering, data discussion, action planning and action. Figure 10.3 details French's action research model for organization development.

The Organizational Development Matrix

One of the important aspects of change is developing an appropriate strategy. This involves creating a matrix of change diagnosis and initiation associated with behaviour, structure and context at four levels, the organization as a whole, inter-group, group, and individual levels. The importance of this matrix concerns the two main factors that have to be identified in the organizational development process. These are:

At what level do we focus our analysis?

How much change has to take place?

Figure 10.4 details an organization development matrix conceptualized and developed by Pugh (1986). The matrix is one the keys for organizations in developing their OD strategy. Go over the matrix slowly at first and be prepared to break it into its constituent parts. It will be useful to do so by writing it out several times in individual areas. For example, take a specific case from your own organization (you will probably be able to cite an example at the individual level fairly easily) and work through the matrix.

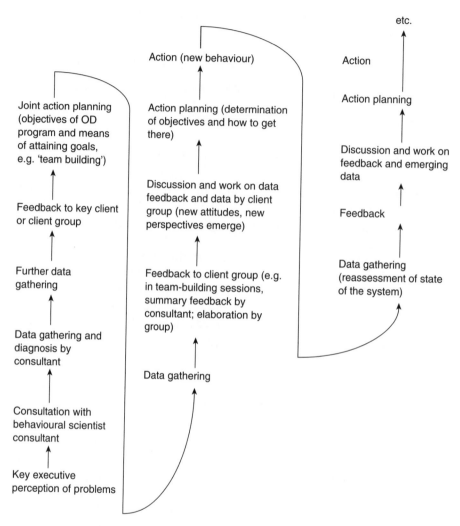

Figure 10.3   The action research model

Source: Copyright 1969 by the Regents of the University of California. Reprinted from *California Management Review*, XII(2):26, Figure 1. By permission of the Regents.

If we were to identify any one part as being crucial to your understanding of organizational development – this is it! Pugh's analysis of the most common strategies used in OD provides an excellent example of diagnosing and initiating change. These are strategies that apply to organizational development, which depend on the level within the organization at which change is contemplated, and the approaches taken which correspond to these levels. Action at the organizational level is

Diagnosis and methods of initiation of change

	Behaviour (What is happening how?)	Structure (What is the required system?)	Context (What is the setting?)
Organizational level	General climate of poor morale, pressure, anxiety, suspicion, lack of awareness of, or response to, environmental changes. *survey feedback, organizational mirroring*	Systems goals – poorly defined or inappropriate; strategy inappropriate and misunderstood; organization structure inappropriate; centralization, divisionalization, standardization: inadequacy of environmental monitoring mechanisms. *change the structure*	Geographical setting, market pressures, labour market, physical conditions, basic technology. *change strategy, location, physical set-up; culture (by saturation OD)*
Inter-group level	Lack of effective co-operation between sub-units, conflict, excessive competition, limited war, failure to confront differences in priorities, unresolved feelings. *inter-group confrontation (with third party as consultant), role negotiation*	Lack of integrated task perspective; sub-unit optimization, required interaction difficult to achieve. *redefine responsibilities, change reporting relationships, improve co-ordination and liaison mechanisms*	Different sub-unit values, life style, physical distance. *reduce psychological and physical distance; exchange roles, attachments, cross-functional social overlay*
Group level	Inappropriate working relationships, atmosphere, participation, poor understanding and acceptance of goals, avoidance, inappropriate leadership style, leader not trusted, respected; leader in conflict with peers and superiors. *process consultation team building*	Task requirements poorly defined; role relationships unclear or inappropriate; leader's role overloaded, inappropriate reporting procedures. *redesign work relationships, (socio-technical systems), autonomous working groups*	Insufficient resources, poor group composition for cohesion, inadequate physical set-up, personality clashes. *change technology, layout, group composition*

Continued

	Behaviour (What is happening how?)	Structure (What is the required system?)	Context (What is the setting?)
Individual level	Failure to fulfil individual's needs; frustration responses; unwillingness to consider change, little chance for learning and development. *counselling, role analysis, career planning*	Poor job definition, task too easy or too difficult. *job restructuring/ modification, redesign, enrichment, MbO*	Poor match of individual with job, poor selection or promotion, inadequate preparation and training, recognition and remuneration at variance with objectives. *personnel changes improved selection and promotion procedures, improved training and education, bring recognition and remuneration in line with objectives*

There are two dimensions to the matrix which represent the two main factors that have to be identified during the diagnosis stage of the OD process: level of analytical focus and degree of required intervention.

Figure 10.4   The organization development matrix (Pugh, 1986)

Source: 'Organization development training: proposal for skills council funding' (an in-house proposal for training managers in OD techniques and capabilities)

likely to be different from that at the individual level, although there are areas where overlap exists. There are a number of aspects of the matrix that you may be unfamiliar with. For example, Table 10.1 details some of the methods of initiating change.

If there is one underlying theme of organizational development, then it is related to the need to be able to manage change. Taking care of the process by which an organization moves from an unsatisfactory state of affairs, through the recognition of this, identification of alternatives, communicating these and receiving feedback, educating the changes required, reviewing development in the light of experience, and progressing the change process forward is both a lengthy and messy process. Therefore, there is a need to manage this positively. Organizations go through what can best be described as interlocking layers of perpetual change management which reflect aspects such as the trigger layer where opportunity or threat triggers responses for change in the organization. This can sometimes create a vision of where the organization might be able to go. This visionary state then has to be communicated to individuals and groups and their commitment gained. Having gone through this process of change, what can best be described as a maintenance and renewal layer closes up the loop. Revision of what the organization sets out to do, and whether this is appropriate at this point in time leads to a further process of change analysis. This is related to the basic rules for managing a change process:

Table 10.1 Methods of initiating change in organizations

Method	Level	Explanation
Survey feedback	Organization	Organization-wide review of attitudes and morale used as basis for discussion of change
Inter-group confrontation (Third party present)	Inter-group	Bringing together groups in presence of an external consultant to discuss and attain change
Role negotiation	Inter-group/individual	Review process on the appropriate areas of concern for individuals and groups and levels of interaction between groups
Cross-functional social overlay	Inter-group	Attaining movement between groups which enhances cohesion through continuous interaction
Process consultation	Group/individual	Review of work patterns and relationships to develop effective organization forms
Redesign work relationships (socio-technical systems)	Group	Effective co-ordination of people and technology in organization for a 'best fit' solution
Autonomous work groups	Group	Self-managing team approach to job design

Rule 1   Establish that there is a need.
Rule 2   Think it through thoroughly.
Rule 3   Discuss it informally with those likely to be affected.
Rule 4   Encourage the expression of all objections.
Rule 5   Make sure you are willing to undertake change yourself.
Rule 6   Monitor the changes and reinforce them at all points.

Phases of an OD Intervention

In terms of the process of OD, there are a number of phases that an organization will go through. Lewin (1958) describes these as unfreezing, changing, and refreezing the organization into its new state. Warner Burke (1994: 72) identifies seven phases which the organization experiences during a typical OD change process. These are described below with appropriate examples, from our own experience.

Phase 1: entry

At this point an initial contact is made between the organization and the consultant to begin the entry phase. There may be many reasons for this initial contact, but largely this will be based on the organization's initiative, as it has perceived a need for change. Both the organization and the consultant will explore the issues and establish a rapport or capability for working on the OD intervention. From the organization's perspective it has to be sure that it has the right person for the job and whether they will be able to work with the consultant. The consultant also has a number of criteria that have to be satisfied. These relate to factors such as, whether they can work with the organization, whether or not there is a readiness for change, the motivation and values of the individual(s) calling on the consultant, their position power within the organization as a leverage point for instigating change, and the amount of resources at hand for change (Warner Burke, 1994: 73).

It is also useful for both the consultant and the organization to check that there is a clear understanding of the roles to be adopted by each prior to the establishment of the contract stage. In our experience it is useful to leave the first meeting and then provide the client with a copy of what we understand to be the salient points of the meeting and how both consultant and organization should proceed. This should be done as soon as possible after the first contact to maintain the flow and to check for any possible misinterpretations on the part of either party.

Phase 2: formalizing the contact

The second phase is the drafting of a contract that explains and clarifies what will be done. This is a two-way process in which the consultant lays out what they intend to do but which also explains what the organization is contracting to do. At this point, the client organization will internally discuss the consultant's proposal with its key people and may propose amendments before agreeing the terms. We would encourage organizations to view this phase as similar to any other negotiations that take place with any other type of supplier. Unless the consultant has a clear specification of what the client desires in terms of an OD intervention, then they are unsure of issues such as, what each expects of the other, how much time will be involved, the associated costs and the ground rules which will operate. Most organizations treat the OD intervention by an external consultant in this way, even to the point of issuing a purchase order.

Phase 3: information gathering and analysis

Having successfully negotiated a contract, it is then up to the consultant in conjunction with the client to begin the diagnosis phase. There are two important elements here – getting the information required and being able to make sense of it. However, the two do not necessarily follow on from one another. The consultant will have begun the diagnosis phase from the initial entry point based on the information gathered, observations, gut feelings about the state of play in the organization, and in many cases from previous experience with other similar issues. French and Bell comment that, 'organization development is at heart an action program based on valid information about the status quo, current problems and opportunities, and effects of actions as they relate to goal achievement. An OD program thus starts with diagnosis and continuously employs data collecting and data analysing throughout' (1998: 63).

Formal information gathering is therefore necessary and this usually comes in the form of interviews, staff surveys and organization records associated with the issue being analysed. Margerison argues that this is a crucial stage in terms of what could be considered the diplomacy and partiality displayed on the part of the consultant related to whom they gather information from:

> A former colleague once gave me a phrase which has stuck with me as an important principle in all my work. 'Selection implies rejection' he said. This is absolutely right. Make sure you don't offend people by ignoring their opinion. (1988: 64)

We would recommend that when gathering data, the consultant whether, internal or external glean information from all those likely to be affected by the OD change programme, from a political and/or content perspective.

Phase 4: feedback

Having gathered the data, it is then up to the consultant to analyse it, summarize the information, and organize it into a format which can be readily understood by the organization's members to enable action to take place based on that information. This is the point where the OD consultant will use their previous experience to draw conclusions, from what they have observed, to feedback data in a form, which is both understandable and acceptable, to the organization and gets the necessary messages across. We would recommend two mechanisms for accomplishing these tasks: first, the preparation of a report of the work carried out and the consultant's conclusions from this, issues for the future and proposals for change. This is distributed to all who took part in the data gathering stage for their information and commentary, and acts as a further source of information or feedback. The second is a presentation to the management body initiating the OD change programme. This is likely to include those to be affected by any change proposals and the consultant needs to be prepared to enter into what one might consider a 'lion's den' on many occasions. The important point here is to facilitate discussion of the data being presented.

The feedback session must contain three basic elements – summary of the data gathered and the consultant's initial analysis, a general discussion which clarifies points of confusion that may have arisen on the organization's side, and interpretation of what has taken place and how this will be carried forward. The consultant must also be flexible during this process as changes to their analysis and interpretation will often be generated in light of the feedback session.

Phase 5: planning the change process

This is the second stage of the change programme – the action phase of the OD intervention. The basis of all OD programmes is to improve the organization's processes from what they are now, to what they will be in the future – the unfreezing, change, refreezing process. There are two possibilities here. First, the planning for change stage may take place towards the end of the feedback session as the consultant and organization get a clearer picture of the steps that are likely to be needed. However, for more complex, larger organization development issues the planning process may be lengthened in time and incorporate those likely to be involved in the process itself. The whole point of the planning for change phase is to look at what alternative actions there are open to the organization in terms of response to the feedback given by the consultant, and to consider the best way forward or plan of action to take.

We would recommend that the consultant move through this phase in collaboration with the organization in order to gain commitment to both the plans for change and their implementation. The consultant should act both as an idea generator, putting forward alternatives and getting the organization to consider the consequences of each proposal, and as a sounding board for the organization's proposals for the way forward, using his/her experiences of similar attempts at change. This is a crucial

phase, but it is the organization, above all, that has to live with the consequences of decisions made during this phase. They should need to fully
agree with the proposals for the way forward.

Phase 6: implementing the changes

Once the organization has decided what action it will take then the
implementation of change can take place. The consultant may or may not
be involved at this stage depending on the actions to be taken, the degree
of experience required within the organization to take these actions, and
the consultant's own assessment of his/her role at this stage. We would
suggest here that the consultant, even if not actively involved in the
intervention phase, keep an eye on the development of this phase. It is
difficult to force an organization to change; those most likely to be negatively impacted by change will resist the strongest. As Warner Burke
noted, 'the OD practitioner continues to work with the client system to
help make the intervention successful' (1994: 78). This is most effectively
done with the consultant still involved as most failures at the implementation stage result from unanticipated consequences of the change
process and it is here that the consultant may be able to help anticipate
likely outcomes.

Phase 7: assessment

The final phase of the OD process of change is to evaluate the results of
what has taken place. Margerison (1988) argues that this should take the
form of a review and that the principle of establishing a review stage
would assist in preventing all the previous work going astray. The
process of assessment also assists the change effort by focusing attention
on what has taken place. In our introduction to this book we referred to
the layers of transition management. The final layer was associated with
maintenance and renewal. The assessment phase is useful here in looking at what has gone, what the current state of play is, and what action
steps need to be taken to move the organization forward.

Guiding Values and Philosophy

Before moving on to an analysis of the role of the consultant in the OD
change process, it is worthwhile considering what we have looked at
over the last two chapters. It is crucial here to summarize why we place
such emphasis on people management and the OD process of change.

This is a guiding value and belief that organizations should have as the cornerstone of their operating philosophy – all successful organizations do. Margulies and Raia (1972: 3) argue that the values of a fully functioning organization could be stated as:

1 Providing opportunities for people to function as human beings rather than resources in the productive process.

2 Providing opportunities for each organizational member, as well as the organization itself, to develop to full potential.

3 Seeking to increase the effectiveness of the organization in terms of all its goals.

4 Attempting to create an environment in which it is possible to find exciting and challenging work.

5 Providing opportunities for people in organizations to influence the way in which they relate to work, the organization, and the environment.

6 Treating each human being as a person with a complex set of needs, all of which are important in work and in life.

Individually, we each have our own sets of values or personal philosophy for life. However, for the organization this is often lacking. The organization needs a philosophy, a description of basic principles guiding its behaviour. The values are the beliefs that flow from these basic principles. Philosophy and values apply to human behaviour in organizations. All organizations have their own philosophy and values about human behaviour but seldom are these charted and used as a guide to organization design and development, as a guide to managerial and people policies, or as a checklist for daily practice.

We make no apologies for repeating what Megson (1988) describes as examples of the beliefs inherent in two plants:

> They are based on a philosophy that I describe as follows: People are the most important asset we have. They want and need to grow – without growth interest wanes and talents waste away, with growth interest flourishes and talents develop. People really do care; they do exquisite work if it is designed to enable them to grow. *In other words, personal growth is the engine that drives organization performance.*

Through the process of organization development it is possible to put expressions of values and philosophy such as these into practice at individual, group and organizational levels – to let the engine itself develop enough momentum that it drives effective performance. Margulies and

Raia sum this up as, 'the usefulness and effectiveness of OD is dependent upon the degree to which organizational values become consistent with the core values of organizational development' (1988: 9).

In the next chapter we describe the role of the consultant or change agent in the OD model. The consultant can either be internal or external to the organization depending on the level of experience with OD techniques, the strategy being adopted, and the level of change. What the consultant is, however, is the driver – the change agent. They drive the change process, and as such occupy a linchpin role.

11 | The Objective Outsider

The use of organization development in stimulating and implementing change rests very much on the way it is handled. The successful use of the ODM is influenced by a number of factors, not least of which are the purpose and process of change itself. One of the key underpinnings of this process is the role of the consultant acting as a facilitator of change. More often than not, an outsider is needed to move the part of the organization contemplating change to its new position. However, this outsider may well come from another part of the organization and thus be an internal figure. To this end, we prefer the term change agent. Whether internal or external, the change agent facilitates change in the particular area in which it is needed.

Why is an outsider needed? What does facilitation mean? Why bother when the manager of the department in question knows what they want and knows how to get there? Good questions! But again the underlying assumption is that of pre-destination – the manager, in his or her infinite wisdom knows best. Schein (1988) argues that managers in organizations need assistance in managing the process of change in order that they learn how to do it more effectively the next time round. He cites seven reasons for using a change agent:

1 Clients/managers often do not know what is wrong and need special help in diagnosing what their problems actually are.

2 Clients/managers often do not know what kinds of help consultants can give to them; they need to be helped to know what kind of help to seek.

3 Most clients/managers have a constructive intent to improve things, but they need help in identifying what to improve, and how to improve it.

4 Most organizations can be more effective than they are if they learn to diagnose and manage their own strengths and weaknesses.

5 A consultant probably cannot, without exhaustive and time-consuming study or actual participation in the client organization, learn enough about the culture of the organization

to suggest reliable new courses of action. Therefore, unless remedies are worked out jointly with members of the organization who do know what will and will not work in their culture, such remedies are likely either to be wrong or be resisted because they come from an outsider.

6   Unless the client/manager learns to see the problem for himself and thinks through the remedy, he will not be able to implement the solution and, more importantly, will not learn to fix such problems should they recur.

7   The essential function of process consultation is to pass on the skills of how to diagnose and remedy organizational problems so that the client is more able to continue on his own to improve the organization.

Regardless of where the trigger comes from it has to be viewed as a destabilizing agent and has to be taken seriously. Kudray and Kleiner (1997) suggest that to recognize the impact of change triggers early, every organization should have a change agent who is typically a member of staff who assists in the initiation and implementation of the change process. These individuals are deemed crucial in minimizing the resistance to change. People generally tend to have a low tolerance to change and as such will resist a change even when they think it is a good one.

When we look at who should be a change agent, we are concerned with the personality and style of the individual. Margulies and Raia (1972) note that there are three attributes that the individual needs to enable them to take on a consulting role in the area of organization development:

1   *Personality*   As a result of the need to establish, maintain and work on relationships with people within the organization, the change agent needs to show an awareness and sensitivity to social issues. This means more than it actually says. The change agent has to feel comfortable with people, that is, have an ability to get on well with people, and be able to understand and recognize their worries and fears as well as their hopes and aspirations. In particular, you must not pay scant or transient attention to fears and aspirations as part of the process of accomplishing the change task. To do so, the change agent has to have an ability to listen to others and show empathy. This means that the change agent has to have numerous people-oriented skills. In essence, this is flair or a natural empathy. The theory X manager, described in Chapter 10 has few of these skills.

2   *Change agents require both analytical and diagnostic skills*   This enables them to identify and solve problems by using techniques that are available to them to facilitate the change process. However, change agents have to be conscious that they are using these skills as part of the change process and not as an exploitative mechanism, as a means of going through the motions.

3   *Finally, change agents need to have client-related experience*   The, 'been there, done that' school of experience related to expertise.

There is a degree of both expertise and facilitation associated with the change agent. The change agent has to come from outside the social system where change is being contemplated. The reasons for this are fairly straightforward. It allows the individual to have an unbiased viewpoint of the need for change, and also allows them to take a non-controversial line in considering actions for change. In addition, this is a mechanism that allows for all views within the change setting to be taken into consideration. The potential change agent has to be able to recognize and reconcile what type of person they intend being. Change agents like most managers are people occupying a role for a particular period of time. To do so, they have to be able to determine what that role entails.

What Type of Change Agent is Required?

The first issue that needs to be clarified when looking at the role played by the change agent in the change process is how that role is defined and implemented. The type of role adopted has a significant bearing on the results that one can expect to achieve using the organization development model. The most widely used model by organization development practitioners is that of a collaborative approach which helps the client organization define, understand and act on process events which occur within their own environment (Schein, 1988). There are a number of characteristics associated with this model, which follow on from Schein's assessment of the need for a joint change agent/client relationship. Margulies and Raia (1978: 111) argue that these are based upon the following assumptions and beliefs:

1   Managers often do not know what is wrong and need special help in diagnosing what their problems actually are.

2   They do not know what kinds of help to seek. Consequently, they need help in this regard.

3   Organizations can be more effective if they learn how to diagnose their own strengths and weaknesses.

4   The consultant cannot hope to learn all he or she needs to know about the culture of an organization to suggest reliable solutions. Therefore, it is necessary to work jointly with organization members who *do* know.

5   Since the decision is the client's, it is important that the client learns to see the problem clearly, to share in the diagnosis, and to be actually involved in generating solutions.

6   The consultant is an expert on how to diagnose processes and how to establish effective supportive relationships with clients. Effective process consultation involves passing on *both* of these skills to the client system.

(Margulies and Raia, 1978: 111)

Based on these assumptions, what might one traditionally view as the role of the consultant? The popular view of the consultant is that associated with the doctor–patient model of consultation. In this model, the organization brings in a consultant to find out what is wrong with it and the consultant then recommends change. This type of expert–client relationship has a number of problems when applied in an organization development setting. For one, it may hamper the individual's willingness to open up to the doctor. The patient is not totally involved in the diagnostic process and therefore, feels left out of the solution. Finally, the patient may be unable to understand the proposed solution or the mechanisms of achieving it.

Lippit and Lippit (1975) argue that the behaviour of the change agent runs along a continuum of eight different roles depending on whether the change agent is being directive or non-directive. These roles are not mutually exclusive and may vary according to the stage the change project has reached. They range from advocate, technical specialist, trainer or educator on the directive side to collaborator in problem solving, alternative identifier, fact finder, process specialist and reflector on the non-directive side. What Lippit and Lippit emphasize is the multiple role nature of the change agent, the situational focus which determines these roles, and the need to work in close conjunction with the client organization no matter what role is being used.

Tearle (2007) argues that it is difficult for an individual to be skilled in all these roles. For those who are, she argues that they have a number of attributes which classify these individuals as change masters. The ideal change master would have the following qualities:

- common sense, and the courage to use it;

- credibility and trust – the ability to work at all levels in the organization;

- a wide range of business knowledge – preferably someone with experience in three or four different areas, or an MBA, or a general management experience;

- knowledge of change management;

- the ability to work with teams of people both inside and outside the organization; this includes the ability to work with people across all departments;

- the ability to do very unstructured work;

- creativity – the ability to customize design processes to meet the goals of the organization;

- self-confidence offset by humility;

- facilitation skills;

- design skills;

- coaching skills;

- a love of innovation and new ways of doing things;

- a sense of humour and a sense of fun;

- a spirit of caring;

- the ability to inspire people – to bring out the magic within every individual and every team.

The collaborative nature of the process model of organization development defines the role to be adopted by the change agent. When taking up this role the change agent needs to be fully aware of a number of key criteria. First, in defining the problem the change agent works with the client organization to verify this. Second, the relationship between change agent and client is crucial to developing the change process and needs to be nurtured and developed. Third, the change agent's focus of attention is in helping the client organization discover and implement solutions to the problem. Fourth, the change agent's expertise is in diagnosing and facilitating the process of change – steering the organization through. Fifth, the change agent helps the organization improve its own diagnostic and problem solving skills. Finally, the change agent assists the organization to a position where it can manage change itself (Margulies and Raia, 1978: 113).

The effective change agent takes on a number of roles:

- to help the organization define the problem by asking for definition of what it is;

- to help the organization examine what causes the problem and diagnose how this can be overcome;

- to assist in getting the organization to offer alternative solutions;

- to provide direction in the implementation of alternative solutions;

- to transmit the learning process that allows the client to deal with change on an ongoing basis in the future.

The type of change agent you are is dependent on the change situation with which you are faced. Broadly speaking, the change agent will tread a line between expert and process facilitator depending on their individual approach to the process, the skills and competencies which they possess, the values and assumptions they make about change in the organization, and their own personal characteristics. However, the experience of the organization in terms of its past dealings with change, their willingness to change, and the size and complexity of the problem will also influence the change process. Early on in the process the role of the change agent is that of information-seeker. As the process develops and solutions emerge, the role of the change agent becomes one of being more directive in terms of moving the organization through learning to the accomplishment of new procedures that solve the particular problem. In general, the change agent should try taking a position within the process that serves to assist the organization in every way possible. This involves assessment of problems, attempts at resolution and implementation issues.

Moving Towards Change

In Chapter 10 we noted that there were four situations where organization development is needed:

1   The current nature of the organization is leading to failure to meet objectives.

2   Change is required to react faster to external alterations.

3   Where the introduction of one form of change (for example, new technology) requires change in other parts of the organization (work organization, reward systems, etc.).

4   Where the introduction of change acts as the trigger for consideration of other new approaches.

We would like to give you the opportunity here to look at a situation where a change process has to be managed, and ask you to work your way through it, in terms of how you, as a potential change agent, would approach this situation. This is to be treated as a non-threatening, simulated example. There isn't a right answer to it, but there are a number of different approaches, each with their own consequences. Read through the case described below, and think about how *you* would tackle this situation.

READER ACTIVITY: MAKING FRIENDS AT QUILTCO

Making friends at Quiltco.
Bob Smeaton, the Managing Director of Quiltco, a West Midlands textile manufacturer, was quite pleased with himself. It was Friday afternoon and his flight from Tokyo was just about to land at Heathrow. In conjunction with his Sales Director, Peter Wilson, he had just returned from Japan where he had managed to successfully complete negotiations on a £2.5 million order from the Japanese golfing equipment manufacturer, Kokuna. The order was for the manufacture of a new range of golf sweaters and accessories and was the biggest single order that the company had dealt with in their five-year history. They had come up

(Continued)

(Continued)

against stiff competition from other sportswear manufacturers in the United Kingdom and Japan.

To secure the order, Quiltco had to promise delivery of the first batch of newly designed golf wear within six weeks and bulk order shipments of 10,000 pullovers every two months. This created a problem. At maximum production, Quiltco could only manufacture and meet these order requirements by dropping 80 per cent of its ongoing business. It also meant that three new computer controlled manufacturing machines and a new computer aided design system would be put to work to come up with the new styles and design and to manufacture the sweaters. These had been recently purchased at great expense. The problem was who would operate the machinery and design systems to meet the order requirements, and what to do with Quiltco's current workload.

Still it had been a good trip and Bob had the weekend to plan the future development of the company.

Patricia Kennedy, Production Director at Quiltco was called into the board meeting on the Monday morning. 'It's like this Pat', said Bob Smeaton, 'We need the new designs in a matter of weeks and they have to be computer-generated to fit straight into our new machinery. Our people haven't been trained on them yet so we'll have to subcontract this to some freelance designers who specialize in this field. They'll do the designs for us and we should be able to meet the six week deadline with some ease.'

Patricia paused, 'So who is going to actually make all these lovely new golf sweaters then, and who will tell Parks and Dencing that we can't provide them with any knitwear for the next nine months? You just can't tell the design shop that they are surplus to requirements for the next couple of weeks, and then tell P&D that we're sorry but they'll just have to wait. That's not how we do business is it?'

Bob's reply was succinct and to the point, 'Pat, this is a new millennium. If this company is going to survive it has to become an international concern. Sure, P&D are a big contract for us but we'll deal with that problem when it arises. As for the designers, I'm going to have a meeting with all operating staff this afternoon and let them have the good news.'

Work stopped at Quiltco at 4.30 p.m. that day. Bob Smeaton accompanied by Peter Wilson and Patricia Kennedy addressed the staff in the company cafeteria. Bob started off in ebullient mood, 'Well the situation facing us is one that I'm sure other companies would like to be in. I am sure you are aware by now that we have managed to win the biggest order in this company's short history, with the Japanese golfing company, Kokuna. This assures our future and means that jobs are secure. However, it does put us all under a bit of pressure. To this end I have made arrangements for an outside design and production team to join us temporarily to design and manufacture the Kokuna sweaters on our new equipment. This should allow the rest of you to carry on your normal duties allowing us to meet the tight deadlines Kokuna have set. The outside team will be independent but will gradually bring in our own staff on design and production matters when they feel that the time to pass on the contract is right. To me it's the best of both world's and with a little bit of a squeeze we can do both the Kokuna work and satisfy the needs of our other customers like P&D. There are some good times ahead, lots of hard work but I'm sure you'll agree with me that it'll be worth the struggle in the end?'

Smeaton's comments were met initially with stunned silence. However, it did not take long for murmuring to begin. The first came from one of the designers, 'Are you saying that we aren't good enough to do the design for the new sweaters?' 'Yeah, and we can't handle the new machinery so we'll buy in some smart Alecs from outside, is that it?' The meeting soon deteriorated into a slanging match from the floor with comments such as, 'We're only good for the simple stuff', 'Who are these outsiders anyway?, and 'Don't you trust us to be able to deliver this for you?'

As the meeting finally began to get out of hand, Bob Smeaton turned to the assembled group and said, 'Who do you people think you are? We bring in the biggest order we've ever had and all you can think about is yourselves. Obviously we'll have to get this situation resolved before we go anywhere.' At that, he closed the meeting. However, on his way out of the cafeteria he turned to Patricia Kennedy, 'This bolshie lot need a good sorting out. Come and see me tomorrow morning first thing and we'll get to the bottom of this.'

Questions

- Was Bob Smeaton wrong? How should he have approached the situation?
- What advice would you give Patricia before the Tuesday morning meeting?
- How should Quiltco try to recover the situation?

Case analysis

Quiltco is a good example of managing the process of change and also dealing with the potential for resistance to change. The manner in which change is brought about is an important determinant of the level of success associated with it. Huse (1975) argues that there are eight factors associated with reducing the level of resistance to change. One of the more important factors is that associated with allowing those likely to be affected by change a participatory role. So when considering the Quiltco case above, or any change process, three options are available.

(Continued)

(Continued)

Option one is likely to be the most unsuccessful. This is where change is introduced in a top-down manner with no consultation with those about to be affected. In this sense, the effect of change is likely to be more negative in its orientation. It is logical that those about to be affected for example, by the introduction of new technology, should have their views and feelings taken into consideration prior to the change process taking place. Resistance to change is not resistance to the change itself, more, it is a reaction to the way in which change is introduced and the levels of consultation and information provided related to that change.

Option two is likely to create the greatest chance of success, but is also likely to be time-consuming. This involves full participation by all likely to be affected by the forthcoming change. As Huse (1975) points out:

> The amount of opposition to change is reduced when those people who are to be changed and those who are to exert influence for a change have a strong sense of belonging to the same group. Change that comes from within is much less threatening and creates less opposition than change that is proposed from the outside. There are varying degrees of participation in this context.

The argument that Huse makes is relevant to the use of organization development as a model for instigating change in organizations because of its participatory nature, and the use of the change agent, especially one from within the organization. Full participation allows all to become involved and even enthused by change. However, it is a slow and time-consuming process and may not be appropriate where the need for change has been left too late, as in the Quiltco example.

Where change has to occur rapidly, for example to ensure company survival or growth, then option three, limited participation is a more effective strategy. This is accomplished by targeting, selecting, and involving key members likely to be affected by change, and using them as a short term project group to assess and implement the change process. This allows participation to occur as well as keeping to specific deadlines when these are crucial. The most obvious (but not the only route) is to involve departmental managers, trade union representatives and a number of key staff. So Patricia Kennedy might recommend the adoption of an option three type solution.

The learning element for the change agent in terms of moving the organization with which they are dealing with towards change is that of allowing and taking advantage of participation. The individual problem will determine whether options two or three are pursued. However, in an OD setting, option one is an anathema to successful change interventions. As Warner Burke (1994) notes:

Thus the primary though not exclusive function of OD consultants is to help clients learn how to help themselves more effectively. Although consultants occasionally provide expert information and may sometimes prescribe a remedy, their more typical mode of operating is facilitation.

Dealing with change is one of the most crucial factors that a manager will have to experience within an organization. More often than not, it is resistance to change as a result of insufficient attention being paid to the process of change that causes problems. Change is a common occurrence within organizations, and resistance to change is just as common. There are several types of resistance to change. Understanding these different types can help in understanding ways to reduce resistance.

Resistance can occur at three levels:

1   *Organizational*   This would include resistance which is being triggered by power and conflict (perceived or real), changes to function, structure and culture.

   - *Power and conflict*   Resistance to change due to power and conflict occurs when a change may benefit one department within the organization while harming another department within the organization. One of the outcomes of power and conflict within organizations during change process is organizational politics which we will examine in some depth in the next chapter.

   - *Function*   Resistance to change due to differences in the way separate departments see problems and issues. Thus making it harder to come to an agreement regarding change.

   - *Organizational structure*   Resistance to change caused by recommendations because employees working 'within a mechanistic structure are expected to act in certain ways and do not develop the initiative to adjust their behaviour to changing conditions (George and Jones, 2007).

   - *Organizational culture*   Resistance due to organizational culture occurs when organizational change disrupts the values and norms within the organizational culture.

2   *Group*   which would include resistance due to group norms, group cohesiveness and groupthink.

   - *Group norms*   Resistance due to group norms occurs when change alters interactions between group members due to changes in task and role relationships within a group.

   - *Group cohesiveness*   Resistance where the group members want to keep things the same within the group.

   - *Groupthink*   Janis (1972) classifies this as:

   A feeling of invulnerability creates excessive optimism and encourages risk taking.

   Discounting warnings that might challenge assumptions.

An unquestioned belief in the group's morality, causing members to ignore the consequences of their actions.

Stereotyped views of enemy leaders.

Pressure to conform against members of the group who disagree.

Shutting down of ideas that deviate from the apparent group consensus.

An illusion of unanimity with regards to going along with the group.

Mindguards – self-appointed members who shield the group from dissenting opinions.

3 *Individual*   individual-level resistance includes resistance to change due to uncertainty and insecurity, selective perception and retention, and habit.

Huse (1975) suggests eight ways to reduce resistance to change:

1 Any change process needs to take into account the needs, attitudes, and beliefs of the individual(s) involved as well as the forces of the organization. The individual must see some personal benefit to be gained from the change before he or she will be willing to participate in the change process.

2 The greater the prestige of the supervisor, the greater the influence he or she can exert for change. However, the official leader of a group and the actual (although informal) leader need not be the same individual. Frequently, an unofficial leader with high prestige and influence within the work group can be highly influential in the change process.

3 Strong pressure for change in behaviour can be established by providing specific information desired by the group about itself and its behaviour. The more central, relevant and meaningful the information, the greater the possibility for change. For example, if properly used, data obtained through a survey questionnaire may be much more meaningful to a particular work group than data about attitudes in general.

4 Strong pressures for change can be established by creating shared perceptions by the group members of the needs for change, thus making the pressure come from within the unit. In particular, the participation in analysis and interpretation helps to reduce or by-pass resistance which comes from proceeding either too rapidly or too slowly.

5 The amount of opposition to change is reduced when those people who are to be changed and those who are to exert influence for a change have a strong sense of belonging to the same group. Change, which comes from within, is much less threatening and creates less opposition than change that is, proposed from the outside.

6 Group cohesiveness or 'togetherness', may operate either to increase or reduce resistance to change, depending on the issue and the way in which the group sees the change as being valuable or harmful.

7 A group that has a continuing psychological meaning to an individual has more influence than a group with only temporary membership. Therefore, a change process that involves

bringing individuals together, off the job, in temporary groups, has less force for lasting change than those change processes that involve the individual in the immediate job situation.

8   All relevant people in the group must share information relating to the need for change, plans for change, and consequences of change. A change process ordinarily requires the specific and deliberate opening of communication channels. Blocking these channels usually leads to distrust and hostility. Change processes which provide specific knowledge on the progress to date, and specify the criteria against which improvement is to be measured are more likely to be successful.

At this point it is important to be able to relate the concepts of what is involved in the change process to your own organization, as well as highlighting that change is messy, affects many, requires systematic diagnosis and needs an effective strategy. Before moving on to examine the rules and procedures to be adopted by the change agent during the lifetime of a project, it is worthwhile considering the implications of selecting a change agent from within the organization.

The Internal Change Agent: Pros and Cons?

Many organizations have invested resources to establish their own internal organization development consultants as a means of instigating change. For example, staff at an American computer manufacturer prepared an organizational development training proposal. The purpose of this document was to secure internal company funding for the establishment of a training programme for internal OD consultants. Part of the introduction is reproduced in Figure 11.1. Why would a company wish to become so heavily resourced in the area of organization development? One reason is that it is an investment in getting ahead and being able to manage change. Similarly, the costs involved in external change agents getting up to speed with the culture and values of an organization is expensive in time and money. There are several organizations willing to invest heavily in this field as a means of forgoing external costs via change consultants.

The benefits of using an internal change agent are linked directly to two key issues – cost factors and access to information. By comparison, the costs associated with training an employee in the techniques and practices of OD are minimal when the alternative is the use of an outside consultancy firm over a lengthy period of time. External consultants charge by the day and more often than not, the cost of one change project can run into tens of thousands of pounds. The external consultancy firm has to build in overhead costs, which run up the bill.

> The purpose of the Organization Development training is to help increase the effectiveness of manufacturing by providing expertise and skilled resources to help manage the massive changes now taking place in our manufacturing operations in Europe.
>
> The amount of change going on in manufacturing – the type of work, the type and mix of skills, structures and systems, response times, performance measurement of operating units and people, and in the way the manufacturing operations are designed and operate – is already high and is increasing. Manufacturing must change the way it operates in order to correspond with changes going on in customers, vendors, marketing and sales, engineering. Products and processes are changing rapidly. Manufacturing also needs to influence the operations and style of these other organizations.
>
> Training internal consultants drawn from existing, experienced employees is preferred. This has the great advantage of providing resources who know how our company works and who can actively re-design and make changes in the organization rather than just consult. The learning and the experience become embedded in the organization.
>
> From: Organization Development Training: Proposal for skills council funding (An in-house proposal for training managers in OD techniques and abilities.)

Figure 11.1   Purpose of training

The internal change agent may also have the benefit of having access to information that the external agent cannot hope to get, no matter how long the project runs. However, as Margulies and Raia (1978) point out, to be effective the internal consultant is required to maintain a marginal status between being internal and being objective. The value of the internal change agent rests with being inside the organization and able to have information at hand whilst remaining objective with regard to the problem and the client organization. This is a particularly difficult situation for an employee of an organization to be in. There are a number of factors which may hinder the internal change agent's objectivity:

- being too close to see what the problem is;
- being part of the problem;
- being willing to confront issues when promotion and pay issues are forthcoming;
- being part of the power system being examined;
- being aware of the needs and demands of superiors.

The use of internal change agents, who have been effectively trained in the techniques of managing change, will obviously benefit the organization. However, there are a number of issues that the change agent should be aware of that may inhibit their ability to influence change within the organization. Two of these relate to the method of entry into projects and, the nature of the voluntary relationship.

In terms of entry into a change management process as a facilitator, the internal change agent has to convince management and employees within a particular part of the organization of their expertise in this area. There is also a need to display the willingness to help. These issues are no different from those experienced by the external change agent and confidence and trust will come from successful change management projects within the organization over time. However, the internal change agent needs to use these successful interventions as an open education process for the organization far more than the external ever has to.

The voluntary nature of the relationship between the change agent and the client is one of the golden rules outlined below. The internal change agent may not be given the opportunity to pick and choose clients from within the organization. Nor can they always expect to be free in their choice of the manner and mode of facilitation employed. The internal change agent is constrained by his/her involvement and participation in the organization and by their specified role which others may seek to exploit to their advantage.

The internal change agent must not and cannot become involved in change within his/her own area. For most internal change agents this rules out the development of projects for change in the personnel area, but leaves them free to deal with issues related to sales and marketing, manufacturing, etc. Ideally, any organization training internal change agents would select a number of them from different departments to be able to deal with this difficulty.

In assessing the need for internal and external change agents, Margulies and Raia argue that,

> Organizations must learn to use external and internal consultants in more effective ways. Perhaps the best approach consists in the use of both. External consultants can bring objectivity, expertise and fresh approaches to organization problem solving. Internal consultants provide knowledge and understanding of organizational processes, information about current issues, and continuity of effort ... a collaborative relationship provides an opportunity to transfer the external consultant's skills to the client system ... since the capacity for organization development must ultimately emerge from the organization itself. (1972: 477)

The Golden Rules

The issues related to participation become apparent when we look in closer detail at the role and positioning of the change agent in the process of change itself. In essence, there are four 'golden rules' (Lippit, 1959) that the change agent has to observe.

Rule 1: the nature of the relationship

This has to be seen as a voluntary one between the professional helper (the change agent) and the part of the business classified as the help needing system. The most clear-cut example is that of a consultant from one of the large consultancy organizations who is brought in to assist the process of change in an organization.

In our work with organizations we make a point at the start of the process of stressing that it is a voluntary link between two parties which can be severed, at any time, by either party. We make the point of continually reiterating this at stages in the relationship and to all concerned in the change process. The reasons for this are that it allows those who feel uncomfortable with the relationship to express their discomfort openly, allows both parties to begin to address this, if possible, and maintains an open and honest atmosphere. It also has the benefit of allowing the change agent to withdraw if they feel that the assistance being provided is not what is needed, or wanted.

Rule 2: to action an organization development process within any organization the change agent has to help solve a current or potential problem

The obvious is important. There are two issues here. First, the organization itself must recognize that a problem exists. This should come from senior management as the instigation of change stands a greater chance of success with top management support. Recognition of a need for change can take several forms. For example, an increase in employee absence figures should be recognized as an issue for concern that needs to be addressed. Absenteeism over a period of time costs money. Similarly, major changes in organization structure, the introduction of new technology being one example, are also situations where problems may occur and some form of OD analysis may be required.

The second issue relates to the help the change agent can provide. To help solve a problem, the change agent has to be able to offer some form of expertise. Traditionally, this is based on knowledge of the subject area. However, for the organization development agent, the knowledge, more often than not, is in dealing with people and helping the organization find its own solutions to structuring, absenteeism, etc. This is a skill that few have, and fewer still use effectively.

Rule 3: the relationship is a temporary one and the change agent and organization must accept the temporary nature of the assistance being provided

In effect this means recognition of withdrawal from the system as a fact of life. One of the main criticisms of consultants is that they get others to solve their own problems, charge them for the privilege, leaving the organization to manage the mess. Any change agent worth his salt cannot expect to stay in business long using this approach. The old adage that if you ask a consultant the time he'll ask if he can borrow your watch may have a grain of truth to it and can be applied in this context to the change agent. The important point is that the change agent has to be temporary but needs to see the project through to satisfactory completion. They are not employed, full-time by the organization, and in the case of internal change agents, may have a day job! Both parties must recognize the need to sever the relationship at some point. This does not prevent the change agent from returning periodically to see how the organization is coping with the changes introduced, and some form of neutral or objective audit of change helps the process. However, this should occur after the initial change process has been completed and the change agent has withdrawn to allow the organization to manage its own affairs.

Rule 4: the change agent must be an outsider who is not part of the hierarchical power system in which the client organization is located

Why? Three main reasons immediately spring to mind. The first concerns the nature of being an objective outsider. Again, the obvious choice here is an external change agent. There is no particular axe to grind and therefore the nature of the assistance provided is that of being truly impartial. Change agents are from within the confines of the organization, but from another department may also be able to remain impartial, although the obstacles are greater. Second, as change agents are from outside the immediate hierarchy, they are less likely to be influenced by the machinations of power, and therefore more likely to remain fair-minded. Third, to be truly effective in helping the client organization, the change agent has to be *seen* to be non-partisan by those within the client system.

In our dealings with client organizations we make a point of stressing to all we come into contact with that we will remain objective, open-minded, and above all, free from influence. This is a difficult situation to maintain balance from. At the end of the day, the change process often involves payment to the change agent, and there is an argument that one has to be aware of whom one is working for. This would also be true for the internal change agent in terms of the intrinsic or extrinsic rewards associated with a successful change project.

These, then are the rules which the change agent must accept as guiding the change process. Remember that it is a voluntary relationship in which you, as the change agent, are attempting to solve a current or potential problem on a temporary contract with the client organization as an outsider.

The Change Agent's Approach to Change

In Chapter 10 we set out the process the change agent has to go through from the beginning to the end of a project in terms of negotiating access, undertaking the intervention, etc. In this section we outline, in more detail, the issues that the change agent will have to deal with in terms of each stage of the process. Where possible, we have tried to use examples from our own experience to highlight some of the issues that one can expect to encounter. We have also tried to relate these to some of the difficulties that an internal change agent can expect to meet under similar circumstances.

The first problem facing the change agent is one of definition. They have to ask the following:

What is causing the problem?

This should be in terms of trying to define:

What is going wrong?

What/who is causing the problem?

Why does it continue to be a problem?

At this point, it is essential to be able to describe to oneself what the current situation is, why it exists, and what is going on, etc. This ability to be able to apply a descriptive-analytical capability combines with the skill of diagnosis to enable the change agent to focus on the symptoms of the problem before drawing attention to the causes.

In our experience, this is where the change agent can make their first and perhaps fatal mistake. Under the doctor–patient scheme of system intervention, you tell me the symptoms and I prescribe the remedy. However, diagnosis using expertise may not be the most appropriate form of action in an organization development sense. This is related to why and how the change agent becomes involved in the process. At this point the change agent should ask whether he or she wants to enter into this relationship.

Why do I want to enter into this relationship?

If the answer is to provide the solution via analysis, diagnosis and application of a cure by a fairly standard and mechanized means, then the damage inflicted may be greater than that which the actual problem warrants. The change agent has to be clear about their own goals and the reasons for motivating and influencing others. This is related to who sets the goals for the change process. The client organization and the change agent should define these together. In an organization development mode it has to be both because of the nature of what is being changed. More often than not, this is people within a particular setting within the organization, and the change agent has to assist in helping people change themselves. Therefore, description of what the problem is, what is causing it, and how it can be remedied has to come from both parties to this process. The doctor–patient relationship denies mutual exchange as a two-way process.

In one of our first projects as external change agents, one of us was set the task of determining ways of making a customer sales department 'work smarter'. The definition of the problem was set by the client organization as a simple one of finding out how the people resources of that department could be better utilized. In the naivety of youth, the description of the problem and its analysis were accepted as straightforward. The answer simply meant talking to the department's main internal customers to find out what better service they could provide. This ignored the fact that the customer services department could find its own way of working smarter, and that these ideas could and should be taken into consideration. The fundamental flaw was the process by which diagnosis was sought. This was externally driven and discounted the importance of getting those within the department involved in defining the problem and looking for solutions to it.

Having begun the process of defining what the problem is, in alliance with the client organization, the change agent should also look at what potential there is for change. The change agent needs to be sure that there is, within the organization, a motivation towards change. Otherwise, all attempts at instigating change with the client system may be hampered. The motivation can come from two main sources – ambition or dissatisfaction. Lippit, noted that in terms of the motivation for change among individuals:

> Pain and dissatisfaction with the present situation are most frequently the dominating driving forces for change, but with groups very often one of the most important motivations is a desire to improve group efficiency ... even though there may be no critical problems in the present situation. (1959: 8)

Often the motivation for change by one part of the client system may be hampered by other parts of the organization. The change agent has to be aware of the potential for resistance from other areas, has to be aware that they may be viewed as 'on the side' of the immediate client organization, and has to be aware of the impact that both factors may have on the change process. The change agents should at the outset ask themselves who is likely to be affected and how they would react.

Who is likely to be affected by change in this client system, and how are they likely to react?

Answers to these question may go a long way in determining how successful change is likely to be, who is likely to be impacted by them, and how motivated the organization, as a whole is, to change.

Another important issue that the change agents need to look at, and be honest about is their own capabilities to manage the change process. In this sense, change agents need to ask what they can do to help the organization change.

What can I do to help this organization change?

This brings us back to the temporary nature of the change process and the full role of the change agent. The change agent in their role of facilitator is more often than not seen as being an individual who diagnoses problems and offers recommendations for improvement. However, the role is a temporary one and the change agent must also be seen to offer continuity in interpreting the consequences for change made in their recommendations. The logic behind this is fairly straightforward. Having assisted the organization to define its current problem, and helped it consider alternative solutions, the change agent should also assist in the process of working out the meaning of change for the organization in terms of practices, procedures and resultant design.

Change can create a level of disruption within the organization which, if not handled adequately, can lead to demoralization. Having gone through the diagnostic process and outlined the changes needed, the organization may also feel that it has insufficient capabilities to cope with the implications for change without the assistance of the change agent.

It is therefore necessary, as a change agent, to be able to offer both diagnostic and application skills. Lippit (1959: 9) recommends that a consultative team is best placed to offer such solutions. Either way, walking away from the process halfway through would appear to be an inadequate means of dealing with change.

In our dealings with organizations we have often called on the resources of our own outside observer for a neutral standpoint. In this sense, what we get is the viewpoint from someone that has not been closely involved with the organization and may be able to look at the implications of change from a fresher viewpoint. More often than not, this confirms our diagnosis and assessment of the implications of change, but it would assist the change agent greatly, especially if they have a 'sounding board' to bounce ideas off. What we recommend here is that organizations invest their resources in more than one individual as change agent, to provide the security and efficiency associated with a team.

There are two other important issues that the change agent needs to take into careful consideration during the course of managing a change project. The first relates to their role during the different phases of the project. The second is linked to establishing change as the norm within organizations.

In terms of the developing role of the change agent, the important question for the change agent is one of being in the appropriate role at certain points in time.

Who should I be at certain points in time?

In essence this involves movement from information gatherer towards a more active training role. Lippit et al. (1958) identified seven phases of change within what they term the consultant–client relationship:

1 development of the need for change;

2 establishment of the consultancy relationship;

3 clarification of the client problem;

4 examination of alternative solutions;

5 transformation of intentions to actual change;

6 generalization and stabilization of a new level of functioning or group structure;

7 achieving a terminal relationship with the consultant and the continuity of change-ability.

The first crucial area is the move from change agent as information and opinion-seeker towards that of facilitator and adviser/trainer. This occurs between stages 4 and 5 and involves taking on a more directive role with the client organization. This prevents the organization regressing backwards by allowing individuals to focus on the application of the alternatives they helped develop. In this scenario, the change agent takes on more of a driving role for change. In this way the client organization will see what happens during the change process and will be able to learn from it, and hopefully, apply the techniques the next time.

In our experience, it is better for the change agent to deliberately separate the information gathering from the diagnosis and recommendation stages. In our dealings with organizations we make a point of using the summary session at the end of the information gathering stages 1 through 4 to get commitment that we can move forward in a different mode. This involves a form of contract renewal where we seek permission to either lead the transformation of intentions into actual change or, offer to act as observers of how the organization is managing this stage itself. The latter is preferable in terms of gaining the commitment from those being affected by change. It also assists in the termination of the relationship for the organization to be seen to be taking a greater participatory role. However, the change agent still has a part in terms of helping the organization learn new procedures and skills associated with the alternative solutions they have helped to establish. You must be acutely aware of the change in role. Do not to hide behind the information-seeker phase. Be prepared to move on to the training and guidance role with the ultimate aim of removing the need for the change agent.

The second issue directly concerns the question of learning in the organization. The change agent should, during the change process, ask how to get constant change within the organization.

How do I get constant change in this organization?

The process of working through definition of the problem and possible solutions helps the organization learn to cope with the problems that initiated the need for change. It now knows what the causes were and is hopefully in a position to remedy them on its own should they occur again. However, if the change process has been successful, the organization will also have learnt how to go about defining problems and clarifying them as they emerge. In this sense, they are learning directly from the change agent about the mechanisms they used to clarify problems as they emerged – the types of questions asked, the way in which meetings were run, the way the change agent communicated and got the involvement of all concerned. The organization learns in this way when it has reached its own limits in dealing with problems, and hopefully learns about making decisions on when it needs to seek outside help.

We were asked by the computer chip business of a major computer manufacturer to undertake a short review of the development of semi-autonomous work teams. This was a fairly straightforward process that involved the design of an opinion survey questionnaire, the running of a number of workshops on issues of concern and critical success factors with operating staff and conversations with managers within the business. We worked through the process of information gathering and analysis and provided feedback on how the teams were operating, what were the critical success factors and a number of issues that gave cause for concern. However, one of the unexpected success criteria from our perspective was that having used the teams to help design and run the questionnaire and the workshops, the organization decided that this method of data collection and analysis could be successfully adopted inside the business and used as a mechanism for assessing where they were, what changes were likely to affect them, and what issues staff felt were likely to be problematic. The change agents, ourselves, had left the relationship, but the mechanisms for making change ongoing remained and had been built into the business. This example is dealt with in greater depth when we examine OD cases.

Conclusion: OD and the Effective Change Agent

We pointed out earlier that experience suggests that creating a sense of involvement with those likely to be affected by change encourages their commitment to change and higher levels or standards of performance result. The mechanisms used during the process of change and the change agent, by ensuring participation and involvement in the changes being contemplated, can increase the likelihood of a successful change intervention.

Many organizations now involve people through consultation, participation and communication. However, this still creates a degree of controversy related to timing, effectiveness and applicability. Schein (1988) comments that:

> As long as organizations are networks of people engaged in achieving some common goals, there will be various kinds of processes occurring between them. Therefore, the more we understand about how to diagnose and improve such processes, the greater will be our chances of finding solutions to the more technical problems and of ensuring that such solutions will be accepted and used by members of the organization.

The effective change agent has to be able to manage the bridge between the manager's desire to solve the problem immediately and the time it takes the organization to solve its own problems via the change agent and their facilitation process. The effective change agent also has to remain on an unstable borderline, or what Margulies and Raia (1978) classify as 'marginality' between being in the organization and remaining aloof. Similarly, the change agent has to strike a balance between being the 'technical' expert – the person assumed to have the answers, and the process facilitator – the person with the techniques to allow the organization to find its own answers. Most effective change agents need to find a balance. This lies between what they know is the correct solution, having done it before and thus knowing what types of answers and solutions are likely to emerge, and the processes by which they get the organization's members to find their own answers to their own problems – a tricky task!

In our experience, many managers will readily accept the overall argument for a need to change organization structures and management styles for more effective performance. However, they feel that there is a lack of adequate guidance on how this transformation takes place. This reverts back to the desire for instantly applicable, off-the-shelf solutions to their problems. The real world, even from an OD perspective, is less clear-cut. The concept of perpetual transition management, as an approach to implementing and sustaining organizational change is an example of dealing with change as it is lived. To this end, it is the job of the effective change agent to get those involved with the change process to pay attention to how it is lived. It is only in this respect that the experience of change can be learnt from, and applied effectively at a later date. The change agent to be effective needs to constantly work on the basis that they are doing themselves out of a job, and that the client is big enough to be able to handle their own problems – another tricky task!

12 Organizational Politics and Change

> 'Comrades', he cried. 'You do not imagine, I hope, that we pigs are doing this in a spirit of selfishness and privilege? Many of us actually dislike milk and apples. I dislike them myself … It is for *your* sake that we drink that milk and eat those apples.'
>
> (George Orwell, *Animal Farm*, 1945)
>
> Power is the pivot on which everything hinges. He who has the power is always right; the weaker is always wrong.
>
> (Niccolo Machiavelli, 1532)
>
> In the real world of organizations: the 'good guys' don't always win.
>
> (S. Robbins, 2007).

Organizational politics traditionally gets a 'bad press'. It has generally been under-researched mainly because of concerns about image. Managers dislike discussing subjects such as organizational politicking, believing that it reflects badly on themselves as managers and on their organization and they cling to a purely rationalist model of decision making. Sometimes, even the presence of politics is denied. But, as we suggest in this chapter, while some managers may claim to have no taste for politics they readily engage in it and justify it. The processes of managing organizational change more often than not result in conflict and resistance, requiring political engagement in response.

Political behaviours in organizations are an acceptable and pervasive dimension of organization life. There is a growing body of literature that views organizational politics as central to our understanding of the workings of the organization (Pettigrew, 1985; Mangham, 1979; Kakabadse and Parker, 1984; Kumar and Thibodeaux, 1990; Frost and Egri, 1991; Hardy, 1996). Drory and Romm (1990) provide a useful process of distinguishing between the purpose of the political act (outcomes), the behaviour itself (means deployed) and the relevant context (situational characteristics). They conclude that organizational politics occurs, 'when goal attainment is sought by informal, rather than formal means of influence in the face of potential conflict' (1990: 1133). However, when examining the political behaviour of managers there is a tendency to draw attention to the 'dark side' of activities that are deemed negative: against the organization and self-serving (Ferris and Kacmar, 1992: 93). There are obviously elements of politics, which can be seen as self-serving actions against organizational goals, covert means, and situations where conflict and uncertainty exist. However, Buchanan and Badham (1999a) suggest that political behaviour is acceptable and, 'can serve organizational goals as well as personal career objectives; and that while specific actions may appear unacceptable when considered in isolation, political behaviour is potentially defensible in context'.

On a related theme, it appears that organizational politics suffers from an affliction to the extent that we all know that it exists in organizations, but it is rarely discussed openly and brought explicitly into business decision making. Even though academia is increasingly prepared to engage with questions of ethics and politics there are methodological problems associated with examining the political activities of individuals. The very nature of the subject matter means that getting beyond the socially desirable response and organizationally acceptable message is a major barrier to proper scholarly investigation. Buchanan and Badham (1999a) refer to the clear difficulties of investigations into organizational politics given the sensitivities of disclosure. Business ethics research similarly faces obstacles to accessing motives, actions and expectations of business behaviour (Robertson, 1993).

When examining the political behaviour of leaders there is a tendency to draw attention to the 'dark side' of activities that are deemed negative, against the organization and self-serving (Ferris and Kacmar, 1992: 93). Such judgements are implicitly and sometimes explicitly ethical in nature. The macro- and microanalysis of organizational behaviour seems to run into difficulty in reconciling the ethical with the political. If the open consideration of both politics and ethics are individually under-represented and under-researched, then dealing with the ethics of politics is inadequately addressed in academic literature and business practice.

It may also be worthwhile viewing the political behaviour of change managers in the context of organizational ethics rather than the attainment of organizational goals and career development. In this sense we should seek to examine the engagement of managers in political processes, and in relation to this examine three key questions:

1 Are political interventions in change programmes characterized by illegitimate, self-serving actions or organizational good?

2 Can the political behaviour of change managers ever be deemed ethical and, if so, under what circumstances?

3 What types of political activity and tactics do managers engage in?

Defining Organizational Politics

Maclagan (1998: 127-8) argues that, 'it is practically impossible to arrive at a general theory of organizational politics; and this undoubtedly applies also to the ethical dimension to such behaviour.' In order to make sense of these two difficult concepts we adopt frameworks to aid understanding and application. We analyse what Buchanan and Badham (1999a: 27-8) define as 'turf game tactics'. Utilizing Gray and Starke's (1984) headings of how organizational politics are undertaken; they define a series of managerial behaviours classified as political actions. We then can assess whether each turf game tactic can be deemed ethical. These moral stances are then counter-pointed from an organizational politics perspective. Finally, we offer a suggestion of how politics can realistically and ideologically be brought into the open.

What do we define as organizational politics and the act of politicking? It is difficult to apply a universal perspective. However, certain broad similarities exist among the definitions of what constitutes organizational politics (Drory and Romm, 1990). There is acceptance that in examining organizational politics there is a need to break free from the confines of traditional rationalist arguments. By examining the differences between economic models of organization and more pluralist perspectives, Ferris and King (1991: 59) argue that, 'politics is what takes place between the perfect workings of the rational model (efficiency) and the messiness of human interactions.' Gandz and Murray (1980: 237) suggest that managers perceived that politics was happening, 'when people were believed to be trying to advance or protect their own self-interests in the face of actual or potential opposition from others in the organization.' They also highlight two main types of political behaviour – conflictual manoeuvring and blatantly self-advancing/protecting actions. Palmer and Hardy (2000: 75) suggest that work on politics has restricted the reach of power by defining its use as, 'unsanctioned, self-serving, informal, illegal, illegitimate, conflict-ridden, duplicitous and anti-organizational behaviour.' Politics in this sense is seen as being negative.

In short, politics may be defined as the use of power through influencing techniques and tactics (sanctioned or unsanctioned) aimed at accomplishing personal and/or organizational goals. Our concern is less with the ethics of political tactics that are deemed legitimized by organizational sanction and used by dominant groups to maintain the status quo, and more with the morality implicit in the use of organizational politics.

Why Do People Engage in Politics?

Figure 12.1 (based on Pfeffer, 1981 and illustrated here from the teaching materials of Buchanan and Huczynski, 2006) outlines a model of why politics occurs in organizations. It starts with some underlying assumptions associated with differentiation. Because different parts of the organization compete for scarce resources and may often disagree about the goals and objectives to be aimed for, and the means by which these can be accomplished, a degree of conflict is a natural state of being. This belies the 'we're all in this together' notion of corporate culture but still recognizes through interdependence that people in organizations need to work together. The process where conflict gets triggered into politics depends on the importance of the issue at hand and on the nature and distribution of power. The wider the distribution of power in organizations the greater the opportunity for politics.

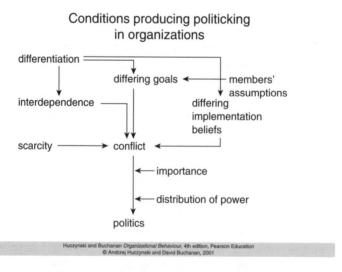

Figure 12.1 Conditions producing politicking in organizations
Source: Pfeffer, 1981.

By examining the politics of organizational change Buchanan and Badham (1999b) suggest that political behaviour is acceptable and, 'can serve organizational goals as well as personal career objectives; and that while specific actions may appear unacceptable when considered in isolation, political behaviour is potentially defensible in context.' Similarly, Appelbaum and Hughes (1998) argue that far from having a negative connotation, political behaviour is quite neutral and can be either helpful or harmful to members of an organization or the organization itself. Stone (1997: 23) notes that, 'When people have a choice between a rational decision and their ego, they always choose their ego!' Therefore, the prevalence of political behaviour is the norm rather than the exception (Buchanan and Badham, 1999b). In some senses it may also be seen as desirable. Frost and Egri (1991) argue that political behaviour is both inevitable and necessary in stimulating creativity and debate and that it should be seen as a positive mechanism for change.

Power and politics have generally been under-researched in organizations. Thompson and McHugh (1995: 132) suggest that most textbooks ignore power and politics or subsume it under other headings such as leadership. The main recognition of the importance of politics comes from the contextual/processual approach (Pettigrew, 1985, 1987, 1988; Dunphy and Stace, 1988). By recognizing that change is non-linear the contextual/processual approach focuses on the enabling and constraining characteristics and hence to the political arena in which change is made. Lee and Lawrence (1991: 143) argue that, 'There is much power in being able to affect the political context, often more, and with longer-term effects, than possessing strong power bases and adopting effective strategies within that context.' Others are less willing to accept the processes and behaviours associated with organizational politics. In reviewing the field of organization development (OD), Buchanan and Badham (1999b) argue that many authors either deny the relevance of 'power-coercive strategies' or recommend action within a legitimate domain of politics. Here individuals are advised to pursue the moral highground for organizational well being instead of 'dirty tricks' and other dubious tactics for self-enhancement (Greiner and Schein, 1988; Egan, 1994).

Much of the politics literature avoids spelling out the kinds of actions, which are under discussion explicitly. An exception is the work by Gray and Starke (1984), who have devised headings of how organizational politics are undertaken. They define a series of managerial behaviours classified as political actions, which have been developed by Buchanan and Badham (1999a: 27–8) and are defined as 'turf game tactics'. Buchanan and Badham identify eight turf game tactics used by managers (see Table 12.1).

Yet there is a need to draw attention to organizational politics as it affects the management of change. Buchanan, Claydon and Doyle (1997) provide evidence that 70 per cent of managers felt that the more

Table 12.1   Turf game tactics

Image building: actions which enhance reputation and further career; appropriate dress, support for the 'right causes'; adherence to group norms; air of self-confidence.

Selective information: withhold unfavourable information from superiors; keep useful information from your competition; offer only favourable interpretations; overwhelm others with complex, technical data.

Scapegoating: make sure someone else is blamed; avoid personal blame; take credit for successes.

Formal alliances: agree actions with key people; create a coalition strong enough to enforce its will.

Networking: make lots of friends in influential positions.

Compromise: give in on unimportant issues to create allies for subsequent, more important issues.

Rule manipulation: Refuse requests on the grounds of 'against company policy', but grant identical requests from allies on grounds of 'special circumstances'.

Other tactics: these seem to be concerned with the apparently more covert and ruthless aspects of political infighting.

Source: Adapted from Buchanan and Badham (1999a: 27–8)

complex and wide-ranging change was in an organization, the more intense the politics became. Similarly, these managers felt that the change agent who was not politically skilled would eventually fail. Buchanan and Badham (1999b) suggest that, 'change drivers acting as political entrepreneurs can justify their behaviour in terms of benefit to the organization.' They also argue in favour of a greater depth of analysis of how politics affects the change agent: 'the contemporary nature of political intervention in organizational change, however, has attracted less attention and commentary. Little seems to be known about the motives, conduct, manoeuvring, tactics, "power plays", perceptions, and self-justifications of change agents at the level of the lived experience.' By examining four case studies of organizational politics within a change context they conclude that political behaviour is an acceptable dimension of the change agent's role, implies a considered and creative approach, can be deemed reasonable and justified in context, and occurs through a combination of organizational circumstances, personal motives and the behaviour of others. Simplistic dichotomies between legitimate and illegitimate are not deemed appropriate.

Others have chosen to look elsewhere for assistance in understanding the principles behind organizational politics. Cavanagh, Moberg and Velasquez (1981) suggest that work in the field of normative ethics, and in particular, theories of utilitarianism, justice and rights offer useful insights, 'that may reduce the ethical uncertainty surrounding the political use of power.' They suggest a decision tree associated with ethical behaviours, which determines whether political alternatives are deemed acceptable. The decision tree embodies three ethical criteria:

- *Utilitarian:* the action results in the efficient optimization of the satisfactions of interests inside and outside the organization.
- *Rights:* the action respects the rights of all the affected parties.
- *Justice:* the action respects the canons of distributive justice (equality, fairness and impartiality).

Behaviours, which meet all these criteria, are deemed acceptable politically. Political activities that violate these ethical tests can also be deemed acceptable where there are what are classified as 'overwhelming factors, double effects or incapacitating factors'. Cavanagh et al. suggest that these concern behaviours 'that may, in a given case, justify overriding one of the three ethical criteria: utilitarian outcomes, individual rights, or distributive justice.' Overwhelming factors are defined as:

- Conflicts between criteria: for example, behaviour undertaken for the greater good that will mean the violation of an individual's rights. This leads to a 'double effect', one good and one bad. The act is acceptable if the dominant motivating factor is to achieve the good effect.
- Conflicts within criteria: conflicts between utilitarian consequences or the means chosen to accomplish goals; conflicts between the competing rights of individuals; conflicts between different canons of justice.
- Lack of capacity to employ the criteria: three examples are cited. First, an ethical criterion is abandoned where there is no freedom to use it, such as when peer pressure causes the abandonment of ethics. Second, lack of adequate information means ethical criteria are – out of ignorance – not followed. Third, the ethical criteria are conscientiously rejected.

The existence of overwhelming factors is said to enable the decision maker engaging in the political activity to justify their actions within acceptable parameters.

Double effects involve negative and positive outcomes. Negative outcomes are acceptable if the dominant purpose is to achieve positive outcomes and they outweigh the negatives.

Incapacitating factors are those which prevent the decision maker from applying the ethical criteria – pressure from colleagues, inadequate information, doubting the relevance of the ethical criteria in a given context.

Political behaviour is deemed to be ethical if it is entered into for the good of the greatest number of organization members, does not interfere with the rights of others affected by the action, and is deemed to be just in terms of equity, fairness and impartiality. Buchanan and Badham (1999b) in reviewing a number of examples of organizational politics conclude that: 'The overwhelming factors box is thus full of potential excuses, mitigating circumstances, escape clauses and "fudge factors" ... The "ethics test" is artificial, and the penalties flowing from it are often insubstantial.'

The Politics of Change – Some Evidence

McCalman (2001) researched 15 individual case studies and argued that they seemed to reveal that organizational politics is a pervasive part of management life. The cases seemed to confirm three aspects of managing change and the ethical nature of organizational politics.

First, they tended to confirm the findings of Buchanan and Badham that organizational politics are regarded as an acceptable dimension of managing change. The data also suggested that managers often play the role of the political entrepreneur.

Second, there appeared to be a tendency, again confirming the findings of Buchanan and Badham, to view political activity as being undertaken via a formal warrant associated with the organizational change agenda, a tacit personal warrant for political activity, and the maintenance of personal reputation as a credible change driver.

Third, change agents deemed organizational politics ethical when they assessed it in terms of utilitarianism, rights and justice. Most academic definitions of politics have adopted a neutral stance towards the morality and ethics of politics. The majority of the case studies examined were justified quite clearly on ethical grounds. They appeared to be more a matter of conflictual manoeuvring than serving blatant self-advancing or self-protecting aims. Those that did not match up to such lofty criteria also had overwhelming factors that acted as extenuating circumstances. Actions aimed solely for personal gain appeared to be rare in these instances. One might argue that individuals may use utilitarianism to mask self-serving actions and although political engagements were entered into for the organizational good, in most instances this did protect or promote the reputation of the individual. However, this was not reported as the prime motivator.

Following on from McCalman's (2001) cases we undertook a research study in 2003/4 in collaboration with the UK Institute of Directors (IOD) to examine the impact of organizational change on the leaders responsible for instigating change. The study took the form of a research questionnaire which participants were asked to complete as part of their attendance at the IOD's 'Leading and Directing Change' module. This module formed part of the IOD's Chartered Diploma in Company

Direction and the respondents reflected a relatively broad range of managerial roles and industry categories in UK based organizations. Operations managers, business managers, financial directors, marketing managers, commercial business managers, and company owners were well represented. Occupying a leading position in their organization they were constantly engaged in managing change. Regardless of industry, company size or even their position the managers could be described as being energetic, keen to see their ideas implemented and in search of new ways of doing things as well as seeking out new challenges. Respondents thus appeared to have had extensive experiences of organizational changes.

The survey results

The focus of the research was the identification of trends in organizational change and current opinions about fundamental aspects of the change process. In searching for a better understanding of organizations we touched on three different dimensions of change management which were considered as 'problematic':

Strategic planning and implementation of change

To be able to recognize the threats and take advantage of the opportunities in major turnarounds, today's organizations face a need for dramatic, strategic and cultural change and for rapid and continuous innovation in technology, services, products and processes. Regardless of the type or scope of organizational change the main aim of it is the achievement of strategic advantage. For a change process to be successfully implemented managers must make sure that every change undertaken has a definite need, implementation strategy and resources. Also key managers and employees need to be in agreement to support the change. Implementation of change often becomes the most difficult part of the change process. Bain (1998) suggests that during the implementation of any change process social defences are developed against anxiety which is created because of the unknown. This usually happens when managers tend to spend their time in fragmented, problem-solving activities rather than trying to establish a sense of urgency and encourage bottom-up creative processes within the organization.

Communication of the change processes

The way in which change is communicated is also a significant element associated with successful adoption.

Change and organizational politics

Management of change in any organization is normally a blend of art and politics. The political dimension of change is increasingly being recognized as an area in need of further research and one which organizational change agents need to be adept at operating within. Frost and Egri (1991) argue that political behavior is both inevitable and necessary in stimulating creativity and debate and that it should be seen as a positive mechanism for change.

One of the main difficulties in looking at politics in organizations is in gaining access to research evidence associated with the behaviors of individual managers. Buchanan and McCalman's (1989) research on 'organic organizational designs' focused their attention on the contemporary rhetoric of the *entrepreneurial hero* as a new model of competitive requirement in the interests of responsiveness to high performance and rapid innovation. Later in the 1990s the focus shifted to the 'team leader' (Zenger et al., 1994) and 'real change leaders' (Katzenbach and Smith, 1993; Katzenbach, 1997, 1998). At that time organizational change and innovation called for a shift from charismatic leadership to participative leadership where top managers performed inspirational leadership by *leading others how to lead themselves* (Buchanan and Badham, 1999a: 135).

We were interested in looking at the current management view of organizational politics and in what ways *politicking* could be a facilitator or inhibitor of change management.

This section is divided into the four main areas associated with change that we sought to investigate – planning and implementation, communications and the impact of organizational politics. We have deleted questions where no significant results were attained.

Quantitative analysis – survey results for the whole sample

Planning and implementing change

Respondents agreeing and disagreeing with the statements that:

> **My organization has problems planning effective implementation strategies for change.**

There appeared to be a strong indication here that the majority of respondents felt that their organizations had problems with the strategic planning and implementation of change (Figure 12.2).

> **When implementing rapid and radical change, participative approaches are inappropriate.**

The results here tend to suggest a strong preference in favour of a more participative approach to the change implementation process. This is particularly true where change is both radical and rapid (Figure 12.3).

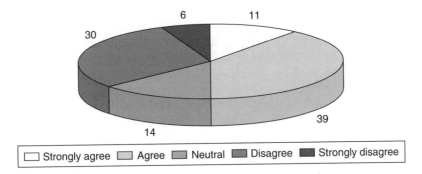

Figure 12.2   My organization has problems planning effective implementation strategies for change

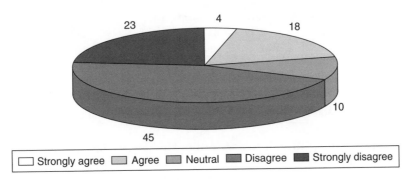

Figure 12.3   When implementing rapid and radical change, participative approaches are inappropriate

I find people in my organization suffer from change fatigue.

There seems to be a reasonable group within this sample who make the argument that change fatigue in organizations is not an issue (Figure 12.4).

It is difficult to stay out of the day-to-day management of change initiatives

This is a significant indication of the inability of company directors to divorce themselves from the management activities associated with change. Seventy-six per cent of the sample had difficulty separating their leadership of change from the day-to-day management of change activities and this tends to support previous arguments (Garratt, 2003) that one of the main difficulties associated with the successful implementation of any change process is the ability of directors to pass on to management the responsibility for change implementation (Figure 12.5).

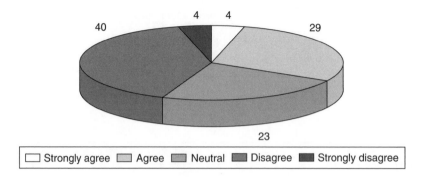

Figure 12.4   I find people in my organization suffer from change fatigue

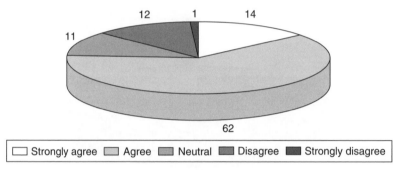

Figure 12.5   It is difficult to stay out of the day-to-day management of change initiatives

Communication issues

Respondents agreeing and disagreeing with the statements that:

> Communication is seen as a two-way process.

> We never have the time to consult with the staff properly before or during change!

Once again there appears to be a desire on the part of the majority of respondents to ensure time is made available before and during the change process to undertake consultation. This again would confirm a more collaborative framework for change (Figures 12.6 and 12.7).

We also sought to determine whether for small firms the communication process was somewhat easier.

> It is easier for a small firm to communicate change than it is for a larger organization!

Two-thirds of the population felt that company size affects strongly the development of communication processes (Figure 12.8).

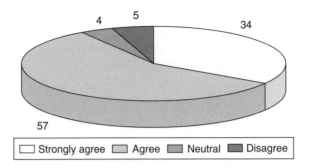

Figure 12.6   **Communication is seen as a two-way process**

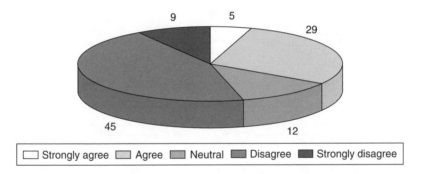

Figure 12.7   **We never have the time to consult with the staff properly before or during change**

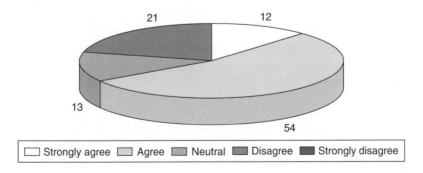

Figure 12.8   **It is easier for a small firm to communicate change than it is for a larger organization**

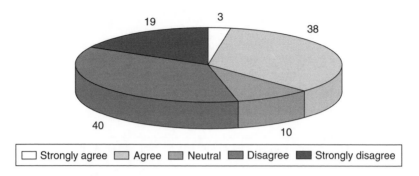

Figure 12.9 Being honest and open with some stakeholder groups isn't a wise idea

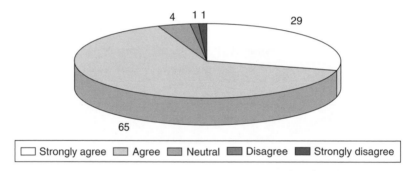

Figure 12.10   One of the main sources of resistance to change is people trying to defend their personal territory or 'turf'

Change management and organizational politics

This area produced some surprisingly strong and confirmatory results in relation to the impact of politics on change. It also provides us with the strongest areas of agreement/disagreement related to the experience of organizational politics and change. Once again, respondents agreeing and disagreeing with the statements that:

Being honest and open with some stakeholder groups isn't a wise idea.

This tends to imply that respondents felt that engagement with stakeholder groups during the change process is a beneficial activity (Figure 12.9).

One of the main sources of resistance to change is people trying to defend their personal territory or 'turf'!

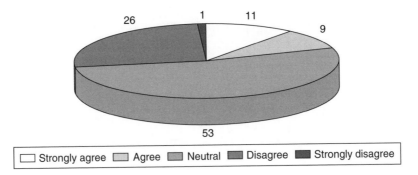

Figure 12.11 **When it comes to getting people to change in my organization I personally would rather tell than sell**

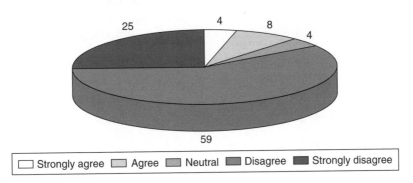

Figure 12.12 **Most change in my organization has been triggered by current management trends rather than business needs**

This statement provided the strongest level of agreement from the survey. Clearly, there is a distinct association between resistance to change and the impact on the individual's own future in relation to that change (Figure 12.10).

> When it comes to getting people to change in my organization I personally would rather tell than sell.

The level of disagreement with this tends to reinforce earlier views associated with a more collaborative/participative approach to change (Figure 12.11).

> Most change in my organization has been triggered by current management trends rather than business needs!

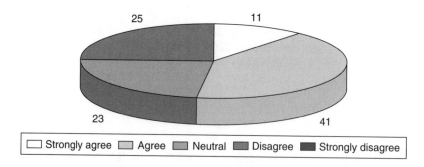

Figure 12.13   The more complex the change, the more intense the politics become

Responses here tend to signify that change management in the sample survey is not seen as a response to current management trends or fads but is associated with speficic business needs (Figure 12.2).

The more complex the change, the more intense the politics become.

Results here tend to imply agreement with the idea that change and uncertainty intensify the politics game (Figure 12.3).

But Is It Ethical?

Some steps have been taken in applying ethics to organizational politics. Most of the discussion to date is influenced by a wealth of literature drawn from the United States. Authors such as Pfeffer (1992), Brayman (1967) and Zahra (1984, 1985, 1987) offer a choice of theories, which are deeply embedded in the dominant US perspective on business ethics (Spence 2001). Jackall (1988) has done seminal work on the complexities of managers in the workplace, but an American organizational culture perspective dominates the companies on which he focuses. While his participant observer method of gathering intricate sensitive data is to be applauded, the contextual findings are not at all readily transferable to a European context. Watson's (1994) ethnographic study 'In search of management' offers a view of British management in the early 1990s, but takes as its main focus how management can best be understood rather than taking a particularly political or indeed ethical perspective.

At best the US contributions could be considered to be relevant to the US where they are in keeping with prevailing liberal individualist theoretical perspectives, but it is questionable whether such a narrow range of perspectives would be appropriate to multicultural business operations both within America and around the world. More recent work by Wijnberg (2000) counters this difficulty to some extent by introducing Aristotelian virtue theory into understanding ethics and politics, suggesting that an Aristotelian approach to business ethics would focus on allowing *potentially* good business people to be sufficiently empowered to actually *be* good business people.

Zahra's work on ethics and politics utilizes empirical survey work to begin understanding US managers' views of organizational politics (1984, 1985). Zahra also uses 55 manufacturing organizations as the unit of analysis in a third piece of research (1987). The individual survey work concluded that managers believe that organizational politics can help accomplish organizational goals. The organizational work revealed the importance of establishing a culture in which self-interest is congruent with organizational advancement. For the cynic, neither of these conclusions sheds much light on ethics and politics. It may be that managers justify any dubious political activities by failing to acknowledge their ethical side, or that the aspiration for good business is simply keeping activities, ethical or otherwise, in line with organizational goals. Neither of these perspectives is satisfactory from the point of view of business ethics.

Ralston et al. (1994: 995) also focus on ethical perceptions of organizational politics, making a comparison between American and Hong Kong managers. They found that, 'in the West, ethical behaviour is an absolute that applies universally, while in the East, "face" and ethical behaviour depend on the situation.' These findings do not, however, go much beyond cultural comparisons, which could and have been done on other topics.

Maclagan notes that a key concern for business ethicists is the potential tension between acting to further one's self interest and forwarding the needs of others and the group (1998: 129–30). He supports the idea that politics in organizations need not be 'nasty', quoting French et al.'s (1983: 373) notion that, 'organizational politics can have a positive and a negative face. The negative face is characterized by extreme pursuit of self-interest ...The positive face of politics is characterized by a balanced pursuit of self-interest'. Maclagan further emphasizes the assumption that political activities are motivated by egotistical self-interest may be incorrect. He suggests that where actions are motivated by altruism, for the wider good and out of generosity to another, they can be regarded as both political and ethical.

Uneasy Bedfellows?

There are some general perspectives on ethics and politics, which we can posit prior to looking at the detailed level of 'turf tactics'. Using theories of utilitarianism, ethical egoism and virtue theory, stances of politicking as generally ethical or generally unethical can be taken.

Politicking is ethical

A number of theories, notably ethical egoism and utilitarianism, view the variety of politicking tactics as potentially ethical. The clearest perspective, which has already been considered by others, is the perspective of ethical egoism as a justification for political action. Egoists argue that an ethical position is one where the individual acts in such a way that they forward their own needs (self-interest) above everyone else's. Hence it is not only justifiable, but also ethically necessary for individuals to act to their own ends in business life, as elsewhere. Any type of political activity, be it forming tactical alliances with colleagues in different departments or massaging rules for one's own convenience, is quite correct. There are limits to this behaviour, however. Egoists will for example bend rules – maybe even contravene them – but will not do so if they judge that they may be caught out, since this will result in sanctions and work against their own best interest. If everyone operates by ethical egoism then we could justify politicking easily: politics and ethics become quite comfortable alongside each other and very ready bedfellows.

However egoism is theoretically inconsistent: the political activist who is an egoist should pursue his or her own goals and thwart others but would simultaneously approve of others doing the same – which in turn will thwart them, hence challenging the consistency of the theory. Furthermore, within the business organization, we assume that people come together with some degree of overlap in terms of a common goal. Certainly organizational mission statements and contracts would suggest loyalty and commitment to a particular set of causes. If it is accepted that every individual will work for their own ends rather than any group, organizational or social goals (unless these are a coincidental outcome of acting egoistically) then notions of organizational objectives, targets, and even a standard culture become highly problematic.

Some would no doubt argue that the enlightened ethical egoist will be aware that acting to forward his or her own goals, for example by pursuing a particular deal which in the short term would bring individual gain, may not always result in the best long term self-interested outcome. Accepting a different deal, which forwards the organizational, or colleagues' interests may still be more beneficial for the individual in terms of good will owing (from the colleague) and reflective benefit (from the organizational advancement – maybe an across the board bonus). This enlightened self-interest form of egoism which sees the benefits of acting for other immediate reasons than the self, but which will also have self-interested outcomes – certainly exists widely in business. But it is highly unlikely that egoistic actions can always have a wider enlightened perspective. There are, by definition of ethical egoism, bound to be cases where acting in one's own self-interest runs contrary to the interests of colleagues and the organization.

The utilitarian principle operates on the basis that an ethical decision is one that benefits the greatest number of people to the greatest extent. What is of interest, when applying utilitarian theory, is the sum of impartial utility of a particular act – the act that maximizes the sum total being ethically preferable. This theory is commonly used as a justification for some individual injustices or questionable activities where 'the ends justify the means'. In the case of organizational politics, for example, manipulation of rules – perhaps insulting the competitor's products contrary to the organizational code of conduct – means that sales targets can be met, which is good for the organization and shareholders (although not so good if consequences for the competitor are taken into account, or the fact that the customer may have the less beneficial product). Hence from an act utilitarian point of view, politicking can be justified where the action results in the greatest good for the greatest number (i.e. everybody wins, or at least more people win than lose). This form of utilitarianism will routinely allow for the disregard of individual rights because of the overwhelming good that is expected to result from the particular act. There are, however, measurement problems with the use of utilitarianism to assess the ethics of an action. Quantifying the value that individuals will put on the outcome of a given act is difficult and subjective. Predicting outcomes of an act is also arbitrary, as are the definitions of 'costs' and 'benefits', which may differ between cultural and other groups.

John Stuart Mill attempted to overcome the disadvantages of act utilitarianism by considering the utility of a rule rather than an act, and hence developed the rule-utilitarian principle. This reconfigures the focus on happiness through a two-stage procedure to establish the criterion of right action. Hence for the rule-utilitarian, rules would be fashioned on utility; conduct on rules. When considering whether an act is right or wrong, one would assess its tendency to, or likelihood of, improving happiness if acts of this type were generally done rather than generally not done (Mackie, 1977: 136). This allows for consideration of political acts in general rather than in the specific act of a specific case. When applying rule utilitarianism to the turf game tactics, the utilitarian application becomes less crude, allowing for more generalizable rules of conduct. Ethicality becomes a function of whether a rule can be constructed which will result in the greatest good. For example, manipulating rules is unlikely to be ethical according to rule utilitarianism since fiddling established codes will not normally or consistently result in the greatest good, although this depends on the content of the rules in the first place!

Politicking is unethical

According to Aristotle, it is through being virtuous that an individual flour-ishes and is happy, and thus ethics is about the character of the individual actor, not the universal correctness of acts or preferred outcomes. Hence we would consider what type of person it is that would act politically and what characteristics they have if they so do. Classic Aristotelian virtues are courage, justice, wisdom and temperance; modern day virtues are wider in scope and might include generosity, honesty, friendship, conscientiousness (Sorell and Hendry, 1994: 46), faithfulness, kindness, co-operativeness and commitment (Beauchamp and Childress, 1994: 68) although there is no definitive list. The virtues are fundamentally socially oriented and consider the support of the weak rather than the self-promotion of the strong. For example, the use of someone else to take the blame for your own mistakes, scapegoating, would be seen as cowardly, and the manipulation of rules to one's own advantage, unjust. In this respect, politicking for self-promotion could be considered the act of an unvirtuous person. It could be argued that commitment to career progression and conscientiousness could be in keep-ing with both the political actor and one expressing positive virtues. However, it is not the case that one can be virtuous by demonstrating one or two virtues. The virtuous person is magnanimous, not self-centred, although their actions are expected to lead to self-satisfaction because of the result of achieving their own happiness.

Applying Ethics to Turf Game Tactics – Points and Counterpoints

Here we apply the range of ethical theories to Buchanan and Badham's (1999a) 'turf game tactics'. Each tactic is considered by pointing to the ethical concerns it might raise, and counterpointed by an assessment of political realities of everyday life.

Image building and selective information

Points

Image building and selective information can be viewed very similarly from an ethical standpoint. They both concern the information we allow others to see, image building being in respect of ourselves, in terms of 'expressions given off' (Goffman, 1959: 16). We are bound to be selective in information presented, whether it be personal or data form – there is not enough time in the day to tell everyone everything, and besides it is hard to argue that we do not legitimately have different roles – brother, mother, boss, subordinate, colleague, friend – wherein different behaviour and presentation of image is highly appropriate. Similarly, in selecting information and data to present within an organization, it is no surprise that the whole story cannot always be told and some selection will be made. Not being selective about information, for example a manager telling the cleaner her personal medical problems, will tend to cause embarrassment and discomfort and may be deemed insensitive or indeed unethical.

Nevertheless, a Kantian would argue that we must always act in such a way that we could will that it becomes a universal law. A clear consequence of acting in accordance with this 'categorical imperative' is the requirement to tell the truth. While Buchanan and Badham do not go as far as to suggest that image building and selective information require outright lies to be told, or false images built, they clearly suggest misrepresentation and the telling of part of the truth as political activities. Where these versions of untruth have been motivated by anything other than good will, that is where the intention behind the politicking was, for example egotistical, then Kant would argue that the actions are unethical.

Counterpoints

The development of image within an organizational setting does not imply the development of false image. Gray and Starke (1984) and Buchanan and Badham (1999a) view image building as a series of actions, which are aimed at enhancing reputation and career. Appelbaum and Hughes (1998: 85) suggest that by using impression management, 'an individual can make a positive impression on influential members of the organization.'

The use of selective information again does not imply misrepresentation or the telling of untruths but is rather a matter of *informed improvisation* (Buchanan and Badham, 1999a: 30) where the individual seeks to use information in a manner, which is beneficial to him/herself and to the organization as a whole.

Scapegoating

Points

Scapegoating, avoiding blame and taking credit for success has elements of image building and similar aspects of Kantian unethical behaviour such as misrepresentation of the truth apply. In addition, however, is the highly unethical use of others for one's own gain. This is again a Kantian formulation of the categorical imperative such that people should be treated as ends in themselves; no one should use someone else exclusively as a means to their own ends. Identifying a scapegoat to take the blame for an event for which one is partly responsible would be quite clearly unethical according to the 'respect for persons' maxim.

Counterpoints

It is difficult to justify the scapegoating of one individual by another. However, is it unethical for the individual to seek to distance him/herself from failure? One might also suggest that attempting to apply a Kantian universalism such as respect for persons is highly problematic in an organizational context where others abandon such rules.

Formal alliances, networking and compromise

Points

From the point of view of discourse ethics, we would expect ethical actors to take actions, which are governed by unrestrained, fully participative argumentative dialogue or discourse (Kettner, 1996). In current business practice this relates reasonably well to the notion of encouraging wide-ranging, genuine stakeholder dialogue with serious expectation and willingness to reach a consensus. In a similar vein, the characteristics of a 'good' conversation as a resolution to ethical problems and as an effective means of strategic management are that it is vocal, reciprocating, issues-oriented, rational, imaginative and honest (Quinn, 1996).

Part of a discourse perspective would certainly be to build alliances and networks in order to ensure wide ranging input into far reaching decisions. Where the discourse perspective would view formal alliances and networking as clearly unethical is where they are built on the basis of bringing the most powerful and influential on side for personal gain. Discourse theory, in contrast advocates the importance of bringing the disempowered and those who are not 'useful' into the discussion, because they have a legitimate right to a voice. Networking and alliance building have the result of blocking full participation, strengthening the 'club' of people who have input into decisions and sabotaging the efforts of those outside of the alliance or network to have an input.

It should be stressed that discourse ethics theory does not advocate sophisticated compromises as a means to conflict resolution. The political actor, who compromises on one issue in order to gain favour for another, is not acting ethically according to discourse theory. He or she should take each discussion in isolation and consider the merits of all relevant arguments, without taking into account 'you scratch my back and I'll scratch yours' arrangements. Discourse theory promotes open, honest, transparent dialogue with all relevant individuals. A successful exchange would be considered to be an argument, in the form of a thorough, constructive discussion, which enables the building of a new normative basis for a decision. Hence in this respect, compromise, networking and alliance building could not be seen as ethical.

Counterpoints

March (1962) defines the organization as a series of political coalitions and as such the notion of consensual discourse must always come up against the *realpolitik* of alliance formation and coalition (Allison, 1971). Part and parcel of any stakeholder involvement as a decision making process involves analysis of the players. Egan (1994) suggests that politics can be positive where they begin with a legitimizing, institution building agenda. This process involves welcoming open scrutiny and entertaining competitive agendas as well as recognizing the value of competition and collaboration. However, Egan also suggests that players need to acquire the power to compete and this will necessarily involve the creation of coalitions. Consensual approaches to goal attainment or conflict resolution are to be welcomed and applauded. However, we also need to recognize the plurality of organizational life and accept that it is not unethical to work with allies to achieve what are deemed to be worthwhile personal and organizational goals.

Rule manipulation

Points

In terms of ethics the most pertinent perspective on rule manipulation is the self-interested interpretation of codes of conduct. One of the criticisms of codes of conduct is the difficulty of interpreting them consistently. Where there is natural room for varied interpretations, the malleable use of the rules to one's own advantage may be difficult to distinguish. Again in this case we come back to Kantianism as the clearest position against rule manipulation as being ethical. Kant's universal law demands that the same action must be taken in every circumstance, breaking, bending and stretching the rules are entirely inconsistent with this formulation of the categorical imperative.

Counterpoint

There is little to justify the ethicality of rule manipulation. It rests with a managerialist perspective of organizational life which sees the use of power or rules to manipulate situations as legitimate on the part of management but illegitimate by others. However, in the real world of organizational rules, structures and conventions bending and manipulation are bound to take place. They need not be applauded but certainly need to be recognized and challenged.

Ruthless

Points

Buchanan and Badham's final category is a catch all for political activities they refer to as, 'covert and ruthless aspects of political behaviour' (1999a: 28). The category includes wide ranging perspectives including the use of coercion, attacking, and warring metaphors. While this is in keeping with some analogies with business, for example the Machiavellian perspective on successful management (Machiavelli, reprinted 1993), and Sun Tzu's, 'The Art of War' (reprinted 1990), the suggestion is that the end point is really the systematic undermining of others, not just the promotion of the self. The suggestion in terms of Machiavelli was that a ruler, or powerful person, cannot rely on prudence and caution alone, but must be prepared to take bold action in order to maintain power – even if cruel and violent actions are required (Germino, 1972: 22). There has to be a point, however, at which this is inconsistent with the idea of the organization where not all those seeking power are the legitimate leader. How can an organization possibly prosper, even survive, if it is being dismantled by internal antagonism, where even force is acceptable? In current Western business environments even ethical egoism does not justify such behaviour, since threatening the existence of the company is highly likely to go against individual self-interest, and breaking the law which, the extremes of the 'ruthless' activity suggests, is clearly detrimental to the self, assuming one is caught sooner or later.

Counterpoints

Can 'dirty tricks' ever be condoned. Buchanan and Badham (1999a: 222) speculate that, 'The flat, flexible, fluid and organic organization offers considerable scope for emotional arousal, for direct social interaction, for improvisation. In other words, organizational trends appear to be creating conditions in which the Machiavellian manager will thrive.' What they refer to as 'the ongoing action' of ploys and plots, wheeler-dealing, scapegoating, etc., is dependent on the accounts and outcomes of a specific political behaviour and how this affects the reputation of the individual manager within his or her organizational setting. In this sense, the ruthlessness of individual action might be deemed ethical where it takes place against unacceptable provocation. The notion of

'I did it because I was provoked' or 'I did it because she started it' seems to offer some form of tacit personal warrant for political activity (Buchanan and Badham, 1999a: 33).

Conclusion

In concluding, we would like to draw particular attention to discourse theory as a way forward in helping practical development of ethical politics. Many of the turf game tactics become irrelevant and indeed useless as ways of achieving things if discourse is given primacy in an organizational culture. This might be deemed to move analysis of politics away from the negative perspective and towards discussion of the behavioural repertoire of political entrepreneurs and the practice of positive politics.

If discourse is privileged in an organizational culture as a sensible background to organizational behaviour and politics, we argue that both ethics and politics will be surfaced and actively acknowledged in organizational life. The requirement for honesty and full disclosure will mean that image building is superfluous and the supplying of *appropriate* selective information the norm. The need for transparency means that scapegoating, rule manipulation and certainly ruthless tactics are taken outside the realms of acceptable behaviour. Alliances and networking become legitimate as long as they allow for open dialogue with all parties who have an interest – closed groups who support each other with mutual favours are not acceptable. Finally, compromises are not enough. What is needed in resolving different viewpoints is a new normative basis in which everyone relevant has a stake and with which they are content.

There are, however, some national cultures, which are more predisposed to adopting a discourse perspective than others (French and Mühlfriedel, 1998). In Germany and the Netherlands, for example, consensus building and inclusion are accepted modes of business practice. Such approaches are far less familiar, and may even be seen as radical, in US and UK contexts. These complications not withstanding, openness and transparency are, we propose, extraordinarily effective diffusers of divisive political behaviour.

Merely putting forward a discussion of how different ethical theories view turf game tactics offers no real help to organizational actors. However, discourse ethics is a useful way of making sense of politics and ethics in organizations. The hybrid nature of discourse ethics means that, in doing this, we do not wish to promote one epistemological perspective over others. A focus on discourse allows for the unique context, yet has consistent rules. What remains is undeniably a privileging of process over consequences. The value of this in particular needs further research and investigation.

Organizational politics is deemed ethical when measured against normative judgements such as utilitarianism, rights and justice. Most academic definitions of politics have adopted a neutral stance towards the morality and ethics of politics (Drory and Romm, 1990). One might argue that individuals may use utilitarianism to mask self-serving actions and although political engagements are entered into for the organizational good, in most instances this will protect or promote the reputation of the individual. A wider understanding of political behaviour may assist moves towards more collaborative and participative change strategies by getting what has been previously spoken of in hushed tones into the public arena. What may also be more interesting in future is whether discourse ethics begin to change the political agenda away from the macho side of politics and how more consensual models of organizational politicking begin to emerge.

More open discussion of politicking through discourse analysis may highlight the specific behaviours of managers which are deemed to be unethical, self-serving and against the notion of collaboration. At least this should enable others to have a greater awareness of the tactics pursued and to develop responses to them, hence levelling the political playing field.

13 | The Learning Organization

It would be erroneous to chart the development of OD without giving some consideration to the learning organization. This terminology, or possibly more accurately the underpinning philosophy, often attributed to Peter Senge, has become increasingly popular with both management gurus and leaders of change. Learning organizations have joined the litany of corporate buzzwords. The learning organization with its roots firmly in the 1990s can be seen as a precursor to, or at least a contributing factor to, the development of many other 'routes' to corporate success and survival, such as, the knowledge or artful worker, knowledge management approaches, innovation and creativity based business solutions, and services science and innovation. Before continuing with an exploration of the concepts and practices that underlie the learning organization it is perhaps appropriate to give some consideration to whether they are the invention of the corporate marketing world, or whether indeed there is some substance and justification to support such a claim. It is important to make a distinction between fads and trends. Fads exist to respond to short-term changes in demand such as business process re-engineering or outsourcing. Trends by contrast are the consequence of long term patterns of change, which are indicative of the changing nature of society, such as increased health consciousness and the need for increased flexibility of organizational resources.

To what extent then might learning organizations be considered as a fad, in response to some wider corporate trend, or indeed as a trend in themselves? There is little doubt that the term itself is widely used both as an external marketing vehicle, and internally as a means of developing staff consciousness and awareness of the need to be more receptive to opportunities for service or product improvement. There is however a general trend, not only at the organizational level, but also at the level of society at large, to realize the full potential of the working community. From a human resource perspective, one might argue that there is nothing new in such a notion; however, the realization of such an ideal in practice requires nothing less than a *cultural revolution*.

Management theorists constantly portray the external environment as 'turbulent'. Rapidly-evolving technology, dynamic markets and increasingly sophisticated customers and competitors combine forces to challenge the traditional notions of successful businesses. It is a widely accepted belief that successful organizations of the future will be those who are sufficiently flexible to respond to these constantly changing demands and have the ability to redirect, focus and resource effectively, appropriately and more quickly than their competitors. Argyris and Schon (1996) describe the conventional wisdom that suggests all organizations need to draw lessons from the past, detect and correct errors, anticipate and respond to impending threats, engage in continuing innovation and build and realize images of a desirable future. They suggest that a virtual consensus exists and that we are all subject to a learning imperative. Clearly, it is not enough merely to respond to the changes but to develop the capability to predict what they may be, to develop a corporate understanding of a range of possible futures and position the organization appropriately to meet any of these potential demands.

Developments in the field of strategy, where strategic thinking may be rethought of in terms of organizational change, has also triggered the interest in how organizations learn. Reflecting the growing agreement that development of strategy as an active, iterative process, involving whole organizations, it strongly suggests a requirement to understand the processes of institutional learning and what creates a learning organization (Argyris and Schon, 1996).

Drucker (1998) suggests that the development of information technology will have a significant effect on the internal appearance of organizations of the future. He argues for a reduced hierarchy as fewer managers are required to act as conduits for information. He also describes the enhanced dissemination of information that he predicts will shift the responsibility for decision making further down the organization. This movement creates the need to develop the skills of those who use data, convert it into information and then use that information to acquire knowledge that guides the organizational response to the external environment. It is not only the terminology he uses, but also the process he describes that suggests learning. This is further supported by his advocacy of executives and specialists who, 'need to think through what data they need – first to know what they are doing, then to be able to decide what they should be doing and finally to appraise how well they are doing'.

Despite its appeal, the concept of a learning organization is not new. A number of initiatives and models have been developed to guide organizations to an enhanced level of effectiveness that can be translated into competitive advantage. Such programmes include continuous improvement (CI), business process re-engineering (BPR), total quality management (TQM), and even the balanced score card (BSC), all of which suggest a consideration of what organizations need to do differently to maintain their competitiveness.

Garratt (1994) suggests that the major ideas underlying the concept of a learning organization have been in place since the 1940s. He cites the pioneering work of Revans, the proponent of action learning, the economist Fritz Schumachker and the cybernetic research of Norbert Weiner, Ross Ashby and Jacob Bronowski. He argues that through their work developed the notion that the sole source of organizational learning is people, that learning has an intrinsic (personal development) value and an extrinsic (organizational asset creating) value, and that multiple feedback loops of learning are required for developing continuous organizational learning. He argues that the recent acceptance of the concept of a learning organization is a result of economic recession in the West and fierce competition from Asia.

The learning organization concept has been suggested as way of moving an organization towards improved performance on the understanding that improvement depends on learning something new, on seeing things with a different perspective and that to continuously improve requires a commitment to learning. The risk of not learning is that old practices will be repeated and any changes will be merely cosmetic. If it can be said to have a central theme, the notion of the learning organization is one that relates to formally acknowledging and providing for feedback as a basis for change.

There are many definitions of what constitutes a 'learning organization' and much of the literature emphasizes 'aspirational' theory, with little focus on the practical aspects that organizations need to consider. As Garvin (1993) describes, academics are partly responsible for the plethora of definitions and he criticizes them for their, 'reverential and utopian ...near mystical terminology.' He argues that the recommendations of leading theorists such as Senge and Nonaka are often too abstract and too many questions remain unanswered. For example:

How will managers know when their organizations have achieved the lofty heights of the learning organization?

What concrete changes in behaviour are required?

What policies and programmes must be in place?

How do you get from here to there?

Defining the Nature of the Beast

There is an abundance of literature surrounding the concept of the learning organization that can be divided into two distinct categories. The first addresses the conceptual aspects relating to the theory of organizational learning and to opinions on learning types, the process of learning, and seeks to differentiate between individual and organizational learning. The second category of work has developed as a result of the experiences of practitioners who have attempted to introduce these concepts into organizations.

It has long been argued that there are two types of learning: single- and double-loop learning. Single-loop, or instrumental learning, is described by Senge (1990) as adaptive learning, which changes the 'theory of action' and response to a problem but not the 'theory-in-use' (Argyris and Schon, 1996). It pertains to the detection and correction of error within the boundaries of current thinking that, potentially, allows the problem to re-emerge in the future. Within an organization, this is a process by which an entity learns to do better what it is currently doing; adaptive learning is about coping. This basic form of learning is restrictive and non-challenging. The problems of the day are solved without taking time to understand their root cause and taking action to ensure that they will not be repeated. The term learning organization has been used by some as implying a transformational approach to change that comes from double-loop learning. Incremental change or adaptation via such processes as TQM is the outcome of single-loop learning. This narrow frame of reference can, over time, transform the perceived core capabilities of an organization to 'core rigidities' as members consistently fail to challenge existing patterns of thinking and behaviour, resulting in an inflexible, reactive company, characterized by short-termism (Slater and Narver, 1995). This perpetual cycle, whilst it exists, can be a source of comfort to organizations who enjoy a sense of security in their ability to repeatedly solve familiar day-to-day issues. Much of the literature in fact makes no such distinction and uses the terms interchangeably. The potentially different outcomes for organization change from single- and double-loop learning are really the essential implication of Argyris and Schon's work.

Double-loop learning, or generative learning (Senge, 2006), occurs when there is a willingness to challenge long held assumptions and create new ways of looking at the world. Generative learning is about creating knowledge. The two feedback loops connect the observed effects of action with strategies and the values served by those strategies and may be carried out by either individuals or organizations. This 'framebreaking' approach within organizations is most likely to lead to competitive advantage because it focuses on reviewing and changing business systems rather than functional efficiency (Slater and Narver, 1995). It is more challenging to organizations because it forces them to consider that their accepted ways of thinking and behaving may no longer be appropriate and this process of review can be painful. Nevertheless, if organizations

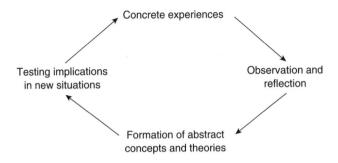

Figure 13.1   The Kolb learning cycle

are to develop the capability to renew themselves to meet the demands of the emerging environment then they will need the capacity for generative learning.

Carr (1997: 224–31) in reviewing the work of Argyris and Schon argues that

> single-loop learning has had the practical effect of diverting attention away from the possibility of double-loop learning and has in this context. This is an interesting point, for in recent years some in the literature have actually made a distinction between the terms 'learning organization' and 'organizational learning' on the basis of the conservatism implied in single- and double-loop learning for organization change.

Fulmer (1996) argues an alternative but complementary approach to the understanding of types of learning. His theory of maintenance learning relates to single-loop learning as does his theory of shock learning, a response to crisis, both of which are short term, reactive learning systems involving little creativity or challenge to developed thinking. Conversely, anticipatory learning is more akin to generative/double-loop learning in that it is participatory, future oriented and long term in its outlook.

Argyris and Schon (1996) present a schema for learning:

- informational content – *the learning product*;

- *the learning process* – acquiring, processing and storing of information;

- *a learner* to whom the process is attributed.

The learning cycle developed by David Kolb (1976) is often used to describe phase two of this schema; the 'natural process of learning' (see Figure 13.1).

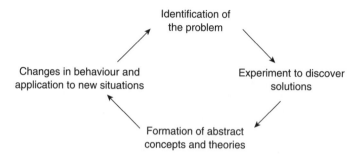

Figure 13.2   The Buckler model

A four phase process based on concrete experience, reflection and observation and the development of theories and concepts which are tested for their relevance and validity, it is closely aligned to the Deming cycle of PLAN-DO-CHECK-ACT and the model presented by Buckler (1996), which prescribes the identification of problems, experimentation to discover solutions, development of new theory, change in behaviour and application to new situations (see Figure 13.2).

Both models emphasize learning from experience, reflecting on that experience and forming new ideas that are then tested in a reiterative process.

The Kolb cycle was initially developed to represent the process of individual learning. However, he describes how this can be adapted for organizational learning. Building upon the notion that individuals have diverse learning styles and will therefore have unique capabilities that lend themselves more closely to specific phases; he recommends the development of teams that incorporate the specific skills required at each phase.

Kolb's argument suggests that organizational learning be differentiated from individual learning by the nature of collective experience. This is accepted by Argyris and Schon (1996) who argue that for action and inquiry to be truly 'organizational', it must be within previously agreed boundaries and parameters of policy that turn a group of individuals into an organization. Van der Heijden and Eden (1994) extend this by distinguishing individual and organizational learning by an alignment of thinking. Supporting the idea of learning from experience, they suggest that learning from uncoordinated activity will remain an individual affair. They argue that Kolb's model emphasizes the proactive approach required for organizational learning – the need to consciously create experiences from which to learn – but stress that an alignment of thinking will direct the creation of experience and encourage joint reflection and testing of theory, developing common understanding and consensus as to the required response to the problem. This argument echoes Senge (2006) who presents shared vision and mental models as prerequisites for organizational learning.

It has been argued that the distinguishing factor between individual and organizational learning is information dissemination (Slater and Narver, 1995). Initially this seems a simplistic theory, but on closer examination supports the previously presented arguments. They argue that information is shared with the objective of increasing its value via the process of feedback, providing a broader context from which to view the world and providing new insights into potential solutions to problems. It is only by disseminating information that a shared interpretation can be achieved and a consensus reached as to the meaning and implication for the business that will shape future activity.

Organizational enquiry

Van der Heijden and Eden (1994) and Argyris and Schon (1996), suggest that learning will only occur when the results of organizational enquiry are different from expectation, which triggers further thought, reflection and challenges the current 'theory-in-use'. To become organizational, learning must be embedded in the images of the organization held in the minds of its members or the physical artefacts embedded in the environment. The challenge may trigger changes in organizational activity in order to realign with the new system of beliefs. This element of change is the learning product, and interestingly, Argyris and Schon argue that it is not always positive. Individuals can learn collectively to respond to error by scapegoating, using systematic patterns of deception, camouflage of intention and maintenance of taboos. They argue that productive learning takes place when organizational enquiry is pursued for the improvement of business performance and when values and criteria that define 'improvement' shape that enquiry. Finally, productive learning enhances the capabilities for future learning as individuals practise the process of enquiry and development of commonly held definitions.

Conversation and shared language

For an organization to take effective advantage of learning opportunities, members must identify and break down the barriers that inhibit productive learning. There is a need for meaningful, open conversations, and developing the capabilities for conversation is not easy, but essential if learning is to take place by challenging deeply held assumptions (Senge, 2006). Van der Heijden and Eden (1994) expand upon this by arguing the need for a shared language, developed through collective experience, to facilitate productive verbal exchange. They describe the existence of labels and jargon as manifestations of the process of language building and they refer to the way concepts of strategy have been codified in management text books to aid effective conversation. Nevertheless, they argue that language can only represent yesterday's problems and will evolve as organizations seek for new responses to the new reality.

Arguing from the context of strategy development, they contend that through institutional action, the alignment of mental models and facilitated by shared language, planning becomes a joint activity and learning experience. Stata (1989) develops the concept of a collective experience and introduces organizational memory. This depends on the mechanisms used to retain knowledge; policies, strategies and explicit models – documentation, information systems, etc. Reliance on individual memory clearly constitutes a major risk as personnel change roles or leave the business.

To sum up these ideas on organization and learning:

- Learning takes place as a result of experience and the key differentiator between individual and organizational learning is the collective nature of experience, and the joint testing of potential responses to that experience to develop a shared view of what constitutes appropriate action.

- Organizational learning does not occur when individual members of the organization learn; there is a major emphasis on the sharing of information and establishing a shared interpretation. Thus organizations can only learn as quickly as the slowest link learns.

- Change is blocked unless all the major decision makers learn together and are committed to the actions necessary for change.

- Learning only happens if the results of experience are different from expectation and it is facilitated by a shared language and enhanced capability for meaningful conversation.

- Meaningful conversation takes place when there is a willingness to challenge assumptions that trigger change in behaviour. It is this environment that is most conducive to double-loop/generative learning.

The Relevance of a Learning Organization

If the need for increasing flexibility and adaptability for most organizations is accepted one might argue, then the need to change within an organization should stem from a desire to create competitive advantage and there is a strong link with organizational learning. Stata (1989) is often quoted:

> I would argue that the rate at which individuals and organizations learn may become the only sustainable competitive advantage, especially in knowledge-intensive industries.

Competitive advantage can come under different guises. Senge (1995) argues that it is generated within organizations committed to marrying individual development with superior economic performance to improve quality, to delight customers, to energize and motivate employees and to manage change. It is further argued that learning provides a buffer between the organization and its environment to stop a reactive response to every event (Slater and Narver, 1995). Despite being built from a platform of past experience, a company committed to learning is inherently forward looking which reduces the frequency of major shocks and fosters an enhanced level of flexibility with which to respond to, and predict, emergent opportunities. This develops the rationale for a learning organization by presenting the view of learning as a natural human process, and that to encourage it will unleash previously unharnessed individual, and thus organizational energy. It suggests that it stems naturally from previous thinking in organizational development, and that it is reflected in the modern Japanese management approach. Because of these influences, development of learning is essential to create superior performance and sustain competitive advantage.

Senge builds upon the belief that 'human beings are designed for learning' and that the major institutions and their processes which are designed to control stifles that natural learning process. He comments that by focusing on performance for someone else's approval, corporations create the conditions that lead to mediocre performance. He quotes W. Edwards Deming, leader of the quality movement:

> Our prevailing system of management has destroyed our people. People are born with intrinsic motivation, self-esteem, dignity, curiosity to learn, joy in learning. The forces of destruction begin with toddlers – the prizes for the best Halloween costume, grades in school, gold stars, and on up through university. On the job, people, teams, divisions are ranked – reward for the one at the top, punished at the bottom. Management by objectives, quotas, incentive pay, business plans, put together separately, division by division cause further loss, unknown and unknowable.

Senge (2006) contends that a young child entering school soon discovers that the name of the game is getting the right answer and not making mistakes. This manifests itself in organizations of individuals who also understand the game and avoid making mistakes or, at least, avoid admitting to them. This prohibits the superior learning that Senge believes is required for superior performance. He also challenges the role of the leader who 'learned for the organization', arguing that it is no longer feasible to 'figure it out at the top' and a dynamic, interdependent and unpredictable world requires integration of learning and acting at all levels. Senge attributes the rise of the Japanese manufacturing companies to a recognition of the need to integrate. Recognizing that the key to reducing cost was the elimination of process delays, they worked extensively to build networks with trusted suppliers and to reduce delays in materials procurement, production set-up and in-process inventory. The attitude of continuous improvement and total quality management is essentially a generative learning process geared today towards understanding the latent needs of customers – what they really value but have never experienced and would never think to demand.

The evolution of learning organizations: impact on training and development

Pedler et al. (1991) offer a different perspective to the contemporary relevance of a learning organization which is seen as an evolutionary process, combining the phases of organizational development with significant impact on training and development. This supports the view of Garratt (1994). They describe the movement from primal to rational phase, where the organization develops from the entrepreneurial form, characterized by charismatic leadership, flat structures, and limited specialization, to a more complex organization with hierarchical structures, increasing levels of specialization and where commitment to the profession outweighs that to the organization. Energy becomes focused on building systems and structures to cope with the increasing requirements for analysis and recording.

This leads to a bureaucratic crisis and increasing alienation from both customers and fellow members of the organization. One potential response is the matrix organization where horizontal, temporary project teams supplement the original vertical authority relationships in an attempt to break down the barriers and team-building, conflict resolution and customer care programmes are the norm. This is followed by the differentiated phase of organizational development and the integrated organization – one that has been described as a shamrock (Handy, 1989) and a cloverleaf by others. The key factor is that throughout the organization, at all levels and in all directions, there is increasing integration between people, functions and ideas. An example of practice in this type of organization is the increasing collaboration with external suppliers and customers, which is mirrored internally. Similarly, there is an emphasis on aligning the espoused values of the organization with its business processes.

Movement in training and development mirrors these developments in organization design. The rational phase is complemented by a systematic approach to training illustrated by establishing best practice, job descriptions, job analysis, behavioural objectives and systematic evaluation. As alienation and frustration become more pronounced, the response is geared towards organizational development, self-development, and the pursuit of excellence (Peters and Waterman, 1982), which has manifested itself in a plethora of initiatives (TQM, CI, BPR). Many organizations facing this evolutionary phase have found their training and development programmes unfocused, individualistic, and without longevity. There has been an increasing sense of the organization not actually getting anywhere despite the level of activity. The evolutionary response to this, argue Pedler et al., is organizational transformation. The response to self-development and action learning is the concept of the learning organization

Organizational transformation (OT) has been described as 'the extension to organization development that seeks to create massive changes in an organization's structures, processes, culture and orientation to its environment' (French et al., 2005). It is the application of behavioural science theory and practice to effect large-scale paradigm-shifting organizational change and usually results in totally new paradigms or models for organizing and performing work.

In trying to develop a relationship between the learning organization, OD and the management of change one can identify three key linkages:

- The concept of a *learning organization* is increasingly relevant as businesses seek to deal with complex environments.

- It is a natural evolution from earlier forms of training and development as organizations evolve new behaviours and structures.

- It harnesses the belief that humans are designed for learning.

The emerging challenge is how to accelerate organizational learning, build consensus for change and how to facilitate the change process. The concept of a learning organization seems to fit comfortably with this challenge, but there are many models, definitions and characteristics which are used to illustrate what a learning organization might look like, and how to achieve one. The next section presents some of the more influential ideas.

Building a Learning Organization

The body of work relating to definitions, characteristics and models for creating a learning organization seem to fall naturally into three categories:

1 the application of the academic theory of systemic learning to business;

2 the presentation of definitions followed by prescriptive, practical solutions;

3 the work of practitioners who decry a prescriptive approach but offer guidelines and practical hints as to how organizations can develop a bespoke approach.

Academic theory of systemic learning – the Senge model

Peter Senge and colleagues at the Massachusetts Institute of Technology pioneered efforts to apply academic theory of the learning organization to business. Senge has been described as the 'intellectual and spiritual champion' of the learning organization by *Fortune* magazine and his philosophy is based on a humanist view of organizational change: that businesses should pay more attention to the conditions that motivate people to do great things for themselves and for their companies.

> Our organizations work the way they work, ultimately, because of how we think and how we interact. Only by changing how we think can we change deeply embedded policies and practices. Only by changing how we interact can shared visions, shared understandings and new capacities for co-ordinated action be established. (Senge, 2006)

This involves a commitment to lifelong learning and Senge's (2006) work has led to the development of the *five disciplines*, which he describes as artistic rather than traditional management disciplines, aimed at enhancing an organization's creative capability.

- *Personal mastery*   The ability to clarify what one most desires in life and work and to apply the principles and values most important to achieving those goals. Essential to the process is building self-awareness and understanding personal strengths and weaknesses. He also argues that managing the creative tension between the vision and the current reality is a critical dimension.

- *Mental models*   These are the assumptions that shape one's view of the world, developed from past experience, and feed the judgements and perceptions that influence what one hears, says and reacts to others. Senge argues that it is not easy to articulate these models because people naturally seek evidence consistent with prior beliefs and this blindness provides a resistance to change. In organizations, mental models shape the views of the market and influence the development of strategies. In an organization it has been established that success is more likely to stem from an alignment of thinking, therefore it is not necessarily important in the first instance to judge whether they are right or wrong, but to understand what they are and how they influence thinking.

- *Building a shared vision*   Senge argues that whether a vision is created by an entire company or a team of two, is not important. The key factor is that it is created collectively because the collective capability to realize the vision is more powerful than that of a single individual. Nevertheless, it follows that in an organization the more members that have been actively involved in the process of developing a shared vision the higher the degree of ownership and the greater the commitment to achieving it. Furthermore, it is less open to misinterpretation as it is communicated to members of the business.

- *Team learning*   This is based on the acceptance that people who work well together can learn more and accomplish more than is possible individually. It builds from the previous three disciplines, because not all teams can generate the power of collective thinking, and they are essential to team communication which leads to productive learning and action. Senge suggests that effective group learning involves listening to others without confirmation bias, being receptive to new ideas and being comfortable with not knowing the answers to every question.

- *Systems thinking*   This refers to a conceptual framework that defines a system as a set of interrelated parts. The key to understanding is to understand how all the parts connect and interrelate. Naturally a business organization is a complex system with many subsystems and applying systems thinking means viewing each function as part of the larger system rather than as a collection of isolated tasks. It is the nature of the relationship between these subsystems that influences the performance of the whole. This was based on a detailed and proactive review of organizational systems and their interrelated parts. Similar issues and approaches were introduced in Chapter 6.

These disciplines have emerged from the belief that for sustainable success, contemporary leaders need to adopt new roles and develop new skills that signal a movement away from the authoritarian decision maker. He argues that complex environments require leaders to become designers, teachers and stewards.

As *teachers* they are required to act as coach, guide and facilitator, encouraging members of the organization to gain more insightful views of the current reality – to bring to the surface those assumptions which influence thinking and behaviour but which usually remain tacit. He argues it signals a movement away from short term response to events (single-loop learning) to an investigation of the systemic structure of long term trends which reveal the underlying causes and pave the way for successful change.

As *stewards*, he argues, leaders are responsible for establishing the attitude towards members of the organization and towards the essential mission of the business. They need to act as role models, displaying commitment to the espoused values and behaviour they expect to witness in others.

It is in his description of leaders as *designers* that the most interesting perspectives are given. Leaders are responsible for designing the governing ideas of purpose, vision and core values. Furthermore, they are responsible for designing the policies, tasks and structures that translate those ideas into business decisions. It is this process, he argues, that can stimulate effective learning. We can relate this directly back to Chapter 9 where we discussed the need for organizations to develop purpose, vision and guiding values and beliefs.

Senge notes that the process of strategy development is changing and can be seen as an iterative process and therefore attention should be given to developing the process of strategic thinking rather than the publication of a carefully developed document. This is supported by de Geus (1988) and his experience at Royal-Dutch Shell where corporate planners, after failing to convince the decision makers that the stable world of rising demand for oil was changing, adapted their role to one of fostering learning rather than devising plans. The rise of scenario analysis engaged the key decision makers in the process of understanding the business implications of a range of possible futures. In doing so, they leveraged institutional learning processes as, 'management teams shared their mental models of their company, their markets and their competitors.'

Senge's work is popular because it draws on a range of disciplines – psychology, physics, education, and systems dynamics – in a powerful form. It is aligned to much of the theory espoused by Argyris, Schon, Van der Heijden and Eden and builds upon the values of a collective, participative approach, the alignment of thinking and shared interpretation and quite clearly espouses double-loop or generative learning. But he offers little in the way of guidance as to how to master these disciplines in a business environment or how to recognize the achievement. To a considerable extent this criticism is answered in his *Fieldbook*; a collection of essays, case studies, personal insights and practical suggestions to guide the business leader towards a successful learning environment (Senge, 1995). It is not designed to be prescriptive, rather an encyclopaedia or reference work from which to develop an appropriate approach for individual organizations.

In general, Senge's work reinforces the core message of this book. People, in particular the way in which they are organized, determine through shared and forward looking strategies, the degree to which an organization will succeed in a rapidly changing environment.

The Nonaka and Takeuchi Model (1991) distinguishes between organizational learning and knowledge creation, insisting that the former is an assimilation of existing knowledge and the latter constitutes 'breakthrough thinking' which leads to new knowledge and innovation. Breakthrough thinking is dependent on the interplay between tacit and explicit knowledge i.e. the relationship between unarticulated, intuitive knowledge and the knowledge that is captured in written documents and computerized data banks.

They attribute the success of Japanese companies to the mechanisms and culture developed to harness tacit knowledge: on-the-job training, employee autonomy, long term employment and a cultural tendency to internalize experience. When tacit knowledge is made explicit it can be used in product or process innovation. This new knowledge is internalized which becomes part of the tacit knowledge base of the company. They argue that the Western practice of rendering work practices explicit in manuals and detailed analyses generates little room for creativity. Their model depicts five requirements for knowledge creation.

- *Organizational intention* Identified in the organization's strategic vision, which should be sufficiently broad to allow room for interpretation, but provide a cohesive direction.

- *Autonomy* All employees should be trusted to act independently; teams can share ideas generated by individuals. Teams should be encouraged to pursue innovation even when they challenge conventional wisdom.

- *Fluctuation and creative chaos* Fluctuation describes the concept of challenging mental models or behaviours and creative chaos refers to the sense of urgency to stimulate efforts to generate breakthrough thinking and is the result of leaders intentionally disturbing the environment through new goals or missions.

- *Redundancy* This refers to the intentional overlapping of information and management responsibilities based on a theory that duplication spreads information more widely and accelerates the knowledge creation process. In Japan this is demonstrated by competitions between different development teams working on the same project. Another example would be functional rotation to broaden employees' understanding of the business system and improving cross-functional communication.

- *Requisite variety* The creation of environments which facilitate the sharing of diverse perspective and a variety of information. This is most readily witnessed in the creation of multi-functional project teams, to pool varied skills and to minimize the number of surprises as the product is handed from design to production and marketing.

Nonaka and Takeuchi share Senge's commitment to human dynamics and build upon the theory of organizational learning and the notions of team effort, shared vision, the balance between individual freedom and organizational discipline, and the continuous testing of assumptions about how things get done. It may be argued that their definition of knowledge creation is akin to Senge's generative learning: both constitute a proactive approach in order to dramatically change the status quo. Nevertheless, the model gives little guidance on how to bridge the gap between theory and practice and, does little to address the inherent difficulties of national cultural differences.

Once again these themes seem similar to the early work on OD and the development of models of motivation such as autonomous teamwork.

Definitions and prescriptive, practical approaches

The Garvin (1993) model attempts to address this shortfall. Garvin's five component model is designed to create an organization, 'that is skilled at creating, acquiring and transferring knowledge, and at modifying its behaviour to reflect new knowledge and insights.'

- *Systematic problem solving* A scientific method rather than guesswork, building on data not assumptions and using statistical tools to organize data and draw inferences. He recommends specific training in small group activities and problem solving techniques designed to generate ideas, analyse and display data and plan action. Furthermore, he recommends that these tools be imposed at all meetings.

- *Experimentation* The systematic searching for and testing of new knowledge; a scientific method akin to the problem solving techniques. The key to success is that opportunity and the desire to expand horizons, not as a response to crises, should motivate this activity. Experimentation can be witnessed in continuous programmes of small experiments to ensure a steady flow of new ideas and need to be supported by commitment to developing the skills necessary for experiment design, process analysis and creativity techniques. Furthermore, they need to be tightly focused and tailored to employees' needs so one would not necessarily expect the same development programme to be offered to manufacturing engineers and development personnel alike. Experimentation can also be encouraged via demonstration projects that involve holistic, system-wide approaches and are designed to transform superficial knowledge into deep understanding. They have the benefit of embodying the principles and approaches that will be adopted in the future; they establish policy guidelines and decision-making criteria and test the commitment of senior members of the organization. They are usually developed by multi-functional teams, but have little impact if they are not accompanied by a strategy for transferring the learning.

- *Learning from past experience* Garvin insists that companies must review their successes and failures, assess them systematically and record them in a form that employees find open and accessible. He cites the post-project appraisal unit at British Petroleum, responsible for writing case studies following major projects, as an example of learning from the past and recognizing the value of productive failure when contrasted with unproductive success. Other, less costly, methods to capture learning include enlisting the help of universities and business schools to bring a fresh perspective.

- *Learning from others* Powerful insights can be gained from looking outside one's immediate environment. Businesses in different industries can be a fertile source of ideas and catalysts for creative thinking. Benchmarking, a disciplined process and search for best practices via site visits and interviews concludes with the analysis of results and a series of recommendations and implementation plans. Structured customer contact also invariably stimulates learning.

- *Transferring knowledge* Ideas carry maximum impact when they are shared. Garvin recommends written oral and visual reports, site visits, personnel rotation programmes and education, but stresses that each medium should be tailored to meet the needs of the audience. Reports are popular but cumbersome and he acknowledges that it is difficult to become knowledgeable in a passive way and emphasizes the benefit of transferring personnel with expertise to other areas and education programmes linked to live problems.

Unlike the previous models, Garvin discusses how to measure a learning organization and suggests learning audits by using questionnaires, surveys and interviews to assess attitudes and depth of understanding. This should be supplemented where possible with direct observation to assess behavioural changes, and the development of performance measures such as the half-life curve (a method of measuring the time it takes to achieve a 50 per cent improvement in a specified performance indicator), to test how cognitive and behavioural changes have produced results. Without this, he argues, organizations will lack a rationale for investing in learning and the assurance that learning is serving the organization's ends.

He continues to recommend first steps:

1   Foster an environment conducive to learning: free up time for reflection and analysis, and training in the required skill base.

2   Open the boundaries to stimulate the exchange of ideas: establish project teams and conferences that cross organizational levels or link the company with its external environment (customers, suppliers, industry associations).

3   Create learning forums: programmes or events designed with specific learning goals in mind. Strategic reviews, systems audits, internal benchmarking and study missions are examples.

The first two steps can be seen within the total project management model outlined in Chapter 7 where emphasis is placed on ensuring analytical approaches, employed by project teams are utilized in managing complex problems. As we discussed earlier, the use of external change agents, the objective outsider, can assist in learning from others and transferring knowledge. In addition, by ensuring that the external agents bring with them the ability to disseminate and transfer previous knowledge and understanding, the organization can foster a creative learning environment.

Garvin's model does not ignore the theory of organizational learning. It incorporates the concepts of learning from experience, working through teams and supports the belief implicit in the works of both Senge and Nonaka, that productive learning is dependent on the development of a distinctive mindset and pattern of behaviour. It differs in its emphasis that the creation of learning organizations will only be truly successful if these elements are supported by systems and processes integrated into the fabric of daily life. They serve both to create and sustain a learning culture. His contention that commitment to learning will be maintained only by demonstrating its value to the organization is a realistic, if cynical, viewpoint. Importantly, he promotes the value of an external focus to developing learning opportunities, which is missing in the earlier models.

Guidelines and practical hints

Garvin's work is essentially prescriptive but this style has been criticized by practitioners such as, Pedler et al. (1991) and Pearn et al. (1995). These works suggest that a definition of the learning organization cannot exist. Pearn et al. suggest that learning is a process not a state and that the possession of a number of characteristics does not necessarily entitle an organization to be called *the* learning organization. Pedler et al., prefer to use the term 'company' rather than organization, insisting that the latter is a mechanical word sounding abstract and lifeless, and suggest that the learning company is a vision of what might be possible and have developed a list of eleven features of that vision:

The learning approach to strategy

The formation of policy, implementation, evaluation and improvement are structured as learning processes, with conscious experiments and feedback loops.

Participative policy making

This encourages debate and fosters the airing of differences as a way of reaching business decisions that all members are likely to support.

Informating

This is the state of affairs in which information technology is used to inform and empower people rather than just measuring performance.

Formative accounting and control

These ensure that the systems of accounting, budgeting and reporting are structured to assist learning.

Internal exchange

This involves all departments recognizing themselves as customers and suppliers with the aim of 'delighting the customer'. This encourages constant dialogue regarding expectations and feedback on performance. It fosters the spirit of collaboration, a systemic view and an overall optimization of performance.

Reward flexibility

This relates to the examination of the reward system, understanding the values and assumptions about the basis of pay and ensuring they are consistent with the characteristics of a learning company, where, perhaps, there has been a redistribution of power from the 'top pyramid' to the wider company.

Enabling structures

Flexible departmental boundaries that can adapt in response to change and loosely structured roles to meet the needs of internal customers and suppliers and which also encourage personal development.

Boundary workers as environmental scanners

This is the external version of informating, and although there may be specialized departments it is the accepted role of all members of the organization.

Intercompany learning

This would be demonstrated by joint training, shared investment in research and development, job exchanges and benchmarking.

A learning climate

Managers see their primary task as facilitating experimentation and learning from experience. Mistakes are allowed and there is no such thing as a failed experiment. Senior managers lead by example and openly question their own ideas, attitudes and behaviours.

Self-development opportunities for all

A range of resources and facilities are available to all members who are encouraged to take responsibility for their own learning and self-development.

As a vision it is aspirational, but unlike the models of Senge and Nonaka, they have attempted to model it to illustrate its relevance and value to an organization. Again, although not explicit, their model builds upon the theory of organizational learning and their recommended approach to strategy and policy making is closely aligned to the thinking of Senge, de Geus and Van der Heijden and Eden. Nevertheless, through a natural desire to avoid a prescriptive approach some of their descriptions of features are nebulous. 'Temporary structures that can flex in response to changes' are eminently desirable but perhaps difficult to design.

Importantly, they introduce the process of self-development missing in Garvin's model but share his commitment to business processes and systems that facilitate and sustain learning. They balance an internal perspective with an external orientation and support Garvin and Nonaka and Takeuchi in their attitude towards continuous experimentation to generate innovation. Like Senge, they recognize that the role of the leader is changing. Furthermore, like Senge and Nonaka, they recognize the power of diversity and its potential value to creativity.

A similar approach is suggested by Pearn et al. (1995) who provide a framework and range of tools to guide thinking as to what a learning organization might look like. Rather than provide a vision, definition or list of characteristics, their approach facilitates the process by which an organization can develop its own view. They suggest 10 building blocks for use to develop a tailored working approach:

1 Examine the concept at top management level.

2 Analyse the current state of learning.

3 Devise an implementation plan.

4 Examine the role of training and trainers.

5 Equip managers to encourage learning.

6 Support learning.

7 Develop group and team learning.

8 Upgrade the learning skills of all employees.

9 Promote open learning.

10 Analyse jobs in terms of learning needs.

Although their recommendations are built from their combined experience and knowledge, their underlying philosophy is to create commitment through shared understanding and participation which they believe has a greater impact and longevity than imposing the views of an external 'expert'. This would match well with the participative role of the external change agent, by not imposing solutions but helping the organization develop its own.

Conclusion

The models and visions of learning organizations presented here have common themes. They emphasize a collaborative, participative approach centred on team processes. They demonstrate a commitment to the creation of a shared vision of the future direction of the company and the necessary steps, structural and behavioural, to achieve that vision. They stress a proactive approach to learning, creating new experiences with which to challenge the status quo and a culture that encourages continuous experimentation and risk-taking. Finally, they each emphasize the role of leaders to facilitate the change process and to foster a commitment to learning primarily by leading by example.

Interestingly, in each case the concept of creating a learning environment, however it is expressed, is seen as a holistic process and not the preserve of HR specialists or limited to training and development.

Emerging from the most recent thinking is the value attributed to an external orientation, both in scanning the environment for emerging opportunities, cultivating productive relationships with customers, suppliers and other appropriate businesses, and in establishing sophisticated benchmarking processes.

There is growing recognition that the humanist approach to organizational learning needs to be supported by appropriate business and managerial systems: IT architecture, knowledge systems and management, networks, communication strategies, and organization structures. Appropriate changes in mindset and behaviour, although most critical, form only part of the answer. Increasingly management researchers and practitioners are turning towards services science solutions to the ever-increasing organizational complexities facing the global enterprise and the associated need to address bespoke knowledge worker support (Paulson, 2006; Spohrer et al., 2007). No one branch of management science can offer all the answers. Today's organizations must seek to integrate engineering, science and managerial offerings in a manner that both support the knowledge worker while maintaining organizational alignment.

It is apparent that there is no 'one best way' to approach the development of superior learning in organizations. This is supported by research conducted by the Economist Intelligence Unit who concluded that for success, organizations need to establish an approach that is best suited to their culture, orientation and their perception of performance requirements.

The learning organization assumes managers will work in a learning partnership with other members of the organization. This involves trust and open dialogue as a climate that can engender a greater sense of development and empowerment for the workforce. This has significant implications for the nature of management within organizations. As was seen in Chapters 9 and 10, much of our thinking related to management is control oriented with an emphasis on job design, performance appraisal and supervisory activity, and the merit of hierarchy in organization design and function. New forms of organization structure, processes and workplace relationships will need to be developed which are more in keeping with the different values and beliefs. These need to stress a more collaborative, learning framework. The skill base of managers needs to be enhanced in such a setting. Knowledge acquisition, management and exploitation forms the basis of organizational learning: it drives learning, change and success. The knowledge worker and their operating environment must be supported through bespoke IT solutions that facilitate communication, sharing, learning and growth (McLaughlin et al., 2006; Maglio and Spohrer, 2007). Chapter 14 explores both the role of knowledge and its subsequent management within a change context.

The question related to the impact of the learning organization is similar to managing OD in general. How do organizations and their management unlearn the old ways, challenge the past and in doing so minimize resistance to change? In seeking to transform the culture of the organization, transformations need to take managers along too. It would be impossible to shift cultural norms without first changing management mindset. Similarly, in creating an environment of learning where problems are openly declared, managers need the skill of being able to do so in a manner that will encourage the workforce to embrace the learning mode and feel comfortable with change.

Much of the literature on the learning organization assumes that the only area that organizations work within is that of rationality. Neglecting the political and emotional aspects of change in a learning context is a major oversight in the sense that change may be met with resistance if it does not appear logical. We all have comfort zones which when challenged lead to an emotional response. It may well be that the development of strategies to address such factors are beyond the scope of individual managers and traditional human resource departments and may require the more expert assistance of the change agent. Here the change agent would call on their social and behavioural skills.

PART 4

PRACTICAL CASES IN CHANGE MANAGEMENT

14 Managing Knowledge and Change: an IBM Case Study

The concluding chapter of Part 3 dealt with the learning organization. The basic theme being that change, indeed almost any aspect of management, will be more effectively managed within an open and progressive environment, an environment shaped by a need to learn and develop. Interest in both knowledge management and the knowledge economy stems in many ways from the underpinning logic associated with the learning organization. Combining learning, knowledge, management and most importantly the power of information technology provided an attractive model for competitive advantage to many enterprises as they entered the new millennium. The case presented in this chapter deals with both the need, in today's global market place, to manage supply chain logistics as efficiently and effectively as possible and the requirement to drive innovation, and therefore change through knowledge acquisition, manipulation and exploitation.

Organizations, since the late 1980s (Porter and Millar, 1985; Troyer, 1995) have increasingly recognized the need to harness the power of the supply chain as a means of developing and sustaining competitive advantage. By the 2000s many enterprises now base their business model around a supply chain capability. The supply chain is not simply a support function, but is in fact the key capability from which a competitive advantage can be developed (Kulp et al., 2003). This chapter considers the inhibitors to change through a study that investigates the barriers to knowledge and information transfer within supply chain processes. A detailed literature review identifies 25 potential barriers, which are then evaluated in relation to IBM's supply chain processes.

READER ACTIVITY

Prior to reading further; based on your own experience what do you think the five major barriers will be? Try to identify at least one for each of the categories noted below:

1 technological
2 personal
3 organizational.

Process Alignment

Organizations are now familiar with the core components that combine to form their supply chain; indeed these components are often well established and embedded. Yet, many organizations find it difficult to effectively align these components (Day, 1994; Teece, 1998). A functionally aligned organization, can of course, understand and independently manage the supply chain components; however performance can only be maximized when it successfully transforms into a process aligned organization. A process aligned organization focuses on core process performance as opposed to functional business unit performance. Process alignment unleashes the power of the supply chain and is therefore a change worth pursuing (van Weele, 2002). Nonetheless, this shift in focus does not come easily to many organizations, as internal business unit boundaries can be difficult to remove. Moreover, the problem is exacerbated within complex organizations where capabilities such as manufacturing, logistics, and procurement have been outsourced. The alignment of these core components becomes all the more difficult as external business boundaries such as organizational, technological, and people barriers (Barson et al., 2000) need to be negotiated and managed.

As the performance of core supply chain processes are vital to the overall success of the supply chain, and therefore, the overall success of the organization, the manner and extent in which barriers impact along core processes needs to be understood. It is no longer sufficient to know how barriers impact across the whole organization, or indeed how they affect each particular function; senior management needs to understand how barriers impact at different stages along core processes. The core business process, irrespective of where in the organization it operates, is in effect a core knowledge highway. Identified barriers will impact upon how information is accessed and shared, and also on how knowledge is created. If innovation and organizational learning are valued then consideration must be given to how barriers impact across an organization's 'arterial' business processes.

The IBM Case Context

This chapter examines a core supply chain process, the integrated supply chain (ISC) within IBM and identifies barriers that are impacting performance. The type and impact of the barriers can be seen to vary along the core supply chain process. This, in effect, identifies different information and knowledge creation and sharing practices across the organization. How is knowledge created and shared, from a process alignment perspective, within a complex organization and what barriers may impede knowledge creation and transfer? These questions, indeed this case, were associated with a major IBM initiative that was investigating the way organizations view the inter-connected relationship between information technology (IT) and knowledge systems, people, process, and the prioritization of change through an integrated decision-making process.

The case is based on research conducted by Dr Stephen McLaughlin as part of his doctoral studies (McLaughlin et al., 2006). At the time Stephen was a manager at IBM, Greenock, Scotland and was supervised by Professor Robert Paton. There is little academic research on actual barriers to information and knowledge transfer along process pathways, so the researchers had to rely on pre-understanding based upon experience (Gummesson, 1991). The research was exploratory in nature and a case study (Yin, 2002) methodology was used to support this line of inductive theory building. The research and analysis outlined in this chapter was conducted using qualitative and quantitative methods with all data gathering complying with validation criteria as outlined by Yin (2002).

Delivering Knowledge Throughout an Organization

To ensure that a knowledge management (KM) initiative is successful an organization must develop within their employees a desire for knowledge (Quinn et al., 1996). According to Kluge et al. (2001) if a knowledge programme is to be embraced by the workforce every individual needs to be thirsty for knowledge. Employees should see knowledge management, or to be precise the active application, distribution and cultivation of knowledge throughout the whole organization, as a fundamental part of their personal success and satisfaction.

The emphasis on the importance the individual plays in the creation and sharing of information and knowledge is a widely supported view (Krogh et al., 2000; Kluge et al., 2001). Consequently, if one accepts the importance of information access and sharing, and knowledge creation as part of an organization's ability to learn and be innovative (Krogh et al., 2000; Davenport, 2005) then the interaction individual employees have on core processes will have a significant impact on process performance.

In order to develop a 'learning' mentality within the organization a knowledge, or information 'pull' culture needs to be encouraged over a knowledge, or information 'push' culture. An important aspect of the knowledge or information 'pull' delivery mechanism, is that it focuses heavily on the softer aspects of management. As a result many organizations fail to engage in successful 'pull' and do not achieve the benefits of a bottom-up knowledge delivery system (Kluge et al., 2001).

Identifying Barriers to Knowledge Creation and Sharing

Researchers and authors have approached the issue of barriers to information and knowledge transfer from many different perspectives, and as such there are different, non-contradictory, views.

Kluge et al. (2001) identify two main barriers to developing a knowledge creating and sharing culture:

1 *Not invented here*   The 'not invented here' syndrome describes the tendency to neglect, ignore or, worst still, disparage knowledge that is not created within an individual's department. This problem can arise from a genuine mistrust of outside knowledge.

2 *Knowledge is power*   The 'knowledge is power' syndrome refers to a mindset that places the values of knowledge to the individual ahead of its value to the company.

At its most basic, knowledge sharing starts by taking the time to help others. In a successful company there is always time pressure but the extra 10 minutes spent with a colleague explaining something will be repaid later. In spite of this, just as people distrust external knowledge, they also see their own knowledge as a part of their personal competitive advantage. McKinsey's 'Corporate prisoner dilemma', a modification of game theory's 'prisoners dilemma', illustrates this point as illustrated in Figure 14.1.

From Figure 14.1 we can see that the ideal solution is for employees A and B to share knowledge, as this is where the most significant gains are expected. Conversely, if one decides to hoard knowledge whilst the other shares knowledge then the power balance is shifted in favour of the employee who hoards. As no employee wishes to be taken advantage of, or if the culture is one where individual performance is rated above team performance, the expected behaviour will be one where both employees will hoard. This will maintain a status quo where employees are keen to ensure their personal competitive advantage is not eroded. That said, the overall effect within the organization is one where knowledge is selectively shared

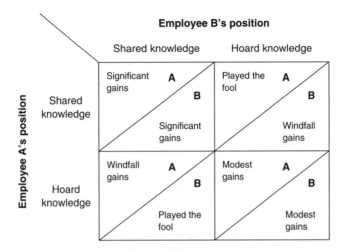

Figure 14.1   Corporate prisoner dilemma

Source: McKinsey Co. (reprinted with permission from Palgrave Macmillan)

resulting in modest gains in performance for the organization. If this is the norm the hoarding process will be counter-productive. This is one of the critical changes that should be targeted by any knowledge management programme, and one that should have positive repercussions beyond purely the exchange of knowledge.

Kluge et al. (2001) acknowledge the importance of technology in delivering information. However, the deciding factor as to whether an organization will benefit is down to how the employees pull and share the information and knowledge. Their research shows that successful organizations use a combination of both push and pull. Push systems are top-down in design and dependent on technology for the flow of information. Pull systems are bottom-up in design and more dependent on an individual's innate desire for knowledge. It is this desire coupled with a culture of co-operation that determines how successful the pull delivery mechanism will be.

Szulanski (1996) also supports the view that relationships between employees contribute to knowledge transfer failures. Nevertheless, he points out that prior research suggests that four sets of factors are likely to influence the difficulty of knowledge transfer:

1   characteristics of the knowledge transferred;

2   characteristics of the source of the knowledge;

3   characteristics of the recipient of the knowledge/information;

4   context in which the knowledge/information is transferred.

Some authors place an almost exclusive emphasis on the attributes of the knowledge transferred (Zander and Kogut, 1995; Winters, 1987). Others stress the characteristics of the situation in which the transfer occurs (Arrow, 1969). However, all four sets of factors can be used together in a model that allows their relative influence to be measured.

Szulanski (1996) states that contrary to conventional wisdom that places primary blame on motivational factors, the major barriers to internal knowledge transfer are shown to be knowledge related factors such as the recipient's lack of absorptive capacity, causal ambiguity, and an arduous relationship between the source and the recipient. Although Szulanski's research was carried out using manufacturing sites it cannot be assumed his findings will map on to the IBM supply chain. That said, there is no reason to believe that the barriers described will not impact knowledge transfer to a greater or lesser degree.

Gupta and Michailova (2004) found that knowledge sharing among departments within the same organization is in reality not as natural as it may appear. In fact knowledge sharing hostility is a phenomenon that widely dominates organizational reality (Husted and Michailova, 2002). Gupta and Michailova (2004) identified three difficulties with the process of sharing knowledge:

> *Knowledge is developed at a local level*   By definition knowledge is embedded in a certain cognitive and behavioural context. Without understanding the context one cannot inquire into the reasoning and the assumptions behind the particular piece of knowledge.
>
> *Knowledge is asymmetrically distributed*   Often those who possess the knowledge are not inclined to invest time and effort to share it without expecting reciprocity, as resources are finite and scarce (Davenport and Prusak, 1998; O'Dell and Grayson, 1998).
>
> *Knowledge sharing is voluntary*   Efficient knowledge sharing depends on the willingness of individuals to identify the knowledge they possess and to share the knowledge when required (Nonaka, 1994).

Moreover, Gupta and Michailova (2004) believe that an individual's ability to appreciate new knowledge is a function of their absorptive capacity (Cohan and Levinthal, 1990; Szulanski, 1996). What is interesting about Gupta and Michailova's (2004) research is that it does not look at the organization as a single entity but as a collection of departments working together, and the different demands they place on knowledge creation. Through their research they identified three aspects of the complex organization that can hinder knowledge creation and sharing:

The nature of the different businesses means different knowledge management requirements   Some departments or business units will operate within different environments; some more stable then others. Therefore, KM systems may need to be modified by each department in order to support the internal knowledge creation process.

The different nature of the different business activities   The nature of the different businesses predispose different requirements to the type of knowledge sought as well as different preferences to how the needed knowledge is obtained.

The way codified and personalized systems are used within each department or business unit   Although the common practice is to assess organizations for codified or personalized knowledge systems, at a department level, depending on the mission and expected deliverables of the department, the best fit from a codified or personalized strategy may not fit with the overall organization's assessment.

This is an important view as the reality of today's organization, especially a complex supply chain, is that roles and expected deliverables will vary between departments or business units. Therefore, when defining a knowledge strategy, an understanding of how departments, or business units that make up the organization, use information and create knowledge needs to be taken into consideration.

Interestingly the literature suggests that when technology is the primary focus of the knowledge delivery system sub-optimal results are achieved (Barson et al., 2000; Gupta and Michailova, 2004; Marwick, 2001; Pawar et al., 2002). The assumption that knowledge management relies heavily upon social patterns, practices, and processes goes far beyond computer-based technologies and infrastructures (Coleman, 1998; Davenport and Prusak, 1998). Empirical evidence on barriers to knowledge sharing stresses the importance of behavioural and cultural factors rather than outlining reasons associated with technology (De Long and Fahey, 2000; Skyrme and Amidon, 1997). Spender (1996) and Tsoukas (1996) also question the value of technology driven approaches, in particular, those directed towards knowledge codification.

Pawar et al. (2002) also question the effectiveness of a purely codified (technology driven) approach to knowledge management. It is their belief that modern management practice has only tended to focus on centralizing, controlling, and standardizing knowledge. Such codification allows the marginal cost of knowledge acquisition to be reduced by economies of scale. This underlying philosophy in the business environment has motivated an immense interest over the last decade in knowledge management. Pawar et al. (2002), at the same time realize the place technology has within the effective co-ordination of knowledge. Nonetheless, they feel that humans play more of a central role in the identification, acquisition, generation, storage, structuring, distribution, and assessment of knowledge. It is interesting that Pawar et al. (2002) although taking the softer aspects of knowledge management into consideration, do not really look at how organizations get their employees to 'pull' knowledge.

Malhotra (2001) also believes in line with Kluge et al. (2001) that there is an overarching need for the building of a KM culture within organizations, and the responsibility for developing this culture does not rest with the information technology specialists. To achieve this Malhotra (2001) believes organizations should focus on rewarding employees for what they contribute, and ensuring organizations track intellectual assets to show staff that knowledge is regarded as a valuable commodity; views which are supported by Kluge et al. (2001). A study carried out by KPMG (1998) highlighted that there is not only a lack of understanding about KM and its benefits, but that there is also a lack of skills within people regarding specific KM techniques.

Barson et al. (2000), using the TOP (technological, organizational, people) socio-technical systems classification (Brandt and Hartmann, 1999), investigated knowledge related barriers to change, the results of which are shown in Table 14.1.

Table 14.1   Barriers to knowledge sharing and management

Technology	Organization	People
Existing resource	Existing resource	Existing resource
Available technology	Need for rewards	Need for rewards
Legacy systems	Culture	Culture
	Targeting	Internal resistance
	Costs	Self-interest
	Proprietary knowledge	Trust
	Distance	Risk
		Fear of exploitation
		Fear of contamination

Source: Barson et al. (2000) reprinted with permission.

This is an interesting perspective, because as many organizations fail to maximize on knowledge management performance due to failure to tackle the softer issues, it can be equally detrimental to performance if technical and indeed organizational issues are also neglected. A common theme that has emerged is that knowledge management must be viewed from a holistic perspective. Failure to do so will result in an organization's failure to realize the potential it has to create and share knowledge. Although the literature reviewed in this chapter looks at the barriers to knowledge creation and sharing from slightly different angles there is a lot of commonality in their published findings. The barriers outlined by Barson et al. (2000) encompass those already outlined in the literature review:

CROSS-CATEGORY BARRIERS

Existing resource If an organization wishes to engage in knowledge creation and sharing then the required resource must be available. The organization must also have employees who can implement and develop the knowledge that has been accrued. This is implying a 'pull' knowledge culture.

Need for rewards Rajan et al. (1998) cited by Scarborough et al. (1999) suggest that employees must be able to see the link between sharing and immediate gains. The need for rewards is a people issue whereas the mechanism for conferring rewards is an organizational one.

Culture A company's culture may not support sharing and the reuse of knowledge. It is important also to look at culture from a push or pull perspective as this determines largely how employees will access and use the information available. If the culture is predominantly either 'push' or 'pull' this is maybe seen as a barrier as either the soft aspects of KM are being overlooked or the IT systems are not in place to support information routing and sharing.

Technological barriers

Available technology Swartz (1999) and Marwick (2001) suggest that technology still is unable to provide a single knowledge solution, and that an organization's codified solutions are usually a combination of applications cobbled together.

Legacy systems Swartz (1999) identifies legacy systems as a significant barrier to knowledge management. Connecting the systems of multiple departments, especially when there is no common standard approach to IT deployment makes it difficult to resolve an efficient knowledge transfer system.

Organizational barriers

Poor targeting of knowledge Scarborough et al. (1999) point out that 'information needs to be targeted if it is to serve knowledge'. Therefore, if a knowledge management system is to be effective it must be clear

(Continued)

(Continued)

about what information it needs and what it expects to generate by way of knowledge.

Cost management of knowledge transfer   Farr and Fisher (1992) point out that a barrier to inter-organizational knowledge transfer is the cost of managing collaboration.

Protection of proprietary knowledge   Sharing of proprietary information with collaborators leaves an organization open to the risk that the information will be revealed. The consequence of this belief is the resistance within an organization to sharing proprietary information with suppliers.

Distance   Nonaka and Takeuchi (1991) suggest the most efficient means of transferring knowledge is through face-to-face communications. However, the distributed nature of today's organization may make this difficult to do, as can cultural, legal, and linguistic factors.

People barriers

Internal resistance   This is where knowledge is hidden or its flow restricted in order to protect the interests of the organization.

Self-interest   This is when customers may not be willing to supply information to a supplier for fear that the information will filter through to competitors.

Lack of trust   This impacts the way we perceive received information and the value we place on it, and also the manner in which we share information.

Risk   This is related to both trust and proprietary knowledge barriers. Inter-organizational knowledge sharing inherently involves an element of risk, particularly when proprietary knowledge in being shared.

Fear of exploitation   According to Lucas (2000) a fear of exploitation starts with the premise that one expects something in return for sharing. Although Barson et al. (2000) see this as a 'people' barrier the solution to resolving this problem is very much an organizational one.

Fear of contamination   This barrier refers to when organizations with up-market brand issues are nervous about getting together with people they perceive as more down-market (Lucas, 2000).

Barriers and the IBM Case

Although Barson et al. (2000) provide a comprehensive list of issues that support the findings of previous research they do not provide any empirical evidence as to how the barriers impact knowledge creation and sharing within a complex organization such as IBM's ISC. There are also aspects of Kluge et al. (2001), Pawar et al. (2002), and Szulanski's (1996) research that are not taken into account. Of particular interest is the impact an imbalanced 'push–pull' knowledge strategy can have on information flow and knowledge creation. Szulanski's work on identifying barriers which effect knowledge 'stickiness' within an organization also needs to be considered when assessing barriers in any large complex organization.

Many of the barriers identified so far clearly overlap and they also employ different terminologies to describe relatively similar features or outcomes. In addition, a few are also cloaked in academic ambiguity. Given that the intention is to test the validity of the barriers within a practitioner environment, the IBM ISC, the list of barriers needs to be both simplified in terms of terminology and de-cluttered. Table 14.2 summarizes the revised list.

Barriers and the Learning Organization

What is interesting is how the 25 barriers identified impact on the learning organization, as Nonaka and Takeuchi (1995) perceive it. Each barrier was assessed as to how it could impact upon any of the knowledge transfer mechanisms – tacit to tacit, tacit to explicit, explicit to explicit, explicit to tacit. If any one of the barriers had the ability to impact on the aforementioned mechanism it was listed in the respective quadrant. Figure 14.2 shows Nonaka and Takeuchi's organizational learning model with the 25 barriers mapped to the quadrant that they influence.

READER ACTIVITY

Consider for a moment your own personal reaction to situations in which you have felt uncomfortable sharing your knowledge. Why has this been the case?

Can you recall a situation relating to a knowledge transfer when disinformation has been given? Once again, why was this done?

What are your experiences of technologically driven change? What characterized the successes and failures?

It is important to note that whilst the barriers are unevenly distributed across the learning organization model it does not mean that the barriers

Table 14.2   Concise list of barriers

Source	Cross category barriers
Barson et al.	Existing resources (Money, time, technology, skills, data transfer)
Barson et al./Kluge et al.	Rewards (individuals rewarded for sharing/creating K)
Szulanski	Arduous relationship
Barson et al./Kluge et al.	Culture (K strategy)
	Technology barriers
Barson et al.	Available technology (does IT support K requirement?)
Barson et al.	Legacy systems (are legacy systems impacting K transfer?)
	Organizational barriers
Gupta and Michailova	K strategy implementation
Szulanski	Causal ambiguity
Barson et al.	Poor targeting of knowledge
Barson et al.	Knowledge cost
Barson et al./Pawar et al.	Proprietary knowledge
Barson et al./Pawar et al.	Distance (geo, culture, language, legal)
Szulanski	Unprovenness (is knowledge rated as being of value?)
Szulanski	Organizational context
Szulanski	Information not perceived as reliable
Szulanski/Kluge et al.	Lack or motivation (knowledge as power syndrome)
	People barriers
Barson et al./Kluge et al.	Internal resistance (protect interests of org/BU)
Barson et al.	Self-interest (expose knowledge to competition)
Barson et al.	Trust (trust for individuals sharing knowledge with)
Barson et al.	Risk (fear of penalty, losing profit)
Barson et al./Pawar et al.	Fear of exploitation
Szulanski	Lack of motivation (not invented here syndrome)
Kluge et al.	Fear of contamination
Szulanski/Gupta and Michailova	Lack of retentive capacity
Szulanski	Lack of absorptive capacity

Nonaka's learning organization model

Socialization (tacit to tacit)		Externalization (tacit to explicit)	
1 *Existing resource(skill)*	17 *Internal resistance*	1 *Existing resource(skill)*	18 *Self interest*
2 *Reward*	18 *Self interest*	2 *Reward*	19 *Trust*
3 *Arduous relationship*	19 *Trust*	3 *Arduous relationship*	20 *Risk*
9 *Poor targeting*	20 *Risk*	5 *Available technology*	21 *Reciprocity*
10 *Cost*	21 *Reciprocity*	9 *Poor targeting*	22 *Motivation*
11 *Proprietary knowledge*	22 *Motivation (K is power)*	10 *Cost*	*(K is power)*
12 *Dist (Culture/language)*	23 *Contamination*	11 *Proprietary knowledge*	23 *Contamination*
13 *Unprovenness*	24 *Retentive capacity*	12 *Dist (Culture/language)*	24 *Retentive capacity*
14 *Organizational context*	25 *Absorptive capacity*	15 *Reliability*	
15 *Reliability*		16 *Motivation (not invented here)*	
16 *Motivation (not invented here)*		17 *Internal resistance*	
1 *Existing resource(skill)*	14 *Organizational*	1 *Existing resource(skill)*	
2 *Reward*	*context*	5 *Available technology*	
3 *Arduous relationship*	15 *Reliability*	6 *Legacy systems*	
4 *Knowledge culture*	16 *Motivation*	10 *Cost*	
5 *Available technology*	*(not invented here)*	11 *Proprietary knowledge*	
6 *Causal ambiguity*	17 *Internal resistance*	20 *Risk*	
9 *Poor targeting*	20 *Risk*	23 *Contamination*	
10 *Cost*	24 *Retentive capacity*		
11 *Proprietary knowledge*	25 *Absorptive capacity*		
12 *Dist (Culture/language)*			
13 *Unprovenness*			
Internalization (explicit to tacit)		**Combination (explicit to explicit)**	

Figure 14.2 Learning model with barriers

Source: Adapted from Nonaka and Takeuchi (1995).

will always be present in these areas. What Figure 14.2 shows is that these barriers may impact to a greater or lesser degree in these quadrants. What can be inferred is that the barriers will impact on the organization's ability to identify, create, and share information and knowledge. Hence, a more accurate view of the learning spiral is shown in Figure 14.3.

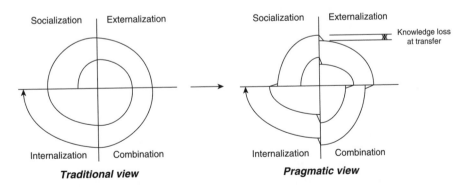

Figure 14.3 Knowledge losses

Source: Adapted from Nonaka and Takeuchi (1995)

Figure 14.3 shows the traditional view as proposed by Nonaka and Takeuchi (1995) juxtaposed with a more pragmatic view showing the effect the quadrant related barriers might have on the learning process. Taking the pragmatic view a step further, if the barriers within the organization are allowed to impact knowledge creation and transfer without being identified and managed the learning spiral may conceivably collapse. Barriers can and will impact to different degrees across the organization so the knowledge loss at transfer will vary through the different quadrants.

Therefore, organizations that simply see knowledge management as the implementation of bigger and better IT systems are possibly only addressing barriers within the 'Combination' section of the learning model. If organizations are to stand a better chance of achieving their knowledge management requirements they will need to identify, and understand how the different barriers exist within their organization, and impact on the learning process across the four quadrants.

Existence of Barriers within IBM

Following the identification of the 25 barriers to knowledge and information sharing it was important to see how these barriers impact across an organization. The core IBM process selected for test purposes was the order flow process. This process followed customer orders for computer hardware from initial receipt through the fulfilment, scheduling, manufacturing, and distribution components of the supply chain.

If the barriers did not appear uniformly across the organization this would indicate differences in knowledge and information access, creation, and sharing practices amongst employees involved in operating a core process. If this was the case, then the deployment of a 'blanket' knowledge management strategy could fail to address key aspects of how employees work together. The relevance of the 25 barriers was tested by an online survey of staff from across the order fulfilment process.

The survey

As the intention was not to determine a level of barrier variance or frequency across the process, the survey was deliberately structured to provide categorial, in particular, ordinal answers. The type of variable response, or answer, is important in determining the type of non-parametric test to be used to analyse the responses. The actual type of non-parametric testing is further determined by the number of groups to be compared, and whether the groups will be tested independently, or dependently (Diamantopoulos and Schlegelmilch, 1997). The IBM process under consideration comprised of eight work groups and all staff were to take part in the survey. Each individual was questioned once as part of a pre-defined group and the groups were 'independently' tested. Using these criteria the test selected was the Kruskal-Wallis one-way ANOVA test (Diamantopoulos and Schlegelmilch 1997). Another important attribute of the Kruskal-Wallis test is its ability to analyse and compare data from groups of different sample size. This was important as the groups identified were not all of the same size, nor, more importantly could the return rate be guaranteed to be the same for all groups.

The hypotheses

The non-parametric test adopted required for data analysis that a number of hypotheses were generated. To enable the analysis the following null hypothesis was assumed:

HO: the impact the barriers have within the groups is uniform across the different groups.

The alternative or test hypothesis is therefore as follows:

H1: the barriers impact or ranking between the different groups is not uniform.

If this null hypothesis is to be tested then a significance level must also be assumed. For the purpose of this experiment the significance level of $\alpha = 0.05$ was set. If the Kruskal-Wallis (K-W) test provides a significance level $p \leq 0.05$ then the result will be seen as being significant with a high probability that the null hypothesis is not proved, thus allowing its rejection in favour of the alternative hypothesis (*H1*).

The results

What resulted was confirmation that the 25 barriers, as identified in the literature, existed to greater or lesser extents throughout the different parts of the organization involved with the process. Although all the barriers appear to a greater or lesser extent across the organization, Kruskal-Wallis analysis (Table 14.3) shows that not all barriers act uniformly across the organization.

Table 14.3   The Kruskal-Wallis analysis

Barrier	p	(α = 0.05)
Existing resource	1.000	
Rewards for sharing /creating knowledge	0.584	
Arduous relationship	0.0240	
Culture (knowledge strategy)	0.120	
Available technology	0.008	
Legacy systems	0.000	
Knowledge strategy implementation	0.000	
Causal ambiguity	0.016	
Poor targeting of knowledge	0.280	
Knowledge cost	0.000	
Proprietary knowledge	0.392	
Distance	0.008	
Unprovenness	0.000	
Organizational context	0.304	
Info perceived as reliable	0.168	
Lack of motivation (not invented here)	0.120	
Internal resistance	0.224	
Self-interest	0.760	
Trust	0.024	
Risk	0.000	
Fear of exploitation	0.072	
Lack of motivation (knowledge as power)	0.736	n = 125
Fear of contamination	0.048	N = 540
Lack of retentive capacity	0.696	
Lack of absorptive capacity	0.720	

From the significance levels reported, the following barriers are perceived to impact on knowledge creation and sharing differently across the core process.

- arduous relationships;
- available technology;
- legacy systems;
- knowledge implementation strategy;

- causal ambiguity;

- knowledge cost;

- distance;

- unprovenness;

- trust;

- risk;

- fear of contamination.

The remaining barriers when tested had a significance level >0.05. This meant for these barriers no conclusion could be drawn as to whether or not they impacted differently across the different groups employed along the core process. However, what could be determined was whether or not the barriers were actually seen to exist across the organization. When considering the overall results, it is clear that all the barriers outlined in Table 14.2 were seen to exist, albeit to varying degrees of impact.

Barrier Impact and Change

The outcome shows that the 25 barriers identified earlier in this chapter exist, and are seen to impact across a complex supply chain. However, this in itself is not the key point of interest concerning this chapter. This research demonstrates that the barriers themselves impact differently across the organization. This, in effect, means that employees' information and knowledge creation and sharing practices will vary, not only within the organization, but also along core complex process pathways. It is also important to note that an assessment of how barriers exist and impact along core complex processes would be expected to vary from organization to organization.

Nonetheless, the way in which organizations create and share information and knowledge is vitally important if an innovative, responsive business is to be developed. As core complex processes are the mechanisms by which business performance is driven, information and knowledge creation and sharing along these arteries must become a key focus point for business success. Therefore, barriers that impact along these processes must be understood and where possible managed.

Another consideration this raises for organizations with complex business processes is that different barriers will need different solutions. The manner and level in which barriers impact the tacit-explicit-tacit transfer mechanism along a process will determine the type of solution needed at that part of the process. Thus, the deployment of a generic IT or business solution across the organization cannot now be expected to fully support the operational needs of employees along a complex process. For organizations to effectively manage their supply chains they must consider the operation of their core supply chain processes. From this point they should then look to understand how employees create and share information and knowledge along this process and which barriers are seen to impact. Similarly this lesson can be applied to any change situation. To effectively manage change, a change agent must fully understand the existing context and culture of the organization as well as the desired ethos. Moreover a participative environment that encourages two-way communication must be supported in order for the change agent to fully appreciate and subsequently manage prospective barriers to the change.

Many of the barriers identified and explored in this chapter could be associated with any complex change event. Knowledge lies at the heart of good decision making and effective learning. Understanding how to acquire, manipulate and disseminate knowledge in a timely manner is as important a manager of change as it is to an IT specialist or accountant. However, as ever, by understanding how others may receive one's quest for knowledge mastery and competitive advantage the likelihood of success will be enhanced. Further, as noted earlier in this chapter, barriers may also impact upon learning potential. At the point of knowledge transfer certain barriers may cause 'leakage' from the knowledge system. Organizations and managers as agents of change must pay heed to the growing evidence that knowledge management mastery is not a panacea in itself – managing the barriers to change will pave the way for subsequent success. The theme of identifying in a timely fashion the potential barriers to change and proactively managing them is returned to in the following chapter which deals with a case relating to business growth.

15 A Case Study in Business Growth: Change at Smokies

Throughout this book we have highlighted numerous techniques, models and concepts that aim to aid the management of change. In this chapter we illustrate, using a detailed case study, the inherent difficulties in managing complex change situations. As far as possible the case study follows the change situation as it occurred. The case demonstrates the complexity of building and sustaining successful partnerships and highlights the dynamic nature of change.

The Company

Smokies was established in the 1980s and is essentially a family business that takes pride in its heritage and community setting. Smokies, along with the associated fisheries, is based in a rural Scottish setting. The business has developed in an organic fashion exploiting the 'value chain' and steadily growing a reputation as a quality producer of traditional foods. The company developed from the family owned fisheries, consisting of several well stocked trout lochs as well as interests in both trout and salmon farms, into a fishery and Smokies. The next natural step on the supply and value chain was to retail the smoked product (Porter, 1985). Initially, this was done by mail order based on mailing lists gathered from family and friends; however, this service rapidly grew into a significant mail order business. Retail now includes both online and mail order services covering discrete and packaged (gift hampers) product ranges, plus an on site shop and café facility.

The company has a diversified product range based around a deliberately loosely defined marketing strategy which aims to develop, and acquire, products associated with the core Smokies produce and package this offering in a manner attractive to customers who appreciate (and can afford) traditional, quality and lifestyle goods and services. They have deliberately chosen to focus on high margin niche markets where direct competition has hitherto been weak (Jobber, 2007). Core products are prepared on site in a traditional manner in which an age-old method of smoking is used to produce a high quality product. This case deals, with an expansion project initiated by the company. It is important to note that the company chose to facilitate the project through an external, government funded, partnership. Essentially external consultants and researchers were engaged.

Background Information Specific to the Change

In many ways Smokies could be regarded as an embryonic lifestyle brand. A brand that would like to consider itself as the custodian of traditional values, packaged in a refined way, and brought to the discerning palate by people who care and in a manner reflecting superior quality. The company, given the limited resources at their disposal, have managed to develop a niche brand with high national recognition and a limited international presence. They would evidence such factors as industry awards, national quality awards, growing sales value, partnership enquiries, brand transfer successes, and repeat custom as signs that product lines have been developed well beyond the core smoked products to include a wide range of branded, but externally sourced fine food products as well as non-food ranges aligned with food preparation and serving. To date, to ensure consistency of image and quality, the company have produced, packaged and distributed form their rural idyll. The directorate and owners have also insisted in playing a major role in all aspects of the business.

Nevertheless, in the early 2000s the company had come to that all too familiar crossroads on the road to corporate and business growth. Turnover was being comfortably maintained at around £2 million with a very respectable bottom line. However, attempts at maintaining, or stimulating, the organic business growth of the past were not proving to be as successful as they had once been. In many ways equilibrium had been reached and they were finding it difficult to break free. Pascale (1999) terms such a state as the 'precursor to death'. With 'new blood' coming into the business in the shape of the owners' offspring the company realized that in order to grow, it would have to go beyond the status quo and adopt a more planned and professional expansion strategy. Thus, a decision to significantly modernize and expand the production facilities was taken and plans were drawn up for a larger smoking facility. The company had its trigger for change and was about to enter a new world which would involve engaging with and managing environments with which they were unfamiliar. In many ways they were about to create dis-equilibrium in an effort to emerge both commercially and managerially stronger (MacIntosh and MacLean, 1999).

As mentioned earlier the expansion project was supported by a government initiative, which aims to stimulate knowledge transfer between research institutions and commercial enterprises. The programme provides the majority of the funds required to appoint an experienced 'consultant', who also acts as a bridge to additional external resources, as well as a researcher and project manager. By engaging with the government supported partnership, they hoped it would secure access to the appropriate knowledge bases and funding.

The Problem Owner and the Definition Phase

In 2002 a consultant was appointed who would be the main conduit through which knowledge between the partners would flow and would be responsible for the day-to-day running of the project. Consequently, this person was in effect the problem owner. It is worth noting that prior to the appointment the external partners, the company and the funding agency all agreed the core deliverables of the project as well as a project plan. The initial consultant's task was to provide the answers to some important questions, such as:

What market(s) were they in and what was the potential?

Who were the competitors and what was their profile?

Were there any other markets for their products?

What were customers' perceptions of the Smokies brand? Was there a brand?

What were Smokies' strengths and weaknesses – both operationally and commercially?

In brief, the consultant was to provide a strategic overview, focusing on marketing capability and potential, combined with at least an initial analysis of their operational capability to meet future growth expectations. Once this was done and agreement reached on the 'way forward', the consultant would move on to implementation, moving from the role of researcher to project manager.

READER ACTIVITY
How would you have approached the initial 'contracting' phase of this consultancy? How would you have attempted to show both quick wins and develop trust?

Evaluation Phase – Preliminary Research

Customer and market profiling commenced, based on existing customer information and a range of secondary information sources. A series of 'face to face' customer interviews (mail order and trade) were conducted which were then followed up by a more extensive market research exercise. The aim was to develop a clear picture of the demographic and psychographic make-up of the customer base. Research clearly indicated that the product appealed to the middle aged to elderly customer with a penchant for *The Daily Telegraph* and a 65 per cent chance of living in the South of England. They were affluent, often retired or semi-retired and tended to like or be involved in gardening, shooting and fishing. More importantly, perhaps, they appeared to be, within reason, insensitive to 'price'.

The figures and tables below provide a summary of the market environment.

There were 40 suppliers operating in the mail order sector, which represented 74 per cent of the supplier total (54) (Figure 15.1), and this represented 2.5 per cent of all salmon sales with a monetary value of £1.8 approximately. The vast majority of sales revenue was through the supermarket multiples. This sector, although financially attractive, is price sensitive and the smoking process employed by the company places their product in an uncompetitive position. Further research showed the company to have 32.8 per cent of the mail order market and 5.3 per cent of the wholesale sector. The international market for smoked salmon was more difficult to specify in monetary terms but research did show that only 4 per cent of UK producers had targeted the USA with 15 per cent active in France.

Smokies 'suffered' from a seasonal sales peak at Christmas within the mail order business. This peak was highly pronounced. As one can imagine Christmas figured prominently on everyone's minds (Figure 15.1). Wholesale, with little resource dedicated to it, performed on a reasonably constant basis throughout the year. Approximately £0.75m sales revenue could be attributed to wholesale. Figure 15.2 charts the relative performance of both wholesale and mail order over the past few years. The rate of mail order growth is declining, with an increasing resource utilization,

Table 15.1   Smoked salmon market profile

	No. of producers selling per location		% of total sales
Location	1999	2001	2001
Scotland	58	51	9
Rest of UK	60	46	57.1
France	26	27	13.4
Italy	29	21	6
Belgium	15	13	3.4
Switzerland	15	9	1.1
Germany	20	18	1.4
Netherlands	9	10	2
Other European countries	4	12	1
USA	17	17	3.8
Far East	14	11	1.5
Canada	4	3	<0.1
Other	5	6	0.3
Total	60	54	100

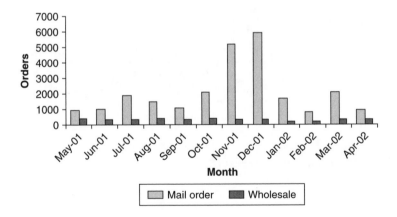

Figure 15.1   The Christmas peak

while wholesale is enjoying some growth with a reasonably static support infrastructure. It is worth noting that the company was a major player in the already competitive mail order sector and the cost of sales

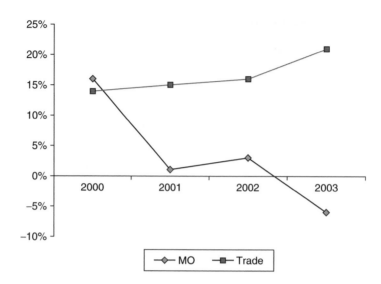

Figure 15.2   Rate of growth trade and mail order

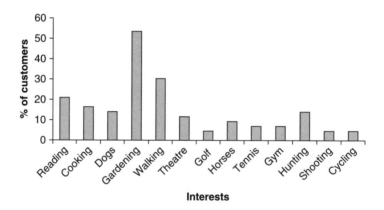

Figure 15.3   Customer interests

was rising, whereas, the much larger wholesale and associated sectors are both far larger and relatively untapped.

Figure 15.3 examines the existing customer bases' interests. There can be few food brands that can boast such a well-defined market segment. The hunting, fishing and shooting fraternity appear to be well represented. The market research also focused on the customers' motivation to purchase. Interestingly the taste and quality of the product impacts far more than its Scottish-ness, with external quality marks coming well down the scale. The market research also quizzed respondents whether, or not, they would consider purchasing from a local quality retail outlet and over 80 per cent said that they would.

The customers' interests are particularly homogeneous but when taken with the readership interests, in terms of national daily newspaper, they shed an even greater light on the customer base. With 47 per cent of the customer base active readers of *The Daily Telegraph* and over 50 per cent of them retired or semi-retired they are almost unique in today's day and age (Figure 15.4).

Although initial research suggested that the company had indeed found an attractive market niche it also highlighted a rather worrying trend. The customer base was unlikely to grow rapidly. Internal and external data sources suggested that the mail order market niche was under threat:

- The traditional customer base was, as one would expect, dwindling (literally dying).

- New customers were costing more to attract.

- The traditional market was changing.

- Industry research suggested room for growth but not necessarily at the quality end of the market.

- Industry research also indicated little room for growth in the mail order sector.

- Business was becoming increasingly seasonal with the lucrative Christmas market both growing (gift related sales) and becoming more central to 'bottom line' success.

- The product offering was highly regarded and they had a loyal and affluent customer base within a rather limited niche market.

When the above are combined with more general research findings regarding factors relating to an economic down turn and low interest rates; UK pension scares, US health concerns and import restrictions; social trends moving against the traditional hunting, fishing and shooting fraternity (within the UK); and, lastly the unacceptability of an age related product profile to the 'new' old (Wolfe, 1997), it became apparent that the growth aspirations would have to be satisfied from outside the traditional customer base.

The research outcomes were not all negative. The traditional market was not going to suddenly disappear and it was robust. The 'gift business' was expanding, but mainly on a seasonal basis. However, there appeared to be scope for expansion across the seasons (Easter, Spring and Autumn product and events related packaging) and within the highly attractive corporate gifts market. Moreover, additional market

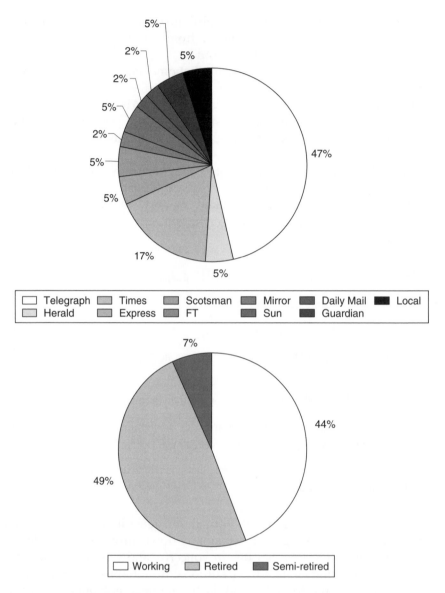

Figure 15.4   Readership and occupation

research indicated a clear opportunity for expansion in the trade sector and potentially also in export. It was sales to the delicatessens, fine food halls and catering establishments, combined with lucrative export contracts that could potentially provide the desired growth. The trade market was worth, in potential revenue, more than ten times that of the traditional mail order sector for smoked salmon.

The company, in particular its senior management, would have to face up to the challenges associated with 'strategic change'. The traditional and much loved, mail order business was still thriving, but opportunities for real growth were limited. New customers would have to be attracted to mail order/online offerings but more significantly the real opportunities lay in trade and export. Trade and export activities had always come second to mail order. Breaking with the old tried and tested beliefs and approaches would not be easy. (MacIntosh and MacLean, 1999).

Having apparently resolved to pursue new market opportunities and to fine tune the mail order approach to welcome more readily new customer profiles, the next task was to develop and gain approval for a clear strategic and operational strategy for market development. It was recognized by the consultant and external partner that, in many respects, the real work lay ahead and success would be determined as much by the 'winning of hearts and minds' as it would by the gaining of sales opportunities.

Implementation Phase – Dealing with Reality

By the end of 2002 all concerned knew where the future lay and the first tentative development of trade and export opportunities had commenced. In addition, catalogues, sales and order processing, merchandising and marketing within the mail order business operations were all being reviewed in the light of market intelligence. It is always easier to map out a vision than to gain the support and action required to make it a reality. To make things happen one must first identify and address the 'games people play' and manage the 'organizational politics (Buchanan and Badham, 1999a). Once the initiative turned its attention to internal operational and managerial considerations it became apparent that:

- It is often easier to plan than to act.

- Agreement in principle is not enough.

- Old ideas and working practices die hard.

- Myths and legends live on.

- 'The not invented here' syndrome is alive and well.

The old adage 'talk is cheap' seemed to pervade all attempts at 'kick starting' the programme. Knowledge transfer requires at least two-way communication and there was a great deal of evidence to suggest that initial discussions were producing a plethora of ideas, along with attempts at evaluating their worth. There were even agreed actions and performance milestones. However, it soon became apparent that there was a great deal of concern, possibly uncertainty and even signs that the overall programme objectives were not what they appeared initially to be. Agreement in principle would be reached, generally relating to initiatives of a commercial nature. Actions would be sanctioned but once the necessary groundwork had been completed and real decisions had to be made there would be a great deal of 'back pedalling'. Old inhibitors for change would rear their heads once more, such as the Christmas rush and peak, or the need to attend a particular country show, or a re-appraisal of the original decision would occur, thus delaying action once more. Old working practices and traditional, embedded, belief systems would return to the fore, and staff, including the consultant, would be reined back. In short, all the predictable inhibitors to change were to be found with the added disadvantage that the programme was not addressing the basic enablers of change: such as active committed leadership, effective sharing of purpose and the empowerment of others (Pascale, 1999).

READER ACTIVITY

Please return to Chapter 2 and consider Figure 2.2 in relation to the case before continuing.

It should be noted that the company was not wholly to blame for this initial lack of progress. The external partners were geographically remote from the programme so the majority of communications had to be by telephone or email. This is not ideal when trying to build a relationship, trust and mutual understanding (Boddy and Paton, 2004). All parties underestimated the need to fully involve other management and supervisory staff in the process. The programme needed to be better understood by all concerned if the transition was to be made. Senior management had to cease defending (Miles and Snow, 1978) and free their staff from the organizational paradigm that inhibited involvement and devolved decision making (Stacey, 2000).

On the positive front there were some clear signs that with a more visible on-site presence things were beginning to move forward on the commercial front. For example, appointments on the trade side were being made and IT support, including call centres, investigated. It sometimes appeared that what was required for action was for the company to take ownership of joint 'programme' initiatives – reinventing ideas and initiatives as their own – then acting. This was taken as a very good sign of progress as ownership lies at the heart of effective change management (Pettigrew, 1987).

Implementation Phase – the Successes

As work continued on the commercial front, attention turned to addressing the enablers of change. In particular how should the company and the initiative address:

- process and systems change?

- managerial styles and attitudes?

- skills and competency gaps?

- moving from vision to commitment?

The work surrounding the organizational transformation required to manage and deliver business growth was highly challenging and interesting. Indeed the key to unlocking a successful knowledge transfer lies not in the arena of the proposed business outcomes but rather in securing and delivering an impetus to change (MacIntosh and MacLean, 1999; Boddy, 2002). Although transformation was, at this point ongoing, the partnership had already addressed issues relating to:

- product costing

- margin/contributions

- overhead recovery

- stock management

- service quality

- team building

- project management

- professional career development

- new product development.

Identification of the above requirements was achieved through multi-functional management discussions and reasonably formal and open evaluation. There were open and frank discussions by all concerned and everyone willingly engaged in a number of management and strategic development events. It was anticipated that by involving the entire team the problem owner would 'learn' how best to proceed from everyone rather than from a select few (Senge, 1990). The outcome of the change, focused management development events, was a realization that various 'things' internal to the business had to improve, or more accurately be realigned with market led operational requirements, if new opportunities were to be fully exploited.

Additional revenue and contributions had to be found to justify the capital expenditure plans for the new facilities. Stock levels were higher than one might have expected and service level quality showed signs of being under threat as a result of increasing sales. There was a belief that margins were high across the whole product range and throughout the market segments, however, costing data was reasonably old and did not always reflect the current operational environment. Communications throughout the organization tended to be informal and based on a 'need to know basis', very much top-down, and more appropriate to what the company had been rather than what it aspired to be, namely, a high quality and margin professional enterprise operating within a sustainable market niche.

The Smokies' management team along with the consultant decided to approach the managerial and operational challenges by using co-ordinated autonomous and high profile project teams (Buchanan and McCalman, 1989). These teams, or task groups, first underwent some basic team-building development and then moved on to task specification and the determination of working arrangements. They then set about addressing an assigned task. Initial results and ongoing developments suggest that Smokies is well on the way to taking ownership of the 'challenges' and has shown the ability to work together towards making the future a professionally supported reality. The teams formed dealt with:

1 product costing – to find out what the real margins were;

2 stock – to design and introduce effective stock control linked directly to forecasted orders;

3 communications – to let all in the company 'know the score';

4 business plan – for the proposed new facilities;

5 Christmas – to plan for and manage the process throughout the year;

6 service delivery – to ensure the ordered product reached the customer – intact and on time.

The most appropriate staff member, rather than one of the directors, facilitated the teams. The teams were managed according to a set of pre-agreed ground rules, which are essential for the basic structure for moving forward (Eisenhardt and Sull, 2001):

- Understand task and objective.

- Listen first.

- Review team and individual skills.

- Plan to be flexible and adaptable.

- Review and reflect.

The teams, although initially slow to perform, produced some very good results. Stock levels were reduced, margins identified with pricing and product deletion managed accordingly. Christmas was managed and customer complaints were significantly reduced.

A number of strategic appointments were also made. The main appointments have been a trade sales manager, a management accountant and most recently a general manager. The latter position was necessary to fill the vacuum, on the production management front, created by the departure of the production director. Moreover, operational issues such as service quality have been dealt with through initiatives such as the reviewing of service level agreements with suppliers. A new call centre provider has been appointed and distribution arrangements reviewed and realigned.

Commercial activities continued to be pursued. It was decided to develop market potential through brand management and expansion. Trade and export were identified as potential sources of additional revenue. Various activities were undertaken in support of these new markets, for instance, the packaging and point of sale material was revamped in line with an updated merchandising strategy. Through consultation with Scottish Development International, Food From Britain (an independent food marketing consultancy), and British embassies, overseas export leads were identified and acted upon.

The initial market research identified a great deal of growth potential in the trade and catering market. The revamped merchandising and promotional efforts, combined with additional trade sales resource, saw real sales grow by over 25 per cent within a year. Export, as anyone in the food trade knows, is a difficult 'nut to crack'. Health related import regulations are varied and food related scares are far more prevalent than they once were. However, the company has seen an increase in export sales and are working hard to develop international partners. Lastly, the mail order promotional and marketing endeavours have been, and continue to be, revamped in light of market research and product mix analysis. The new product development group has been extremely successful; and 2004/5 saw the launch of a new organic food line. There is now clear evidence that they are beginning to move beyond their traditional customer base.

Christmas 2003/4 provided the first tangible proof that from a managerial standpoint the initiatives were delivering the foreseen benefits. From a commercial standpoint, as noted above, the company was progressing well; a new informed customer driven ethos was permeating throughout the organization. Every effort was being made to harmonize internal and external customer expectations. However, as yet it was difficult to identify whether this was due to simply revenue drivers or a more deep-seated desire to manage differently.

In late December the marketing director, in many ways the backbone of the company and the custodian of the 'Christmas peak' became unwell and as a result would be out of circulation until at least February 2004. Would the company cope?

There was no need for concern. The Christmas planning team had done its job. New shift working arrangements, pre-packaging, enhanced work flow systems, improved work in progress and stock systems and a general advance in communications practices, combined with updated call handling and order processing, made for one of the best Christmas performances the company had ever enjoyed. Volume, cash flow and margins were better, while customer complaints were significantly down and delivery times improved. A professional management team, combined with a well-informed and highly motivated workforce, coped with the busiest period of the year and graduated from the experience with 'honours'.

Epilogue – the Closing Stages of the Partnership

As the consultancy and growth programme wound down there was significant evidence that Christmas 2003 was not an exception but rather the new model for success:

- A new designer is tackling the product and brand image – placing all aspects of the product/service customer interface within the context of the Smokies brand. A brand is being shaped by ongoing market research and firmly placed within the growing lifestyle market place.

- The Web packages are to be revamped with the aim of creating a more contemporary feel, one that will retain existing clients but encourage newer, younger, customers by placing the products within a contemporary setting.

- Pricing and advertising are being more actively employed within a pre-agreed marketing plan to encourage purchases throughout the year.

- Tactical and strategic partnerships are being considered with organizations operating within complementary value chains, for example, up-market hotel groups and self-catering establishments.

- Corporate gift markets have been identified and are presently being targeted with much success.

- New product lines featuring organic ranges are being launched in an effort to address concerns expressed over the health of farmed salmon.

On the commercial front much was achieved. Revenues were up, in real terms by 20 per cent and margins have been stabilized. The mail order market share has increased by 4 per cent and trade sales have increased by over 100 per cent. All this has been achieved while increasing managerial overhead. The company enjoys national brand recognition within a high value niche market. It is upon the foundations of superior quality and attention to detail in production that Smokies will base its future success.

Managing a Partnership

It is often the case, just as it was in the one outlined above, that the organization seeking to grow and change engages and seeks external support and advice. Experience suggests that all stakeholders should note:

- The three T's – *t*rust *t*akes *t*ime.
- Also, TDQ – *t*rust *d*isappears *q*uickly.
- Results take time.
- Understand the 'terms of engagement'.

The transfer of any valuable asset from one party to another will only take place once the parties involved trust each other. Trust involves openness and letting go. This is never easy, and trust takes time. Over time and through discussions that result in actions the various partners can by dint of past successes steadily build up a trusting relationship. However, the opposite is also true, one mistake and all the good work will be lost. Failure to deliver, to meet you obligations, will result in a swift loss of trust. For knowledge transfer partnerships to be effective the trust must be built into the relationship as early as possible. Unfortunately, especially in commercially sensitive partnerships, everyone wants to see results as soon as possible. Quick wins that will cement the partnership also take time and effort. They may in fact detract attention from the much-needed bonding by focusing effort on understanding external considerations, such as, competitors, markets, legislation and sales revenue. Attention drifts from 'each other' on to 'whoever' or 'whatever' and trust takes a back seat for a while.

One way of minimizing the impact of the first three factors noted above is to ensure that all stakeholders understand and agree the terms of engagement. Expectations have to be measured from day one and revisited when appropriate. It is also worth noting that:

> Change is an untidy, non linear, quaisi-rational, unpredictable process, intrinsically iterative, politicised and contradictory. (Doyle et al., 2000)

The quote above sums up the experience of change with regard to this case rather well. The case provides an interesting insight to the dynamic and unpredictable nature of life and change and offers many lessons. It reiterates many of the ideas discussed within this book. For instance it reminds us that change is a perpetual process that needs to be continually evaluated. It highlights the need for managers to assist those involved to adapt to change through continued communication and negotiation. Moreover, it demonstrates that by fully understanding the culture, taking a systematic approach and re-evaluating the aims and objectives as the project evolves managers can successfully overcome any issues.

16 Intervention Cases

We have tried, throughout the previous chapters, to illustrate models, techniques and concepts by the use of mini-cases, reader activities and examples. The last two chapters introduced more complex, strategically orientated change events or cases, dealing with topical issues such as barriers to knowledge management and business growth. It is hoped that you, whether a practising manager or not, have found them of some use. They have been selected from a wide variety of change management projects covering a range of issues, sectors and situations. The cases and examples introduced and developed in Chapters 5 and 6 illustrated various features and attributes associated with the intervention strategy model (ISM). In this chapter we will return to a number of the ISM related examples and cases with a view to developing them more fully, the aim being to enable the reader to sample ISM cycles in their entirety. However, as always, the best way to learn and evaluate, is by doing and experiencing. We strongly suggest that you try out for yourself the techniques, models and approaches covered in this book.

Three cases taken from a range of diverse organizations have been selected. The first comes from the National Health Service and illustrates the use of the ISM on an externally imposed change. Caledonian Airmotive Ltd provides the second case, which involves a considerable reorganization of a manufacturing system; this organizational change was tackled successfully by employing a systems interventionist approach. This case exhibits many features associated with total project management (TPM). The final case involves an externally imposed change, with organizational implications, within British Gas. They have been selected not for their topicality, as has been the case with many of the more tactical and strategic examples previously encountered, but rather to illustrate ISM in action.

Each case will be described, as far as possible, as it happened. The reader will follow the change management route taken by each problem owner and their associated team of change agents. At the end of each case there will be a brief review of the key points to be noted and the lessons learnt. Previous chapters have used mini cases; here, however, as the cases form the core of this chapter they will be fully integrated within the text.

Case study 1: the Argyll and Clyde Health Board

The Scottish Health Boards were required to submit their morbidity records, the Scottish Morbidity Records (SMRs), to the Common Services Agency (CSA) of the National Health Service. Under the old system the performance target was rather relaxed: the SMRs need only be submitted on an annual basis, with returns being required by the following summer of any given year. In response to the government's White Paper entitled *Working for Patients*, the SMR returns were required to be submitted within two months of the end of any particular month.

SMRs were much more than statistical returns; they detailed the case histories of each patient treated within an NHS hospital. They detailed individual treatments; in effect, SMRs provided an audit trail. With an audit trail, management, at hospital, board or national level, can compare and contrast performance across facilities and regions. More importantly, when treatments are aligned with costs, then SMRs provided a means of measuring planned against actual budgetary expenditure. The importance of these documents to each Health Board cannot be overstated. The CSA collates the data for all the Health Boards in Scotland and funding is then allocated according to the numbers, costs and categories of patients treated.

Background information specific to the change

An admission to a NHS hospital initiated an SMR document, one for each patient, with a member of medical records staff performing the task. At this point the document contains basic patient information and demographic details. On discharge, clinical codes detailing diagnoses and any operating procedures carried out are assigned and recorded by coding staff in the Medical Records Department. The information required to complete this final section of the SMR is taken from the discharge letter, which must be completed for patients by their medical consultant.

In the case of the Argyll and Clyde Health Board the use of a fully computerized patient administration system, by each of the major hospitals, obviated the need for hard copy SMR documentation. Completed SMRs were stored, having been categorized, on magnetic tape. (Note that the case described occurred in the early 1990s: operating units, health boards and national centres were only beginning to move towards electronic data transfer and/or communication.) The tapes from each hospital were submitted to a central computer centre at which the tapes are input to the SMR standard system. After a cyclical process, involving the production of error and query reports followed by data resubmission, the standard system produced aggregated and validated data for the Board.

This output was then forwarded to the CSA to await further analysis, which might have involved further communication to fully validate the statistics. When the analysis of the national SMR returns had been completed, various comparisons were made and informed discussions took place, after which funding allocations were decided and granted.

The problem owner and the definition phase

The problem, which as far as this case is concerned relates to the need to accelerate SMR processing speed while maintaining data integrity, was assigned to a member of the board's Information Services Division (ISD). ISD was ultimately responsible for centralized data processing and provided an information and internal consulting service to the board. The change situation had, on the appointment of the problem owner, been effectively entered. The problem owner then set about clarifying the change environment. A number of diagrams were developed to define the systems processes and environment under review.

It was at this point of systems specification that the Argyll and Clyde case was first visited. Figure 4.6 deals with the activity sequences associated with SMR production and Figure 4.7 describes the inputs and outputs from the SMR standard system.

READER ACTIVITY

Please return to Chapter 4. Consult and carefully review Figures 4.6 and 4.7 and then return to this case.

In addition to the diagrams illustrated in Chapter 4 the problem owner also produced an input/output diagram. Figure 16.1 summarizes the situation as seen from the position of the problem owner.

The investigation then moved on to consider the relationships that existed between system components. In the old system, magnetic tapes

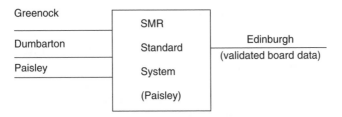

Figure 16.1   Geographic sources (computerized hospitals only)

were produced at hospital locations and ISD staff arranged collection by any member of staff who happened to be on site. Alternatively, tapes were entrusted to the internal transport system. The outputs of the SMR standard system were similarly treated. ISD's role was one of facilitation and co-ordination. Figure 16.2 depicts the relationship map used to identify all those who may, to a greater or lesser extent, be involved in the existing SMR system and have some interaction with any proposed changes.

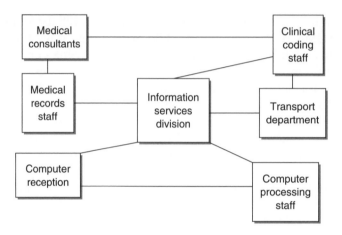

Figure 16.2   Relationship map

The information flows and staff involved were well defined. As the objective, namely, 'to have the SMR data for month n validated, processed and submitted to the CSA by the end of month $n+2$', had come from government and as such was not negotiable, attention was then turned to the factors that would impact upon this objective. The new performance criteria affected the whole of the country. The problem owner, along with other senior management, was involved in discussions at a national level. All agreed that there were three key factors that had to be addressed:

1   the length of time after discharge before diagnostic details were available;

2   the travel time of the magnetic tapes and associated follow-up error and/or query reports;

3   the number of resubmissions of data before finalizing validated SMR returns.

The third factor was to be addressed by a separate study, undertaken at a national level, which dealt with the quality assurance issues associated with the integration of a new computerized coding system with the existing patient administration systems. The problem owner was therefore left with the first two factors. Both studies knew of each other's existence and were working towards the same overall goal.

The problem owner was fortunate that clear and, at least at a senior management level, uncontroversial objectives existed. In addition, the objectives relating to both factors had associated quantifiable time measures, which would provide a means of assessing potential options. All concerned, at a local senior management level, agreed that any systems changes must be achieved at a minimal cost.

Evaluation phase

Up until this point the problem owner had essentially been working alone. Systems investigations had really only been informed by the problem owners and senior management's knowledge and understanding of the situation. On entering the design phase it was decided to involve representatives from those departments highlighted within the relationships map. A meeting was organized and structured around the two factors previously identified. After a brainstorming session and protracted discussions, a number of options were generated. Options were then evaluated, once again by the key players led by the problem owner. Table 16.1 details both the options generated and the group's evaluation of them.

Table 16.1   Option generation and evaluation

	Option A: Consultants code diagnoses and enter them	Option B: Consultants write diagnoses on interim discharge form	Option C: Consultants write diagnoses letter immediately upon discharge	
Factor 1: To minimize from discharge to diagnostic coding (coding time)	Lack of training and no access to the system	Additional work for consultants	Operationally difficult to achieve	
	Option D: Networking of hospital system to SMR standard system	Option E: Special van driver hired by ISD	Option F: Negotiate with board transport department	Option G: Improve data quality
Factor 2: Speed up SMR processing (travel time)	Technically difficult at present, plus costs	Extra recurring cost, leave cover, maintenance	Special arrangements needed	Ongoing subject of another study

It was eventually decided that option B, the interim discharge form, would be selected to influence factor 1 and that option F would be selected for factor 2.

Implementation

The problem owner tackled the implementation strategy as follows:

- *Factor 1*   An interim discharge form was designed by medical records staff and inserted in the patient's case notes. Consultants were requested to complete this at the time of discharge and return it to the clinical coding staff via the internal mail. The target was to have coding performed within three to five days of discharge.

- *Factor 2*   A meeting was held with the transport manager and it was agreed that a system known as 'data in transit', would be attempted. This involved making use of the existing transport runs but with the addition of the following three features:

  1 specifically designed multiple part forms to allow tracking of tapes and error and query reports;

  2 specially purchased colour-coded transport bags for ease of identification;

  3 special arrangements for pick-up and delivery directly to and from the clinical coders at each hospital.

The necessary items were then ordered and forms designed. The new scheme was explained and communicated to all staff likely to be affected by the change. All communications stressed that the amended system had been designed and evaluated by a multi-disciplinary team drawn from across all operating units. There was no visible opposition to the proposed changes. A consolidation period followed. ISD staff monitored the new system, lending support and encouragement when necessary.

Epilogue

The transport system as envisaged within option F, designed to tackle factor 2, was fully implemented. There were no unforeseen difficulties and it significantly reduced SMR travel time. Performance levels associated with factor 1, tackled by option B, only slightly improved. The coding target of three to five days after discharge was not being attained. Once again the problem owner consulted those directly involved, detailing the problem, explaining the rationale, recruiting appropriate senior management support, and involving those at the 'coal face' in providing a solution. The medical consultants seemed to be the problem. They simply were not following procedures. It should be noted that as a group they had been represented on the change management team and were not being asked to do anything that they did not already do. But they were being asked to perform a task at a different time using amended documentation.

Case analysis

On the surface this case appears to be well suited to a systems investigation. The success of the new transport system bears testimony to the appropriateness of ISM. A well-structured and systematic solution was developed to answer a particularly hard problem.

Throughout the case the problem owner followed the ISM approach, except in the definition phase, in which the need to formally address the issue of constraints appears to have been ignored. The financial constraint was an obvious one to those concerned and could be taken for granted, in so much that all knew a minimum spend was required. What appears to have been less obvious was the constraint placed on the solution by the medical consultants. This was an organizational constraint and should have been dealt with accordingly. The implementation strategy for factor 1 did not fully address it. Involving a representative of the medical consultants in the design process did not guarantee acceptance of the implementation strategy.

In effect the 'Epilogue' describes an iteration. It was required to address the failure to fully involve, persuade and stimulate the medics. They had to be tactfully educated and cajoled into acceptance of the change. Change creates multi-disciplinary problems, which often require a blend of the systems and organizational approaches to be applied, especially within the implementation phase.

The key lesson that should be drawn from this case relates to the management of powerful stakeholders. One tries to address such issues by involving them in the change; however, very often those who volunteer are simply viewed as management puppets, or fail to make meaningful contributions. There are no easy answers to such problems. Employing effective change agents who possess the necessary skills and attributes, both from a process and interpersonal perspective, can assist in identifying, managing and ultimately winning the support of powerful stakeholder groups.

Case study 2: Caledonian Airmotive Ltd

The core business of Caledonian Airmotive Ltd (CAL) is the overhaul and maintenance of aero-engines. It is a highly competitive industry and CAL competes in a global market place. The principal production facility is based within the precincts of Prestwick Airport. The company is well established and has developed a reputation for excellence. An extremely dynamic operational and organizational environment was developed in response to ever increasing customer expectations and requirements. CAL's customers compete in an extremely competitive and volatile market place, one in which time is indeed money. An under-utilized piece of expensive resource, such as an aircraft, cannot earn optimal revenue.

The ability to readily adapt to customer requirements, and manage any associated changes or disruptions, is seen by the company as a distinct competitive advantage. Responding to externally driven change, in an effective manner, has become routine for the company. CAL's main customer grouping, the airlines, require two main classes of engineering support:

1   provision of serviceable engines after a repair or overhaul in as short a time as possible;

2   provision of a repair service with respect to line replaceable units (LRUs), which are removed at the operator's base and sent for repair independently of the engine.

This case deals with the second class of engineering service, namely the LRUs. There are a variety of engine components that can be classed as LRUs. Such a diversity of potential components requires that a flexible production response be adopted. Management is therefore faced with the problem of maintaining mainstream engine overhaul and repair whilst dealing with disturbances to the operating system caused by processing LRUs. In the competitive environment of aero-engine overhaul and repair, in which the minimization of engine turnaround time is crucial, the production system must favour the mainstream flow- and process- oriented work. Any disruption to this system results in downtime and thus extended engine turnaround cycles, so value is therefore lost not added. Although lucrative, and a necessary business service within the aero-engine market, servicing LRUs necessitates disrupting the production line. For this reason CAL were always willing to consider production or business systems changes which could potentially minimize disruptions and maximize mainstream productivity.

The accessory shop that was responsible for LRU repair was also an integral part of the mainstream production process. It was dependent on such services as the machine shop, general provisioning, non-destructive testing (NDT) inspection and stores. As one would expect, priority status always went to mainstream engine overhaul and repair activities. The net result being that LRUs suffered delays and clients responded accordingly. The situation may be seen as a mismatch between customer requirements, namely, quick turnaround on both engine and LRU repairs, and the company's norms that seek efficient production flows and a minimization of costs. Over time clients could become dissatisfied and either LRU business would be lost or the company could try some-how to maintain a balancing act between its two principal services. The company aims to be more capable than their competitors at identifying and correcting such mismatches and by so doing maintain a competitive edge. The LRU problem was therefore treated seriously and formed the basis of an extensive change management exercise.

The change objective, or project brief, was clear: to modify the current accessory shop system with the aim of changing it from being one of dependency to one of self-sufficiency, and to create a stable new envi-ronment which can support both shop engine and single item LRU requirements.

The problem owner and the definition phase

Senior management decided to commission an analysis of system rela-tionships and workflow patterns. In particular they were interested in determining the precise causes of turnaround time delays. They appointed a project manager, in effect the problem owner and principal change agent, with direct knowledge of the problem and the necessary skills and position to facilitate the change. In Figures 4.10 and 4.15 the accessory shop relationship and influence maps were produced.

READER ACTIVITY

Please return to Chapter 4 before continuing. Consult and carefully review Figures 4.10 and 4.15 and then return to the case.

In addition to these figures the project manager also produced a multiple cause diagram for LRU delays. A summary of this is illustrated in Figure 16.3.

The project manager's initial reaction was that there was one obvious solution: a truly autonomous accessory shop, operating as a satellite plant.

This conclusion was based not only on the diagrams so far covered but also on highly detailed flow diagrams detailing virtually every activity and link associated with the existing accessory shop system. The detailed, technical and, most importantly, commercially sensitive nature of these diagrams precluded their publication. The investigations relat-ing to the proposed systems intervention were conducted in an open and collaborative manner. In addition to the systems studies the project man-ager also spoke informally to the existing client base. The market expressed enthusiasm for the proposed provision of a dedicated LRU service.

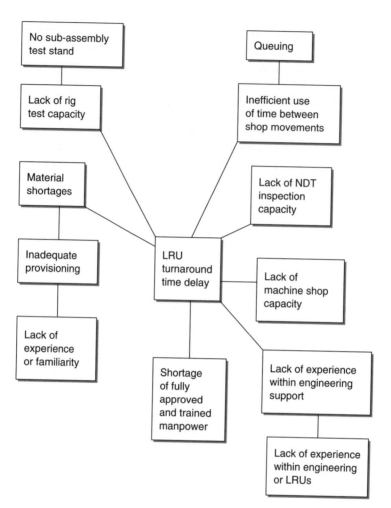

Figure 16.3   Multiple cause diagram for LRU delays

Indulging in a *forward iteration* the project manager decided to evaluate what appeared to be the one and only obvious solution. Representatives of finance, marketing, production and engineering were called upon to form an investigative team. Their brief was to evaluate the costs and general viability associated with the formation of a dedicated LRU facility. After careful study it was decided that this was not a viable option due to both logistical and cost constraints. Essentially the detailed cost-benefit analysis came out against an autonomous LRU facility.

The assembled group then turned their attention, having seen the potential production and service benefits of the proposed change, to a derivative of the original proposal. A semi-autonomous system could be created within the existing plant, with the control of critical areas passing over from mainstream production to the new LRU accessory shop. The only services to be shared with mainstream production would be of an administrative and functional nature, such as systems, personnel and quality. Analysis and evaluation of this option proved more favourable. Proposed expenditure could be justified against the anticipated increase in orders for both LRUs and engines, which would be gained through a reduction in turnaround time. In addition, less downtime and the rationalization of services and responsibilities would also lead to reduced operating costs. Market research was commissioned to ensure that orders would be forthcoming and detailed financial analysis was conducted which confirmed the cost savings. In terms of the 'bottom line' the proposed change had been justified.

Evaluation Phase

In reality the project team had entered the evaluation phase. They had decided what they wanted to do and justified their decision. Armed with a validated solution the project manager set about the actual task of detailing the practical requirements and actions. Several factors associated with the successful implementation of the change still had to be addressed and evaluated:

1 shop layout;

2 equipment requirements;

3 organizational structure;

4 training requirements;

5 disruption to the current production cycle.

The company and the project manager knew that the success of the change would rely on the willing support of all those concerned. Diagrammatic representations detailing the old and new systems, along with updated organizational charts, were produced in consultation with the key stakeholders and players. This material was then used to communicate the change to the rest of the organization. The project manager actively sold the concept first to senior management and then with their support to the other management levels and functions. Having gained widespread support additional change agents were identified and charged with addressing the factor raised above.

Implementation Phase

An incremental and logical implementation plan was initiated. It proposed that both the old and the new system should run in parallel, with the phased handover from old to new occurring in a planned sequence over a specified time period. The actual work groups, who would form the new semi-autonomous accessory shop, would be involved throughout the process. Not only would they be trained, if required, but they would also play a major role in defining the working environment. The CAL implementation plan was used in Chapter 6 to illustrate the generic issues associated with the implementation of change within the ISM.

READER ACTIVITY

You should now return to the section on the implementation phase in Chapter 6. Review the CAL example carefully (Mini Case 6.4) and then return to this case.

The implementation phase was completed and the project has been consolidated. The semi-autonomous LRU approach is now an established feature of the CAL operating strategy and did indeed provide the expected benefits.

Case analysis

The CAL project represented a major change-management exercise. The sheer scale of the project cannot be done justice to within an illustrative case study framework. Operating, organizational and business systems and cultures were impinged upon. Old ideas were challenged and a multi-faceted competitive edge developed. The change was successfully managed by adopting an approach that successfully combined both systems intervention strategies and more traditional project management methodologies. However, within this systems oriented management approach the problem owner ensured that, when appropriate, the wider stakeholder body was involved. The rationale, proposals and consequences of the change were effectively communicated. Active participation and support was sought and integrated into the change process. Senior management were brought on board at an early stage and their support fully exploited.

The project manager did not follow the ISM in a logical manner. The approach taken was in many ways more along the lines advocated by the TPM. The definition phase concentrated on developing an understanding of the systems environment and bringing on board the appropriate expertise to solve the problem. As the project had to be validated prior to commencing change activities there was no choice but to corrupt the ISM approach to facilitate the early generation and evaluation of a solution. The TPM stresses that in project management the solution to the problem generally has to be agreed prior to engaging in detailed planning. The CAL case was no exception. However, it may have been possible to avoid the initial proposition, that of the totally autonomous accessory shop, had the constraints associated with the project been more fully defined. Given that the desired solution had been both found and validated prior to the formulation phase there was no need for evaluation of options. Instead the project team set about analysing and planning for the key factors associated with the project solution. Again this process reflects the second phase of the TPM. Implementation involved the development of a logical, integrated and sequential plan that lent itself to the adoption of network-based activity scheduling.

The major lessons for the practitioner that may be drawn from this case concern the actual application of intervention strategies. First, an optimal solution can still be achieved even when the format of the model has been corrupted to reflect both practical and commercial considerations. Second, care should be taken that the modifications to the format do not result in the complete omission of key process steps. Intervention strategy models are designed to reflect best practice as defined by both researchers and practitioners. Finally, when dealing with projects which are likely to gain the support of key stakeholders, it may be better to adopt the TPM derivative.

Case study 3: British Gas Plc

This case concerns the Scottish operations of British Gas Plc and in particular the region's central purchasing department. Each region serves a customer base that has its own unique appliance population. Regions held local stocks of frequently ordered parts and could therefore offer their customers what may be termed an 'off-the-shelf' service. All other spare parts were known as 'one-time-buys' or OTBs for short. OTBs had to be ordered directly from the suppliers. This process, depending on the supplier and their location, could take on average 15 days from order placement to delivery.

Background information specific to the case

As part of a drive to improve standards of customer service, British Gas, at corporate level, decided to set up their own stockholding facilities for OTBs. Two national stockholding centres, one at Manchester, the other in London, opened for business in March 1991 and provided the regions with approximately 80 per cent of their OTBs. By centralizing the purchasing and holding of such stocks, economies of scale would be available to British Gas as a whole, and there would be no cost disadvantage for the regions trading with the new central resource. Central stockholding costs would be offset by lower initial purchasing costs. Regions were instructed that on the opening of the new facilities they should all be in a position to commence ordering immediately. Lead times for OTBs were expected to drop from 15 days to three or four, thus improving customer service.

The problem owner and the definition phase

The problem owner within the Scottish region was the purchasing manager, who was given the following change brief: 'to change the current OTB ordering system to enable the purchasing department to make optimal use of the new national facility.'

Following the initial stages of the problem the problem owner quickly involved the other key players, namely, the departmental systems development officer and the spares buyer. The steps taken by this group of change agents when defining the systems environment were detailed within the ISM definition phase, which may be found in Chapter 6.

READER ACTIVITY

The reader should now return to the definition phase of Chapter 6. Consult and review the British Gas example (Mini Case 6.1) and then return to this case.

A number of diagrams are referred to within the British Gas example in Chapter 6 (Mini Case 6.1). The additional figures illustrated in this chapter represent the change agent's total investigative diagrammatic output. The first diagram, Figure 16.4, deals with the OTB flow chart. It was produced to further the management group's understanding of the present system.

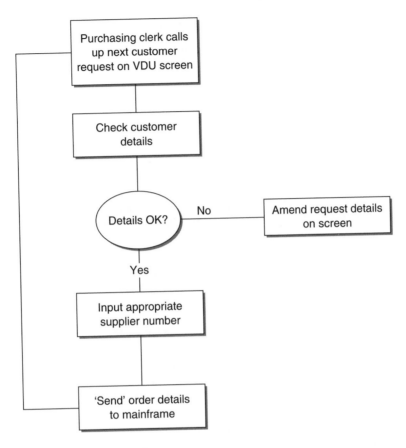

Figure 16.4 OTB flow chart

From the flow chart the group moved on to develop an activity sequence diagram, Figure 16.5, depicting the situation before and after the change. This was a useful analysis exercise and provided a means of communicating the exact nature of the proposed change to the ordering clerks. It would be the clerks who would be most directly affected. It was possible at this stage to define the process elements of the new system due to the detailed information that was provided by corporate head-quarters relating to the change as a whole. In addition, the process activities were unlikely to alter drastically as the change essentially involved altering only the source of supplies.

The activity sequence diagram highlighted the need to consider all the parties involved as there were going to be additional external links after the change. Again, 'before' and 'after' relationship maps were produced and these are shown in Figure 16.6.

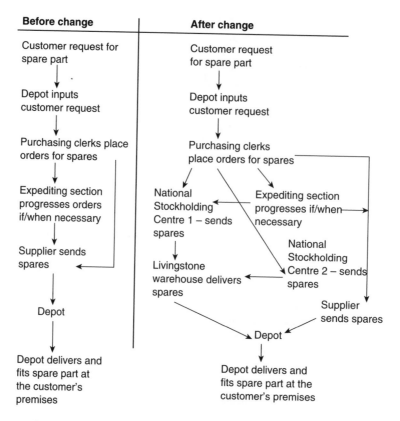

Figure 16.5   Activity sequence diagram

The systems definition stage was completed by the construction of two systems maps as shown in Figure 16.7.

With the actual systems definitions completed to everyone's satisfaction the problem owner then turned the managing group's attention to the change forces at work within the operations environment. A number of force field analysis diagrams, as depicted in Figure 16.8, were produced which both assisted in describing and evaluating the forces acting upon those involved.

It was evident from a number of the diagrams produced that the workload of the expediting section would be reduced by the proposed systems changes. They were consulted and the changes were explained and the likely impact was described. All concerned staff, both the ordering clerks and expediters, were given assurances that no one would lose their jobs as a result of the changes. Redeployments to related disciplines were sensitively managed. These were used to overcome the problem of reduced workloads and operative resistance. The staff accepted both the

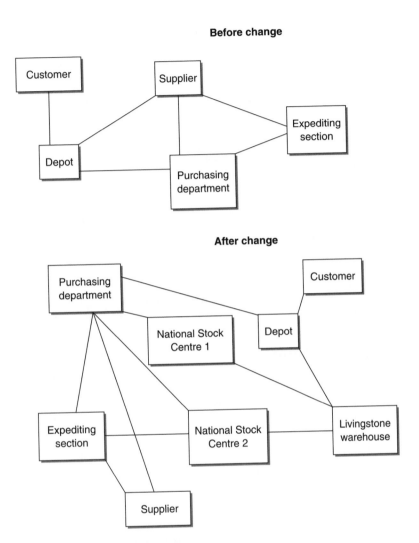

Figure 16.6   Relationship maps

assurances and the potential redeployments. Full co-operation and support was gained.

The problem owner, confident of staff support, now turned his
attention to the constraints acting upon the change situation. To this
end an objectives tree was produced, as illustrated in Figure 16.9, into
which priorities were included. These are indicated numerically within
parentheses.

The performance indicators were identified from the objectives tree.
They fell into two categories associated with the financial and human

Before change

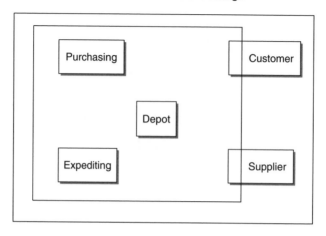

After change

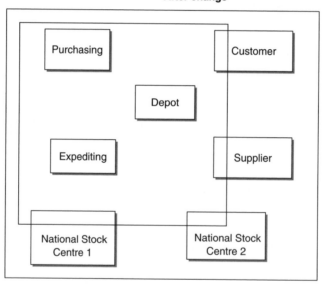

Figure 16.7　Systems maps

resource. First, with regard to finance, budgetary constraints would produce financial measures for training, systems programming and equipment. Second, relating to the human resources, information systems staff were in high demand and therefore their services were difficult to secure. In addition, there were performance targets associated directly with the change itself. A target had been set, by which time 80 per cent of

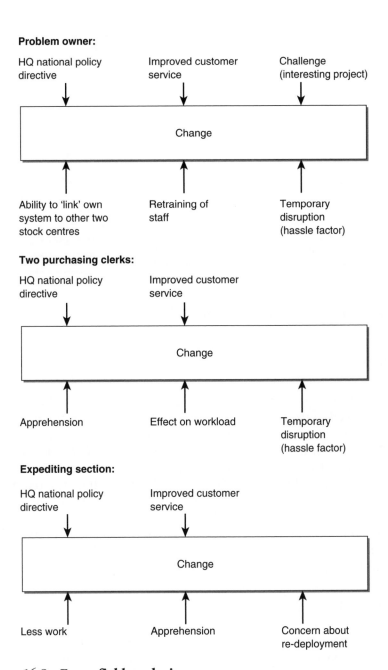

Figure 16.8 Force field analysis

all OTBs had to be ordered from the new facilities. There was also an imposed delivery target of three to four days from receipt of the customer's order.

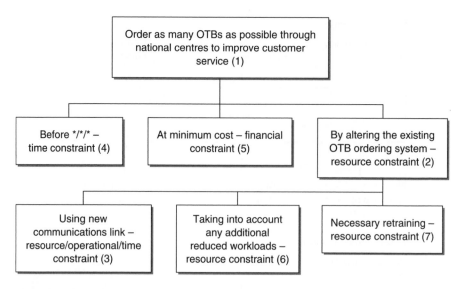

Figure 16.9   Prioritized objectives tree

Evaluation phase

The actual process activities required for the new system had been previously detailed in the definition phase. The management team, along with the ordering clerks, now set about generating options. This involved a detailed study of the existing computerized system. After much deliberation only one feasible solution could be identified. Each ordering clerk would require an additional VDU and PC linked into the stockholding centre. Existing processing kit could not deal with the additional load and still maintain an effective service. Such a solution satisfied the main objectives and constraints. The problem owner, wary of implementation difficulties, contacted the systems people and confirmed that their resources were indeed stretched, but they would do all they could to help.

Implementation phase

The implementation strategy comprised three stages. The first involved the acquisition and installation of equipment, which was immediately, followed by the setting up of external communications links. During this time the operatives entered the second stage. They were given access to dummy screens to allow them to become familiar with screen layout and input requirements. The third stage, once the new system was operational, involved a series of pilot runs. These tested the system, as well as the operatives, and also satisfied the management team of the benefits associated with the new system and the efficiency of the central warehousing resource.

A number of minor iterations were made as a result of the operator training phase and the pilot runs. These resulted in useful screen layout changes. Consolidation was never an internal issue and the national system OTB ordering system achieved its objectives.

Case analysis

The British Gas case is a textbook example of how to successfully apply a systems intervention strategy. Certain details were omitted within the evaluation phase due to their highly technical nature, but they were dealt with according to the ISM methodology.

The lessons to be learnt from this case are all positive. The first concerns the initial selection of a solution methodology. This was a 'hard' systems problem that, although it had significant people implications, was best tackled by a systems-based approach. The human resource implications were dealt with at an early stage in the change cycle. Involvement was sought and participation gained. Redundancy fears were dispensed with and effective systems training provided well in advance of final commissioning. Time spent defining the old and new operating system is generally never wasted. In this case the clear objectives, quantifiable performance measures, fixed target dates and the well bound nature of the change environment, all pointed in the direction of an ISM solution methodology.

The second lesson concerns the forward loop from the formulation to the implementation phase. The need to be aware of the pressures facing the systems resource was built into the implementation strategy. Parallel implementation was achieved by ensuring that the operatives had access to dummy screens while the installation was going ahead. This both avoided potential implementation delays and allowed minor systems updates to be incorporated while the systems people were on site.

17 | Organizational Development Cases

This chapter introduces, in a reasonably traditional manner, a number of OD case studies. However, the sixth of these, a group performance review, is much shorter and far more reflective. It aims to get you to reflect on how you would go about tackling a particular form of organization development with the information provided.

These case studies have been designed both to satisfy the needs of the individual reader, and to act as group exercises in a more formalized setting. To the extent that they try to satisfy two needs at the same time there is a degree of compromise. In the organization development case studies, we have compromised in favour of the group learning approach. In our teaching on the management of change, we have found that a greater degree of thought and discussion is generated through group analysis of situations. Therefore, if you are reading these cases as an individual, it may be worthwhile thinking of some means of relating your personal reflections to past or current group based situations, and/or finding some means of introducing the cases within a group context. Within your own organization, this could form part of an exercise prior to discussion of an actual change event that is likely to take place. You may also be considering some of the changes described in the cases. In this sense, they will act as a form of organization analysis.

Case study 1: Experience at GlaxoSmithKline (GSK)

The merger between Beecham Pharmaceuticals (UK) and Smith Kline (USA) in 1989 was a landmark event not only for the mergers and acquisition fraternity but also for observers of globalization and students of change. SmithKline Beecham (SKB) was hailed as the first truly transactional pharmaceutical and healthcare company. The new executive team

Figure 17.1   SKB initiatives

saw both the need for a shared vision and focal point for stimulating and assisting in formulating the following: a new company culture; leadership approach; and values. The term 'simply better' was generated in a company wide communications process as the way in which things should be done on a day-to-day basis.

As the 'simply better' initiative was cascaded down and throughout the new organization each SKB site addressed what the initiative meant for them and also how best to proceed. One of GSK's sites in Irvine, Scotland detailed a number of key initiatives that fell under what they termed the 'simply better' umbrella. They fell into three main categories that formed a triangle as shown in Figure 17.1.

Some of the initiatives had already been underway, nevertheless this certainly was the first time that they had been grouped together and indeed set in the overall context of organizational change.

The opportunity was taken by the plant management at Irvine to intimate that employees would be expected to become more involved in the change process and they were assured that the implementation would not result in any compulsory redundancies. A commitment was also given to train the employees in any new skills required. Although there were sceptics and dissenters amongst the workforce, generally the roll out sessions were well received due to the job security factor. The success of the roll out took some by surprise given there were some genuine fears of a 'slash and burn' approach being adopted by the acquisitive Americans.

This participative management approach within the company was developed further in 1994 as the focus switched from corporate level restructuring to reorganization specifically at the Irvine site. On this occasion senior site managers were initially taken out of their job roles for a period of several months to concentrate entirely on the transformation to a cellular structure. External change agents were employed extensively during this initial period and in due course the results were communicated to the plant staff. The change from traditional departments to more autonomous cells was announced along with the appointments of new Cell Leaders. It was explained that this was only the first step in the process which would take a further one to two years. This time employees were invited to volunteer for 'design team activities' to help the cell leaders reorganize within each cell.

Again the company had adopted an OD approach to organizational change by involving employees in the process. At the same time the talk was very much of radical changes within the cells, perhaps employing some of the attributes of Business Process Re-engineering (BPR). A significant amount of training was carried out for those involved in the design team activities. Another output of the simply better initiative was the promotion of teamwork and the identification and development of internal facilitators. New areas of training included process mapping, problem solving, analytical tools and so on.

The year that followed was a very busy one for many people on the site as many struggled with the issues of design teams while others were burdened with additional responsibilities to ensure production levels were maintained. Overall, the morale on site actually fell during this period as the workforce showed a significant reluctance to the changes that were being proposed. In the production areas in particular, the unions suspiciously viewed the design teams as a vehicle to reduce manning levels. Non-value-added activities were closely scrutinized and attempts made to design them out.

In terms of results, the prescribed changes from design team activities remained largely unfulfilled as insufficient resources for implementation were made available.

Questions

1   What was the main management lesson in introducing change at SKB?

2   What were some of the key OD lessons at the Irvine plant?

Analysis

Change has become a feature of organizational life and although individuals have a natural tendency to feel uncomfortable and to resist change, further exposure leads to a degree of acclimatization. This would appear to be the experience at SKB, Irvine where the rate of introduction of change had accelerated since the merger. The workforce and management appeared to be more relaxed about tackling change as a result of a no redundancy policy and the widespread communications process.

There is a learning curve that the individual and the organization has to pass through, not only on acceptance of change but also on the process of change. The tried and tested activity-driven processes which had been the main experience at SKB had been found wanting in respect of the resource requirements to complete implementation. Frustration and disillusionment can be the order of the day as limited progress is achieved inside the design team, whilst outside, others struggle to maintain the status quo. On the other hand, a BPR approach would have been completely inappropriate if the needs of the workforce were bypassed to deliver reduced costs with fewer, but less motivated and highly stressed employees. There can be a balance where both individual and the organizational effectiveness are increased within a well-managed and resourced programme. The time frames for results must be controlled and this can be related to the work of Schaffer and Thomson (1992), 'By marrying long-term strategic objectives with short-term improvement projects, management can translate strategic direction into reality.'

Crucial to delivering the required change process is the change agent, who must be suitably equipped with the appropriate skills and the necessary charisma to tackle the complex issues head-on. SKB like many others started off with external change agents and then developed, with limited success, its own team of internal facilitators. They can be called upon, or so it was hoped, to offer their expertise at any time. However, in SKB's experience there have been problems in change agent accessibility due to their normal work activities.

Case study 2: Ethicon Ltd

An example of a company that appears to have successfully implemented a change is Ethicon Ltd, a medical device company who, at the time, manufactured sutures for medical applications. The late 1990s saw the company restructure; one of the aims at the time was the relocation of the research and development function to Germany with the UK site to concentrate on manufacturing.

In managing this change, Ethicon set up new in-house systems to refocus people's ideas on three main goals:

- to improve process cycle times;
- to decrease costs, and
- to improve quality.

Throughout the change process the company communicated well with employees and made them aware of the intentions and the benefits. A number of project managers were put in place to drive through change. Ethicon also introduced cross-functional teams that broke down interdepartmental barriers and encouraged open forum discussions. They managed to involve the workers in the project and made them believe that there were gains to be made by changing the way they worked. This initiated change across the whole company. They also set in play a system of measurements against objectives in order to translate them into tangible business benefits. It is believed that one of the greatest achievements gained from this redesign project was the true sense of teamworking. The end result was a measured increase in productivity levels. The new ways of working were implemented throughout the company and the hope was that they would produce positive results and cost savings to the company to ensure that Ethicon remained competitive.

Questions

1 How did management at Ethicon 'get it right'?

2 What particular aspects have encouraged the successful change?

Analysis

The change implementation process proved successful at Ethicon because of the following factors:

- The management team shared their vision on how it was going to be implemented.

- They employed project managers as change agents who were responsible for the initiation and implementation of the transformation process and monitored these changes.

- The progress of the implementation was communicated to the employees both directly and through newsletters that highlighted improvements made as a result of the changes.

- They encouraged the formation of coalitions, to work together in teams towards a set of common goals.

This is a textbook example of how to manage a complex change situation. Vision was shared, communicated and implemented in a holistic manner. The OD changes may also be seen to be further evidence of the value of integrative, participative and iterative planning as detailed in the TPM introduced in Chapter 7.

Case study 3: United Kingdom Atomic Energy Authority (UKAEA)

After the closure of the Fast Breeder Reactor Programme, there had been considerable redundancies at the UKAEA's Dounreay facility. These were largely voluntary, and accompanied by well funded civil service redundancy packages. This was followed by the contracting out of certain elements of the site organization to the private sector. The UKAEA had successfully implemented a Managing Agency system for the decommissioning work for Windscale Pile 0. 1. In order to improve efficiency and to bring in commercial management practices, they had decided to install a similar system at Dounreay.

The approach taken by the incoming Managing Agency team (for which key members were transferred from Windscale) was autocratic. When problems were encountered, decisions were often made rapidly as to how they were to be resolved. Initiative was not encouraged, and it seemed that a decision did not stand for long before being reversed or modified.

One example of this best illustrates the confusion caused by the change. Project managers had initially been expected to produce quarterly progress reports. These were usually fairly detailed, and supported by financial information. In turn, these were supported by 'short-form' monthly progress reports, which included exception reporting where appropriate. The difficulty was caused by the fact that the 'short-form' reports were not supported by the financial information system or by any of the project management tools available on the site. They relied on manual tracking of contracts and projects by spreadsheet.

The Managing Agency staff issued new formats and content requirements for the quarterly financial and earned value reports, requiring an additional level of detail (partly in order to support their own claims for incentive payments). This involved a considerable amount of extra effort. Although the declared aim was to reduce the amount of effort which went into reporting there was little evidence that this was being achieved.

The local management team did not have the power to make their own changes. The Managing Agency staff made matters worse by requiring further changes to these reporting formats and requested that they be submitted monthly. Moreover, they then changed the requirements each month for several months. The rearrangement of spreadsheets to meet these new requirements became far and away more time consuming than the production of the reports themselves. 'What's the new monthly format for the monthly reports?' became a frequent query. The required changes were achieved but at a cost of diverting significant amounts of effort from productive operations and reduced the credibility of the Managing Agency. Project team leaders at Dounreay were fast becoming experts at accommodating change in reporting requirements, rather than on project management.

Another instance of a non-participative attempt at change concerned the implementation of the construction (design and management) regulations. The regulations required the appointment of a principal contractor to be legally responsible for the management of safety on relevant worksites. The managing agency's view was that the UKAEA could not legally delegate responsibility for safety on a nuclear licensed site. Therefore, UKAEA would have to retain the position of principal contractor, rather than contracting it out, as any other client might do. There were already individuals appointed to take full control and responsibility for safety within specific site areas. The holders of what was termed 'ATO' (Authority to Operate) had absolute authority. The logical organizational stance, was that the ATO holder should also be appointed principal contractor. This quite sensible approach was rejected by the ATO holders, who felt that:

- The new change was being foisted upon them with virtually no discussion.

- Their workload was already excessive: it was inappropriate to add a further legal and mandatory duty to their task list.

- They had insufficient training in the requirements of the CDM regulations, and had very little idea as to what the principal contractor's duties are.

Whilst it should be stressed that there was never any safety problem, or contravention of any legal requirement, there was no attempt to win the hearts and minds of powerful stakeholders in the organization. The objections stated above could have been resolved very simply, by education, discussion, training, jointly establishing a strategy for implementation, and provision of a marginal quantity of staffing resource. The ATO holders were highly qualified and experienced personnel. They already had the vast majority of the skills and training needed for the role, which need not have added excessively to their duties. The lack of consultation simply served as another illustration of a management style which they did not appreciate, and built up resentment and resistance to change in a key segment of the site management.

Analysis

At Dounreay, Managing Agency was employed to achieve cost savings. The trigger for Managing Agency implementation was simply that 'it had worked at Windscale, so it should work here.' There was no evidence that a detailed study of the required change processes was undertaken. Certainly there was no clarity as to how cost savings were to be achieved. The UKAEA appeared to think that Managing Agency would achieve the cost savings for them. Few of the employees saw it as being in their interest to support the change process where decommissioning work was involved. Clearly, it was important to identify and communicate the reasons for change if support was to be generated for it.

The treatment of the ATO holders is a classical illustration of change management being introduced through lack of consultation or effective communication. This resulted in resistance to change and could have been more effectively handled. ATO holders already had responsibilities in this area and the formalization of this through a consultative process would have made the introduction of increased role responsibilities more straightforward.

The method of change management used by Managing Agency was clearly of the project management genre (the change agent's expertise lay in dealing with contractors rather than change management). This approach had worked at Windscale where fewer stakeholders had been involved, but at Dounreay there was a considerable resistance to change in powerful segments of middle management, and Managing Agency did not have the power to simply drive through the changes in the way it had planned.

Not only had the process of change taken control of the strategy and rationale originally envisaged, the trinity discussed in Chapter 2 had clearly broken down. Roles, focus and goals had become confused and lacked purpose.

Case study 4: the National Health Service (NHS)

The NHS has found itself at the forefront of change over the past decade or so. Successive governments, executives and various other stakeholders have contrived to ensure that the NHS is 'fit for purpose'. After nearly 50 years of a very rigid bureaucratic regime the NHS has been finding itself having to adapt very quickly to internal and external pressures.

This case deals with a cultural change that occurred after the appointment of a new general manager at Grampian Health Board. At the time Grampian provided healthcare to half a million people living within 3,360 square miles. The population was not evenly distributed. However, 43 per cent of inhabitants lived in or around Aberdeen. As a result, major acute, obstetric and psychiatric services were based in the city with Elgin providing a secondary centre. Peripheral hospitals and clinics provided additional services. Grampian employed 13,500 staff and received a budget of about £170 million per annum.

The general manager was determined to develop a more proactive, responsive and inclusive culture. An external change agent was engaged to assist in a review of the organization's current position. The review concluded that there were a number of issues to be addressed. On the positive side, 'people in the organization were devoted, capable, and enthusiastic, but they have been bound up in a bureaucratic system of indecision.' However, there were a number of recommendations related to the need to adopt problem solving approaches capable of dealing with issues associated with costs, responsiveness to customers, expectations and strategic direction.

The review highlighted a number of motivators for change:

1   the external pressures of new government legislation – contracting for services, devolution of responsibility, and an emphasis on competitiveness;

2   internal pressures from staff in the form of complaints about poor communication, lack of creativity, low motivation, unclear strategy, unclear structure, systems not understood, lack of teamwork;

3   new standards of delivering services;

4   a new general manager.

The style they decided to adopt was one of an OD driven intervention. This involved utilizing a toolkit of intervention methods including:

•   process consultation

•   survey feedback

•   changing the structure

•   teambuilding

•   inter-group development.

Price Waterhouse were used as process consultants. One of the first steps was to answer the question, 'Where are we now?' This involved an attitude survey of over 1,000 members of the staff. From this, the following issues came to light:

•   *Communication*   Information was not disseminated throughout the organization in a way that allowed it to be understood and accepted.

•   *Creativity*   Ideas for improving the way in which the organization worked were not being put to good use and this led to stagnation.

- *Motivation*   People did not feel greatly concerned about the organization and were not willing to expend much effort to further common goals.

- *Strategy*   The reasons for doing things were unclear and/or poorly communicated. The systems to support management were inadequate and/or not understood.

- *Teamwork*   People who should have been contributing to common tasks did not wish to work together or found too many obstacles to do so.

- *Training*   People were not learning to do things that would materially affect their performance.

This feedback suggested that at the time Grampian tended towards being a monolithic bureaucracy which was unable to cope with rapid and unpredictable change; the increasing complexity of modern organization; the diversity of specialist expertise; and participative management styles.

Further workshops and meetings followed to look at, 'Where do we need to be?' after which the senior management produced three documents: a vision, a mission, and a management approach, which stated the desired future culture at Grampian. A programme was then developed to address these issues as follows:

- A ten-year strategy for healthcare was developed through a highly participative process.

- Each of the units produced a five-year plan.

- Many teambuilding workshops were held throughout the organization but particularly at senior management level.

- The board structure was changed towards one more firmly based on consumer groupings.

- A team process was introduced and the in-house magazine was revamped.

- A comprehensive quality programme was devised, including patient surveys, quality standards and customer care training.

- A rigorous review of overhead costs was conducted which enabled over 15 per cent to be saved and relocated.

- Personal objectives, appraisal and performance-related pay were cascaded through the management hierarchy.

- New training programmes were introduced, covering areas such as problem solving, planning and leadership.

- The whole senior management team went through a development process designed to identify personal potential.

- Twenty-one line managers were seconded for up to 70 per cent of their time to undertake the role of in house consultants.

Analysis

Two years after the OD process was initiated, the original questionnaire was again sent out to see if the people in the organization felt that the objective of cultural change had been achieved. The results showed that at senior and middle management levels there was a definite view that cultural change had taken place, but supervisory and basic grades had a negative and neutral attitude respectively. This outcome, according to the management team, was 'a matter of timing'. They stated that, 'Cultural change takes a long time: it seeps down and permeates management structure from above.' Looking at this it could be suggested that the participative techniques used had focused mainly on senior and middle management. As this change took place over a long period of time there were a number of issues that could possibly have been addressed to avoid this negativity and neutrality.

Dunphy and Stace (1988, 1990) looked at the scale of change and the leadership styles required to facilitate this. The scale of change in this example lends itself to their description of corporate transformation. They described this as, 'involving radical shifts in strategy, revolutionary changes throughout the organization, to structure, systems and procedures, to mission and the core values and to the distribution of power.' They argue that with this scale of change the required leadership style would be one of 'charismatic transformation' and as part of this the organization would require support for the radical change. It is unclear whether Grampian truly had this commitment from the supervisory and lower grades. Perhaps this left them lacking in trust and not fully understanding the purpose of the change. The vision in this case was clearly stated to the organization, but from the outcome the middle and senior management grades appear to be the only ones who had taken it on board. The impact was concentrated at that level, gaining their trust but leaving the lower grades with a neutral feeling.

Change of this magnitude does take time to diffuse throughout the whole organization. However, one would have expected a greater degree of commitment to the change process from all grades. The emphasis on the management levels appears to have been at the expense of the total organization buying into the change process and may have created or exacerbated an 'us and them' syndrome. Too much stress may have been placed on developing management skills rather than enhancing Grampian's management processes.

Case study 5: MTC Ltd

Change is a continuous process of confrontation, identification, evaluation and action. The overlap between systems thinking and OD emerges in Pugh's (1978) article and in Rickards (1985). Both approaches have a great deal in common and it appears the theories are converging, with both emphasizing the importance of the process of intervention and the need for any change strategy to have self regulating loops.

In this particular case the problems are basically people oriented and therefore tend towards the 'soft' end of the change continuum resulting from changes made necessary through the rapid growth the company was experiencing.

In applying the OD model, this case study has used, by way of illustration, the changes that were necessary as a result of the company expanding into another sector of the market, namely, the provision of a national training programme for accountants. The success of this was in part responsible for the significant growth experienced by the company.

Political behaviour often emerges before and during organizational change due to the fact that any reorganization is usually feared by some, welcomed by others and often initially ignored by many! This case study is no exception to this and due to very rapid growth displayed all the classic symptoms.

MTC Ltd was a substantial diverse and financially sound organization operating from 20 locations and employing around 150 people. They were primarily involved in providing a wide range of training programmes. MTC identified a market opportunity for a 'technician' level of accountant. The firm commissioned consultants to conduct a market research survey to determine the likely level of demand for such a training programme. Their findings indicated that there was a very significant level of demand and that none of the company's main competitors were currently involved.

In order to capture the lion's share of the potential market the company had to move swiftly:

1 To establish links with the Association of Accounting Technicians (AAT) who were the London based body responsible for the award of the professional qualification, which was recognized and indeed sponsored, by all five major accountancy bodies in the UK.

2 Similarly, to establish links with the Scottish sponsoring body namely, The Institute of Chartered Accountants of Scotland (ICAS).

3 To negotiate a contract for the provision of a government sponsored training scheme.

4 Based on market research, to quantify the resources that would be required in terms of additional premises, location of premises, equipment, timing, funding and manning.

5 To deal with the scale of the operations meant that the company's administrative and personnel procedures had to be reviewed and upgraded with more formalized procedures being introduced.

6 To deal with the organizational changes meant reorganization was required which with the anticipated increase in manning levels, etc., meant that certain roles had to be changed.

It is a paradox of organizational life that situations and problems that cry out most strongly for change are often the very ones whose resistance is greatest!

The OD process

The philosophy of organizational development is one of long-term change and organizational change efforts that are based on inconsistent strategies tend to run into predictable problems. An effective manager is one who anticipates, diagnoses and manages the change process over a period of time to ensure it is effective. In this case perhaps the use of a change facilitator or consultant would have been helpful in giving an unbiased 'helicopter' view of the organization. However, the organizational change was approached in the following manner.

First, at the planning stage, consideration was given to the four principles and six rules given by Pugh (1978) as a guide to understanding organizational change together with the OD loop, which emphasizes the recurrent nature of change. In order to adequately explain the process that was employed a series and sequence of questions and prompts were formulated as a guide.

Second, if the proposer or problem owner has sufficient power, the change can be pushed through but at the cost of conflict, resentment and reduced motivation. It was always anticipated that resistance to the change would be a major obstacle; the problem owner had to predict what form the resistance might take. The four most common reasons why people resist change are:

1 a desire not to lose something of value;

2 a misunderstanding of the change and its implications;

3 a belief that the change does not make sense for the organization;

4 a low tolerance of change.

Managers who initiate changes often assume that they have all the relevant information required to conduct an adequate organization

Table 17.1 People's objection to change

How can change benefit their job?	How can change appear threatening?	What do people require from their jobs which change can threaten?
Enriching	De-skilling	Interest in their job:
Broadening	Impoverishing	– using a skill
Given discretion	Removing discretion	– having mental challenges
		– using their discretion
Upgrading	Blocking promotion	Growth in their job:
Increased responsibility	Removing jobs	– to more important work
Change of scene	Revising jobs	– to harder work
Improved reward	Rejecting earlier work	– to different work
Improved status	Rejecting ideas	A worthwhile job:
		– recognized by self
		– recognized by others
Training for the job	Increased apparent difficulty	A secure job:
Easier job	Appearing stupid	– ability to handle the job
Permanence of job	Redundancy	– fear of losing face
Better conditions	Degrading	– fear of losing job
		– fear of losing possessions

analysis, and that those who will be affected by the change have the same facts. Neither assumption is correct and again because of the messy nature of the problem it was decided to diagram the 'people problems' in order to understand better the fears and objections of the individuals involved. The people problems and objections are detailed in Table 17.1 and Figure 17.2.

On organizational grounds, resistance to change can be best understood when it is accepted that from the behavioural viewpoint organizations are coalitions of interest groups in tension and there is an interesting parallel here with the Cyert and March (1963) behavioural theory of the firm.

In overcoming an individual's resistance to having their job redesigned there is a motivational opportunity to be gained. Internalized motivation is implicit in McGregor's Theory Y and is reinforced by Herzberg (1966) with his motivational factors that concentrate on the 'satisfiers'. These aspects were given considerable emphasis in order to overcome resistance.

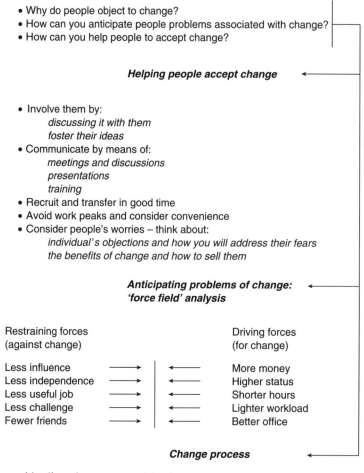

- Why do people object to change?
- How can you anticipate people problems associated with change?
- How can you help people to accept change?

Helping people accept change

- Involve them by:
    discussing it with them
    foster their ideas
- Communicate by means of:
    meetings and discussions
    presentations
    training
- Recruit and transfer in good time
- Avoid work peaks and consider convenience
- Consider people's worries – think about:
    individual's objections and how you will address their fears
    the benefits of change and how to sell them

**Anticipating problems of change:
'force field' analysis**

Restraining forces (against change)			Driving forces (for change)
Less influence	⟶	⟵	More money
Less independence	⟶	⟵	Higher status
Less useful job	⟶	⟵	Shorter hours
Less challenge	⟶	⟵	Lighter workload
Fewer friends	⟶	⟵	Better office

Change process

- Identify and remove restraining forces
- Carry out the change
- Freeze the situation by reinforcing the new behaviour

Figure 17.2　Management of change (people problems)

In summary, the actual OD process model used was as follows:

1　*Confrontation with environmental changes, problems, opportunities*　The decision to diversify into accountancy training would result in a considerable upheaval as there were significant stakeholder influences at play. For example:

External	*Internal*
AAT	Environment
ICAS	Resources
Training commission	Training

Sponsor companies

Competition

Geographical spread

Ethnocentrism

Communication

Motivation

Funding

2 *Identification of implications for organization*   The implications of these changes were far reaching but the most important element by far was how to overcome people's resistance to change. The process described in Figure 17.2 dealt this with.

3 *Education to obtain understanding of implications for organization*   It was evident that attention had to be focused at the individual level and certain actions would have to be taken for those directly affected:

- training;
- communication/involving;
- career planning;
- job enrichment;
- re-establishment of a degree of loyalty.

The fact that this process was interactive was recognized especially when at the implementation stage other factors were identified and the 'loop' would therefore continue.

4 *Obtaining involvement in the project*   It was felt that involving people in carefully planning the change and considering how it would affect them was the best way of overcoming resistance to help develop a change philosophy.

5 *Change and development activities*   The process of change was accomplished by unfreezing, changing and refreezing (Leavitt, 1965). These terms can be explained as follows:

- *unfreezing* – developing an awareness of the need for change and establishing the relationships needed for successful change;
- *changing* – defining problems; identifying solutions; implementing solutions;
- *refreezing* – stabilizing the situation; building relationships.

6 *Evaluation of project and programme in current environment and reinforcement* The evaluation was carried out by determining both what the benefits were and what had been learnt from the process. Some of these were as follows:

- increased profitability;
- more accurate forecasting;
- increased motivation;
- increased propensity for change;
- clearer role perceptions;
- reduced inter-group confrontation.

READER ACTIVITY

Using an example from your own organization, comment on the applicability of Figure 17.2 to the resolution of people problems during the management of change.

Analysis

Few organizational change efforts tend to be complete failures but few tend to be entirely successful either. This was stated by Kotter and Schlesinger (1979) and reinforced by Pritchard (1984): 'There is no right strategy, different combinations are likely to suit different company needs.'

In this particular case, whilst the changes were deemed to have been successful it was recognized that the core measure of success would be the 'bottom line' impact (unfortunately a commercially sensitive piece of information). However, there was ample objective evidence of significant success and the people who were directly affected felt that this style of management approach had been worthwhile, and the enterprise continued to grow.

In reality, if you operate in an aggressive expanding environment, change is continuous and little time is left for formal planning. Management of change remains a fashionable topic but in essence the processes described here are merely the application of a logical and common sense approach. Common sense when applied by informed and competent managers will often suffice. This approach to the organizational development process as illustrated was constructed using a 'logical' approach and yet it contains all aspects of the OD model.

In conclusion, it is important to look both conceptually and practically at managing change and particularly at the interdependence of political, cultural and technical aspects of diagnosing, planning, implementing and evaluating strategic changes.

Case study 6: The Group Performance Review

This final case takes the form of a group performance review. Please note there are no correct answers. There are numerous approaches and techniques associated with undertaking a group performance review. The difficulty that this case study poses to the reader is that it requires *you* to develop your own OD approach. Read through the case study problem, as it is set, and design your own strategy.

During 2005, OILCo, a major oil company, established a number of empowerment workgroups (EWGs) throughout the organization. Six of these EWGs attended a training event during the latter part of 2006 on basic teamwork skills. EWGs are now approaching the end of their first year of operation and it would appear appropriate to undertake some form of review of their operation. Within OILCo, the pilot EWGs' experience has led to questions being asked, in particular, should EWGs be cascaded throughout the whole organization?

As the internal change agent responsible for the initial training of the EWGs, you have been asked to outline a proposal based on: examining the impact of EWGs, staff and management attitudes related to EWGs; a performance review of EWGs, to look at more detailed issues; and an analysis of the likely implications of the move towards wider application.

The remit

The basic remit for this proposal is to establish what stage of development EWGs have reached within OILCo. There are four issues associated with this analysis.

First, there is a need to determine whether the EWGs that are already in existence have resulted in accomplishments that benefit the individual member, the EWGs themselves, and the organization as a whole. It is the intention here to characterize the EWG at work by showing levels of success and/or failure, and relating these to greater employee involvement within OILCo.

Second, there is also a need to examine where EWGs are developing to, and the levels of surety within the groups that they have capability to develop. This issue is related to whether the EWGs are a temporary or permanent phenomenon within the organization, and whether those within the EWGs believe that they are worthwhile enough to be taken forward.

Third, what levels of skills and competencies do the EWGs contain? This issue relates to whether the groups feel confident amongst themselves that they have the necessary skills to be able to function as a coherent group and sustain accomplishments. A related issue here is the level of support that OILCo itself can offer EWGs to optimize their effectiveness, and what form this should take.

Fourth, there are physical indicators to OILCo of the value of workgroups. This issue is linked to the overall benefit of EWGs to the organization as a whole by improvements in the way work is undertaken.

Questions

1 How do you intend approaching this problem? Draft a proposal outlining the way you intend carrying out the remit.

2 Using the organizational development model, what are likely to be the major benefits that OILCo can expect to gain from undertaking the proposal you put forward?

Analysis

Although there are no correct solutions to this case study, a proposal and project were carried out by the authors in conjunction with staff at OILCo. These can be seen as indicators of the ODM approach to managing change in organizations. The important learning points are associated with three specific criteria:

- designing the process for involvement;

- being able to acquire the necessary information to complete the project;

- being able to provide both hard and soft data on the performance of EWGs.

A short summary of the proposal presented and accepted by the organization is outlined below.

The proposal

It is envisaged that the project will contain three stages.

Stage 1: EWG workshops and opinion survey

The starting point for the project will be an opinion survey, designed by the author, and distributed among EWG members. The author will conduct the survey with EWG members through an informal workshop session to obtain feedback on their views related to development of the EWGs. Some form of formal data gathering will take place via the opinion survey but it is envisaged that more relevant information may be obtained by an informal discussion session held immediately after the survey has been completed.

The mechanism for data gathering will be for the author to visit each of the EWGs and managers that took part in the training events at their workplace. This would then be followed in the afternoon by a workshop to look at how the EWGs feel they are progressing. It is envisaged that each workshop will take a half-day to complete. The focus of the latter part of the workshop will be on evidence of success that EWGs can identify as benefiting OILCo. Each EWG will be asked to make a short presentation on whether they have been able to make a greater level of contribution to OILCo as an EWG, situations where the EWG has generated greater profits or cost savings that would not have occurred otherwise, and projected plans for the future with an indication of the costs and benefits linked to these plans.

This stage will provide a good source of both quantitative and qualitative feedback on how well EWGs are currently working. It will also highlight problem areas that need to be addressed. The survey data will be analysed by the author with feedback provided at stage 3.

Stage 2: managerial issues

Stage 2 involves a number of informal discussions with managers working within OILCo who have EWGs within their own remit/organization. It is envisaged that these interviews will act as a managerial perspective on EWGs and will provide ideas and guidelines on their effectiveness and the best way to move forward. This would involve a number of visits to the EWG workplaces and discussions with the relevant managers in these areas. This would be done on a confidential basis and selected (unattributed) commentary from these discussions will be incorporated into stage 3.

Stage 3: product delivery

Stage 3 is the production of a short (25–30 page) analysis of EWGs at OILCo that will include:

- a one-page management summary;

- the results from the opinion surveys;

- workshop feedback on critical performance measurements;

- managerial commentary; and

- a concluding assessment on overall group performance.

Opinion surveys are one of the key techniques/approaches in the OD toolbox. They provide information on factors likely to influence the OD change effort. They also have the benefit of allowing greater levels of contribution by those likely to be affected by change. However, a word of warning. Many organizations use the opinion survey as window dressing. That is, a large number of surveys take place but very little is done to action the results. Feedback of results from the opinion survey is an obvious mechanism for encouraging greater participation in the change effort. Participants have to be able to see, however, that the organization is taking their views seriously, is paying attention to the trends, and more importantly, is taking action based on these. Otherwise, the gathering of data in this way becomes an exercise in public relations that the public, those within the organization, view as phoney, and over time, worthless.

Epilogue

Burdett (1998: 28–9) argues that organizations are approaching a new era and that era requires a new response. In particular, he argues that organizations need insightful thinking and that there are three potential means to respond better to change:

1 'a belief that at the centre of every storm there needs to be an area of calm' – a need to define and manage with a set of well stated organizational values;

2 'at all times keep it simple' – complex theories and solutions take time and can lose touch with reality;

3 'the need for and the benefits of systems thinking' – an holistic and grounded perspective on change.

Karp (2006) stresses the importance of a systematic response to complex change situations. Once again there appears to be a need for a blended approach to change management. In many ways Burdett and Karp, along with many others, seem to be suggesting what we have been attempting in this book – a synergy between two different modes of managing change.

Dealing with the Future

Managers, organizations and the societies they serve would be foolish, even fatalistic, if they failed to realize the necessity of planning for the future. Planning for planning's sake must be avoided. The ultimate failure of centralist planning initiatives, such as those adopted by the former Soviet Union and Maoist China, along with many corporations in the 1960s and 1970s, illustrates the need to be realistic, responsive, proactive and grounded. Plans must be flexible and in tune with the environment in which they are to be implemented. Operating environments, in the broadest sense of the term, must be understood and managerial actions reflect their complexities and intentions.

There is no evidence to suggest that the rate and the nature of change are likely to alter dramatically in the near future. Technologies, industries and societies will continue to converge. Organizations will continue to seek strategic alliances and maximize the benefits associated with an integrated and well-managed supply chain. Managers and employees in general, will be judged, as they are now, on their ability to cope with and implement change. Adaptability, continuous improvement, life long learning and sustaining competitive advantage are and will remain crucial.

Corporate winners will be characterized by a desire to succeed through progressive, dynamic and challenging initiatives. Strategies and cultures that welcome, address and imaginatively manage change will continue to triumph. This is echoed by John Cotter, from the book entitled *The 20% Solution* (1995):

> The first law of the jungle is that the most adaptable species are always the most successful. In the struggle for survival, the winners are those who are most sensitive to important changes in their environment and quickest to reshape their behaviour to meet each new environmental challenge.

Part of the adaptability equation is recognition that the environmental factors will be monitored by not only you, but by your competitors. It is not enough to simply evolve; successful organizations need to evolve at the speed of light. Organizations are reshaping to respond to their environment. Successful organizations are the ones that identify not only the need for change but also the requirement to steal a march on their competitors. They achieve this by:

- innovative responses to triggers;
- holistic solutions;
- visionary leadership;
- committed support;
- never resting!

From this we can begin to identify some of the aspects of change that management in the future will have to confront.

First, all organizations have to be able to effectively identify and manage the triggers of change. Megson (1988) criticized the analytical and mechanistic approaches managers use to solve problems in organizations: such approaches tended to reflect current or past thinking styles – cognitive baggage. His recommendation was the development of systemic thinking, an ability to see the whole picture rather than its functional parts. This stresses more innovative responses to triggers. These must reflect the future not the past. As Sir James Goldsmith put it, 'If you see a bandwagon, it's too late.'

Being alert to the potential triggers is the first step an enterprise can take on the road to effectively managing change. Early identification and classification permits the creative, or at least proactive, management of subsequent events. According to Kanter (1983) effective organizations, or at least the masters of change within them, are adept at handling 'the triggers of change', namely:

Departures from tradition

The worldwide web has enabled many organizations to challenge old assumptions and ideas and as a result consumers now enjoy more choice, of both product and delivery modes, than ever before. Why travel to the shops when they can come to you? Why use a travel agency when you can organize your holiday online? Banks, supermarkets, car dealers and service providers have all challenged their customers to embrace the 'new technologies'. Global supply chains, optimizing their resource utilization, search out new partners and markets – using knowledge and technology to reshape organizational structures and guiding principles.

The crisis of a galvanizing event

The events of 9/11 and the subsequent war on terror leading to military operations in Afghanistan and Iraq has possibly changed the world for the foreseeable future. Travel, security, immigration, educational exchanges and much, much more, have been impacted upon by 9/11. Global warming, or more accurately the results of it are already impacting upon world weather patterns and in turn on industries, economies and societies. The quest for a carbon neutral footprint will be at the forefront of innovation drives for many years to come. Corporate responsibility and governance debacles of recent years, for example Enron and Arthur Andersen, have shaped the minds of many policy makers and legislators. For many it will certainly not be business as usual.

Strategic choice

For example, the sale of IBM manufacturing capability and associated knowledge to Lenova of China, and the subsequent strategic alliance. Each partner wins with IBM free to concentrate on developing a competitive advantage through the solutions philosophy and Lenova gains usage of the IBM brand and international credibility. Was Mercedes' acquisition of the Chrysler group in the 1990s and its subsequent sale in 2007 a strategic choice or error? Was Virgin group's move into the pension, PEP and banking sectors, extending the lifestyle branded image?

Prime movers

Rupert Murdoch's single minded, almost unique, approach to corporate empire building leaves many competitors stranded on the sidelines. For example, his proposed purchase of the *Wall Street Journal* in 2007 startled many an establishment onlooker. Sir Richard Branson is Virgin and through his high profile life he maintains and develops the brand reputation. The new millennium saw the return of the philanthropist, with Microsoft's Bill Gates leading the charge. Business tycoons are shaping and supporting both social and economic infrastructures.

Action vehicles

British Telecom's 'for a better life' programme (Mason, 1998); British Airways' Waterside headquarters is a physical embodiment of the partnership way of working; reorganization within the NHS taking care to the people, reshaping the professions as well as structures, on the back of continued underperformance data and poor health statistics; and, lastly the British government's desire for identity cards as a by-product of the war on terror, are all examples of action vehicles.

These responses need not be revolutionary; they can be evolutionary. Doing something just slightly better is an innovative response to change. Organizations need to develop and stimulate creative thought. In a strategic sense, the identification of triggers must focus on multiple scenarios of the future. Pascale (1994) classifies this as, managing the present from the future. Organizations have responded to this need for enlightened, but realistic, responses to change by developing structures, processes and cultures that encourage employees to question past assumptions and promote innovatory thought.

Second, having developed responses to change triggers, or indeed enacted proactive vision, the subsequent solutions that one proposes have to be holistically managed. In Chapters 5 and 6, we stressed the need to view the change situation in terms of systems linkages and the environmental impact. The triggers and the consequences have knock-on effects for all. Kanter (1983) regards this as a need to develop an integrative approach to solving problems:

> To see problems integratively is to see them as wholes, related to larger wholes, and thus challenging established practices – rather than walling off a piece of experience and preventing it from being touched or affected by any new experiences ... Companies where segmentalist approaches dominate find it difficult to innovate or to handle change.

Third, to be effective, change management needs to be supported from the top and be characterized by 'full-blown' participation. Senior management needs to be seen to be making the time to be fully involved. There is also a need for this involvement to permeate throughout the organization, to gain commitment to the changes being made. For example, when Delta airlines were faced with significant redundancies in 1994 they took positive steps to control and manage the situation. A communications centre, with freephone numbers, was set up to provide immediate responses to employee questions. Open forums were organized and Vice Presidents dispatched to allay fears. In addition, the senior management team visited all Delta sites within two days of the announcement. Those ultimately responsible for the well being of the corporation, division, or operating unit must support strategic, tactical or operational change.

Ten Key Factors in Effective Change Management

We have expanded the themes discussed above, namely, innovative responses to triggers, holistic solutions, and visionary, committed support into ten factors, which must be addressed and actioned if change is to be effectively managed. By ensuring that these factors have been considered, prior to initializing change, the problem owner and associated change agents will be in a position to confidently manage the process of transition from that which is inadequate to that which is desired.

First: change is all pervasive

Any process of change is likely to have an impact greater than the sum of its parts. A holistic view must be taken to ensure that the full environmental impact is understood. When you consider making change in your organization, from redesigning the staff canteen to acquiring a new company, look at change in terms of its impact on the organization as a whole. Forget the parts; look at the whole picture.

Second: successful change needs active senior management support

Whether you believe in a top-down or bottom-up approach to change, one thing is vital: visible and active senior management support is a must. This is self-evident. Without senior management support three things will be missing. First, the change will lack vision. In most organizations, it is senior management's responsibility to look forward, examine changes in the environment, and determine the future state of the business. There are numerous examples of senior management vision from Branson at Virgin, Gates at Microsoft, Soutter at Stagecoach to Murdoch everywhere!

Second, you'll need effective allies. Senior management backing for the change process is crucial in recruiting the desired level of support to instigate change at all levels. Problem owners need someone to help them open doors and gain support. Senior management support is essential. It will allow you and/or the change project to cross the functional boundaries that often impede change.

Third, you'll need power. When the problem owner or change agent communicates the recipients must realize that it is senior management that is really speaking out. Senior management support guarantees that the problem owner 'speaks quietly but carries a big stick'.

Work on achieving senior management support from the outset. Talk out the ideas you have for change with your boss, or his or her boss. The sooner there is senior management awareness of the need and desirability for change, the sooner things will begin to happen.

Third: change is a multi-disciplinary activity

Most successful change projects accomplish their objectives through the project team. No one person can handle all the tasks and they certainly won't have all the required knowledge and understanding. Recognition of the multi-disciplinary nature of change goes a long way in beginning the sequence of events that will realize the transformation. Problem owners are often identified because of their association with the change. Change agents are recruited because of their expertise in facilitating change through its various stages. Their expertise may be based on people skills, technological know-how, or their experience of systems analysis.

When placed in charge of a change project, or when in general contemplating a change, get yourself a team. The successful management of change, which is complex and all-pervasive, will require a multi-disciplinary approach. None of us has the ability to deal with all the aspects of change management that are likely to occur over the lifetime of a project.

Four: change is about people, pure and simple

In Chapter 10, we focused attention on the need to design organizations in a way that created effective performance. The key ingredient in this design was the human element. Remember that people are the most important asset: people want and need to grow, and personal growth is the engine that drives organization performance. Therefore, when

contemplating change, involve the people in the process from the outset. Through active participation you accomplish two things. You gain
commitment and ownership of the change process by all: those experiencing the change will not need to be pushed and they will begin to
drive change themselves.

Change management is about people management. When managing
change, you manage people. Remember the basics:

- openness

- communication

- involvement

- empowerment.

Fifth: change is about success

Faced with competitive environments, which are growing in terms of
both their magnitude and ferocity, organizations must be flexible enough
to rise to the challenges. Creating an organizational culture, which is
receptive to change, should provide a competitive edge that will last the
test of time. Stand still and be complacent if you wish, but you can be
sure that your competitors, both current and future, will be striving
towards greater efficiency and effectiveness.

Make change a way of life. However, watch how you do it. Going
boldly forth where no organization has gone before, discovering new
planets, and seeking out new life forms is all very well, but you need
focus. The challenges created by looking too far ahead may be beyond
the organization's current capabilities. On the other hand, dinosaur
organizations become extinct because they fail to adapt to their environment. Set goals for success that can be accomplished and seen to be
deliverable. Perhaps not all organizations have to go on the five-year
quest; for many a peek round the corner may be a very good start!

Sixth: change is perpetual

How do we explain change that was successful? How do we explain
change that never seemed to get going? How can we explain the change
project that started off well but seemed to fade away after a couple of
years? The answers seem to lie in the attention and resources devoted to
managing change as a perpetual process.

We have cited throughout the concept of perpetual transition management. Change is about identifying triggers, seeking vision, recruiting
converts to the vision, and maintaining and renewing the need for

change on an ongoing basis. The effective management of change demands management action on all these fronts.

You have to be able to identify what is triggering change. This has to be expressed and clarified and communicated throughout the organization to gain understanding. There is also a need for some vision of how the triggers will affect the future of the organization. In this sense, there is a need to define what the future is, in terms of the challenges being faced and the future make-up of the organization. Having set a vision, there is a need to manage change through converting people to that vision. Most successful change programmes work on the basis of persuading people that this is the right way to go. Finally, watch the triggers. Change that fades away does so because circumstances alter: those involved at the start move on, and the triggers become unclear in the minds of those left to carry on. The systems intervention model deals with a dynamic change environment by incorporating, in the design, iterative processes where you can step back and reappraise your position in light of environmental changes.

Perpetual change is what it says: you never get to the end. Something else always comes along to impact the organization and/or business in a new way.

Seventh: effective change requires competent change agents

A change management project has a certain number of needs that must be satisfied. One of these needs relates to the required skills, knowledge and position of the change agents. Analysis of the change situation will determine the appropriate management team in terms of their position and attributes. It will not, however, ensure that the change agents have the necessary competencies to effectively contribute to the process of change. To be fully effective, the change agent must have certain capabilities, over and above their functional skills and knowledge.

The competencies of the change agent were examined in Chapter 11. These relate to being able to communicate with, on behalf of, and through people involved in the change situation. The change agent therefore needs to feel comfortable in dealing with interpersonal relationships, coping with conflict and ambiguity, and the 1,001 different emotions that humans can display as a result of change. Change can upset people; they can also become overjoyed, over-enthusiastic or indeed shy away from it. The change agent has to be able to facilitate those involved through this process by taking their feelings and emotions into account, getting them to address how these emotions relate to change itself, while steering the change forward.

Many organizations have begun to address the management of change within their own organizations as a perpetual process. The competencies of the change agent are being directly dealt with by instigating training programmes to provide them with the necessary staff skilled in the techniques associated with organization development.

Technical skills, such as systems diagramming, network analysis, and charting in general, can be readily taught and acquired. In fact, many of the skills associated with project planning are now dealt with by sophisticated computerized packages.

However, people skills are the more important, and often the more difficult competencies to acquire. If you are a theory X person, you are unlikely to be able to develop good change management skills. You do not appreciate the enormity of the change. The basis of change management rests with the assumptions you make about people in organizations. Make the wrong assumptions and the management of change will not succeed.

Eight: in terms of methodology, there is no one best way

All we wish to say here is: do not adopt a one size fits all strategy. You must not be too blinkered about change management. In essence, there is no single best way. What works for one change situation may not be fully appropriate for another. For example, in takeover situations, the cultures of organizations involved may be seemingly incompatible and require adjustment. The obvious approach is to adopt an organization development methodology. However, such an approach will take time and will not bring about immediate improvements in performance. It may be better to start the ball rolling by adopting a more interventionist strategy. This could provide the quick-wins, whilst over the medium-to-long term, an organization development cycle could be set in motion to accomplish higher level objectives.

Ninth: change is about ownership

Once again we refer back here to people. What makes change happen? When it works beautifully, what causes this? The answers seem to rest with attaining ownership of the change process itself. In terms of the problem owner, change agents, and those being affected by change, there is a need to feel ownership.

The management team must feel that they are responsible for the successful implementation of the change. This responsibility is best discharged through a desire to succeed rather than survive. What we are concerned with here is a movement from control to commitment. When people are being coerced or manoeuvred into change situations, the result is at best indifference and at worst resistance. When people feel ownership of the change process and can see the opportunity it offers, then they will be committed to its satisfactory accomplishment.

Ownership comes from getting involvement. Get involvement through openness and communication; let people live the change.

Tenth: change is about fun, challenge and opportunity

When faced with a challenge, most individuals respond positively. The psychologists would argue that it brings out the best in people. On the other hand, when faced with a crisis people can go one of two ways. They can emerge as strong individuals to meet that crisis or they can become cowering wrecks under its enormity.

We have tried to make this book both interesting and easy to read. We work from the perspective that change management should be a challenging subject that offers the practitioner, the reader, and those associated with change, the opportunity to show their mettle. Change, as it implies, gives you the chance to move on. By providing opportunities you get to learn new and different things. Hopefully, you become a better person and contribute more to your organization. The challenges that you face through change management may be difficult, inspiring, and they may even make a better manager out of you. These challenges should be faced positively. Never shy away from the need for change. Sure, it's uncomfortable in some instances, but change can also be fun.

We use fun, in this instance, to denote an attitude of mind. Throughout the seriousness of it all, the drive for performance, the need to maintain a competitive edge, the desire for a better, more effective organization, there is also a need to show a human face. We teach and research change management because it fascinates us. The specific subject areas of systems and organization development are interesting, practical and challenging. However, if you have ever witnessed the way in which we teach them, you would also recognize that change management can be both gratifying and fun.

Make your management of the change project challenging. Provide those involved in it with the opportunity to develop themselves and the rest of the organization. At all points in time remember, no one ever said that achieving effective change and gaining organizational performance cannot be fun!

References

Ackenhusen, M., Muzyka, D. and Churchill, N. (1996a) 'Restructuring 3M for an integrated Europe. Part one: initiating the change', *European Management Journal*, 14(1):
February.

Ackenhusen, M., Muzyka, D. and Churchill, N. (1996b) 'Restructuring 3M for an integrated Europe. Part two: initiating the change', *European Management Journal*, 14(2):
April.

Ackoff, R.L. (1999) *Ackoff's Best: His Classic Writings on Management*. London: Wiley.

Ackoff, R.L. and Emery, F.E. (2005) *On Purposeful Systems: An Interdisciplinary Analysis
of Individual and Social Behaviour as a System of Purposeful Events*. New Jersey:
AldineTransaction.

Alimo-Metcalfe, B. (1995) 'An investigation of female and male constructs of leadership and empowerment', *Women in Management Review*, 10(2): 3–8.

Alimo-Metcalfe, B. and Alban-Metcalfe, R.J. (2001) 'The development of a new
transformational leadership questionnaire', *The Journal of Occupational and
Organisational Psychology*, 74: 1–27.

Allison, G. (1971). *Essence of Decision*. Boston, MA: Little, Brown and Co.

Alvesson, M. and Deetz, S. (2000) *Doing Critical Management Research*. London: Sage.

Anderson, N. and West, M. (1996) 'The team climate inventory', *European Journal of
Work and Organisational Psychology*, March.

Appelbaum, S.H. and Hughes, B. (1998) 'Ingratiation as a political tactic: effects
within the organization', *Management Decision*, 36(2): 85–95.

Argote, L. (2005) *Organizational Learning: Creating, Retaining and Transferring
Knowledge*. New York: Springer.

Argyris, C. (1970) *Intervention Theory and Method*. Reading, MA: Addison-Wesley.

Argyris, C. and Schon, D. (1978) *Organizational Learning: A Theory of Action Perspective*.
Reading, MA: Addison-Wesley.

Argyris, C. and Schon, D. (1996) *Organizational Learning II*. Reading, MA: Addison-
Wesley.

Armenakis, A.A. and Bedeian, A.G. (1999) 'Organization change: a review of theory
and research in the 1990s', *Journal of Management*, 25(3): 293–315.

Arrow, K.J. (1969) 'Classification notes on the production and transmission of technical knowledge', *American Economic Review*, 52: 29–35.

Bain, P. (1998) 'The 1986–87 News International dispute: was the workers' defeat
inevitable?', *Historical Studies in Industrial Relations*, 5: 73–105.

Balogun, J. (2007) 'The practice of organizational restructuring: from design to
reality', *European Management Journal*, 25(2): 81–91.

Balogun, J. and Hope Hailey, V. (2004) *Exploring Strategic Change*, Second edition. London: Prentice Hall.

Bamford, D.R. and Forrester, P.L. (2003) 'Managing planned and emergent change within an operations management environment', *International Journal of Operations and Production* Management, 23(5): 546–64.

Barson, R., Foster, G., Struck, T., Ratchev, S., Pawar, K., Weber, F., and Wunram, M. (2000) 'Inter and intra organizational barriers to sharing knowledge in the extended supply chain', e2000 Conference Proceeding.

Bateman, T. S. and Zeithaml, C.P. (1993) *Management Function and Strategy*. Irwin, New York.

Beauchamp, T. and Childress, J. (1994) *Principles of Biomedical Ethics*, Fourth edition. Oxford: Oxford University Press.

Beckhard, R. (1969) *Organization Development: Strategies and Models*. Reading, MA: Addison-Wesley.

Beckhard, R. and Pritchard, W. (1992) *Changing the Essence: The Art of Creating and Leading Fundamental Change in Organisations*. San Francisco: Jossey-Bass.

Beer, M. and Eisenstat, R.A (1990) 'Why change projects don't produce change', *Harvard Business Review*, November.

Blickle, G. and Hauck, S. (1996) 'Assertion and consensus motives in argumentation'. Paper presented at the European Business Ethics Network's 9th annual conference: Working across cultures, 18–20 September, Frankfurt.

Boddy, D. (1987) *The Technical Change Audit*. Sheffield: Manpower Services Commission.

Boddy, D. (2002) *Managing Projects: Building and Leading the Team*. Harlow: Financial Times/Prentice-Hall.

Boddy, D. (2005) *Management: An Introduction*, Third edition. London: FT/Prentice-Hall.

Boddy, D. and Buchanan, D.A. (1986) *Managing New Technology*. Oxford: Basil Blackwell.

Boddy, D. and Buchanan, D.A. (1992) *Take the Lead: Interpersonal Skills for Project Managers*. London: Prentice-Hall International.

Boddy, D. and Paton, R.A. (2004) 'Responding to competing narratives: lessons for project managers', *International Journal of Operations Management*, 22: 225–33.

Boddy, D. and Paton, R.A. (2005) 'Maintaining alignment over the long term: lessons from the evolution of a point of sale system', *Journal of Information Technology*, 20: 141–51.

Booth, S. (1993) *Crisis Strategy Management*. London: Routledge.

Brandt, D. and Hartmann, E. (1999) 'Editorial: Research topics and strategies in socio-technical systems', *Human Factors and Ergonomics in Manufacturing*, 9(3): 241–3.

Brayman, H. (1967) *Corporate Management in a World of Politics*. New York: McGraw-Hill.

Brotheridge, C.M. (2005) 'A test of the evolution an predictive capacity for managers' interpretations of change', *Journal of Change Management*, 5(3): 281–94.

Brownlie, D.T., McCalman, J., Paton, R.A. and Southern, G. (1990) *The Glasgow Management Development Initiative: Selected Findings and Issues*. Sheffield: Manpower Services Commission.

Bruch, H., Gerber, P. and Maier, V. (2005) 'Strategic change decisions: doing change right', *Journal of Change Management*, 5(1): 97–101.

Bryman, A. (1988) *Doing Research in Organisations*. London: Routledge.

Buchanan, D.A. and Badham, R. (1999a) *Power, Politics and Organizational Change: Winning the Turf Game*. London: Sage.

Buchanan, D.A. and Badham, R. (1999b) 'Politics and organizational change: the lived experience', *Human Relations*, 52(5): 609–22.

Buchanan, D. and Boddy, D. (1992) *The Expertise of the Change Agent*. London: Prentice-Hall.

Buchanan, D.A. and Huczynski, A.A. (2006) *Organizational Behaviour: An Introductory Text*, Sixth edition. London: Prentice-Hall.

Buchanan, D.A. and McCalman, J. (1989) *High Performance Work Systems: The Digital Experience*. London: Routledge.

Buchanan, D.A., Claydon, T. and Doyle, M. (1997) *Organization Development and Change: the Legacy of the Nineties*. Leicester Business School Occasional Paper 43: De Montfort University.

Buchanan, D.A., Fitzgerald, L., Ketley, D., Gollop, R., Jones, J.L., Lamont, S.S., Neath, A. and Whitby, E. (2005) 'No going back: a review of the literature on sustaining organizational change', *International Journal of Management Reviews*, 7(2): 189–205.

Buckler, B. (1996) 'A learning process model to achieve continuous improvement and innovation', *The Learning Organization*, 3: 31.

Burdett, J.D. (1998) 'Beyond values – exploring the twenty-first century organization', *Journal of Management Development*, 17(1): 28–9.

Burnes, B. (2004) *Managing Change: A Strategic Approach to Organisational Dynamics*, Fourth edition. London: FT Prentice-Hall.

Burns, J.M. (1978) *Leadership*. New York: Harper and Row.

Burns, T. and Stalker, G. (1961) *The Management of Innovation*. London: Tavistock.

Burr, V. (1998) *Gender and Social Psychology*. London: Routledge.

Cahill, L. (2005) 'His brain, her brain', *Scientific American*, 292(5): 40–7.

Calas, M. and Smircich, L. (1996) 'The woman's point of view: feminist approaches to organisational studies', in C. Clegg, C. Hardy, T. Lawrence and W.R. Nord (eds) *Handbook of Organisation Studies*. London: Sage.

Carr, A. (1997) 'The learning organization: new lessons/thinking for the management of change development?', *Journal of Management Development*, 6(4): 224–31.

Cavanagh, G., Moberg, D. and Velasquez, M. (1981) 'The ethics of organisational politics', *Academy of Management Review*, 6(3): 363–75.

Checkland, P. and Scholes, J. (1991) *Soft Systems Methodology in Action*. Chichester: Wiley.

Clark, J. (1995) *Managing Innovation and Change*. London: Sage.

Clarke, C., Hope-Hailey, V. and Kelliher, C. (2007) 'Being real or being someone else? Change, managers and emotion work', *European Management Journal*, 25(2): 92–103.

Cohan, W.M. and Levinthal, D.A. (1990) 'Absorptive capacity: a new perspective on learning and innovation', *Administrative Science Quarterly*, 35: 128–52.

Coleman, S. (1998) *Knowledge Management: Linchpin of Change*. London: ASLIB.

Cooper, D.E. (1996) *World Philosophies: An Historical Introduction*. Oxford: Blackwell.

Cotter, J.J. (1995) *The 20% Solution – Using Rapid Redesign to Create Tomorrow's Organisation Today*, Second edition. Chichester: Wiley.

Cyert, R.M. and March, J.G. (1963) *A Behavioural Theory of the Firm*. Hemel Hempstead: Prentice-Hall.

Davenport, T. (2005) *Thinking for a Living*. Boston: Harvard Business Press.

Davenport, T. and Prusak, L. (1998) *Working Knowledge*. Boston: Harvard Business Press.

Dawson, P. (2003) *Understanding Organizational Change: The Contemporary Experience of People at Work*. London: Sage.

Dawson, P. and Buchanan, D. (2005) 'The way it really happened: competing narratives in the political process of technological change', *Human Relations*, 58(7): 845–65.

Day, G.S. (1994) 'The capabilities of market driven organizations', *Journal of Marketing*, 58(4): 37–52.

De Geus, A.P. (1988) 'Planning as learning', *Harvard Business Review*, January–February.

De Long, D.W. and Fahey, L. (2000) 'Diagnosing cultural barriers to knowledge management', *Academy of Management Executive*, 14(4): 113–27.

Dempster, L. (1998) 'Managing change from a gender perspective'. Masters thesis (unpublished), University of Glasgow, Adam Smith Library.

Diamantopolous, A. and Schlegemilch, B. (1997) *Taking the Fear out of Data Analysis: a Step-by-Step Approach*. London: Thomson Learning.

Doyle, M., Claydon, T. and Buchanan, D.A. (2000) 'Mixed results, lousy process: the management experience of organizational change', *British Journal of Management*, 11, special issue: 59–80.

Drory, A. and Romm, C. (1990) 'The definition of organisational politics', *Human Relations*, 43(11): 1133–54.

Drucker, P.F. (1994) 'The age of social transformation', *The Atlantic Monthly*, November.

Drucker, P.F. (1997) 'The future that has already happened', *Harvard Business Review*, September–October: 20–4.

Drucker, P.F. (1998) 'The coming of the organization, future that has already happened', *Harvard Business Review*, January–February.

Drucker, P.F. (2001) 'The next workforce', *The Economist*, 1 November.

Dunphy, D.C. and Stace, D.A. (1988) 'Transformational and coercive strategies for planned organizational change: beyond the OD model', *Organization Studies*, 9(3): 317–34.

Dunphy, D.C, and Stace, D.A. (1990) *Under New Management: Australian Organisations in Transition*. Sydney: McGraw-Hill.

Durden-Smith, J. and Desimone, D. (1983) *Sex and the Brain*. New York: Arbor House.

Eagly, A.H. (1987) *Sex Differences in Social Behaviour: A Social Role Interpretation*. Hillsdale, NJ: Erlbaum.

Eagly, A.H. and Johnson, B.T. (1990) 'Gender and leadership style: a meta analysis', *Psychological Bulletin*, 108(2): 233–57.

Egan, G. (1994) *Working the Shadow Side: A Guide to Positive Behind-the-Scenes Management*. San Francisco: Jossey-Bass.

Eisenhardt, K.M. and Sull, D.N. (2001) 'Strategy as simple rules', *Harvard Business Review*, 79(1): 107–16.

Enderle, G. (1997) 'Five views on international business ethics: an introduction', *Business Ethics Quarterly*, 7(3): 1–4.

Eriksson, M. and Sundgren, M. (2005) 'Managing change: strategy or serendipity – reflections from the merger of Astra and Zeneca', *Journal of Change Management*, 5(1): 15–28.

Farr, C.M. and Fisher, W.A. (1992) 'Managing international high technology cooperative projects', *RandD Management*, 1(2): 73–9.

Fenton, E. (2007) 'Visualising strategic change: the role and impact of process maps as boundary objects in reorganisation', *European Management Journal*, 25(2): 104–17.

Ferris, G. and King, T. (1991) 'Politics in human resources decisions: a walk on the dark side', *Organisational Dynamics*, 20(2): 59–72.

Ferris, G. and Kacmar, K. (1992) 'Perceptions of organisational politics', *Journal of Management*, 18(1): 93–116.

Firth, G. and Krut, R. (1991) 'Introducing a project management culture', *European Management Journal*, 9(4).

Fletcher, J. (1994) 'Castrating the female advantage: feminist standpoint research and management science', *Journal of Management Inquiry*, 3(1).

Ford, M.W. and Greer, B.M. (2005) 'The relationship between management control system usage and planned achievement: an exploratory study', *Journal of Change Management*, 5(1): 29–46.

Forlaron, J. (2005) 'The human side of change leadership', *Quality Progress*, 38(4): 39–43.

French, W.L. (1969) 'Organization development: objectives, assumptions and strategies', *California Management Review*, 12(2): 23–34.

French, W.L. and Bell, C.H., Jr (1998) *Organization Development: Behavioural Science Interventions for Organization Improvement*. Mahwah, NJ: Prentice-Hall.

French, W.L. and Mühlfriedel, B. (1998) 'Discourse instead of recourse: is it worth using a guided approach to negotiation when working across cultures?', in H. Lange, A. Löhr and H. Steinmann (eds) *Working Across Cultures: Ethical Perspectives in Intercultural Management*, Issues in Business Ethics, Vol. 9. London: Kluwer, pp. 263–85.

French, W., Bell, C. and Zawacki, R. (1983) 'Power, politics and organization development', in W. French, C. Bell and R. Zawacki (eds) *Organization Development: Theory, Practice and Research*, Second edition. Texas Business Publications: 371–8.

French, W.L., Bell, C.H. and Zawacki, R.A. (2005) *Organization Development: And Transformation*, Sixth edition. Illinois: Irwin/McGraw-Hill.

Frost, P.J. and Egri, C.P. (1991) 'The political process of innovation', in L.L. Cummings and B.M. Staw (eds) *Research in Organizational Behaviour*. Greenwich, CT: JA Press: 229–95.

Fulmer, R.M. (1996) 'A model for changing the way organizations learn', *Planning Review*, May–June: 20.

Galbraith, J.R. (1977) *Organization Design*. Reading, MA: Addison-Wesley.

Gandz, J. and Murray, V. (1980) 'The experience of workplace politics', *Academy of Management Journal*, 23: 237–51.

Garratt, B. (2003) *The Fish Rots from the Head, The Crisis in our Boardrooms: Developing the Crucial Skills of the Competent Director*. London: Profile Books.

Garratt, R. (1994) 'An old idea that has come of age', *People Management*, September: 25.

Garvin, D.A. (1993) 'Building a learning organization', *Harvard Business Review*, July–August.

George, J., and Jones, G. (2007) *Understanding and Managing Organizational Behavior*, Fifth edition. London: Prentice Hall.

Germino, D. (1972) *Modern Western Political Thought: Machiavelli to Marx*. London: University of Chicago Press.

Gibson, S. (1993) 'An investigation into gender differences in leadership across four countries', *Journal of International Business Studies*, 26(2).

Goffman, E. (1959) *The Presentation of Self in Everyday Life*. Middlesex: Penguin Books.

Goodman, J. and Truss, C. (2004) 'The medium and the message: communicating effectively during a major change initiative', *Journal of Change Management*, 4(3): 217–28.

Gordon, S. (1991) *Prisoners of Men's Dreams: Striking out for a New Feminine Future*. Little Brown: Boston.

Graetz, F. (1996) 'Leading strategic change at Ericsson', *Long Range Planning*, 29(3).

Graetz, F. and Smith, A. (2005) 'Organizing forms in change management: the role of structures, processes and boundaries in a longitudinal case analysis', *Journal of Change Management*, 5(3): 311–28.

Grant, J.H. and Gnew Yorkawali, D.R. (1996) 'Strategic process improvement through organisational learning', *Strategy and Leadership*, May–June.

Gray, J. (1992) *Men are from Mars, Women are from Venus*. New York: Harper Collins.

Gray, J. and Starke, F. (1984) *Organisational Behavior: Concepts and Applications*. Columbus, OH: Merrill Publishing.

Greiner, L.E. and Schein, V.E. (1988) *Power and Organization Development: Mobilizing Power to Implement Change*. Reading, MA: Addison-Wesley.

Gummesson, E. (1991) *Qualitative Methods in Business Research*. Newbury Park: Sage.

Gunn, L. (1988) 'Public management: a third approach', *Public Money and Management* Spring/Summer: 21–25.

Gupta, A. and Michailova, S. (2004) *'Knowledge sharing in knowledge intensive firms'*, CKG Working Paper No 12/2004.

Hackman, J.R. and Oldham, G.R. (1975) 'Development of the job diagnostic survey', *Journal of Applied Psychology*, 60: 159–70.

Hackman, J.R. and Oldham, G.R. (1980) *Work Redesign*. Reading, MA: Addison-Wesley.

Handy, C. (1989) *The Age of Unreason*. London: Business Books.

Handy, C. (1990) *Inside Organisations*. London: BBC Publications.

Handy, C. (1994) *The Empty Raincoat*. London: Hutchinson.

Handy, C. (1996) 'Understanding power: bringing about strategic change', *British Journal of Management*, 7, special issue: 3–16.

Handy, C. (1997) 'The citizen corporation', *Harvard Business Review,* September–October: 26–8.

Handy, C. (2004) *The New Alchemists*. London: Hutchinson.

Hardy, C. (1996) 'Understanding power: bringing about strategic change', *British Journal of Management*, 7, special issue: 3–16.

Hattori, R.A. and Lapidus, T. (2004) 'Collaboration, trust and innovative change', *Journal of Change Management*, 4(2): 97–104.

Herzberg, F. (1966) *Work and the Nature of Man*. New York: Staples Press.

Higgins, J.M. and McAllaster, C. (2004) 'If you want strategic change, don't forget to change your cultural artifacts', *Journal of Change Management*, 4(1): 63–73.

Higgs, M. and Rowland, D. (2005) 'All changes great and small: exploring approaches to change and its leadership', *Journal of Change Management*, 5(2): 121–51.

Hinkin, T.R. and Tracey, J.B. (1999) 'The relevance of charisma for transformational leadership in stable organizations', *Journal of Organizational Change Management*, 12(2).

Huq, Z., Huq, F. and Cutright, K. (2006) 'BRP through ERP: avoiding change management pitfalls', *Journal of Change Management*, 6(1): 67–85.

Hunt, J. (1979) *Managing People at Work*. Maidenhead: McGraw-Hill.

Huse, E.F. (1975) *Organizational Development and Change*. St Paul, MN: West.

Husted, K. and Michailova, S. (2002) Management International, 2002, knowledge-board.com

Jackall, R. (1988) *The Moral Maze: The World of Corporate Managers*. Oxford, Oxford University Press.

Jacobs, R.L. (2002) 'Institutionalizing organizational change through cascade training', *Journal of European Industrial Training*, 26: 117–82.

Janis, I.L. (1972) *Victims of Groupthink*, Boston: Houghton Mifflin Company.

Jobber, D. (2007) *Principles and Practices of Marketing*, Fifth edition. London: McGraw-Hill.

Johnson, G., Scholes, K. and Whittington, R. (2006) *Exploring Corporate Strategy*, Sixth edition. London: Financial Times Press.

Jones. B.M. (1996) *Financial Management in the Public Sector*. Maidenhead: McGraw-Hill.

Kakabadse, A. and Parker, C. (1984) *Power, Politics and Organisations: A Behavioural Science View*. Chichester: Wiley and Sons.

Kanter, R.M. (1983) *The Change Masters: Corporate Entrepreneurs at Work*. New York: Thomson Business Publishing.

Kanter, R.M. (1989) *When Giants Learn to Dance: Mastering the Challenges of Strategy, Management and Careers in the 1990s*. London: Unwin Hyman.

Kanter, R.M. (1993) *Men and Women of the Corporation*. New York: HarperCollins.

Kanter, R.M. (1994) 'Reach for the top', foreword to N. Nichols (ed.) *Harvard Business Review Book*. Boston, MA: Harvard Business School.

Kanter, R.M., Stein, B.A. and Jick, T.D. (1992) *The Challenge of Organisational Change*. New York: The Free Press.

Karp, T. (2005) 'Unpacking the mysteries of change: mental modelling', *Journal of Change Management*, 5(1): 87–96.

Karp, T. (2006) 'Transforming organisations for organic growth: the DNA of change leadership', *Journal of Change Management*, 6(1): 3–20.

Katzenbach, J.R. (1997) 'The myth of the top management team', *Harvard Business Review*, 75(6): 82–91.

Katzenbach, J.R. (1998) *Teams at the Top: Unleashing the Potential of Both Teams and Individual Leaders*. Boston, MA: Harvard Business School Press.

Katzenbach, J.R. and Smith, K. (1993) *The Wisdom of Teams: Creating the High-Performance Organization*. Boston, MA: Harvard Business School Press.

Kettner, M. (1996) 'Discourse ethics and health care ethics committees', in S. Byrd (ed.) *Annual Review of Law and Ethics (Jahrbuch für Recht und Ethik)*. Germany: 249–72.

Kilman, R. (1995) 'A holistic programme and critical success factors of corporate transformation', *European Management Journal*, 3(2).

Kimble, C. and McLoughlin, K. (1995) 'Computer based information systems and managers' work', *New Technology, Work and Employment*, 10(1): 56–67.

Kimura, D. (1987) 'Are men and women's brains really different', *Canadian Psychology*, 28(2): 133.

Kimura, D. (1992) 'Sex differences on the brain', *Scientific American*, September: 119.

Kimura, D. (2002) 'Sex differences on the brain', *Scientific American Special Edition*, 12(1): 32–7.

Klein, L. (1976) *A Social Scientist in Industry*. London: Allen and Unwin.

Klein, J. (1988) 'The myth of the corporate political jungle: politicisation as a political strategy', *Journal of Management Studies*, 25(1): 1–12.

Kline, P. and Saunders, B. (1993) *Ten Steps to a Learning Organisation*. Arlington, VA: Great Ocean.

Kluge, J., Stein, W. and Licth, T. (2001) *Knowledge Unplugged: The McKinsey and Co Survey on Knowledge Management*. London: Palgrave.

Knights, D. and Murray, F. (1994) *Managers Divided: Organizational Politics and Information Technology Management*. Chichester: Wiley.

Kolb, D. (1976) *Learning Style Inventory: Technical Manual*. Boston: McBer.

Kotter, J.P. (1995) 'Why transformation efforts fail', *Harvard Business Review*, March–April.

Kotter, J.P. and Schlesinger, L.A. (1979) 'Choosing strategies for change', *Harvard Business Review*: March–April.

KPMG (1998) *Knowledge Management Research Report 1998*. http: www.knowledge-business.com/resrep.htm

Krogh, von, G. and Vicari, S. (1993) 'An autopoiesis approach to experimental strategic learning', in P. Lorange et al. (eds) *Implementing Strategic Processes*. Oxford: Blackwell.

Krogh, von, G., Ichijo, K., and Nonaka, I. (2000) *Enabling Knowledge Creation*. Oxford: Oxford University Press.

Kudray, L.M. and Kleiner, B.H. (1997) 'Global trends in managing change', *Industrial Management*, 39(3), 18–21.

Kühl, S., Schnelle, T. and Tillmann, F. (2005) 'Lateral leadership: an organizational approach to change', *Journal of Change Management*, 5(2): 177–89.

Kulp, S.C., Ofek, E. and Whitaker, J. (2003) 'Supply chain coordination', in T. Harrison, H.L. Lee and J.L. Neale (eds) *The Practice of Supply Chain Management: Where Theory and Application Converge*. Boston: Kluwer Academic Publishing.

Kumar, K. and Thibodeaux, M. (1990) 'Organisational politics and planned organisational change', *Group and Organisational Studies*, 15(4): 357–65.

Lane, N. (2005) 'Strategy implementation: the implications of a gender perspective for change management', *Journal of Strategic Marketing*, 13: 117–31.

Langton, N. and Robbins, S.P. (2007) *Organizational Behaviour: Concepts, Controversies, Applications*. Toronto: Prentice Hall.

Lawler, E.E., III (1969) 'Job design and employee motivation', *Personnel Psychology*, 22: 426–35.

Lawler, E.E., III (1986) *High Involvement Management: Participative Strategies for Improving Organizational Effectiveness*. San Francisco: Jossey-Bass.

Lawrence, P.R. and Lorsch, J.W. (1967) *Organization and Environment: Managing Differentiation and Integration*. Boston: Harvard Business School.

Lawrence, P.R. and Lorsch, J.W. (1969) *Developing Organizations: Diagnosis and Action*, Reading, MA: Addison-Wesley.

Leavitt, H.L. (1965) 'Applied organisational change in industry: structural, technological and humanistic approaches', in J.G. March (ed.), *Handbook of Organizations*. Chicago: Rand McNally.

Lee, R. and Lawrence, P. (1991) *Politics at Work*. Cheltenham: Stanley Thornes.

Lempert, H. (1985) 'The effect of visual guidance and hemispace on lateralised vocal-manual interference', *Neuropsycholigia*, 23(5): 691–5.

Lewin, K. (1958) 'Group decision and social change', in E.E. Maccoby, T.M. Newcomb and E.L. Hartley (eds) *Readings in Social Psychology*. New York: Holt, Rinehart and Winston.

Likert, R. (1967) *The Human Organization: Its Management and Value*. New York: McGraw-Hill.

Lines, R. (2004) 'Influence of participation in strategic change: resistance, organizational commitment and change goal achievement', *Journal of Change Management*, 4(3): 193–215.

Lines, R., Selart, M., Espedal, B. and Johansen, S.T. (2005) 'The production of trust during organizational change', *Journal of Change Management*. 5(2): 221–45.

Lippit, R. (1959) 'Dimensions of the consultant's job', *Journal of Social Issues*, 15(2): 5–11.

Lippit, R. and Lippit, G. (1975) 'Consulting process in action', *Training and Development Journal*, 29(5): 48–54; (6): 38–44.

Lippit, R., Watson, J. and Westley, B. (1958) *The Dynamics of Planned Change*. New York: Harcourt, Brace and Jovanovich.

Lloyd, C. and Newell, H. (1998) 'Computerising the sales force: the introduction of technical change in a non-union workforce', *New Technology, Work and Employment*, 13(2): 104–15.

Lockyer, K.G. (1991) *Critical Path Analysis and Other Project Network Techniques*. London: Pitman.

Lorenzen, P. (1987, first published 1968) *Constructive Philosophy*. Amherst: The University of Massachusetts Press.

Lorsch, J. (1986) 'Managing culture: the invisible barrier to strategic change', *California Management Review*, 28(2): 95–109.

Lucas, E. (2000) 'Creating a give and take culture', *Professional Manager*, 9(3): 11–3.

Luecke, R. (2003) *Managing Change and Transitions*, Harvard Business Essentials. Boston: Harvard Business School Publishing.

Luna-Reyes, L.F., Zhang, J., Gil-Garcia, J.R. and Cresswell, A.M. (2005) 'Information systems development as emergent socio-technical change: a practice approach', *European Journal of Information Systems*, 14(1): 93–105.

McCalman, J. (1988) *The Electronics Industry in Britain: Coping with Change*. London: Routledge.

McCalman, J. (1996) 'Technological innovation and work design', in R. Gill, J. McCalman and D. Pitt (eds) *Organization Structure and Behaviour 1*. Glasgow: Strathclyde Graduate Business School, University of Strathclyde.

McCalman, J. (2001) 'But I did it for the company! The ethics of organizational politics during times of change', *Reason in Practice, The Journal of Philosophy of Management*, 1 (3).

McGregor, D. (1960) *The Human Side of Enterprise*. New York: McGraw-Hill.

Machiavelli, N. (1993) *The Prince*. Hertfordshire: Wordsworth Editions.

MacIntosh, R. and MacLean, D. (1999) 'Conditioned emergence approach: a dissipative structures approach to transformation', *Strategic Management Journal*, 20: 297–310.

Mackie, J.L. (1977) *Ethics: Inventing Right and Wrong*. London: Penguin.

Maclagan, P. (1998) *Management and Morality*. London: Sage.

Maclagan, P. and Evans de-Souza, C. (1995) 'Nepotism, politics and ethics in the purchase of organisational consultancy services – two European cases', in H. von Weltzien Høivik and A. Føllesdal (eds) *Ethics and Consultancy European Perspectives*. Dordrecht, Kluwer: 83–92.

McLaughlin, S., Paton, R.A. and Macbeth, D. (2006) 'Managing change within IBM's complex supply chain', *Management Decision*, 44(8): 1002–19.

McLoughlin, I. and Clark, J. (1994) *Technological Change at Work*, Second edition. Milton Keynes: Open University Press.

Maglio, P.P. and Spohrer, J. (2007) 'Fundamentals of services science', *Journal of the Academy of Marketing Science*, July.

Malhotra, Y. (2001) 'Knowledge management for the new world of business'. Available at http://www.brint.com/km/whatis.htm.

Mangham, I. (1979) *The Politics of Organisational Change*. Westport, CT: Greenwood Press.

March, J.G. (1962) 'The business firm as a political coalition', *Journal of Politics*, 24(4): 662–78.

March, J.G and Simon, H.A. (1958) *Organizations*. New York: Wiley.

Margerison, C.J. (1988) 'Consulting activities in organizational change', *Journal of Organizational Change Management*, 1(1): 60–7.

Margulies, N. and Raia, A. (1972) *Organizational Development: Values, Process and Technology*. New York: McGraw-Hill.

Margulies, N. and Raia, A. (1978) *Conceptual Foundations of Organizational Development*. New York: McGraw-Hill.

Margulies, N. and Raia, A. (1988) 'The significance of core values on the theory and practice of organizational development', *Journal of Organizational Change Management*, 1(1): 617.

Markus, M.L. (1983) 'Power, politics and MIS implementation', *Communications of the ACM*, 26(6): 430–44.

Marshall, J. (1995) *Women Mangers Moving On*. London: Routledge.

Martin, G. and Hetrick, S. (2006) *Corporate Reputation, Branding and Managing People: A Strategic Approach to HR*. London: Butterworth-Heinemann.

Martin, G., Beaumont, P.B., Doig, R. and Pate, J.M. (2005) 'Branding: a new performance discourse for HR', *European Management Journal*, 23(1): 76–88.

Martin, J. (1992) *Cultures in Three Organizations: Three Perspectives*. Oxford: Oxford University Press.

Marwick, A.D. (2001) 'Knowledge management technology', *IBM Systems Journal on Knowledge Management*. Armonk, New York: IBM Press.

Mason, R. (1998) 'Switch board', *People Management*, October: 46–8.

Matsushita, K. (1984) *Not for Bread Alone: A Business Ethos, A Management Ethic*. Tokyo: PHP Institute.

Matsushita, K. (1988) 'The secret is shared', *Manufacturing Engineering*: March: 78–84.

Mayon-White, B. (1986) *Planning and Managing Change*. London: Paul Chapman.

Megson, L.V.C. (1988) 'Building organizations for performance', *Digital Equipment Corporation*, unpublished article.

Miles, R. and Snow, C. (1978) *Organisational Strategy, Structure and Process*. New York: McGraw-Hill.

Mill, J.S. (2004 reprinted) *Utilitarianism*, Whitefish, MT: Kessinger Publishing.

Miller, K. (1998) 'He-cells, she cells, brain cells, an interview'. *The Herald*, 22 June.

Mintzberg, H. (1989) *Mintzberg on Management*. New York: The Free Press.

Mintzberg, H. (1994) *The Rise and Fall of Strategic Planning*. New York: The Free Press.

Moir, A. and Moir, B. (1998) *Why Men Don't Iron*. London: HarperCollins.

Moir, A. and Jessel, D. (1991) *Brain Sex*. New York: Carol Publishing Group.

Moorcroft, D. (1996) 'Communicating effectively in a changing corporate culture', *Focus on Management*, June.

Morant, A.J. (1996) 'Video conferencing a tool for business re-engineering', *Management Accounting*, June.

Nonaka, I. (1994) 'A dynamic theory of organizational knowledge creation', *Organization Science*, 5(1): 14–37.

Nonaka, I. and Takeuchi, H. (1991) 'The knowledge creating company', *Harvard Business Review*, November–December.

Nonaka, I. and Takeuchi, H. (1995) *The Knowledge Creating Company: How Japanese Companies Create the Dynamics of Innovation*. Oxford: Oxford University Press.

O'Boyle, W.M. (1987) 'Gender and handedness: differences in mirror tracing random forms', *Neuropsychologia*, 1–6.

O'Boyle, W.M. (1991) 'Brainsex', Discovery Channel, November.

O'Boyle, W.M. and Gill, H.S. (1998) 'On the relevance of research findings in cognitive neuroscience to educational practice', *Educational Psychological Review*, 10(4): 397–409.

O'Dell, C. and Grayson, C.J. (1998) 'If only we knew what we know: identification and transfer of internal best practice', *Californian Management Review*, 40(3): 154–74.

Ogbonna, E. and Harris, L.C. (1998) 'Organizational culture: it's not what you think …', *Journal of General Management*, 23(3): 35–48.

Orlikowski, W.J. (1992) 'The duality of technology: rethinking the concept of technology in organizations', *Organization Science*, 3(3): 398–427.

Palmer, I. and Hardy, C. (2000) *Thinking about Management*. Sage: London.

Pascale, R.T. (1994) 'Intentional breakdowns and conflict by design', *Planning Review*, 22: May–June.

Pascale, R.T. (1999) 'Surfing the edge of chaos', *Sloan Management Review*, 40(3): 83–94.

Pascale, R.T., Milleman, M. and Gioja, L. (1997) 'Changing the way we change', *Harvard Business Review*, November–December.

Pasmore, W.A. (1994) *Creating Strategic Change: Designing the Flexible, High-performing Organization*. New York: Wiley.

Paton, R.A. (2004) 'Knowledge transfer: managing a partnership', Graduate School of Business Administration, Zurich, 13th Zurich MBA Congress, Zurich, March 2004.

Paton, R.A., Southern, G. and Houghton, M.G. (1989) 'European strategy formulation: an analysis technique', *European Management Journal*, 7(3): 305–9.

Paton, R.A. and Southern, G. (1990) *Total project management*, University of Glasgow Business School Working Paper Series.

Paton, R.A. and Dempster, L. (2002) 'Managing change from a gender perspective', *European Management Journal*, 20(5): 539–48.

Paton, R.A. and McLaughlin, S. (2008) 'Services innovation: Knowledge transfer and the supply chain', *European Management Journal*, 27(2): 77–83.

Paulson, L.D. (2006) 'Service science: a new field for today's economy', *IEEE Computer Journal*, August: 18–21.

Pawar, K., Horton, A., Gupta, A., Wunram, M., Barson, R. and Weber, F. (2002) 'Inter-organizational knowledge management: focus on human barriers in the telecommunications industry', proceedings of the 8th ISPE International Conference on Concurrent Engineering: Research and Applications: 271–8.

Pearn, M., Roderick, C. and Mulrooney, C. (1995) *Learning Organizations in Practice*. Maidenhead: McGraw-Hill.

Pedler, M., Burgoyne, J. and Boydell, T. (1991) *The Learning Company: A Strategy for Sustainable Development*. Maidenhead: McGraw-Hill.

Peters, T. J. (1987) *Thriving on Chaos*. New York: Alfred A. Knopf.

Peters, T. J. and Waterman, R.H., Jr (1982) *In Search of Excellence*. New York: Harper and Row.

Pettigrew, A.M. (1985) *The Awakening Giant: Continuity and Change in Imperial Chemical Industries*. Oxford: Basil Blackwell.

Pettigrew, A.M. (1987) 'Context and action in the transformation of the firm', *Journal of Management Studies*, 24(6): 649–70.

Pettigrew, A.M. (ed.) (1988) *The Management of Strategic Change*. Oxford: Basil Blackwell.

Pettigrew, A.M. and Whipp, R. (1993) *Managing Change for Corporate Success*. London: Basil Blackwell.

Pettigrew, A.M., Ferlie, E. and McKee, L. (1992) *Shaping Strategic Change: Making Change in Large Organizations – the Case of the National Health Service*. London: Sage.

Pfeffer, J. (1981) *Power in Organizations*. New York: HarperCollins.

Pfeffer, J. (1992) *Managing with Power: Politics and Influence in Organizations*. Boston, MA: Harvard Business School Press.

Pfeffer, J. (1994) *Competitive Advantage Through People: Unleashing the Power of the Work Force*. Boston, MA: Harvard Business School Press.

Piczak, M. and Hauser, R.Z. (1996) 'Self-directed work teams: a guide to implementation', *Quality Progress*, May.

Porter, M.E. (1985) *Competitive Advantage: Creating and Sustaining Superior Performance*. New York: Free Press.

Porter, M.E. and Millar, V.E. (1985) 'How information gives you competitive advantage', *Harvard Business Review*, July–August: 149–61.

Preuss, L. (1999) 'Ethical theory in German business ethics research', *Journal of Business Ethics*, 18: 407–19.

Pritchard, W. (1984) 'What's new in organizational development?', *Personnel Management*, July: 30–3.

Prusak, L. (1998) *The 11 Deadliest Sins of Knowledge Management*. Boston, MA: Butterworth-Heinemann.

Pugh, D.S. (1978) 'Understanding and managing organizational change', *London Business School Journal*, 3(2): 29–34.

Pugh, D.S. (1986) *Planning and Managing Change, Block 4: Organizational Development*. Milton Keynes: Open University Business School.

Pugh, D.S. and Hickson, D.J. (1989) *Writers on Organizations*, Fourth edition. London: Penguin.

Quinn, J.B., Anderson, P. and Finkelstein, S. (1996) 'Managing professional intellect', *Harvard Business Review*, March–April, 71(2): 71–81

Quinn, J.J. (1996) 'The role of "good conversation" in strategic control', *Journal of Management Studies,* 33(3): 381–94.

Rajan, A., Lank, E. and Chapple, K. (1998) *Good Practice in Knowledge Creation and Exchange*. Tunbridge Wells: Create.

Ralston, D., Giacalone, R. and Terpstra, R. (1994) 'Ethical perceptions of organisational politics: a comparative evaluation of American and Hong Kong managers', *Journal of Business Ethics*, 13(12): 989–1000.

Richardson, P. and Denton, K. (1996) 'Communicating change', *Human Resource Management*, Summer.

Rickards, T. (1985) 'Making new things happen', *Technovation*, 3: 119–31.

Robbins, S. (2007) *Organizational Behavior: Concepts, Controversies, Applications*, Eighth edition. New Jersey: Prentice-Hall.

Robertson, D. (1993) 'Empiricism in business ethics: suggested research directions', *Journal of Business Ethics*, 15(10): 1095–106.

Roethlisberger, F.J. and Dickson, W.J. (1939) *Management and the Worker*. Cambridge, MA: Harvard University Press.

Rosener, J. (1990) 'Ways women lead', *Harvard Business Review*, May/June; 103–11.

Rosener, J. (1995) *America's Competitive Secret*. New York: Oxford University Press.

Roth, A., Moruchek, A., Kemp, A. and Trimble, D. (1994) 'The knowledge factory for accelerated learning practices', *Planning Review*, May–June: 26.

Scarborough, H., Swan, J. and Preston, P. (1999) *Knowledge Management: A Literature Review*. Issues in people management. London: Institute of Personnel and Development.

Schaffer, R.H. and Thomson, H.A. (1992) 'Successful change programs begin with results', *Harvard Business Review*, January–February.

Schein, E.H. (1988) *Process Consultation: Its Role in Organization Development*. Reading, MA: Addison-Wesley.

Segal, A. (1996) 'Flowering feminism: consciousness raising at work', *Journal of Organizational Change Management*, 9(5).

Semler, R. (2003) *The Seven-Day Weekend*. London: Century Books.

Senge, P.M. (1990) 'The leader's new work: building learning organizations', *Sloan Management Review*, Autumn.

Senge P.M. (1995) *The Fifth Discipline Fieldbook: Strategies and Tools for Building a Learning Organization*. London: Brearly.

Senge P.M. (2006) *The Fifth Discipline: The Art and Practice of the Learning Organization*, revised edition. New York: Currency.

Shaywitz, B.A. and Shaywitz, S.E. (1995) 'Sex differences in the functional organisation of the brain for language', *Nature*, 373, February: 607.

Shenhar, A.J., Levy, O. and Dvir, D. (1997) 'Mapping the dimensions of project success', *Project Management Journal*, 28(2): 5–13.

Sherwood, J. J. (1988) 'Creating work cultures with competitive advantage', *Organizational Dynamics*, Winter 1988, American Management Association.

Simon, H.A. (1957) *Models of Man*. New York: Wiley

Singh, V. and Vinnicombe, S. (2001) 'Impression management, commitment and gender: managing others' good opinions', *European Management Journal*, 19(2): 183–94.

Skyrme, D.J. and Amidon, D.M. (1997) *Creating the Knowledge Based Business*. London: Business Intelligence.

Slater, S.F. and Narver, J.C. (1995) 'Market orientation and the learning organization', *Journal of Marketing*, July.

Sminia, H. and Van Nistelrooij, A. (2006) 'Strategic management and organization development: planned change in a public sector organization', *Journal of Change Management*, 6(1): 99–113.

Sorell, T. and Hendry, J. (1994) *Business Ethics*. Oxford: Butterworth-Heinemann.

Spector, B.A. (1989) 'From bogged down to fired up: inspiring organisational change', *Sloan Management Review*, Summer.

Spence, L.J. (1998) 'Comparative European business ethics: a comparison of the ethics of the recruitment interview in Germany, the Netherlands and the UK, using Erving Goffman's frame analysis'. PhD Thesis, Brunel University.

Spence, L.J. (2001) 'Is Europe distinctive from America? An overview of business ethics in Europe', in H. von Weltzien Høivik (ed.) *Business Ethics and Leadership in Action*. Cheltenham: Edward Elgar Publishing.

Spender, J.C. (1996) 'Organizational knowledge, learning and memory: three concepts in search of a theory', *Journal of Organizational Change Management*, 9(1): 63–78.

Spohrer, J., Maglio, P., Bailey, J. and Gruhl, D. (2007) 'Steps toward a science of service systems', *IEEE Computer Journal*, January: 71–7.

Stacey, R.D. (2000) '*Strategic Management and Organisational Dynamics: The Challenge of Complexity*, Third edition. London: FT/Prentice Hall.

Standing, C. and Standing, S. (1998) 'The politics and ethics of career progression in a systems perspective', *Logistics Information Management*, 11(5): 309–16.

Stata, R. (1989) 'Organizational learning – the key to management innovation', *Sloan Management Review*, Spring.

Steinmann, H. and Löhr, A. (1994) *Grundlagen der Unternehmensethik*, Second edition. Stuttgart: Poeschel.

Steinmann, H. and Löhr, A. (1996) 'A republican concept of corporate ethics', in S. Urban (ed.) *Europe's Challenges: Economic efficiency and social solidarity*. Wiesbaden: Gabler, pp. 21–60.

Stone, B. (1997) *Confronting Company Politics*. Basingstoke: Macmillan Business.

Swartz, J. (1999) 'Collaboration – more hype then reality', *Internet Week*, 25 October: 786.

Szulanski, G. (1996) 'Exploring internal stickiness: impediments to the transfer of best practice within the firm', *Strategic Management Journal*, 17: 27–43.

Tannen, D. (1992) *You Just don't Understand*. London: Virago Press.

Tannen, D. (1994) *Talking from 9 to 5*. London: Virago Press.

Taylor, S.S. (1999) 'Making sense of revolutionary change: differences in members' stories', *Journal of Organizational Change Management*, 12(6): 524.

Tearle, R. (2007) 'The role of the change master', http://www.changedesigns.co.za

Teece, D.J. (1998) 'Capturing value from knowledge assets: the new economy, markets for know how, and intangible assets', *Californian Management Review*, 40(3): 55–78.

Thompson, P. and McHugh, D. (1995) *Work Organizations: A Critical Introduction*. Basingstoke: Macmillan.

Thorsurd, E. (1972) 'Job design in the wider context', in L.E. Davis and J.C. Taylor (eds) *Design of Jobs*. Harmondsworth: Penguin.

Tiong, T.N. (2005) 'Maximising human resource potential in the midst of organizational change', *Singapore Management Review*, 27(2): 25–35.

Todnem By, R. (2005) 'Organizational change management: a critical review', *Journal of Change Management*, 5(4): 369–80.

Troyer, C.R. (1995) 'Smart movers in supply chain coordination', *Transport and Distribution*, 36(9): 55.

Tsoukas, H. (1996) 'The firm as a distributed knowledge system: a constructivist approach', *Strategic Management Journal*, 17: 11–25.

Tzu, Sun (1990 republished) *The Art of War*. Hertfordshire: Wordsworth.

Ulrich, D. (1998) 'A new mandate for human resources', *Harvard Business Review*, January/February: 124–34.

Van der Heijden, K. and Eden, C. (1994) 'Managerial cognition, organizational cognition and the practice of organizational learning', presented at the second International Workshop on Managerial and Organizational Cognition.

Van Weele, A.J. (2002) *Purchasing and Supply Chain Management*, Third edition. London: Thompson.

Velasquez, M., Moberg, D. and Cavanagh, G. (1983) 'Organisational statesmanship and dirty politics: ethical guidelines for the organisational politician', *Organisational Dynamics*, 12(2): 65–81.

Vennix, J.A.M. (1996) *Group Model Building: Facilitating Team Learning Using Systems Dynamics*. Chichester: Wiley.

Viewpoint (1993) *A changing workforce*, Income Data Services, Report 640, May: 1

Vinnicombe, S. (1987) 'What exactly are the differences in male and female working styles?', *Women in Management Review*, 3(1): 13–21.

Vinnicombe, S. and Colwill, N. (1995) *The Essence of Women in Management*. Hemel Hempstead: Prentice Hall.

Vinnicombe, S. and Singh, V. (2001) 'Impression management, commitment and gender: managing others' good opinions', *European Management Journal*, 19(2): 183–94.

Vroom, V.H. (1969) 'Industrial social psychology', in G. Lindsey and E. Aronson (eds) *The Handbook of Social Psychology*. Reading, MA: Addison-Wesley.

Warner Burke, W. (1994) *Organization Development: A Normative View*, Second edition. Reading, MA: Addison-Wesley.

Watson, T. (1994) *In Search of Management: Culture, Chaos and Control in Managerial Work*. London: Routledge.

Weiner, E. and Brown, A. (1993) *Office Biology*. New York: Master Media.

Wijnberg, N. (2000) 'Normative stakeholder theory and Aristotle: the link between ethics and politics', *Journal of Business Ethics*, 25(4): 329–42.

Winter, S.G. (1987) 'Knowledge and competence as strategic assets', in D. Teece (ed.) *The Competitive Challenge: Strategies for Industrial Innovation and Renewal*. Cambridge, MA: Ballinger.

Wolfe, D.B. (1997) 'Older markets and the new marketing paradigm', *Journal of Consumer Marketing*, 14(4): 392–402.

Woodward, S. and Hendry, C. (2004) 'Leading and coping with change', *Journal of Change Management*, 4(2): 155–83.

Wren, J. and Dulewicz, V. (2005) 'Leader competencies, activities and successful change in the Royal Air Force', *Journal of Change Management*, 5(3): 295–309.

Wright, M. and Rhodes, D. (1985) *Managing IT: Exploring Information Systems for Effective Management*. London: Pinter.

Yates, D.J. (1985) *The Politics of Management*. San Francisco: Jossey-Bass.

Yin, R.K. (2002) *Case Study Research*, Third edition. London: Sage.

Zahra, S.A. (1984) 'Managerial views of organisational politics', *Management Quarterly*, 25(1): 31–8.

Zahra, S.A. (1985) 'Background and works experience correlates of the ethics and effect of organisational politics', *Journal of Business Ethics*, 4(5): 419–24.

Zahra, S.A. (1987) 'Organisational politics and the strategic process', *Journal of Business Ethics*, 6(7): 579–88.

Zander, U. and Kogut, B. (1995) 'Knowledge and the speed of transfer and imitation on organizational capabilities', *Organizational Science*, 6(1): 76–92.

Zenger, J.H., Musselwhite, E., Hurson, K. and Perrin, C. (1994) *Leading Teams: Mastering the New Role*. Irwin: Business One.

Index

Please note: the letter 'f' after a page number indicates a figure, 'mc' a mini case, 'ra' a reader activity and 't' a table.